MEDIA ETHICS

IN THE NEWSROOM AND BEYOND

D0218136

 McGRAW-HILL SERIES
IN MASS
COMMUNICATION

CONSULTING EDITOR

Alan Wurtzel

MEDIA ETHICS

IN THE NEWSROOM AND BEYOND

Conrad C. Fink
School of Journalism
University of Georgia

McGRAW-HILL BOOK COMPANY

New York St. Louis San Francisco Auckland Bogotá Caracas Colorado Springs
Hamburg Lisbon London Madrid Mexico Milan Montreal New Delhi Oklahoma City
Panama Paris San Juan São Paulo Singapore Sydney Tokyo Toronto

This book was set in Times Roman by the College Composition Unit
in cooperation with Black Dot, Inc.
The editors were Phillip A. Butcher and James R. Belser;
the designer was Suzanne Haldane;
the production supervisor was Salvador Gonzales.
R. R. Donnelley & Sons Company was printer and binder.

MEDIA ETHICS: IN THE NEWSROOM AND BEYOND

1 2 3 4 5 6 7 8 9 0   DOCDOC   8 9 2 1 0 9 8 7

ISBN 0-07-020976-6

Library of Congress Cataloging-in-Publication Data

Fink, Conrad C.
     Media ethics.

     (McGraw-Hill series in mass communication)
     Includes index.
     1. Mass media—Moral and ethical aspects.
2. Journalistic ethics.   3. Mass media—Social aspects.
I Title.   II. Series.
P94.F48   1988   174'.9097   87-21496
ISBN 0-07-020976-6

ABOUT
THE AUTHOR

For twenty-five years, Conrad C. Fink was a reporter, editor, foreign correspondent, and media executive. After a start in small-town journalism, he moved on to cover crime stories for the Associated Press in Chicago and handle other assignments in New York, Japan, Korea, Vietnam, India, Pakistan, and many other countries in Asia, the Middle East, and Europe. He was vice president and secretary of AP at headquarters in New York City and also worked in newspaper and broadcast station management. In 1982, he opened a new career at the University of Georgia's Henry W. Grady School of Journalism and Mass Communication, where he has been cited for superior teaching of advanced reporting and newspaper management and strategy. Fink says *Media Ethics* is a book "field-tested for twenty-five years, then classroom-tested. The ethical questions raised in it include many I have encountered personally on assignments from New York City to New Delhi."

CONTENTS

FOREWORD

There is a lot of discussion these days about ethical standards and the credibility of the media in the nation's newsrooms.

As a journalist with nearly 40 years of experience as a reporter and editor, I know that newspeople today are better educated and better trained than ever before. The public is better informed—and better served—than it was even a decade ago. The media are more responsible and more responsive to public needs today than ever before.

Yet there is plenty of evidence around that the media of this country are undergoing a credibility crisis. Journalists have declined in public esteem. The public questions the believability of newspapers, magazines, and broadcast news. There is obvious public dissatisfaction with our performance in an increasingly complex society. The public perception is that journalists are often arrogant, irresponsible, unfair, biased, and unethical; that we have no standards.

Still, studies also show that the public believes in a free press; that it believes a free press is essential if American democracy is to realize its potential. People recognize that the media have substantial power; that they have a great deal of freedom under the First Amendment and that they have great responsibilities. It is how we use that power and exercise those responsibilities that rightly concerns them. As it must concern journalists.

Conrad Fink, an experienced newsman and educator, brings these issues into clear focus in this new look at media ethics. This book is an important tool for journalism students to build a strong individual ethical base for their careers. Students must start now, in class, thinking about their values and ethics and learning about the difficult judgments they will have to make as writers, photographers, or editors. It is important that they are ready to meet the ethical challenges that lie ahead. It is as essential to a student's career as improving writing, developing editing skills, sharpening graphics techniques, or learning about newsroom management. Professional skills are empty without a clear set of ethical values to guide beginning journalists.

But Professor Fink's book is not only an educational tool for embryonic journalists. He reminds those of us already in the profession that we must have high ethical standards; that we have obligations to perform our jobs with intelligence, accuracy, objectivity, and fairness; that we must make clear distinctions between news and opinion. A unique aspect of Professor Fink's book is that he asks us to look not only at our individual ethics but at those of the corporate organizations for which most journalists work today. He explores our need to consider bringing the publishers, general managers, advertising directors, and circulation directors into our ethical discussions. He reminds us how vital it is for us to consider the impact of the bottom line on newsroom ethics. It also is vital to ask to whom the media are accountable when they misstep, violate their own high public trust. If government should not oversee the press, should anyone? How well does the press monitor itself?

Most journalists are opposed to adoption of any ethical codes or standards that apply equally to all. Similarly, most are opposed to any system of outside performance evaluation, such as press councils, that make judgments on an individual journalist's or news organization's ethics. It is extremely important that those who will lead the media in the years ahead examine these concerns and explore accountability issues fully. Are there acceptable alternatives to media self-policing? Are press councils dangerous to a free press?

I am convinced that journalists must set high ethical standards in our newsrooms, adhere to them tenaciously and enforce them fairly. If we fail to embrace high ethical standards, we will lose our integrity. If we do not have integrity, we have no credibility. And, if we have no credibility, we journalists have little to offer the American people.

Media Ethics: In the Newsroom and Beyond touches on these most critical and sensitive issues. It is a timely and welcome addition to our journalism libraries.

John R. Finnegan, Sr.
Sr. Vice President/Editor
St. Paul Pioneer Press Dispatch
Former chairman, Ethics Committee,
Society of Professional Journalists,
Sigma Delta Chi

PREFACE

For we who teach print or broadcast journalism and mass communication, serious issues of media ethics and social responsibility arise frequently in dialogues with students. Whether we teach stand-alone ethics courses, introduction to mass communication, reporting and writing, management, media and society, or other courses, we confront with our students numerous questions of right and wrong, good and bad, in the conduct of newspaper, magazine, and broadcast journalism.

This book is designed to assist teacher and student in the dialogue—not by presuming to answer those terribly complicated questions (which often defy clear-cut answers) but, rather, by illustrating what is being done in the communications industry today and what others who came before us have done in matters of ethics. The goal is a contemporary framework for discussion and, it is hoped, much introspective thought by aspiring journalists. Of course, our growing concern in the classroom over ethics reflects wider societal discussion of the media and increasingly heated debate among working journalists. So the book also is designed to contribute to current ethical debate in the print and broadcast industries—and to bring into the dialogue other teaching disciplines and members of the reading and viewing public concerned about the crucial role of the media in our society.

In the parlance of ethicists, this book's approach is not one of "metaethics," the study of abstract principles, but, rather, one of "normative ethics," a discussion of specific, present-day media behavior in search of what is correct and what isn't. Attempting to even point at possible answers to ethical problems creates enormous risks, of course. Who, after all, truly knows what is "right" or "wrong" about how newspapers and television operate? This book draws heavily on what individual journalists do when *they* meet ethical challenges. Teachers will note this is done throughout the numerous case studies, quotations (labeled "Viewpoint") from working journalists, and anecdotal illustrations of what happens when ethical ideal meets media world reality.

Case studies are, first, real-life, not fictional. Each is selected carefully to shed light on major ethical questions confronting the media today. Second, case studies present briefly the facts working journalists actually faced in each situation and then ask questions to stir classroom discussion and present how journalists actually handled each situation. Obviously, not even media "pros" always solve ethical problems satisfactorily, particularly under the deadline pressures and space and time limitations of daily journalism. So this text is written for teachers to use in challenging students to create their own responses to some of the pressing ethical questions of our time.

Importantly, this book is structured to assist teachers in illustrating that the ethical strains and doubts confronting journalists don't always begin and end in the newsroom, that they in fact arise during three stages of a career in the newsroom and beyond—as a beginning reporter-writer, then, as a representative of a media institution—an editor, news director, or manager—and, finally, as a representative of the media as a whole in society.

Teachers will note discussions of newsroom ethics are cast against a wider corporate backdrop. Too often (in both industry and academia), we ignore the impact of profit, "image," and other corporate concerns on the ethical conduct and reporting techniques of the man and woman with notebook and pencil or camera and mike in hand. But it is useless for teacher and student to belabor the question of, say, an individual reporter's fairness in covering a story unless we also examine whether that reporter has been given sufficient corporate support and resources to be fair—money and time to chase all sides of the story, the necessary newsprint or airtime to report a balanced account.

Nevertheless, corporations don't solve ethical problems, individuals do— reporters, editors, news directors, publishers, network executives. So, although we will examine the wider corporate or societal context, *individual responsibility in ethical matters is a fundamental teaching theme of this book.*

The book breaks down into three parts:

Part One: Ethics in the Pursuit of News: There is no precise rule book on conduct for journalists, no widely held single code of ethics, so Chapter 1 sketches a philosophical framework for a teacher's initial discussion of professional conscience in the newsroom. We look quickly at a 2,500-year-old mainstream of ethical debate leading into an examination, in Chapters 2, 3, and 4, of how each journalist inevitably meets, early in a news career, serious ethical issues. A teaching theme is that each journalist must build a *personal* approach to ethics within the context of his or her relationship with a supervising editor or news director and the reading or viewing public.

Part Two: Ethics in Pursuit of Profit: Newspapers and television, their credibility questioned, are challenged severely by other media—and public indifference—in the drive for increased advertising and circulation revenues. Managers must examine *corporate* attitudes toward ethics. Whether written or simply laid down by example, ethical codes increasingly guide advertising departments and business offices, as well as newsrooms. Throughout Chapters 5, 6, 7, and 8, teachers will find many examples of how newsroom ethics are affected by what happens in the "countinghouse." A basic teaching theme is that profit, not ethics, often motivates corporate management but that journalists can learn to operate ethically and responsibly within profit-driven newspaper or television news operations.

Part Three: The Media in Society: Public perceptions of the media are changing in fundamental ways. There is serious discussion among influential people of whether, in times of peace as well as war, the Fourth Estate can be permitted to barge about in public and private affairs, to operate independently of legal and societal restraints that govern conduct of other major institutions influencing American life. Public relations—and the ethics of that industry— plays an important role in all this. A fundamental teaching theme in Chapters 9, 10, 11, and 12 is whether society will write new rules for the increasingly powerful media.

Each chapter opens with a "window," bringing into focus questions and issues to be discussed. Summaries for each chapter will stimulate teacher-student discussion.

For those teaching stand-alone ethics courses, assigning students front-to-back reading will facilitate orderly progression from basic newsroom ethical concerns onward to corporate social responsibility and the media in society. However, chapters are written as self-contained units which can be assigned students in other courses such as reporting and writing, introduction to mass media, media management and strategy, and so forth.

Extensive endnotes for each chapter will direct students to deeper reading in scholarly works and research journals and to more contemporary writing in print- and broadcast-industry publications. As aids for teachers and students desiring to stay atop current industry discussion of ethics, the author recommends reading each year's ethics report by the Society of Professional Journalists, Sigma Delta Chi and periodic reports on ethics in the American Society of Newspaper Editors *Bulletin* and the Associated Press Managing Editors *Redbook*. Important periodicals include *Broadcasting, Washington Journalism Review, Columbia Journalism Review,* The American Newspaper Publishers Association's *presstime, Editor & Publisher, Advertising Age.*

Teachers will note that efforts to make this book a comprehensive teaching and discussion resource include reproducing at the end of this book the Statement of Principles, American Society of Newspaper Editors; Code of Ethics, Society of Professional Journalists/Sigma Delta Chi; Code of Broadcast

Ethics, Radio/Television News Directors Association; Code of Ethics, Associated Press Managing Editors; Conflict of Interest Policy, Dow Jones & Company; The Advertising Code of American Business; Declaration of Principles, Public Relations Society of America; sample letter requesting information under Freedom of Information Act.

ACKNOWLEDGMENTS

Memory is vivid of that day during the Vietnam war when I heard, while reporting in India, that Larry Burrows had "bought it." He was on assignment for *Life* magazine when his helicopter was shot down in flames on a U.S. Army raid along the Cambodian border. Later, another colleague, Dennis Lee Royle of the Associated Press, went down on an RAF copter in the North Sea. I had been deeply impressed by the enormous talent of both men and their willingness to repeatedly risk so much to get the story and get it right. Their deaths—and those of others who ran out of luck while chasing the story—were turning points for me. Since then, I have thought a great deal about those who give their careers—sometimes their lives—to covering the news.

Reading and viewing publics little know, perhaps little care, but many who seek the news, in far-off jungle or closer to home in state capitol or city hall, often do so with amazing selflessness, high ideals, and dedication. Not all do, of course. Among us are rampant careerists for whom everything, truth included, must give way before personal gain; for others, journalism simply is a job, devoid of higher motives or ideals, to be performed as quickly and painlessly as possible.

So, a distinction: My inspiration comes from those men and women who try so very hard, who give so very much to get the news and get it right. To those who follow the principled path, I dedicate this book.

For recognizing there was a potential book in all this, my deep thanks to Phillip A. Butcher, editor in chief, Arts and Sciences, College Division, McGraw-Hill Book Company. Barbara L. Raab, a conscientious and discerning editor, was of immense assistance. Dr. Alan Wurtzel, a former university professor now an ABC Television executive and McGraw-Hill consultant, was very helpful and supportive.

My sincere thanks go to those colleagues in academia who reviewed this book in manuscript form: Maurine Beasley, University of Maryland; James L. Hoyt, University of Wisconsin-Madison; Maclyn H. McClary, Humboldt State University and Patrick S. Washburn, Ohio University.

At the University of Georgia's Henry W. Grady School of Journalism and Mass Communication, Dean Tom Russell and Dr. Al Hester have been supportive in my switch from the communications industry to academia. Valuable guidance and support have come from Warren Agee, Scott Cutlip, George Hough, Kent Middleton, and others. Profs. Agee and Cutlip were helpful particularly in giving me guidance on Chapter 11, "Public Relations, the Media, and Society."

As for so many years, in so many places around the world, Sue has been my main support.

Typist Vera Penn has my thanks for splendid assistance on my writing projects.

Finally, in the spirit of openness that I think should characterize any reporter's ethical relationship with readers, I must note that I worked for two companies mentioned in this book. For twenty-one glorious years, I worked in the United States and abroad for the Associated Press, in nearly every job from police reporter to vice president and secretary of the corporation, trying in my own way to add to that organization's principled devotion to the goal of creating the best, most ethical news coverage possible. Then, before turning to academia, I worked three years as executive vice president of Park Communications.

Conrad C. Fink

INTRODUCTION

There is under way in this country a debate over media ethics and credibility that has moved sharply into the public arena. Journalists heatedly convene over whether the public trusts reporters or "likes" the media. Politicians jump into view with strong opinions on newspaper performance and television coverage. Even private citizens choose sides with an intensity customarily reserved for Super Bowl weekends.

Yet, I fear the noisy debate not only loses sight of key issues involving the media, but in fact serves to disguise them. Crucial questions of ethics *do* confront journalists; fundamental changes *are* under way in the relationship of media to society. But the dialogue often misses those questions and changes, and ineffectually wanders astray.

This book is written in the hope it will help focus the debate for young, aspiring journalists, working journalists, and for members of the public concerned with the role of the media in our society. Above all, this book is a call to students of journalism to start, now, their own urgent examination of ethical conduct in American newspapers, magazines, and broadcast news and begin, now, constructing their own personal codes of ethical conduct. Ethical challenges come in many forms, frequently offering no clear-cut distinction between right and wrong. Often, a journalist's only course is a compromise between equally distasteful options. So, I urge students to start deciding now what for them is right and wrong in the practice of journalism and, furthermore, what they personally will do and won't do, in an ethical sense, when they join the ranks of working journalists.

I counsel all due haste. As always, there is the historical, philosophical imperative to improve ethical standards in the media because that is the *right* thing to do. But today, improving standards of professional performance is something the media also *must* do, for the media operate in an increasingly hostile social, legal, and economic environment and, I believe, unless they clean their own house there is in this republic a real and present danger that other institutions will try to do it for them—very likely in a manner not best suited to preserve the crucial role the free media play in our democracy. I suspect, then, there has arrived—in disguise and perhaps generally unnoticed—a watershed era for the media. As institutions of enormous social, political, and economic power, the media are entering an extremely critical new stage in their evolving relationship with the public and other institutions in our society.

To explain: The spirit and basic position of the media today in the American scheme of things arise from a colonial newspaper culture that, if not particularly high-minded or professional, certainly was free-spirited. From that arose libertarian attitudes that newspapers should function as businesses publishing news and opinion, being specially watchful of government and safeguarding personal liberties—but not feeling particularly constrained by performance standards or a sense of responsibility to any individual or group, including the public. Libertarian journalism assumed the citizenry would find the truth if enough news and opinion were published. However, in the 1930s and 1940s, the media began evolving into a second developmental stage, "social responsibility." Many newspapers resisted the concept, but broadcasters were forced by government regulation into at least a show of public responsibility, and the media as a whole came under increasing public pressure to be something more than self-centered, profit-making concerns. Attitudes arising from that hold the media responsible for practicing sound, professional journalism and exercising press freedom wisely in the public's interest. With the rise of the attitude of social responsibility came wider awareness in the media of ethical codes and emphasis upon principled use of media power.

The media now may be evolving toward a third stage, which I choose to call "ethical-reactive," and I regard it as full of dangers to the media and the democracy they serve—thus, my feeling of urgency. Ethical-reactive journalism is defensive, in large part a reaction to societal criticism of the media that arguably is harsher and more determined than any this country's news media ever have faced. For example, when international controversy erupted in 1986 over the Reagan administration's arms sales to Iran, leading American editors quickly warned reporters to consider how history would view their coverage, to avoid excesses that drew so much public criticism following Watergate in the 1970s. As Reagan/Iran began to unfold, a *New York Times* survey found editor James Squires interrupting a news-planning session with his *Chicago Tribune* staff to say that "when history looks back at this event" he wanted *Tribune* coverage to be "cautious, fair, and honest from the beginning." Squires didn't put up warning flags deep into the story, after the press had been in hot pursuit or found guilty of excesses. He voiced caution *one* day after one of the earliest and biggest news breaks in the entire story—charges that payments from Iran had been diverted to Nicaraguan rebels. Squires, a conscientious, highly regarded editor, was a White House reporter during the Nixon era. He told the *Times* his caution stemmed in part from what he regarded as his own excesses on Watergate. Other editors similarly were cautious up-front on Reagan/Iran. Dan

Rather, managing editor as well as anchor of CBS's *Evening News,* said he learned from his own mistakes in covering Watergate, and now "often" talks with his staff about the tone of their coverage and need for accuracy and fairness. Editor William F. Thomas of the *Los Angeles Times* said the press indulged in gloating and self-aggrandizement after Watergate and, "This time we have to avoid all the appearances of being after somebody. What I'm talking about is appearing to like it too much." Ben Bradlee, architect of the *Washington Post's* prize-winning Watergate coverage, said that for a journalist the Iran incident was a "wonderful story" but, "We don't want to appear to be gloating, and anyone who thinks this thing through sees problems (for the media) at the end of it." *New York Times* media reporter Alex Jones noted Bradlee warned his staff to keep a low profile and "avoid such things as television appearances."

Thus, even in the earliest stages of Reagan/Iran, many editors were burdened by memories of public backlash over Watergate coverage. From the first, they looked beyond covering the story to *how the public might react to the way it was covered.*

It all led the *Columbia Journalism Review* to comment in January 1987 that journalists had begun to "fear that the public would believe that the press's real goal was to bring down the president. Editors worried that people would think that reporters were merely having a lark. Most curiously, journalism's establishment repeatedly vowed to avoid what it had done in Watergate." The *Review* suggested "political prudence" was motivating such agonizing self-appraisals, that the press perhaps felt "such pledges of good behavior are obligatory, given the press's sensitivity to accusations that it is unpatriotic. . . ." The *Review* added, "But having thus stated their honorable intentions, reporters and editors should get on with the job at hand."

In a spirited defense of the media and their role in American society (*The War Against the Press,* Dodd, Mead & Company, New York, 1987), *Time* senior correspondent Peter Stoles declares, "To a far greater extent than many of them are willing to admit, editors and publishers and news executives are avoiding the kinds of investigative stories that make headlines while making people angry. Some are turning their editorial pages into mixtures of bland mush, avoiding strong positions for fear of offending someone—readers, advertisers, rivals."

Could the media's concern during Reagan/Iran simply have been commendable caution on a tremendously important story? A sign of professional maturation? Not so, says Hodding Carter III, media commentator and former U.S. State Department spokesman. Carter says many news organizations have been gripped by "insane tentativeness" since Watergate—not due to excesses during coverage of that story, but, rather, owing to an unrelenting campaign since those days by conservatives to paint the media as unfairly liberal. Says Carter: "They've had their brains beaten in on the whole notion of a liberal press."

(The *Washington Post's* Bradlee was accurate, incidentally, in predicting problems for the media over Reagan/Iran. In January 1987, after the story had been actively reported for about two months, a Gallup poll survey showed many

Americans, particularly conservatives, felt the story had been overreported and, as a result, news organizations had lost substantial public esteem and credibility.)

Clearly, the ethical-reactive disposition has two parents: external criticism and pressure, and internal turmoil and self-doubt among journalists themselves, who have a growing preoccupation with whether what they do is ethical, fair, balanced, or constructive—worthy even. It is to some extent an overreaction to criticism that could severely distort the news-reporting process as we know it and, indeed, shift relationships between the media and other institutions of power and influence in this country. Simply put, journalists who once perceived their mission as covering the news and getting the story now spend much time in heated discussion among themselves on self-imposed *rules* for covering the news. Great newspapers that once gloried in their often critical relationships with government and other institutions now stutter in self-doubt, burdened by concern over corporate "image" and profit success in the marketplace. Together with television, they conduct survey after survey on whether they are "liked" by the public or "disliked," respected or not. John Perry, veteran editor of the *Rome (Ga.) News-Tribune,* puts it this way: "No other profession on the American scene today does more public daisy-petal plucking than journalism: 'He loves me. He loves me not.' Concern about what the reader thinks of the writer was never more prominent in the consciousness of the journalists. A stranger to the journalism trade press would think he had come upon a litter of adolescent puppies, hand-licking and floor-wetting, falling all over themselves in their eagerness to be wanted, to be understood, to be loved—to be credible."

It all raises the question whether a journalistic tradition unique worldwide in its independence and vigor is inhibited by self-inflicted wounds.

RISE OF THE MARKETING CONCEPT

In part, the ethical-reactive disposition arises as the media, particularly newspapers, strive to put their business affairs in disciplined, profitable order by employing the marketing concept in media management. Marketing orientation was present in television from its birth and was basic corporate philosophy in other industries before that. But it is relatively new in newspapers. The concept regards newspapers and television news as products to be created in response to marketing research, to be promoted and sold just as any other products are. If the concept is permitted to run unrestricted through management ranks, what news products are created—and for whom—is decided by marketing experts whose goal is not fearless coverage of the news on its merits, but, rather, attracting the right affluent readers and viewers who in turn will attract advertisers. There was a day, not too distant, when experienced editors made such decisions based on their best instincts about what was timely, topical, and important news—and what wasn't. Then, newspapers proudly and confidently thundered out their editorial views; today, most are the only paper in town and, sobered by that responsibility, more likely will *react* to all viewpoints in their market by following a middle-of-the-road course. For example, *USA Today* is a newspaper designed in direct response to market research of reader *wants* (not needs), and it avoids any editorial page endorsement of political candidates. Clearly, many editors and managers believe it is good business to straddle issues, to react to public consensus, rather than to lead.

Within a management context, it must be argued that the marketing concept should be extended into the newsroom. After all, newspaper and television *are* businesses that must succeed financially if they are to serve readers and advertisers as well as shareholders. But neither the marketing concept nor any other internal or external business consideration should warp the news process. Men and women who accept the challenge of being journalists in this country and who devote careers to collecting and disseminating news and opinion have a higher responsibility than the bottom line.

There is need, then, for journalists to react urgently *but* thoughtfully, discerningly to the notions so widespread in our society that something is wrong in the way the media operate. Grevious ethical lapses *have* occurred; problems *do* exist and they *must* be met—but with calm, balanced corrective efforts, certainly not mindless stonewalling or frenetic, unthinking fawning before the latest survey on how to court public favor. Ethical-reactive journalism cannot be permitted to overpower the historic responsibility of doing on the front page and in the 6 P.M. news what, in the judgment of professional journalists, *must* be done.

THE HOSTILE PUBLIC ENVIRONMENT

Opinions differ within the media on whether there is anything new in the current level of public and institutional attacks on the media. Some experienced editors and publishers say the media always have been somewhat unpopular—just stay cool and get on with the job without worrying too much about public perception of how it should be performed.

However, the media do operate today in an increasingly hostile public environment, and if this isn't corrected, the role of the free media in our democracy will change. Along with surveys reporting the media have serious credibility problems comes the occasional poll suggesting, to the contrary, that the media enjoy "believability" among the public or that journalists are more popular than, say, lawyers or U.S. senators, and that things aren't so bad after all. But how, then, to explain such wide public acceptance, for example, of unparalleled White House orchestration of news and image during most of the Reagan administration? How to explain during the "Irangate" story in 1987 unmistakable public feeling that the media had overreported the story, relied too much on rumors and unconfirmed reports, had in fact simply given too much coverage to the story? And, closer to Main Street, how to explain public acquiescence as legislatures, school boards, and city councils chip away at the First Amendment or conduct public business behind doors closed to the media? How to explain private citizens wielding libel law with unprecedented success—

not only to defend name and honor, but to attack and punish the media? Isn't all that in part a reflection of worsening societal attitudes toward the media, a signal that although we can differ on how serious is the problem the media face, there can be no doubt a problem exists?

It is obvious mounting external pressures are contributing heavily to a defensive, reactive posture by the media. For example, the *Washington Post's* Bradlee, secure in journalistic history for his role in uncovering Watergate, ruefully points out that any newspaper forced to spend more than $1 million to defend itself in a single libel suit, as the *Post* was, today must look twice at any story, whatever its news value, if it is likely to draw heavy legal fire. The public has moved off the sidelines, into the fray—and has found weapons, in court and out, to effectively influence the outcome.

With $1 million lawyers' bills feared in newsrooms and public clamour about the media rising, there is considerable danger the resultant noisy palaver may camouflage two important factors: First, much criticism of the media is *not* designed to engender ethical, fair, and balanced behavior; rather, it is designed to win a narrow point on behalf of an individual or special interest group—and never mind being fair. Second, a worsening public climate emboldens special interest critics to attack a newspaper or network with studied indifference to wider damage thus done to the media's historic, unique, and important role in our democratic society. It can be argued the importance of that role should transcend individual and relatively insignificant transgressions by the media. Yet, the public attitude toward the media increasingly is adversarial or, at best, indifferent as special interest groups attempt to weaken the media and force their basic repositioning relative to other institutions in our society. Small wonder government and other institutions feel free to manage the news, to pull even more tightly the reins of power.

Too often, at such moments so dangerous to the future role of the media, arguments rage within the media themselves: Is it press or television that is most responsible for the "credibility gap?" The proposition that television belongs under the First Amendment umbrella would not gain unanimous support today even among journalists. It's eyeball-to-eyeball for media versus critics—and too often the media are blinking or, at least, looking in the wrong direction.

It is imperative the media themselves resolve such credibility questions, for the alternatives are unlovely to contemplate. If the media ignore serious ethical issues now on the public agenda, they can expect, at best, disenchanted readers and viewers; at worst, the media will face deeper intrusion into the news process by government and other institutions of power in our society, which truly could jeopardize the First Amendment and the concept of a free media in the United States.

All this creates, of course, an additional burden for anyone picking up the already heavy responsibility of participating in public affairs as a reporter, editor, or media manager. But that burden must be accepted by any journalist during a career in the media.

In a sense, students of journalism are on their own in searching for a course to follow in matters of ethics and professional conscience. No matter what we can turn up here on how other journalists view ethics, or what newspapers or networks put forward as *their* ethical codes, there really are only very general guidelines to follow. For you young, aspiring journalists, it is a lonely journey ahead if you attempt to define ethical conduct with any precision and personal meaning. But it is a very worthwhile—and essential—journey you undertake.

Conrad C. Fink
Alta Vista Farm
Cherry Valley, New York

MEDIA ETHICS

IN THE NEWSROOM AND BEYOND

ETHICS IN THE
PURSUIT OF NEWS

Part One of this book is structured to help journalism students and beginning reporters in a critical self-examination of ethical conduct in the pursuit of news. It is a subject widely discussed among newspaper editors and broadcast news directors as well, of course, and how we get the story and then write or broadcast it is much debated by media critics, social commentators of all sorts, and our larger constituencies, the reading and viewing publics. But it is with the individual journalist that lies the responsibility—or, it might be said, the agony—of deciding what is right or wrong, ethical or unethical.

To aid the journalist making those decisions, the first chapter of Part One sketches a philosophical framework of recorded debate and writing about ethical matters reaching back 2,500 years. There is a mainstream of thought coming down through the centuries that bears directly on today's discussion.

In our second, third, and fourth chapters, we discuss specific work situations in which principles of ethics and matters of professional conscience arise for every reporter. The problems are as basic as which story a beat reporter selects for coverage (thus ignoring others) and the sources quoted in reporting it (while not quoting some). But we also will range widely into such questions as whether a reporter, to avoid even the perception of conflict of interest, must step aside in private life from activities others participate in without second thought.

THE PHILOSOPHICAL FRAMEWORK

Why do we sometimes read a news story and think, "That writer was not fair?" Why do we sometimes think, "That's wrong; that shouldn't be done" when we see a TV camera linger on the broken body of an accident victim or the grief-stricken face of a widow at graveside?

Why do readers and viewers sometimes arise in amazing unanimity to condemn what they perceive to be unfair coverage or invasion of privacy by the media? What is there inside us—reporter or newscaster, reader or viewer—that even raises such questions?

Well, it's not some sort of genetic transfer down through the generations that plants such sensibilities within us. So, all of us must be subject to external influences that condition us to regard such questions in a certain light. Chapter 1 traces briefly the origins of some of those influences in hopes that this will clarify the common philosophical framework within which the individual journalist and the American media collectively operate today.

In search of what shapes a journalist's ethical thinking, let's put together a blue-ribbon panel of media leaders who began as reporters or copy editors, then rose along varying routes to influence and authority not only in their own organizations, but in the industry, too. We'll pick a group geographically diverse, whose members represent both the business and news sides, and who lead organizations ranging in size from huge media conglomerates to small community papers. Let's ask the group to pinpoint formative experiences—perhaps a memorable crisis or two—in their own careers that helped establish their personal code of ethics.

Warren H. Phillips, chairman of Dow Jones & Company, Inc., publisher of the *Wall Street Journal* and a former copy editor known for dedication to principled, ethical journalism: "[I] have trouble recalling the kinds of watershed incidents you are seeking. The ethical standards at the *Journal* were set before I arrived on the scene....Essentially I worked to maintain standards set by predecessors. I am sure we all faced problems of professional conscience at one time or another, but they were so routine and continuing that they don't stand out, and I would hate to pull out the one or two such recollections and dramatize them. They were no more worthy of note than the questions that come up at newspapers every week, and I certainly would not characterize any as 'memorable crises' that were in any sense 'formative experiences.'"[1]

Harold W. Andersen, chairman and chief executive officer of the *Omaha World-Herald* and a former reporter: "Most often, a challenge to ethical standards, in my experience, [has] been rather subtle—real, but not the type that makes for a story with a moral."[2]

William F. Thomas, editor and executive vice president of the *Los Angeles Times:* "At my age, a guy's attitudes and ethics have been affected by so many singular happenstances it is impossible to pick one out."[3]

Claude Sitton, editorial director and vice president of the *Raleigh* (N.C.) *News and Observer* and *Times:* "My sense of ethical practice is the result of slow maturation rather than any crises."[4]

Robert B. Atwood, editor and publisher, *Anchorage Times:* "I consider ethics mostly a matter of common sense....I can't remember ever having any dramatic incident when we had a big ethical problem in regard to a story. We have judged each one as it occurs and we handle it the way we think is fair and right to all."[5]

Dorman E. Cordell, Associated Press reporter and executive for 23 years, then president of six community dailies in the Dallas-Fort Worth area: "How is a sense of ethics formed? I asked the question of myself and identified four main sources: (1) training as a youngster in the difference between right and wrong and the importance of doing right; (2) formal instruction, primarily by various journalism teachers, in ethics and specifically related to journalism; (3) role models, both supervisors and persons I admired; and (4) experience, the factor that contributes the fine-tuning of the ethical sense."[6]

In sum, in an industry where making judgment calls on ethical issues is a daily, almost automatic occurrence, our panel cannot pinpoint how their own personal sense of journalistic ethics developed. None can recall with any precision single incidents or formative professional experiences, let alone specific philosophical guidelines, that shaped their thinking. Note none of the six even in passing refers to ethical guidelines laid down by industry groups as being central to their thinking on ethics or matters of professional conscience. Clearly, to build the philosophical framework for this book's discussion of ethics in the pursuit of news we must begin outside the media, beyond their current practice, and backward in time. Let's look backward, toward the origin of ethical thought. We will not attempt any definitive review of all that has gone before us. That is far beyond the scope of this book. But let's see if we can detect the early shaping of certain core principles that are reflected in today's discussion of ethics and professional conscience in the media.

THE 2,500-YEAR-OLD MAINSTREAM

Ethics is a system of principles, a morality or code of conduct. It is the values and rules of life recognized by an individual, group, or culture seeking guidelines to human conduct and what is good or bad, right or wrong.

There is a record of humanity debating ethics for nearly 2,500 years, searching for applications of values and rules to everyday life. As cultures and societies evolved, so did ethics and the debate; different ethical codes developed in different cultures and even within the same societies.

Perhaps one constant in ethical debate is that conflict is kin to ethics. Even within a single society or culture, opinions can differ widely on what is right, what is wrong. In a very real sense, a discussion today over, say, the ethical implications of TV's "ambush" interview technique joins a 2,500-year-old mainstream of ethical debate. And if, for example, a *newspaper* journalist complains a *television* journalist is unfair in ambushing people, that is just another illustration of how different viewpoints over ethical matters can develop in the same society among persons who share basic values and principles. In ethical debate it has been ever thus.

The mainstream originates, by general agreement, in Athens, where Socrates, before he died in 399 B.C., is recorded by his student Plato as discussing the meaning of abstract terms such as "justice" and "good." Socrates essentially was optimistic that "good" could be identified and practiced. Plato, who died in 347 B.C., launched into the mainstream the ideal of good that exists however a society might conduct itself at the moment. Thus did the earliest thinkers in ethics pose for today's journalists the prospect that ethical behavior might require adhering to a personal interpretation of what is right or good, even if that means going against the flow of current thought in society. Both teacher and student idealized the search for good even though that might be a lonely task in a generally uncaring society. Both emphasized the need to seek virtue for its own sake, not particularly for reward.[7] Aristotle, a student of Plato, focused on enumerating virtues and vices and placing on the individual responsibility for taking virtuous action through free choice. Aristotle cast this individual responsibility within a wider context, holding that only through contribution to a good society can an individual live the good life. His teachings constitute a warning that virtue doesn't always come easily. In fact, Aristotle felt that doing what is morally right can be measured by the price paid—sacrifices made, happiness given up. These thoughts are not foreign to journalists today who feel a sense of mission, and fulfillment, in a job that informs and enlightens for

VIEWPOINT 1-1

OK. WHAT NOW?

"It's been a worrisome subject since not long after mankind first emerged from caves.

"At least as far back as Socrates, the Greeks wrestled with the problem, finally concluding that it couldn't be separated from aesthetics. The Germans took a slightly more ponderous view, seeing it as some sort of on-going debate between man and God, while the French thought it came down a little closer to a question of whether the wine was properly aged. The British got it all tangled up with the work ethic, and Americans, gen-erally speaking, were too busy conquering a continent to pay it much heed.

"That happy heedlessness came to an end with the vanishing of the last frontier. In more recent times, hardly a profession in the land—certainly including journalism—has failed to give increasing attention to two ques-tions: What in the hell is ethics, and once you define it, what do you do about it?"

Frank McCullough, then executive editor, McClatchy Newspapers, in the preface, *Drawing the Line*, American Society of Newspaper Editors, Washington, D.C., 1984

"Ethics is a curious combination of self-awareness, history, self-criticism, and an-thropology. It begins with a tradition which is as old as western thought itself and ends, necessarily, in the question: OK, what do we do now?"

Robert C. Solomon, *Morality and the Good Life,* McGraw-Hill, New York, 1984

the good of society; or, say, journalists who take stands on matters of profes-sional conscience and pay for it by losing their jobs or, even, going to jail to protect sources.

With the advent of Christian ethics, a momentous turn in our ethical main-stream, there arose the concept that seeking salvation through God was more important than virtuous action. However, Christian theologians, including the earliest of note, Saint Augustine (354–430), left with the individual the respon-sibility of interpreting God's will. Even the most explicit sense of God's will, including the Ten Commandments, must be interpreted in secular life.

By the 1600s, there appeared se-rious investigation into humanity's psychological impulses in matters of ethics. Thomas Hobbes (1588–1679) viewed such impulses as fear and selfishness as prime motivators of conduct. His influential writing, es-sentially pessimistic about human na-ture, indicated he felt each individual must give up certain rights under a strong government if society is to control selfishness and violence, but later Hobbes threw into the main-stream the then radical thought that

VIEWPOINT 1-2

SERVE THE GENERAL WELFARE

"The primary purpose of gathering and dis-tributing news and opinion is to serve the general welfare by informing the people and enabling them to make judgments on the issues of the time. Newspapermen and women who abuse the power of their pro-fessional role for selfish motives or unwor-thy purposes are faithless to that public trust."

American Society of Newspaper Editors "Statement of Principles," adopted 1975

the people possess true power. Hobbes rejected the concept of all-powerful sovereigns pretending to divine rights. It is not much of a leap from that thought to the assumption of journalists today that the people must be informed and that the media, as surrogate of the people, therefore have a special role in society.

John Milton (1608–1674), in his *Areopagitica,* published in 1644, fashioned the concept of an "open marketplace of ideas" in which all would be free to express ideas. He was confident a "self-righting process" would enable truth to survive while false and unsound ideas would be vanquished. This line of thought echoes today among those who advocate publishing or airing *facts* and trusting readers and viewers to ascertain *truth.*

VIEWPOINT 1-3

TRUTH WILL SURVIVE

"Let all with something to say be free to express themselves. The true and sound will survive, the false and unsound will be vanquished."

John Milton, *Areopagitica,* 1644

ENTER UTILITARIANISM AND ETHICAL DUTY

Empiricism, the concept of knowledge through experience and verification through experimentation or observation alone, appeared in the 1700s. A Briton, David Hume (1711–1776), is associated with the emergence of this scientific approach to ethics. Hume, an atheist, was skeptical that good can be found through reason, but argued human beings naturally or instinctively feel charitable toward others. He argued human activity is aimed at achieving happiness and that usefulness—"utility"—is the measure for any ethical principle in determining its place in society. For example, justice serves the good of humanity and thus is utilitarian.

What might be called the modern era of ethical thought opened with Immanuel Kant (1724–1804), who wrote of duty and the "categorical imperative" in what *ought* to be done in ethical matters. He argued that codes of conduct and morality must be arrived at through reason and be universally applicable to all societal environments at all times. Kant, who believed in God, argued each individual is free to act and thus is responsible for measuring up to codes of conduct. He felt strongly that the moral worth of an act is determined by rational intention, the will to be moral, not the consequences of the act. In the context of today's dialogue over media ethics, Kant would place responsibility squarely on the individual journalist to reason out what is good. But Kant probably would be of less help to that individual in relating the process to any wider societal context.

The context for ethical thought was widened by John Stuart Mill (1806–1873) who interpreted utilitarianism to mean ethical conduct should aim at general well-being, creating the greatest happiness for the greatest number of people. Mill objected to Kant's emphasis on the intentions behind an act and argued it is the outcome or consequence of an act that counts. Although Mill asked whether an act created happiness for the greatest number of people, he also spoke strongly in defense of the rights of minorities. The seeming contradiction—or, shall we say, flexibility—in Mill's argument is no stranger in newsrooms today. For example, should a newspaper or TV news team invade the privacy of an individual—thus inflicting unhappiness—in order to serve the larger populace, the larger good, with a story that should see light? Mill probably would counsel looking at the consequences and determining what best would serve the greater number.

LIBERTARIANISM, OBJECTIVITY, AND SOCIAL RESPONSIBILITY

In the late 1600s and early 1700s, in Britain and America, there developed the libertarian philosophy concerning the press and its place in society. This placed great faith in the ability of the people to make rational, intelligent decisions, to find truth *if* sufficient information were available through a free press in a free society that protected free expression. The press in that era assumed the role of enlightening the public, guarding against government infringement on personal liberties, and fighting off all but the broadest outside limitations on how the press operated. That meant, for example, answering to the laws of sedition or libel after publication, but vigorously rejecting attempts by governments or other institutions to exert prior censorship or otherwise threaten fundamental press freedom. The sense of freedom extended even to freedom from any responsibility to the public; the press regarded itself as a provider of information and entertainment to readers and, later, advertising to buyers and sellers—and in that way served both the political and economic systems while making a profit.[8]

Such was the temper of the times that the First Amendment to the U.S. Constitution, passed by Congress in 1789 and ratified by three-fourths of the states in 1791, stated, "Congress shall make no law...abridging the freedom of speech, or of the press...."

In the late 1800s, there developed in the American press a concept still central to media ethics: "Objectivity," the effort to present balanced accounts of all sides of an issue in news stories written as dispassionately as possible by reporters-observers who spurn activist involvement in the news and avoid injecting partisan views into their copy. As we will discuss later, true objectivity was—and is—impossible to achieve. But the *effort* to achieve it became the core philosophy of the influential Associated Press when it was reorganized in 1894 into the forerunner of today's mammoth international news agency. There was a business imperative for AP's efforts at objectivity: as a membership organization serving newspapers of all political persuasions, in every section of the nation, reporting and writing without hint of partisanship was an obvious necessity. Many individual newspapers, serving local audiences equally diverse and following the AP model, later developed the same business reason to strive for the ideal of objectivity.

In the early 1900s, another major development was a rising sense of community conscience among newspapers, a feeling among some editors and publishers that responsibility to society was a corollary to freedom of the press. This became a much stronger impulse, along with an attitude of professionalism among many newspaper reporters and editors, with the creation in 1922 of the American Society of Newspaper Editors (ASNE), still the premier editors' organization. In 1923, at its first meeting, ASNE adopted the "Canons of Journalism," a statement of newspaper ideals—service in the public interest, independence, truthfulness, sincerity, accuracy. (ASNE's canons were supplanted in 1975 by a "Statement of Principles," reproduced at the end of this book, as is the code of ethics of the Society of Professional Journalists, Sigma Delta Chi.)

ASNE's canons had considerable moral force. Many other journalism organizations subsequently drew up codes of ethics, too. Most were sweeping, idealistic statements of principle, not precise codes of conduct, and journalism organizations studiously avoided any suggestion that subscription to the codes be a condition of employment as a journalist. No journalism group made any effort to force its members to comply with the codes. That would have been too much like a first step toward licensing and the shackling of the free press. (To some social commentators, codes of ethics with strict rules of enforcement, including expulsion for infraction, are necessary characteristics of any profession; thus the tendency in some quarters to deny journalism the label of "profession.")

Though vague and completely unenforceable, the early codes were expressions of hope that American journalism would move in a new direction. They signaled clearly that the media were well on their way out of libertarianism and into a new era in which freedom of the press was linked in the minds of many with social responsibility. Rights became tied to duties, and American journalism never was the same again.[9]

As did most significant turns in the 2,500-year ethical mainstream, the move toward social responsibility developed slowly, almost imperceptibly at times, and within the context of wider changes in societal attitudes. For example, the public became better educated and more discerning; it began to look at the media more critically, and by the 1920s and 1930s, it began in significant numbers to seek news and opinion not only from newspapers, but also from a growing number of alternatives. Thus was a new competitive factor inserted into the mix as magazines proliferated in numbers and appeal and as radio emerged as a source of, at least, news headlines as well as entertainment. (Television surfaced as a commercially viable competitor only in the 1950s, of course.)

For newspapers, the new era brought a startling reality: Economic support now had to be found in a wider marketplace, among readers and listeners of varied social status, interests and beliefs, and not simply from narrowly partisan political or economic groups that supported many publications in earlier eras. Many newspapers that developed as voices of political factions and were supported by relatively small partisan groups now needed a wider economic base due to the rising cost of publication and circulation. Significantly, the new era offered undreamed profits for newspapers that widened their appeal. Thus, social responsibility, with its sense of service to a larger constituency, became a profitable philosophy. There developed a *business,* as well as journalistic, rationale for paying closer attention to the needs and desires of the marketplace.

Social responsibility got another boost from growing awareness that government intervention in media affairs was a real possibility, and that the only barrier was support by the public of a free press. Particularly in the 1930s, a period of serious economic dislocation and social unrest, government was intervening in other affairs of Americans as never before, and receiving general applause for it. The meaning was clear: If government could tinker with, say, the supply and demand mechanism of a free marketplace or with the relationship between employer and employee, could not it tinker with the media as well? There was the example of radio being slipped tightly under government regulation, albeit because it uses a finite "public resource," the airwaves, that perhaps only a government agency can regulate properly. But, nevertheless, the example of radio was a precedent for government intervention, and yet another reason for the media in general to reflect a sense of responsibility to the society that sustained them.

In 1942, Henry R. Luce of Time, Inc., provided principal funding for a study that to this day influences strongly many discussions of ethics by the public and journalists alike. Luce commissioned Robert W. Hutchins, then chancellor of the University of Chicago, to study, in Hutchins' words, "the present state and future prospects of the freedom of the press." Hutchins created a study panel of ten university educators, a former U.S. assistant secretary of state, and the then chairman of the Federal Reserve Bank of New York that became known as the "Hutchins Commission."[10] It issued in 1947 a report, "A Free and Responsible Press," that is regarded as the strongest, best focused statement up to that time of the need for a socially responsible press, although the label "social responsibility" never was mentioned by the commission—that came later, notably in the writings of a journalism professor and media watcher, Theodore Peterson.[11]

The commission concluded press freedom was endangered because, first, as mass communication developed, the press (in which the commission included newspapers, radio, movies, magazines, and books) became much more important to the people, yet its very development *decreased* the number of people who could express their ideas and opinions through the press. Second, "the few who are able to use the machinery of the press" stereotyped some groups in society and had not provided "service adequate to the needs of the society." Third, the press sometimes engaged in practices which "society condemns and which, if continued, it will inevitably undertake to regulate or control."

The press, the commission said, was "probably the most powerful single influence today" in shaping American culture and public opinion. Press responsibilities, the commission said, included being accurate, serving as a forum for exchange of comment and criticism, projecting representative pictures of groups within society, presenting and clarifying society's goals and values, and widely distributing news and opinion.

If private ownership was irresponsible, the commission said, government could regulate the press. It added the First Amendment was intended to guarantee free expression, not create a privileged industry, and the press was accountable to its public. Many newspapers ignored, condemned even, the commission report. But the report's main thrust—responsibility—was an idea here to stay.

In language that shaped much of the vigorous discussion following the commission report, Theodore Peterson wrote in 1956 that social responsibility's "major premise" is that "freedom carries concomitant obligations; and the press, which enjoys a privileged position under our government, is obliged to be responsible to society for carrying out certain essential functions of mass communications in contemporary society."

"People's Right to Know"

One seminal idea that entered the ethical mainstream after World War II was enunciated by Kent Cooper, then general manager of the Associated Press. Cooper, a vigorous critic of censorship and barriers to free flow of information around the world, spoke of the "people's right to know."[12] This concept held that while the First Amendment gives the press the *right* to freely print the news, the people's right to know gives the press the *duty* to print it. Thus developed the idea of a press serving as surrogate of the people and demanding access to news, as well as freedom to print it, on behalf of the people.[13]

The people's right to know is a concept not found in the Constitution; neither is the idea that on behalf of the people the media have the right of access to news. Nevertheless, by the 1950s both "rights" were regarded widely in the media and public as implicit. In the minds of many, the idea was firmly fixed that the media were the "Fourth Estate"—a fourth branch of government which (in addition to legislative, judicial, and executive branches) had a real role in governing the country.[14]

Enter Radio and Television

Radio and television, born as commercially viable media much later than newspapers, entered the mainstream of ethical debate under considerably different circumstances. Both began as federally regulated media concentrating primarily on entertainment, rather than news, and so remain today. Matters of *news* ethics were turned to with less urgency.

In 1923, radio stations formed the National Association of Broadcasters (NAB) as a voluntary membership trade association; but not until 1929 was the NAB's first radio code established—and that dealt with a wide range of advertising and programming standards, not just news. There was no workable machinery for implementing the code, which NAB didn't really attempt to rectify until 1958, when it urged members to pledge adherence to a new code. Just 14 percent of radio stations then on the air signed the pledge. Not until 1961 was a code authority established to oversee implementation.

NAB's television code was adopted in 1952, but was virtually meaningless until creation of the code authority in 1961. Still, until 1976, stations could join NAB and reject the codes. By 1974, only 57 percent of stations were NAB members; 41 percent subscribed to the codes.[15] With no requirement for compliance, NAB codes are reduced in effect to suggesting respect for conventional social attitudes such as "sanctity of marriage" and "value of the home." Then, in 1982, following an antitrust suit by the U.S. Justice Department, the U.S. District Court for the District of Columbia held the Sherman Antitrust Act was violated by a section of the NAB television code dealing with length and number of commercials member stations should broadcast within certain time periods. In response, both NAB's radio and television codes were suspended. That ended any industrywide codes for membership organizations of stations and networks (although the Radio and Television News Directors Association has a code for *individual* broadcast journalists).

Government regulation of radio and television, through the Federal Communications Commission, was designed to represent the people's interests, but it, too, usually has been ineffectual, and in recent years the mood in Washington has been to withdraw even more from federal intervention in such matters. Deregulation of broadcast is the trend.

Well, then, where does that leave the ethical debate today in broadcasting?

At both network and station levels, it is a debate generally unable to rise above questions of how to produce inoffensive programming that will ensure widest possible public support which, in turn, will (1) promise just enough self-regulation to prevent government intervention and (2) bring in the most advertising dollars. (And dollars there are aplenty. An NAB survey of 1984 results for fifty-two TV stations in the ten largest markets shows they averaged net revenue of $39,429,300. Pretax profit averaged $14,252,200—for a profit margin of 36.1 percent, extraordinarily high for American industry.)

In radio and television newsrooms, as in newspaper newsrooms, absence of any generally accepted, practical codes of ethics throws onto each journalist the responsibility for ethical behavior. There has been a great deal of debate over ethics down through the centuries. Associations have been formed, codes written, seminars held. But for the American journalist—in broadcast or print— little has changed since Aristotle put on each individual the burden of personal responsibility for virtuous conduct.

THE "CREDIBILITY GAP" APPEARS

Personal responsibility was the thrust of a hard-hitting speech in 1982 by a respected journalist that sparked within the media a new turn in the debate over ethics and what became known as the "credibility gap." The speaker was Michael J. O'Neill, then editor of the *New York Daily News,* which, at 1.3 million circulation, was the nation's largest general-readership newspaper. His speech, "The Power of the Press, A Problem for the Republic—A Challenge for Editors," was delivered at an ASNE convention in Washington, D.C., thus reaching the most influential editors of America. O'Neill lamented the "press's harshly adversarial posture toward government and its infatuation with investigative reporting." There had been "astonishing growth in the power of the media over the last decade or so," he said, and "I am by no means sure we are using it wisely. The tendency has been to revel in the power and wield it freely, rather than to accept any corresponding increase in responsibility." O'Neill warned that some reporters were going too far with investigative reporting. It had "run off the ethical tracks...individuals and institutions have been needlessly hurt when the lure of sensational headlines has prevailed over fairness, balance, and a valid purpose...Is our duty to inform so stern that we must exile ourselves from our humanity? Have we become so cynical, so hardened by our experiences with sham, that we can no longer feel what an official feels, what his wife and children feel, when he is being ripped and torn on TV and in the press?"

O'Neill warned that advocacy journalists were permitting "cultural, visceral, and ideological" biases to slip into news copy. "Editors—myself included—have simply not exercised enough control over subeditors and reporters..." O'Neill concluded:

> In the final analysis, what we need most of all in our profession is a generous spirit, infused with human warmth, as ready to see good as to suspect wrong, to find hope as well as cynicism, to have a clear but uncrabbed view of the world. We need to seek conciliation, not just conflict—consensus, not just disagreement—so that society has a chance to solve its problems, so that we as a nation can find again the common trust and unity—so that we can rekindle the faith in ourselves and in our democracy—that we so urgently need to overcome the great challenges we face in the 1980s.[16]

O'Neill's speech had enormous impact, in part because it came at a time when public opinion polls were revealing beyond doubt that media credibility was in serious trouble with the reading and viewing publics. Poll after poll in the early 1980s showed that public confidence was slipping and that increasing numbers of readers doubted newspapers were fair or unbiased; many viewers were found to reject as sensational and improper much of what television delivered as news. This was the "credibility gap."

In one poll, only 38 percent of respondents said they had a "great deal" or "quite a lot" of confidence in newspapers; 25 percent said that about television. Among institutions, newspapers were ranked sixth in public confidence, behind organized religion, military, banks, the U.S. Supreme Court, and public schools. Television finished even lower, also behind Congress, big business, and organized labor.[17] Repeatedly, studies showed readers were convinced newspapers presented biased or slanted news and too much bad news.[18]

Many polls showed the public quite discerning in attitudes toward media affairs. For example, the Gallup organization found considerable public support for the concept of investigative reporting by newspapers, television, and magazines—but overwhelming disapproval of methods some reporters use, such as quoting unnamed sources or using hidden cameras and microphones. An ASNE survey in 1985 found three-fourths of all adults had some problems with credibility of the media. A Times Mirror Corp. study in 1986, though interpreted by some as showing the news media had unexpectedly strong "believability," was hardly more comforting: only 37 percent of respondents believed the press was "pretty independent"; 53 percent said the press was "too often influenced by powerful interests and institutions" like government, big business, advertisers, and special-interest groups; 73 percent said news organizations were likely to invade an individual's privacy; and 60 percent said the media dwelled too much on bad news.[19]

VIEWPOINT 1-5

THE PUBLIC DEMANDS FAIRNESS

"The First Amendment does not require fairness but I think the American public is beginning to."

Robert MacNeil, *MacNeil-Lehrer News Hour*, Public Broadcasting Service

The public mood was reflected in telling terms in law courts. In the period 1979 to 1983, newspaper defendants in libel cases lost 83 percent of trials that went before juries. In medical malpractice suits, defendants lost 33 percent of the time; in product liability cases, 38 percent. Juries handed down stiff judgments against newspapers that lost—$2.1 million on average in eighty libel cases. In medical malpractice suits, plaintiffs were awarded $665,000 on average, $785,000 was the figure in product liability cases. When newspapers appealed to higher courts and thus removed the issue from the grasp of juries, 70 percent of the verdicts in lost cases were reversed; damages often were trimmed by four-fifths or more. Yet, the point remained: when reflected in jury verdicts, the public's feelings were as fully negative about the media as the opinion polls indicated.

In sum, any discussion of media ethics today must acknowledge that many journalists are deeply concerned that the media have not used their power entirely wisely or professionally and that the transgressions by individual journalists are many and serious. Media ethics must be discussed also within the context of increasingly negative perceptions of newspapers and television held by readers and viewers. Inside the media and out, there is fundamental reassessment under way of the journalist's basic mission, the techniques of reporting and writing, and the morality of the manner in which they are employed. It is not too much to say that many critics feel there must be reexamination of the media and their role in our society.

Let's turn now to the individual journalist and how he or she fits into this overall media review and how ethical issues must be tackled from the first day on the job.

CHAPTER SUMMARY

Many journalists cannot state precisely how they developed ethical guidelines for news work or for managing some of the nation's largest communications companies. Corporate or industry codes are only general statements of principle. So, students of journalism or young working journalists searching for a personal code of ethics should begin outside journalism and backward in time.

For 2,500 years, humanity has debated ethics—a system of principles, a morality or code of conduct. Our detailed knowledge of the debate begins in Athens, where Socrates, before he died in 399 B.C., discussed values and rules of life, seeking guidelines to human conduct and what is good or bad, right or wrong. Different ethical standards developed in different societies, and even within the same society. But core principles entered the 2,500-year mainstream of ethical thought that today constitutes a basis for discussion of media ethics.

Socrates' student, Plato, argued that good exists however a society might conduct itself, suggesting today's journalists must do what their own personal code dictates even though that might differ from current thought in society. Aristotle, Plato's student, focused on individual responsibility for virtuous conduct. Even Christian theologians, though preaching salvation through God, charged the individual with responsibility for correctly interpreting God's will.

John Milton (1608–1674) argued for an "open marketplace of ideas," confident truth would surface if facts were published. In the 1700s, there emerged utilitarianism, measuring an ethical principle by whether it serves the good of society. Immanuel Kant (1724–1804) generally is accepted as opening modern ethical thought when he argued for a sense of duty in what ought to be done in ethical matters.

In colonial America, newspapers adopted a libertarian philosophy that developed in Britain and which rejected responsibility to any institution, including the public. This period gave birth to the First Amendment to the U.S. Constitution prohibiting any abridgment of freedom of the press. In the late 1800s and early 1900s, there developed concepts of "objective" reporting and "social responsibility," which hold the press has responsibilities linked to its rights.

By the 1980s, there was in both the media and public deep concern that newspapers and television were misusing their power and that journalists were arrogant, insensitive, and biased. The "credibility gap" between media and public became a heated issue.

CHAPTER 1

Notes

1 Warren H. Phillips, letter to author, Oct. 17, 1985.
2 Harold W. Andersen, letter to author, Nov. 4, 1985.
3 William F. Thomas, letter to author, Feb. 4, 1986.
4 Claude Sitton, letter to author, Sept. 26, 1985.
5 Robert B. Atwood, letter to author, Nov. 11, 1985.
6 Dorman E. Cordell, letter to author, Nov. 13, 1985.

  7 There is rich material awaiting the reader who seeks more depth in the origins of Western ethical thought. Note particularly Robert C. Solomon, *Morality and the Good Life,* McGraw-Hill, New York, 1984; Crane Brinton, *A History of Western Morals,* Harcourt, Brace, New York, 1959; Alasdair MacIntyre, *A Short History of Ethics,* Macmillan, New York, 1966; Bernard Williams, *Morality: An Introduction to Ethics,* Harper & Row, New York, 1972. For an influential recent writer, see John Rawls, *A Theory of Justice,* Harvard University Press, Cambridge, Mass., 1971. Two books that examine his views in detail are Norman Daniels (ed.), *Reading Rawls,* Basic Books, New York, 1983, and Rex Martin, *Rawls and Rights,* University Press of Kansas, Lawrence, 1985 (note particularly Chapter 7 on conflict of rights such as free press versus fair trial). Also note Henry D. Aiken, *The Age of Ideology,* Houghton Mifflin, Boston, 1957.

  8 Sound discussions of libertarianism are found in Gerald Gross, *The Responsibility of the Press,* Fleet Publishing, New York, 1966; John Calhoun Merrill, *The Imperative of Freedom,* Hastings House, New York, 1974; Peter M. Sandman, David M. Rubin, and David B. Sachsman, *Media,* Prentice-Hall, Englewood Cliffs, N.J., 1976.

  9 The evolution of American media is described particularly well by John Calhoun Merrill, *The Imperative of Freedom* and Gerald Gross, *The Responsibility of the Press.* For a detailed and excellent look at the development of ethical thought in American media see Michael Schudson, *Discovering the News,* Basic Books, New York, 1978. Also note Schudson's *Advertising, The Uneasy Persuasion,* Basic Books, New York, 1984.

10 The Commission on Freedom of the Press, *A Free and Responsible Press,* University of Chicago Press, 1947.

11 Theodore Peterson, Fred S. Siebert, and Wilbert Schramm, *Four Theories of the Press,* University of Illinois Press, Urbana, 1956.

12 Note, particularly, Kent Cooper, *Barriers Down,* Farrar and Rinehart, New York, 1942.

13 For a superb look at modern-day implications of the people's ''right'' to know, see *The Public's Right to Know,* Media Institute, Washington, D.C., 1980.

14 For excellent treatment of this subject see Douglas Cater, *The Fourth Branch of Government,* Vintage Books, New York, 1959.

15 These developments are treated extremely well in Sydney W. Head, *Broadcasting in America,* Houghton Mifflin, Boston, 1976.

16 Michael J. O'Neill, speech to American Society of Newspaper Editors, Washington, D.C., May 5, 1982.

17 Gallup Report, August 1983.

18 Particularly pertinent polling on this subject was done by Belden Associates, a newspaper research consulting firm, 2900 Turtle Creek Plaza, Dallas, Tex., 75219.

19 A Gallup organization poll commissioned by Times Mirror Corp., Times Mirror Square, Los Angeles, Calif., 90053.

2

YOUR PERSONAL CODE:
TROUBLING CONCEPTS

In days bygone, young aspiring journalists prepared for careers in news mainly by developing reporting techniques for getting a story and sharpening writing skills to convey it in clear, understandable language. But times have changed for both individual journalists and the media.

Readers and viewers often are highly critical of what journalists do and the techniques they use to do it. Newspapers and TV news operations can get seriously "out of synch" with their public on ethics and matters of professional conscience. Today's aspiring journalist, therefore, prepares for a career in news under external and internal pressures not only to develop workable reporting and writing techniques, but also to think about ethics and develop a professional stance ethically above reproach.

When all is said and done, readers, listeners, or viewers command the journalist's ultimate allegiance. And, "thinking ethics" requires each journalist to determine how to build a relationship of trust with those consumers of news who depend on the accuracy, professionalism, and fairness of their news medium.

Be prepared for difficulty in building that trust. A survey, "Relating to Readers in the '80s," done for ASNE, finds 50 percent of respondents *disagree* with the statement, "Newspapers are usually fair, they bend over backwards to tell both sides of the story." Of the total number of respondents, 12 percent are not sure about that statement; only 38 percent agree with it. When that same statement is made about television, 63 percent disagree; 8 percent are unsure; and only 29 percent agree.

In Chapter 2, we will discuss broad concepts of concern for any journalist trying to build reader and viewer trust through sound, ethical journalism. We will examine objectivity as a worthwhile goal; conflicts of interest, real or perceived, that can undermine a journalist's objectivity; invasion of privacy; and offenses against "good taste." Let's turn now to how those broad concepts must enter your personal code of ethics as you prepare for a career of giving readers or viewers fair, balanced coverage of the news.

Whatever your personal beliefs or political persuasion, there are publications somewhere in this country that reflect your views. You could happily report and write for one of them under the label "liberal" or "conservative"—or anything in between. Indeed, if you want to express personal views on many topics, you can plan a career of writing editorials for newspapers or television or doing a signed column.

There is nothing wrong with advocacy journalism. It offers exciting, rewarding, meaningful careers. However, if advocacy is your choice, you should consider two factors:

1 It is unethical and irresponsible to blur the distinction between advocacy journalism and the effort to practice the fair and objective reporting that is the core of most newspaper and television journalism today. If you want to be an advocate, work for an advocacy medium.

2 If advocacy is your choice, openly put your advocate's label on now and display it for all to see. Enter a reporting and writing career as an acknowledged advocate; don't masquerade under the title "objective reporter," or secretly carry your crusade into a newsroom that is trying to do an objective job of reporting.

OBJECTIVITY: THE WORTHWHILE GOAL

True objectivity is impossible to achieve. Each of us is shaped by background and experiences that inevitably influence how we see things and act as journalists. That influence cannot be denied; but objectivity is a worthwhile *goal*, and as an ethical journalist you must recognize—and overcome—the very human tendency to let personal feelings influence your reporting and writing. For conscientious journalists, it can be a struggle as long as they are in the newsroom. Be particularly alert at five key points in the sequence of events leading from news development to publication or broadcast of a news story. They are:

1 **Story selection**   Scores, if not hundreds, of story ideas are available to a newspaper or television news department. The *New York Times'* editors look each day at millions of words in news and feature copy; on an average weekday they publish only 200,000 or so. Obviously, some stories must be covered—the hard news about government, accidents, trials, and so forth. Many other stories must be rejected. Thus, the individual journalist often has great discretion in choosing which nonspot or timeless stories will be covered. Will you do a personality profile on a new, rising political star? A feature on abortion clinics? A background piece on crime in the streets? Examine your personal

mindset, your prejudices. Are you selecting, perhaps subconsciously, stories that fit your own way of thinking? Are you intentionally picking stories to prove a point? Or, more properly, are you selecting stories that have news merit and which truly are important to your readers or viewers? Space and time limitations are such that often only those stories of compelling importance and interest to the largest number of readers or viewers can be published or aired. But serving the greatest news needs of most readers or viewers is not always the only yardstick against which a story's news merits should be measured. Your responsibility as a journalist includes spotting, highlighting, and explaining stories *you* know to be significant, even if most of your readers or viewers do not understand that.

2 Source selection   There is danger of subconsciously seeking news from sources who agree with you. If you personally believe abortion is immoral, news sources who agree probably will sound more logical. Whatever your views, beware you don't gravitate unthinkingly toward sources who feel the same way. You must tap sources on all sides of a story, of course. That is just common sense. What often is overlooked, however, is that it is *imperative* that those representing contrasting viewpoints hold equally authoritative credentials. A Democratic dog catcher in your town indeed represents part of the "other side" of a story involving your Republican mayor. But the dog catcher is not an authoritative source for comment on how the mayor is handling citywide expenditure of millions of dollars. A United Press International story on a bank failure in Tennessee quoted "one passerby, who would not give his name," as saying the bank president's "funny paper finally caught up with him."[1] How could any discerning reader trust a reporter who stands outside a bank and grabs a passerby who, under the cloak of anonymity, makes such a serious charge?

3 Fact selection and arrangement   As you arrive back in the newsroom, your notebook full of facts gathered in a day of interviews, you must write a lead and structure a story as objectively as possible. Obviously, not every argument you have heard on, say, abortion can be in your lead. In broadcast, you have thirty or forty-five seconds for a story, and time limitations force greater selectivity in writing or choosing a video clip. You must select facts, gained from equally authoritative sources, that will present a balanced story. Devoting your lead and the subsequent ten paragraphs to the proabortion viewpoint, and quoting the other side only in the twelfth paragraph, is failing your responsibility of presenting the facts in a balanced manner.

4 Language selection   The language you use in writing a story can be highly prejudicial. Consider the different effect upon a reader or viewer if you write that a source "admitted nervously" as contrasted with "acknowledged." What different pictures you paint if you write that a witness "walked" or "strutted" to the stand! What enormous difference there is in describing a person as "antiabortionist" or a "right-to-life advocate." In one story, the *Wall Street Journal* prejudiced readers by stating a woman "began lamely" to explain her viewpoint.[2] Achieving complete neutrality in language is, like achieving total objectivity, arguably impossible; in some cases it may be undesirable. But even-handed, fair use of language must be a goal for any writer dedicated to presenting a balanced account.

5 Timing and context   A spot, or "breaking," news story sets its own timing and rhythm. If the President of the United States speaks on U.S. involvement in Latin America, that is news to be published or aired right now. Reaction from political opponents or comment from Latin American leaders is rushed to the public as it develops. In such cases, a story's timing and the context in which it is published are out of the journalist's hands. But for much news, a journalist selects timing and context. This can be crucial in determining the impact a story will have. For example, a three-part series on crime in the streets of your town might have little political impact if run when no local elections are scheduled; it might have great impact if run two weeks before the mayor is up for reelection. That doesn't mean a journalist's news judgments should be based only on the impact publication will have; it *does* mean a responsible journalist must understand that timing and context can have dramatic effect.

It is simplistic, of course, to limit discussion of objectivity to the preceding five neat categories. The problem is much more complex. Two alternative views, one from inside the media and another from outside, illustrate that:

Jay T. Harris, executive editor of the *Philadelphia Daily News,* argues American journalists are "becoming reluctant to harp on that which is wrong or dangerous in our society and to continue to harp on it until it is made right." Further, he argues journalists should be "conscious, open and continuing advocates for that which is right and necessary..."[3] The weakness in Harris's position is who shall determine what is "wrong or dangerous" and "right and necessary"?

A greater challenge comes from Roberto C. Goizueta, chairman of the Coca-Cola Co., who, with his company, often is the subject of media coverage. Goizueta told an editors' meeting, "...the single most damaging trait in today's journalism, in my opinion, is that in the search for, and preoccupation with, objectivity and balance, the important elements of context, perspective and judgment often suffer. I will even be so blunt as to say that with some reporters and editors, it may be the result of just plain taking the easy road intellectu-

---

VIEWPOINT 2-1

TRUTH AND OBJECTIVITY

"Truth is the ultimate goal.

"Objectivity in reporting the news is another goal, which serves as the mark of an experienced professional. It is a standard of performance toward which we strive. We honor those who achieve it."

"Code of Ethics," Society of Professional Journalists, Sigma Delta Chi, adopted 1926, revised 1973

---

ally. Understanding and reporting the importance of events in their proper context surely is a heavy responsibility to place on anyone, but in fact, I believe the journalist has that obligation.... The consumers of print journalism want to see an editor's opinion on the editorial page, but we need his or her judgment as to significance, relevance and truth reflected in news stories.'' Goizueta thus argues the journalist's responsibility is to not only judge the news merits and facts of an event, but also its truth.[4]

Yes. But Is It True?

Must reporters determine the ''truth'' of stories they report? Is it enough to simply state facts and quote authoritative sources on both sides? Or, must reporters determine the underlying validity of those facts and quotes?

Those questions resurrect a journalistic nightmare out of the 1950s, when a Republican senator from Wisconsin, Joe McCarthy, manipulated reporters through shrewd understanding of what in those days was their very narrow interpretation of ''objective reporting.'' It was sufficient—indeed, for many required—to limit reporting to who said what and when. A U.S. senator could be quoted at length and virtually without challenge if, for example, he scurried about the country, making unsubstantiated charges of communist infiltration in high places, both civil and military, and assassinating with abandon previously unblemished reputations. And that, of course, is precisely what McCarthy did— and what the media did. A U.S. senator was saying it, and that meant it was news; it was somebody else's job to determine whether it was truth.

It was an agonizing experience for reporters of the ''who-said-what-and-when'' school. They could see the senator jumping ahead, from charge to charge, never letting rebuttal catch up. A person attacked today tried to respond tomorrow, but by that time McCarthy was attacking someone else, again seizing headlines. McCarthy, who thoroughly understood the mechanics of news agency and newspaper operations, often timed news conferences just before presses rolled. Day after day, newspapers carried his latest charge before they could obtain balancing comment.

From the McCarthy experience came a true turn in American journalism, a realization that traditional efforts to balance charge with response by quoting the other side a day or so later were inadequate. There evolved a new, much wider definition of objectivity that requires a reporter to provide a dimension of analysis or interpretation in addition to factual reporting. This means balancing the relative validity of charge and countercharge, expanding a ''straight news'' story with some sense of the wider context that lets reader or viewer judge the truth. This is done today by inserting balancing material within a single story, or writing an interpretive story labeled ''news analysis'' for a newspage, often next to the spot news story itself.

Interpretive coverage developed further during the Vietnam war and Nixon presidency, when straight news reporting proved inadequate in revealing official lies and coverups. The sheer complexity of other stories—in politics, science, economics—forced reporters more deeply into analytical writing.

This is dangerous business for a reporter, of course. Where is the line between reporting ''facts'' and inserting your opinion? If you transfer interpretation from editorial page to newspage, how is your reader to differentiate between news and opinion? Some reporters in the 1960s and 1970s went too far. They created the "new journalism," variously considered "impressionistic" and "humanistic," or "participatory" and "activist." Its proponents went beyond reporting and into advocacy journalism, sometimes labeling their work as interpretive and sometimes not. In its worst form, new journalism featured made-up quotes and composite—that is, *fictional*—characters. This was considered acceptable as long as the final result was a story of "truth." Today, it is a technique rejected by newspapers of consequence and most TV news operations.

How—or whether—a journalist should attempt to divine truth can be hotly debated. There can be no quarrel, however, with the proposition that in seeking fairness and balance, the journalist must be open and frank with reader or viewer. For example, an individual accused in a story of wrongdoing obviously should have right of reply in that same story; if that individual cannot be reached, or declines comment, the story should explain. However, the writer who goes beyond that, with a paragraph or two on how a story was researched or which sources were contacted, can add for reader or viewer a dimension of understanding that helps establish trust in the story, and thus in the journalist and the newspaper or television station.

Within the context of the media's current credibility problems, it is not enough to know in your own heart that you are practicing ethical journalism. A journalist must be *perceived by the public as being ethical*. Let's turn now to conflict of interest and how even the perception of conflict can create problems.

CONFLICT OF INTEREST: REAL AND PERCEIVED

A small-town sports writer in south Georgia simultaneously worked as general manager of a local radio station and served on both the school board and county board of commissioners. Nobody in town, including his newspaper employer, seemed to think worse of him for wearing four hats. "I don't see any conflict of interest," said the journalist–radio manager–public official.[5]

At the *New York Times,* the wine critic resigned when it was revealed he had written a book for a wine importer. Said a *Times* spokesperson, "We really don't feel comfortable with a critic doing a subsidized book." Said the ex-critic, "The *Times* clearly overreacted....What I did was write an objective book....I have never endorsed a product...."[6]

The two cases illustrate questions long plaguing journalists: Where does professional life end and personal life begin? Must one dictate how the other is conducted? Must the reporter give up rights—and responsibilities—of citizenship, such as political work, to avoid conflict of interest? Must a journalist become an emotional, psychological, and social bystander in pursuit of dispassionate, objectively balanced reporting and writing?

It clearly is unethical for journalists to let their personal views or interests influence how they report and write the news. But many newspapers and TV organizations go beyond that, insisting journalists avoid any outside activity or commitment that creates *perception* of conflict of interest.

ABC News, in a policy statement to its staff, puts it this way: "Individuals should recognize that the same rules of conduct followed in their professional lives must also be observed in their private affairs. The distinction between professional and private is too fine to admit any essential difference. For example, a compromising offer is no less so if it involves vacation time instead of a work situation. Both must be refused."[7]

The *Charlotte* (N.C.) *News and Observer* treats the subject this way in its code of ethics:

> It goes without saying that no *Observer* staffer would ever show favoritism in the news columns in exchange for gifts or favors. So in most circumstances our concern is the appearance of conflict of interest, not actual conflict.
>
> The best general guide to conduct is that we accept nothing of value for which we do not pay. To be specific: You go to lunch with a news source who picks up the tab. That's fine, and next time you pick up the tab and put it on your expense account. Someone courts you as a pipeline into the paper and wants to give you a bottle of whiskey. Decline, with thanks, as gracefully as you can. We don't want to be sanctimonious about this, but we want our people to carry their weight.
>
> In addition, there's an obvious reason not to write stories concerning outside interests in which you are involved unless your editors know of your involvement and your story discloses that involvement.[8]

The *News and Observer* code also covers outside conduct by journalists:

> You have the right to determine what you do in your private life, and so does your spouse, but that private life might affect what newsroom duties you could take on.
>
> Whenever a potential for conflict between personal and professional activities arises, prudence dictates open discussion with supervisors.
>
> In general, be wary of political commitment, although this need not mean civic isolation. Part of our obligation as citizens is to make decisions about candidates and issues and act on them.
>
> But it is also clearly part of our obligation as journalists to insure that our reputations as objective fact-finders are not blemished by a display of our political views.
>
> Generally that means the public ought not be able to tell by our behavior how we feel about an issue or candidate....[9]

Note these extracts from the *News and Observer* code are preoccupied with public perception of newsroom staffers and their conduct *because of corporate concerns for the image of the newspaper itself.* (Standards for other departments will be discussed later.) Many news organizations similarly write codes essentially to protect corporate image, and only secondarily to present precise ethical instructions for individual journalists attempting to frame personal approaches to ethical issues. That is—again—you are on your own in fashioning a personal code.

In avoiding conflict of interest, several key areas are particularly troublesome.

• *Conflicting public presence*   You will find it difficult to stay independent and objective in your own mind if, like the south Georgia sports writer, you participate actively in, say, a political process or event on which you report or write. And, you cannot expect readers or viewers to accept you as a truly objective, dispassionate reporter if, even in "off-hours," you demonstrate political commitment by, say, working for the local Democratic or Republican party. Can you trust yourself—can any discerning reader or viewer trust you—on the education beat if you are a member of the city board of education? Obviously, no. What perhaps is not so obvious is that high-profile involvement in *any* type of organized political or partisan endeavor outside the newsroom likely will prejudice your position. If, for example, you become a community activist, even in such worthy endeavors as the United Way or a local blood bank, you have joined the structure—the *system*—on which you report; you have left the ranks of observers and joined the activists. For some reporters in recent years, the issue of public presence versus professional detachment has extended even to spouses. A Seattle newspaper warned its managing editor he would be fired if his wife worked as the mayor's press secretary. (She quit.) CBS News warns its staffers they "must avoid any conflict between their personal interests and the interests of CBS," adding that "Each employee will be held responsible for seeing to it that neither he nor she nor any member of his or her immediate family has any interest, or engages in any activity, which is in conflict with this policy."[10]

• *Conflicting personal interests*   With the explosive growth of business news sections across the country, new attention is focused on whether reporters can reconcile, say, personal investments in the stock market with their role as dispassionate observers of the business scene. Obviously, it is grossly unethical for a reporter to manipulate news coverage or use "inside" information for personal profits. A *Wall Street Journal* reporter did this by using his advance knowledge of what the *Journal* was going to publish and how the news would affect prices of stock in certain companies (see Case Study 2-1.)[11]

Such conduct clearly is treason to the higher calling of every journalist, and, of course, a fundamental betrayal of everything a principled newspaper like the *Journal* stands for. But ethical questions arising out of a conflict of personal interest seldom are so clear cut. For example, a business reporter obviously should

---

VIEWPOINT 2-2

JOURNALISTS OR MEDIA STARS?

"Abusing, if not manipulating, the 'public right to know,' they use this city to enhance their reputations and push their incomes, first to six, and then even to seven figures.

"The people of the media are today the wheelers and dealers. Point to any others so skillful at using the machinery of Washington, and so protected from any public challenge of scrutiny."

Henry Fairlie, British journalist, on how Washington reporters become TV "media stars" and command $12,000 or more for a single speech, ASNE *Bulletin,* October 1983, p. 31

CASE STUDY 2-1

THE REPORTER AND "INSIDE" INFORMATION

You are a 35-year-old reporter for a highly profitable newspaper owned by a $1 billion media conglomerate. You are paid $575 weekly, barely enough to live on in your high-cost city.

You frequently write a column reporting what you have heard from stockbrokers and corporate executives about publicly traded stocks. Many "fat cat" speculators on Wall Street make money by reading your column for tips, then trading before the public, always slow in such matters, can trade.

You realize you can make money (and you sure need it) by trading *before* your column is printed and *before* the "fat cats" can act. You also can profit on your advance knowledge of what other reporters will publish.

Your paper warns employees against trading in stocks they write about or telling outsiders about their work. Of course, such work rules are laid down by executives made wealthy in the company's employ (the chairman is paid $1.1 million annually; that's more than $21,000 *weekly,* compared with your $575). And, who's kidding whom about company rules? Everybody knows they are broken daily—editors telephone home and charge the company, executives take a friend to lunch and put it on their expense account as "business luncheon."

Questions: Is it unethical to bend the rules yourself by trading privately on your "inside" information, and beating the "fat cats" to the draw? If you thus augment your income, are there any victims of your action? You gathered the facts for columns under your byline. Who owns the product of your labors? Do your superiors, most of whom have investments of one kind or another, *really* expect you to live on $575 weekly?

That scenario developed at the *Wall Street Journal* in New York City when R. Foster Winans, frequent writer of the popular column "Heard on the Street," was charged with providing advance information to trader friends, and with them enjoying about $675,000 in profits. After an investigation by the Securities and Exchange Commission, Winans was sentenced in Federal District Court in 1985 to eighteen months in prison, five years' probation, and was fined $5,000 on charges of securities fraud and mail and wire fraud for misappropriating privileged information from the *Journal.* His confederates also drew jail terms and fines.

Said the *Journal:* "We are saddened and shocked by this betrayal of trust. The *Journal* has stringent policies designed to protect against ethical abuses, including use of inside information.... When an individual breaks faith and casts a blot on the paper's reputation, it can only inspire a deep sense of hurt and outrage among all who have labored so hard to build that reputation."

What is a reporter's moral obligation to protect an employer's reputation? Were *Journal* readers betrayed?

---

not trade in, say, stock of an auto manufacturing company he or she covers; a single favorable story could raise that stock's price, creating profit for its shareholders (including the reporter). But, does that mean that reporter should not trade in the stock of *any* auto companies? Or, indeed, should the reporter avoid holdings even in companies, such as tire manufacturers, whose fortunes rise and fall with the auto companies? By extension of the argument, does this mean journalists should avoid any outside investments? Some newspapers require staffers, particularly those in business and financial reporting, to reveal to their supervisors any private investments that might create conflict of interest. None require of their own staffers the same *public* revelations of personal finances required of candidates for major government office. John Finnegan, vice president and editor of the *St. Paul* (Minn.) *Pioneer Press and Dispatch,* argues journalists should be required to publicly divulge their private interests, perhaps even publish periodically a statement of net worth listing stock holdings and other investments.[12] Since such forced revelations by reporters logically would compel editors and publishers to likewise tell all, there is not likely to be much support in the news industry for Finnegan's position. Therefore, a journalist serious about establishing a personal position of trust should (1) discuss any possible conflict of interest with an editor/supervisor, and (2) decline any assignment that conceivably could create a conflict.

• *Freebies, junkets, and other disguised bribes*   Whether it's a $900 airline ticket to a South Seas vacation or a $9 bottle of liquor, it can be construed as a bribe if offered you free by a government official, public relations person, or news source. And forget trying to establish dollar limits, such as "anything under $9 is an acceptable gift, anything over that isn't." Whatever their value, such junkets and freebies often are bribes intended to influence news coverage. And, remember, it's not *you* they are trying to capture; they're romancing you only in hopes of capturing your newspaper or newscast (see Case Study 2-2 for an example).

If you're serious about avoiding conflicts of interest, you will reject quickly such blatant attempts to curry favor. And, if you work for a newspaper or TV news operation that *expects* you to accept free press tickets to the opera or free rides on the team bus, you have the option of moving on quickly to a new job where ethical professionalism meets your standard. But, wait. As with all ethical issues, there are gray areas requiring deeper discussion. The author encountered many in his reporting career. For example, there *are* times when free transportation must be accepted. They include riding free into a battle zone on a U.S. Army helicopter whose pilot is reluctant to delay his departure to discuss fees. (That's quite different, of course, from accepting free rides in a press plane following Air Force One and its important passenger, the President of the United States; news organizations pay for seats on that plane.) Another gray area is created when an important news source presses a gift on you in apparent ignorance of the ethical problem thus created. If you fear offending—and losing—the source, estimate the gift's value and send a check to your favorite charity. Advise the gift giver you have made a donation to the Boy Scouts or whatever in his or her name as your way of expressing thanks. And, do it in a *written* thank-you note. Keep a copy for your records.

PRIVACY: A SPECIAL AGONY

If you're sensitive to human suffering, you will feel special agony many times during a news career when you drag into the public spotlight an individual who doesn't want to be there, or when you poke your intrusive reporter's notebook or camera into an embarrassing dark corner of someone's private life.

Your rationale may be "It's news," or "The public has a right to know," but that won't make you feel much better when you comprehend the hurt un-

---

CASE STUDY 2-2

NEWS OR A FREEBIE?

You are a general assignment reporter who doubles as travel editor. Winter is just ahead when you get a tempting invitation: Would you like three days in the sun, all expenses paid, to attend a birthday party of a famous resort? You may bring a guest free. The invitation is equivalent to $2,000 in travel, hotel, food, and entertainment costs. No strings attached; you need not write about the trip. Your paper has no policy on such things.

Question: Will you accept?

More than 5,000 news people from many countries did in 1986, when Disney World in Florida celebrated its fifteenth anniversary. Disney said the $7.5 million in costs were shared with seventeen airlines, twenty-six hotels, the State of Florida, and two county governments trying to enhance central Florida's image.

Question: Does such wider sponsorship change your attitude toward the invitation? Would paying $150 for the trip, or even all costs, change your mind? Disney offered those options.

U.S. Chief Justice Warren Burger was there to talk about the bicentennial of the U.S. Constitution. Also there were other notables, including Nicholas Daniloff, *U.S. News & World Report* correspondent recently freed from the Soviet Union, where he had been accused of espionage.

Questions: Does inclusion of newsy events in the program change your attitude toward a free trip? Isn't Disney World legitimate *news* in your hometown? Don't many of your neighbors dream of taking their families there? And was Disney's publicity director correct in suggesting that ethical standards for hard news, such as government coverage, should not be applied to "entertainment news"? Could you go at Disney's expense but write or broadcast without a pro-Disney slant?

Reactions of journalists varied.

An editor from a small New Hampshire paper told a *New York Times* reporter (covering the affair at his paper's expense) she brought her husband and, "I hope the paper will give me a full page for it."

A Rochester, N.Y., radio station news director told the *Orlando Sentinel:* "We are going back and we are going to talk about it. If you lived in Rochester and it was 50 degrees and rainy, would you turn down a free trip?"

Michael Gartner, president of the American Society of Newspaper Editors: "I am disappointed that so many reporters and editors aren't troubled by the acceptance." A. M. Rosenthal of the *New York Times:* "I thought we had cleaned ourselves up and we haven't. It is astonishing."

Mike Royko, *Chicago Tribune* columnist, condemned "freeloaders" with "no qualms about grabbing a freebie." (He noted freebies often are part of political life, and added: "Who ever thought Mickey Mouse would be acting like a Chicago alderman?")

Question: If you worked for a small paper or station that never could afford to send you on such an assignment would you then be justified in accepting a free trip?

Postscript: It was at Disney World that the Associated Press Managing Editors Association met in 1975 and adopted an ethics code calling on journalists to "accept nothing of value from news sources or others outside the profession." It specifically termed expense-paid junkets as conflicts of interest.

---

wanted publicity inflicts on some individuals, or when you see in the eyes of a new widow the pain caused by your probing questions at that terrible moment in her life.

Few ethical issues will cause you more difficulty than the godlike attempt to balance the individual's right to privacy, the right to be left alone, against your responsibility to inform readers and viewers about matters in which they have justifiable news interest. Public opinion polls show the spirit of trust between the journalist and the public is eroded seriously by the public's perception that the media wantonly invade privacy in search of titillating stories that "sell papers." An ASNE survey shows 32 percent of respondents feel newspapers invade people's privacy; 40 percent feel television news does. Only 30 percent feel newspapers *respect* privacy; 24 percent feel that way about television. The rest—about one-third polled—are neutral on the subject.[13]

For many journalists, the judgment call is less difficult in privacy matters concerning *public officials,* those who seek public office, and *public figures,* such as movie stars and athletes who choose to live in the public spotlight. The public has every right to be informed of an official's conduct, obviously. Yet, that doesn't solve the journalist's ethical dilemma. Has the public the right to know about an official's *private* life? Or, does the right to know extend only to private affairs that might affect official duties? If so, where is the line between private life and official duties? Every journalist who has covered Washington knows of highly placed government officials who are secret alcoholics, secret philanderers. Sometimes, such information breaks into public view through the media, sometimes it doesn't. When it does, the rationale usually is that private misconduct has affected official duty—the U.S. senator no longer can function in the role for which he was elected. When it doesn't, the rationale is that he can drink all night but still function during the day, so why publish the information? But who is qualified to make such judgment calls? You, the journalist? Who elected *you* to play God?

Raging debate over these issues erupted in May 1987 when the *Miami Herald* published a story that Gary Hart, then the leading contender for the Democratic presidential nomination in 1988, had put himself in a compromising position with a 29-year-old woman. Hart, 50, had been dogged throughout his political career by rumors that he was a "womanizer." But, as so often when such personal behavior by public figures is the issue, Hart's relationships with women other than his wife of twenty-eight years had been *talked about* privately more than *written about* by Washington reporters—until the *Herald* broke its story. Acting on a tip, the *Herald* flew reporters to Washington, where, through the night, they "staked out" Hart's townhouse from the street and observed the former U.S. senator from Colorado accompanied by the young woman. Hart's wife was at their Colorado home at the time.

At this point, a familiar scenario went into play: A story about private behavior known to many but published by few was "legitimatized" for widespread publication when one newspaper published it. The floodgates were opened, and Hart's personal behavior became one of the biggest journalistic and political sensations in decades. The 29-year-old woman inevitably was described as a beautiful, blond, aspiring actress. She was pictured on front pages and evening newscasts in a skimpy bikini. The *Washington Post* reported Hart had had a long-standing relationship with yet another woman. Reporters swarmed to the Hart home in Colorado seeking comment from the obviously distraught Mrs. Hart.

Hart fought back, accusing the *Herald* of sloppy, untruthful reporting and charging the newspaper refused to publish his side of the story. Then, with his standing in public opinion polls plummeting, Hart quit his campaign for the presidency with a statement that struck at the privacy issue. He accused reporters of distorting stories about his personal life but ignoring his public policies. His private life had been overemphasized, he said, and "I refuse to subject my family and my friends and innocent people and myself to further rumors and gossip." He added:

> We're all going to have to seriously question the system for selecting our national leaders, that reduces the press of this nation to hunters and presidential candidates to being hunted, that has reporters in bushes, false and inaccurate stories printed, photographers peeking in our windows, swarms of helicopters hovering over our roof, and my very strong wife close to tears because she can't even get in her own house at night without being harassed.

The media's role became an instant issue, discussed by the public and journalists alike as intently as was Hart's conduct. Debate focused on two areas:

First, was Hart's personal conduct legitimate news? Did the media have a responsibility to place it before voters who were attempting to assess the character and judgment of a man who wanted to be President? Or was the coverage unprincipled, sensationalistic prying into sordid details of a man's private life?

Second, should the *Herald* and other media have resorted to secretive techniques—nighttime stakeouts and what *New York Times* columnist A. M. Rosenthal criticized as "hiding in the dark, listening for squeaking bedsprings"—to get the story?

The *Herald*'s executive editor, Heath J. Meriwether, defended the paper's coverage: "With the ethics and morals of our leaders under such intense scrutiny today, people want to know about a candidate's character...we think the issues raised by our stories are germane to any consideration of a presidential candidate."

Meriwether's media colleagues were divided. Many saw the issue of Hart's character as legitimate news but questioned the *Herald*'s reporting techniques and wondered whether the paper rushed into print, to publish an exclusive, without putting the story in proper context. In sum, the Hart incident will be debated for years as a classic case study in how far journalists should go in reporting the private lives of *public figures*.

VIEWPOINT 2-3

TWO VIEWS OF PRIVACY

"Anyone who runs for public office invites public interest in one's private life, family and spouse...."

The *New York Times* commenting editorially on intense coverage of John Zaccaro, husband of Geraldine Ferraro, 1984 Democratic vice presidential candidate, January 8, 1985, p. 25

"You people haven't changed...vultures..."

Ms. Ferraro when reporters covered court appearance by her son on cocaine possession charges, March 24, 1986

The journalist's dilemma is even more excruciating when such judgments must be made about those *private individuals* thrust unwillingly into the public spotlight by circumstances beyond their control. If your camera catches a woman survivor running naked from a hotel fire do you air that footage because it dramatically depicts a news story in which the public has justifiable interest?

Infinite variations of such ethical dilemmas arise in privacy issues. Here, perhaps more than in any other area of journalistic ethics, you will have no precise guidelines, and often will find little solace in what other journalists did in similar past cases. Make your best judgment call, balancing your responsibility to your reading or viewing public against the individual's right to privacy, and expect to awaken in the night, even years later, with the gnawing feeling you made the wrong call (see Case Studies 2-3 and 2-4 for illustrations of how complex this can be).

CASE STUDY 2-3

WAS IT NEWS OR "SLEAZE"?

You hear rumors that twenty-one years ago, as an 18-year-old college freshman in a distant city, a prominent local businessman shot to death his mother, father, and sister. Your investigation reveals he was found mentally incapable of standing trial, and hospitalized. After seven years of therapy, he was tried and acquitted on grounds he was insane at the time of the shootings. He was released from the hospital, won a college degree, and married and took his wife's surname. He moved to your town and, it appears, has lived a blameless life ever since.

There is no "news peg"—no current development that makes this story "hot news." But, the man indeed is prominent—he is publisher of thirteen suburban newspapers with 200,000 circulation and 200 employees.

Question: Will you publish what you learned? Here is how that question was answered in 1986 in Denver:

Patricia Calhoun, editor/publisher of *Westword,* a weekly with 90,000 free circulation that tries to present alternative approaches to news published by dailies, broke the story on her front page "because no one else had done it. . . . It always struck me as being a fascinating and absolutely newsworthy story. . . ."

Editor David Hall of the *Denver Post* also knew details but said, "It's not a story. . . . There was no reason and purpose to run it. . . . There are lots of things people know that they don't put in the newspaper."

Editor Ralph Looney of the *Rocky Mountain News,* Denver's other daily, said, "This is the kind of thing that gives our whole industry a bad name. If you have someone who has led an exemplary life, it gets to the point of sleaze and sensationalism [if you publish]."

Joe McGowan, Denver AP bureau chief, said, "I'm not sure the story should have been published. How did it pertain today? He had paid his debt, done what society required. There was no impropriety. He was not in a sensitive government position."

The *Denver Post* never did run the story; the *Rocky Mountain News* did after *Westword* broke it, explaining it considered the publisher's past private until he spoke out—which he did when the story broke. AP then carried the story, and it was used by hundreds of newspapers and broadcast stations.

The publisher, H. Garrison Cochran of Sentinel Newspapers, told AP: "I have been trying to prepare myself to be strong enough to handle this when it arose." His own papers published a 17-inch story on his past.

What do you think? Was Cochran's occupation as a publisher a factor in whether to publish? *Westword*'s Calhoun said, "I think how the media deals with it is a media story. I do think, in covering the media, the media does use a different set of standards." Also, did the *News,* AP, and other media let *Westword* set the ethical standards on this story?

CASE STUDY 2-4

IS THE MAYOR'S SON NEWS?

The mayor is a hardliner on crime who made local drug enforcement a major issue. You learn his 19-year-old son, who lives at home and attends a local junior college, was arrested for possession of a small quantity of marijuana, a misdemeanor if convicted.

In almost identical language, Michael Davies, editor of the *Hartford* (Conn.) *Courant,* and Heath Meriwether, executive editor of the *Mi-*

ami Herald, wrote columns posing those facts and asking their readers and own staff editors these questions: Would you run a story on the arrest? What if the arrest were for selling a pound of marijuana? Would you run a story if the arrest were for using cocaine? What if the arrest were for selling cocaine?

Compare *your* decisions with responses from readers and editors in both cities:

	Miami Herald		Hartford Courant	
	Readers	Editors	Readers	Editors
Would run a story on the arrest for possessing marijuana	63.9%	75%	61%	60%
Would run a story if the arrest were for selling a pound of marijuana	92.1%	100%	82%	100%
Would run a story if the arrest were for using cocaine	77.7%	85.7%	67%	70%
Would run a story if the arrest were for selling cocaine	94%	100%	87%	100%

In follow-up columns, Davies and Meriwether presented their own decisions:

Davies: "Normally, we wouldn't publish the name of someone arrested on a marijuana charge. Except in unusual circumstances, we wouldn't publish the name even if the teenager was the son of a public official. In this case, however, the mayor has made drug enforcement a major part of his administration....We would

publish the son's name and talk about the mayor's position...."

Meriwether: "I print it. I don't make it a big deal, but play it deep inside the paper. If the mayor's son is selling marijuana or cocaine, I probably bring it out to the front of the local section. Although we don't normally report misdemeanors, I think a politician's family does become part of the public scene...."

GOOD TASTE: BLOODY BODIES AND MORE

Early in their careers, young journalists must decide what their fundamental stance will be on matters of good taste and sensationalism. Both frequently give rise to major ethical crises.

First, as in perhaps no other area of journalism, you will find the public deeply suspicious of your motives. The 1985 ASNE survey found 68 percent of respondents agree reporters "frequently overdramatize the news." There is a widespread conviction that the bloody body is filmed at the auto wreck simply to sensationalize an otherwise dull newscast, that lurid details from a sex crimes trial are published to lend shock value to an otherwise ho-hum front page.

VIEWPOINT 2-4

A PHOTO THAT OFFENDED

"In the first two days we had a total of 500 complaints. There were also hundreds of protest letters, cancelled subscriptions, an attempt to boycott the paper and a bomb threat that forced us to evacuate the newspaper building."

Staff photographer John Harte after his photo of a drowned child was front-paged by the *Bakersfield Californian*, quoted in *Washington Journalism Review*, January 1986, p. 10

Second, many responsible journalists fear the public often is correct in those assessments. Every journalist knows of stories that were overplayed and "hyped" in extremely poor taste; confirmation that the practice continues is as close as tonight's explicitly bloody TV footage of car bombings in Beirut or another famine in Africa.

Often, newspaper and TV journalists must make difficult judgment calls quickly on stories that clearly are news but are horribly grisly. For example, on January 22, 1987, in Harrisburg, Pennsylvania, state treasurer R. Budd Dwyer, due to be sentenced the next day on a bribery conviction, called a news conference and, when reporters were assembled and the cameras rolling, put a .357 Magnum pistol in his mouth and pulled the trigger. The networks had the entire episode on videotape, but declined to use it. CNN said, "You can tell the story without showing the shooting." NBC said, "...too unsettling for our viewers." Some TV stations used it. One that did, WPXI-TV in Pittsburgh, said, "It's an historic event. We've seen JFK (President John F. Kennedy) shot to death 200 times. We've seen Bobby Kennedy shot to death. So it's a reflection of a very important man in Pennsylvania society and what he did." The station later used edited versions of the videotape, letting viewers hear the pistol shot but not see Dwyer's last moments. Stations that used the episode in full reported receiving hundreds of protest calls from viewers. Newspapers had complete still photo coverage—an Associated Press series that gave editors the option of showing the entire sequence or omitting the most graphic parts. Gannett surveyed its ninety-three newspapers and found fifty-one used AP's photo of Dwyer holding the pistol and waving back reporters; twelve used one of Dwyer with the pistol in his mouth; the rest of the papers used other versions or, in the case of seven, no photos at all. There was, then, no clear consensus among professionals that day on news versus poor taste.

Complicating your quest for personal guidelines, societal attitudes shift rapidly on what is "good" taste or "bad," and are difficult to define in advance. Experienced newspaper and TV journalists often cannot be helpful. Many, even after years of wrestling with the issue, have difficulty deciding themselves where the line lies between responsible—or, at least, necessary—journalism and bad taste or sensationalism. For example, consider how wide open ABC News leaves the issue in this statement to its staff on broadcast of objectionable material:

> ABC News believes that good taste must prevail in its broadcasts. Morbid, sensational or alarming details should not be included unless they are essential to the factual report. Obscene, profane or indecent material must also be avoided. The broadcast of material deemed to be obscene by the courts may also run afoul of the law as well as the canons of good taste...Questions of taste cannot be answered in the ab-

stract, but when specific problems involving objectionable material arise, they must be resolved in light of contemporary standards of taste, the state of the law and the requirements of newsworthiness. When these considerations come into conflict, consult ABC News management and request a decision.[14]

Attitudes among journalists on such subjects are nonspecific and, thus, not satisfactorily instructive. But they provide *some* guidance:

Language generally held in poor taste—vulgarity or obscenity—should be used only if central to the meaning of an important story. There was widespread usage in 1986 of a presidential expletive considered important news. Here is what happened: During a "photo opportunity" at the White House, when photographers were permitted to take pictures of President Reagan in the Cabinet room, reporters pressed questions about the Philippines, then in political turmoil. Reagan said to an aide, "Sons of bitches." Videotape was used on television; the language, in quotes, was used by many newspapers. In this case, journalists decided the expletive was indicative of the presidential mood on an important story, the U.S. position on the Philippines, as well as a commentary on the press corps. Whether to use such language is not the only decision to be made. How will it be displayed and where? Many newspapers opt for burying such language deep in a story, or running the story itself on an inside page, not on the front page. Some television newscasters introduce video clips of obscenities or vulgarity by warning, "The following contains language objectionable to some..." Federal regulation limits use of objectionable language by TV and radio but, of course, is not a factor in judgments by reporters and editors for non-regulated newspapers or magazines.

Racial slurs or, even, racial identifications in news stories are widely held in bad taste—except, again, unless germane to an important story. Many newspapers never identify the race of criminals; others do only when, for example, a manhunt is under way and identification is deemed necessary. Yet, many newspapers published Spiro Agnew's offhand reference to a "Fat Jap" in the press corps; they argued the comment, offhand or not, was an important indicator of the character of the man then vice president of the United States (at least one journalist argued using the

---

VIEWPOINT 2-5

GOOD TASTE AND BAD NEWS

"We live in the era of news-media overkill.

"It isn't enough to acknowledge the ubiquity of barbarism; we are forced to see it in color. Local television news assaults our sensibilities with graphic details of incineration, rape, infanticide, gruesome murders, and every horror that the well-developed imagination of a masochist can conceive.

"It isn't that these events don't occur. Everyone living in New York City and every other city is aware of them. The issue is not whether these stories are news—technically whatever occurs is news—but whether they are newsworthy.

"I am not arguing here for censorship, albeit any concern for human decency ultimately involves some limits on what television allows us to observe. What I am demanding is tastefulness."

Herbert London, dean of New York University's Gallatin Division, writing in the *New York Times,* December 29, 1981, p. 21

VIEWPOINT 2-6

GHOULS OR GUESTS?

"In Berlin, Maryland, a Baltimore television crew arriving to interview the family of one Marine victim was greeted by neighbors shouting, 'Here come the ghouls.'

"...According to Major Fred Lash, a Marine Corps public affairs officer in Washington, 75 percent of the families who were assisted by Marine Corps officials decided they wanted press coverage, and some of them called television stations and newspapers themselves to volunteer their reactions when they learned that their sons had been killed."

C. Fraser Smith of the *Baltimore Sun* describing coverage of families of Marines killed in Beirut, the *Washington Journalism Review*, March 1984, p. 21

---

quote was a "cheap shot" because the "Fat Jap" actually was a friend of Agnew, and that the two jokingly traded ethnic slurs when together[15]).

Good taste is a major consideration in covering stories involving grief. Families of U.S. Marines killed abroad *are* in the news; many want to be there so they can make known their feelings about U.S. foreign policy. The widow of a villager killed in a guerrilla war in Latin America *is* in the news; pain inflicted by war on the innocent *is* an important part of the story. But, how to handle that grief, that pain? How to avoid what columnist George Will calls the "pornography of grief," the brutal exploitation of the grief and pain of others? The camera—television's or a newspaper's—is the worst offender; it intrudes, it catches and exploits the tears on the cheek, the tremble across the lips. But word journalists who crowd around a grave, who push into a church as the dead are eulogized are part of the problem, too. Happily, there are many examples of journalists discharging their responsibility to cover a significant story but doing so with consummate good taste. For example, reporters protected the identity of a Houston family whose son was forced to live in a germ-free plastic bubble for twelve years while suffering from a medical phenomenon, an immunological deficiency. This important medical story was covered without the parents' name or address becoming widely known. And, when "David, the Bubble-Boy," died, the parents were left to grieve alone. When covering grief, you must make the initial judgment whether it belongs in the public view or is one of those stories that should not be published. If you must publish, move in with sensitivity, get your story and get back out as quickly and gently as possible.

Good taste is essential in covering sex crimes or trials. Heinous crime *is* important news, and not covering it in the name of good taste is abdication of ethical responsibility. The dilemma is *how* to cover it. Many journalists are guided by whether readers or viewers *need* to know. For example, if a rapist is assaulting women in one section of your town, your readers need to know how and when he operates. If children in a day care center have been sexually abused, parents among your readers and viewers need to know what warning signs to look for, what protective steps to take. Societal revulsion over sex crimes is so great that special ethical problems are created for a journalist covering anyone connected with them—accused or accuser. Most journalists, for example, withhold names of rape victims but agonize over whether to identify the *alleged* rapist. Journalists protect sexually abused children. But should men arrested for, but not convicted of, sex crimes on the testimony of children be photographed being led handcuffed into a courtroom? Repeatedly, as you try to develop a personal code for handling such coverage, you will come down to words such as "sensitivity" and "common sense," in addition to "good taste." Coolly assess in advance the *need* to cover the story, then proceed with utmost care if you determine you must. Language used, details presented, pictures published, timing and context of publication—all must be considered carefully if coverage is to stay within the bounds of good taste (note Case Studies 2-5 and 2-6 for discussion of good taste and privacy in covering sex crimes).

Using good taste in sex crimes can shield the victims' reputations and your public's sensibilities; good taste in covering other types of crimes and suicides can save lives. Some criminals and unbalanced people are subject to "copy-

---

CASE STUDY 2-5

DO WE VICTIMIZE VICTIMS?

You report for a weekly newspaper in a town of 7,500 people. In this town, everybody knows nearly everybody else—and the details of their lives.

Your paper's long-standing policy is to publish each week a "Journal of Records," listing police and fire calls, traffic court records, hospital admissions, and court suits, and to cover felony trials and publish the names of anyone who testifies in open court.

In quick succession, a 16-year-old high school student testifies in court she was raped and a 26-year-old woman testifies in a separate case she was abducted, beaten, and raped. The older woman acknowledges she had been drinking heavily, moving from bar to bar, and says, "I have no recollection of what went on in a part of that evening because I was so drunk. Hey, I was out having a good time." She also acknowledges she is not married to the man with whom she lives.

Questions: Will you publish the student's name? The older woman's name? Will you publish the names of the alleged rapists at their arrest and during the trial? Is there a difference between printing names of *alleged* victims and *alleged* rapists? Is rape just another crime? Or, must print and broadcast journalists cover sex crimes differently? Should television cover rape cases differently than do newspapers? What

would your attitude be if the alleged victim (or rapist) were famous—a movie star, for example?

Henry Gay, publisher of the *Mason County Journal* in Shelton, Washington, where both rape trials were held in 1985, published detailed coverage that identified both alleged victims. Says Gay: "We cover felony trials in Mason County Superior Court and we print the names of people when they get up in court to testify. We see that as fair." Gay and his son, Charles, managing editor, say society must do more to help rape victims, and that it would be improper professionally to cover sex crimes differently than other trials.

The student says she felt victimized three times—once by a rapist, once while testifying at his trial (he was convicted), and once in a 3,000-word account of the trial published in the *Journal*.

The 26-year-old woman complains that "My 8-year-old daughter had to hear at school from other kids that her mother had been raped." One man pleaded guilty in this case and went to prison; a jury acquitted a second man.

Did coverage in fact victimize the student? Did it victimize the older woman's 8-year-old daughter? Does a reporter have a duty to shield such innocents?

CASE STUDY 2-6

IS IT DIFFERENT ON TV?

You report for a television station in a major city where a sensational kidnap trial is under way. Evidence shown the jury in open court includes videotapes of the bound, helpless kidnap victim just prior to being raped. Reporters have been given complete transcripts of dialogue on the tapes.

Questions: Should you show the videotapes on your evening newscast? Does public interest in the trial override the victim's desire for privacy? Do you see greater societal good flowing from screening the tapes of this horrible event? Is publishing transcripts in newspapers different from showing videotapes of the actual event? Should *all* judicial records be available to the media and public?

In Minneapolis, where the trial was held, two television stations asked a federal court for the right to copy and use the tapes. The judge refused—and drew editorial support from the *Minneapolis Tribune.*

Don Dwight, then publisher of the *Tribune,* noted:

"The *Minneapolis Tribune* said the judge 'exercised his discretion rationally and justifiably.' By supporting an individual's right of privacy in this case, did the *Tribune* yield its position in the front lines defending the right of the press and public to judicial records?

"We think not. The tapes had been shown in the courtroom 'for all to see,' as the judge's decision pointed out. Complete transcripts of the dialogue were furnished to the press at that time.

"The *Tribune* did express real concern about precedent setting, but it also noted: 'Even when not compelled to do so, Minnesota news media have usually respected individual privacy when that consideration was compatible with their duty to inform the public. Such responsible behavior is not entirely altruistic. The press usually recognizes that when it abuses its power, it jeopardizes its credibility—and its ability to gather information for which the public has a legitimate need.'

"We think that's another very good way of saying a press that is responsible will help ensure a press that is free and strong."

Who was right—publisher Dwight or the TV news directors who wanted to use the tapes? How far must an editor go in such cases to present the news *but* also protect the sensibilities of viewers or readers?

cat" impulses. Given graphic details of a crime or suicide, they sometimes are triggered to copy. Two days after treasurer Dwyer killed himself in front of the cameras in Harrisburg, Pennsylvania, a teenager in nearby York, Pennsylvania, shot himself to death in precisely the same manner. In March 1987, four New Jersey youths killed themselves in a suicide pact by running a car engine in a closed garage until overcome by carbon monoxide. A week later, two acquaintances tried to commit suicide in the same garage bay—and a series of similar teenage suicides erupted across the nation. The *New England Journal of Medicine* has published studies showing teenage suicides, second only to accidents as a killer of teenagers, increase following a suicide heavily covered by the media. The U.S. Food and Drug Administration finds heavy news coverage of food tampering causes a wave of tampering complaints nationwide. Sometimes, the unwary—or unethical—journalist can risk contributing to copycat behavior in indirect ways. In 1985, for example, a new book specified names and doses of drugs a woman used to help her terminally ill mother commit suicide. Book reviews by the Associated Press and the *Washington Post* reprinted the specifics—a prescription for suicide. In this type of news coverage, your personal code of ethics must consider the likely impact of each story you write.

Now, a warning: As you judge newsworthiness in part by your sense of good taste, there is danger of putting a "reverse spin" on your judgment process and overlooking your first responsibility, the news needs of your readers or viewers. A striking example of this occurred when AIDS burst widely into view in the United States.

From coast to coast, journalists agonized over handling graphic details of how the disease, acquired immune deficiency syndrome, is transmitted. The story was handled so delicately that both reading and viewing publics were denied essential details, and something akin to panic ensued. In sum, high risk of AIDS infection comes from exchange of semen through anal intercourse, thus the high rate of incidence among homosexual men. That preceding sentence contains words—"anal intercourse," "homosexual"—that many journalists would do almost anything to avoid using in a news story. And that's what many did as they tried to explain to their readers and viewers, with euphemistic indirection, what AIDS was all about. One result was a huge health scare that left millions wondering whether they could contract AIDS from drinking fountains, the air they breathed, or from little children who got it quite innocently from blood transfusions.[16]

The lesson: "Good taste" is essential but cannot develop into prudishness that denies your readers or viewers essential information on important stories. Even the most explicit story on a subject normally deemed offensive can be used in a newspaper or newscast if written in considered, responsible language and displayed appropriately.

CHAPTER SUMMARY

Each aspiring journalist must build a personal code of ethics as part of giving readers or viewers fair, balanced coverage of the news. Four general areas of ethics are fundamental:

1 *Objectivity in reporting and writing* arguably is impossible to achieve, but the effort must guide journalists in deciding which stories to cover, selecting sources, arranging facts, writing, and, then, timing publication or airing of the story. Some argue journalists must also decide what is "right" or "truth" in the news, but who is to make those judgment calls?

2 *Conflicts of interest,* real or perceived by the public, can destroy the relationship of trust each journalist must create with readers or viewers. Avoid particularly any outside work or commitment, as in politics, that would prejudice your objectivity. Also beware personal investments and accepting gifts that might influence your news judgment.

3 *Privacy* is a delicate area because it forces you to balance the individual's right to be left alone against the public's right to know about matters of important news interest. It's not difficult to make judgments concerning public officials, those who seek the public spotlight; much of their lives should be open. But it gets tougher when you understand that unwanted publicity inflicts great hurt on many private individuals who want only to be left alone.

4 *"Good taste"* must enter your value judgment on stories involving, for example, vulgarity or obscenity, racial matters, grief, sex crimes, and other types of crimes and suicides that might trigger "copycat" behavior. At times, however, explicit stories normally deemed objectionable must be told—in considered, responsible language—if you are to fulfill your greater responsibility of meeting the public's need to know details of important stories.

CHAPTER 2

Notes

1 "Knoxville Bank Shut by FDIC," a United Press International story published in the *Athens* (Ga.) *Daily News,* Feb. 15, 1983, p. 1.

2 "A Lot of People Listen to Nixon in Washington, D.C., These Days," *Wall Street Journal,* June 30, 1982, p. 32.

3 Jay T. Harris, executive editor, *Philadelphia Daily News,* speech to Society of Professional Journalists/Sigma Delta Chi, Phoenix, Ariz., Nov. 15, 1985.

4 Roberto C. Goizueta, chairman and chief executive officer, the Coca-Cola Co., speech to Associated Press Managing Editors, San Francisco, Oct. 29, 1985.

5 Sam Hopkins, "Conflict of Interest Likely for Journalist Holding Public Office," a detailed report on conflicts of interest on various South Carolina and Georgia newspapers, *Atlanta Constitution,* Jan. 18, 1981, p. 9B.

6 For detailed treatment, see "Wine Critic Corked," *Washington Journalism Review,* May 1983, p. 9.

7 Roone Arledge, president, ABC News, memorandum to ABC staff, March 10, 1982, American Broadcasting Companies, Inc., 7 W. 66th St., New York, N.Y., 10023.

8 "Ethics Policy" adopted in 1980 by the *Charlotte News and Observer,* P.O. Box 32188, Charlotte, N.C., 28232.

9 Ibid.

10 CBS News Standards, CBS Inc., 51 W. 52nd St., New York, N.Y., 10020.

11 For details, see Alex S. Jones, "Insider Trading Reports Focus on Journal Writer," *New York Times,* March 30, 1984, p. 29; Jonathan Friendly, "The Sticky Business of Financial Reporting," *New York Times,* April 8, 1984, p. 22E; and Harvey D. Shapiro, "Unfair Shares," *Washington Journalism Review,* July/August 1984, p. 35—three of the more definitive accounts of the "R. Foster Winans affair."

12 John Finnegan, speech to Morris Communications Corp. seminar on "Newspapers: Conduct and Values," Savannah, Ga., March 9, 1986.

13 "Newspaper Credibility: Building Reader Trust," ASNE, Research Report, 1985, American Society of Newspaper Editors, P.O. Box 17004, Washington, D.C., 20041.

14 Roone Arledge, staff memorandum, op. cit.

15 Dan Thomasson, editor, Scripps Howard News Service, Washington, D.C., at Roy Howard Seminar on Public Affairs Reporting, Indiana University, Bloomington, Ind., Sept. 11, 1985.

16 For a superb study of the AIDS story, see Edwin Diamond and Christopher M. Bellitto, "The Great Verbal Coverup," *Washington Journalism Review,* March 1986, p. 38.

THE ETHICS OF TECHNIQUE: REPORTER, ADVERSARY OR SLEUTH?

Did you ever watch somebody perform an important task and think, "I like what he's doing but I sure don't like the way he's doing it"?

Listen carefully and you'll hear newspaper and magazine readers and TV viewers saying the same thing. They like much of what the media accomplish and regard it as important but often deeply disapprove of *how* it is accomplished. Gallup finds, for example, 79 percent of U.S. adults approve of investigative reporting to uncover corruption and fraud; however, strong majorities disapprove of many investigative techniques—reporters failing to identify themselves as journalists (65 percent disapprove), using hidden cameras or microphones (58 percent), paying informers for information (56 percent), or quoting unnamed sources (52 percent).[1]

Further, news professionals themselves are deeply divided over whether worthwhile journalistic *ends*—say, uncovering official fraud—justify *means* that are, well, a bit sneaky.

In Chapter 2, we discussed broad concepts of probable concern to you in drawing up a personal code of ethics—objectivity, conflict of interest, privacy, and good taste. We now turn, in Chapter 3, to the *ethics of technique,* to ethical concerns over your *methods* of obtaining the news.

Television makes it a familiar sight. The smiling man alights from a helicopter and strides across the White House lawn. A gaggle of correspondents, herded behind restraining ropes like so many honking geese, shout questions.

"Whaaat?" the "Leader of the Free Western World," now smiling broadly, cups hand to ear.

Doubly frustrated by the helicopter's noisy engine and certain knowledge that, once again, they've been had in a superbly staged "photo opportunity," the correspondents shout the questions on which surely turns the fate of that "Free Western World."

We gonna bomb Libya?

Think interest rates will fall?

How about Central America?

For a reporter, the lesson is reinforced: Sometimes, powerful manipulative forces can reduce reporting technique to tragicomic adversarial dimensions. For readers or viewers, there is only bewilderment (or perhaps, disgust): *This* is how they get the news?

Shift scenarios:

It's a dull day, and a business news reporter telephones a source to initiate an interview on XYZ Corp. The resultant "enterprise" story stirs Wall Street. XYZ's stock price leaps upward ten points, and its shareholders profit handsomely. Is that journalist's technique one of reporting news or making it?

Correspondents jump from the secretary of defense's plane the minute it stops rolling and file urgently: the United States is considering a shift in Middle East policy. When a diplomatic storm results, the State Department and White House issue denials. Where, ask puzzled readers and viewers, did reporters get *that* one? Reporters reply simply, "A source told us." The reporters, their collective hands and tongues tied by prior agreement with the "source," cannot reveal it was the secretary of defense himself who launched that trial balloon, knowing full well it could be shot down quickly if reaction was negative. Reporters (who suspected this all along) are in an ethical catch-22. They are bound to their agreement with the source, and thus must leave readers and viewers thinking once more that reporters "make up stories."

An official "linked" to a widening corruption scandal emerges from his home to meet TV cameramen jumping out of hedges and from behind trees in an electronic version of the ambush at Little Big Horn. That night, on the 6 P.M. newscast, you can *see* he's guilty; just look at his astonished face as he protests his innocence. The afternoon paper has a heck of a good story, too; a reporter secretly taped a telephone conversation with the official the day before.

Thus must our Chapter 2 discussion of ethical *concepts* in journalism be followed by discussion of ethical *techniques*. These include the adversarial relationship, involvement in and/or making the news, your relationship with news sources, use of secret recorders and other tools of the "news sleuth," and the "good news versus bad news" syndrome.

ADVERSARIAL RELATIONSHIP: A FACT

It's often cautious, frequently tense, the relationship between reporters and the "structure" they cover—whether that structure be government, business, or even those cheerful volunteers who run United Way fund drives in your town. Sometimes, it bursts into bitterness. Should it be this way? Two views are expressed by Michael O'Neill, former editor of the *New York Daily News,* and Benjamin C. Bradlee, executive editor of the *Washington Post:*

> *O'Neill*—The press has become so adversarial in its relationship with government that it threatens the democratic process.[2]
>
> *Bradlee*—Mike talks about the press's harshly adversarial posture towards government. I'd like to talk about the selling of the presidency, the manipulation of the public, where the press is a captive, if not willing, victim.... Does anyone really want to make peace with government? Do you really want us to formalize a "more positive, more tolerant" attitude with government? More tolerant of what? More tolerant of lying? More tolerant of misrepresentation? More tolerant of manipulation, photo opportunities? That can't be serious. That's a pact with the devil.[3]

Philosophically, you may feel reporters are too adversarial, and that, as publisher Richard Capen of the *Miami Herald* says, they should adopt the perspective of an "associate," not adversary, toward their local communities. Or, you may feel the freely adversarial stance of many American reporters is their major strength in discharging their responsibility to meet the news needs of readers and viewers. Realistically, whatever your philosophical bent, widespread adversarial attitudes—those of your media colleagues and your news sources—will be major factors in shaping your reportorial technique. Like it or not, the relationship between reporters and those who generate news in this country largely is one of tug and pull, push and shove. As you fashion your own reportorial techniques, you must develop personal attitudes toward both the *concept* and *form* of that relationship.

In concept, an adversarial approach is considered by many journalists fundamental to success of the mission. The news must be found, the story must be dragged out, over the objections, often the active resistance, of those who for their own and sometimes nefarious reasons want to keep it hidden. Many journalists, hardened by years of battling for the news, regard "adversarialism" inevitable, natural even, in the relationship between newsmaker and news reporter in a free society. There are innumerable instances in American journalism of the media—and, thus, the people—being led astray, even lied to, on stories of compelling national interest.[4] That causes visceral suspicion among many journalists that the facts simply will not emerge from anything less than head-on confrontation. After decades of high-level (and high-quality) reporting from Washington, James Reston, the *New York Times* columnist, puts it this way: "I believe that the journalistic tradition of skepticism and even defiance toward political power is valid today. After all, the pamphleteers were ahead of the politicians in the fight for the independence of the country, and this tradition still dominates the press, radio and television today."[5]

Opinions differ widely, however, on the *form* the adversary relationship should take. Bluntly, some journalists *start* assignments thinking they must blast their way into the story, confront and even threaten sources, and gut officials. For these reporters, every story is a brawl—and no wounded are taken. Newsmakers often react to this reportorial technique by avoiding contact with reporters. In 1982, after the media hit hard at several factual errors President Reagan made at news conferences, the mood became so tense, in the words of David R. Gergen, then White House director of communications, that each news conference was "like going into the arena of the lions again."[6] On the other, equally unacceptable, extreme are reporters who passively accept, with grateful thanks, the prepared statement—and who swallow hook, line, and handout the official version of the story.

Be comforted. There is, somewhere between those extremes of technique, a more decorous but equally effective relationship you can build with news sources or the "structure" you are covering. It starts with your own strongest possible commitment to an ethical, professional technique, coupled to a bulldog—but polite and responsible—determination to get the news and to fulfill your journalistic responsibilities to your readers or viewers. That means you, the reporter, must get close to them, the newsmakers, but never on their team; you must work with them, at times travel or pal around with them, but always remembering you are there as a surrogate of readers or viewers.

For the unwary, there are traps in all this. A skilled, multibillion-dollar industry is devoted to breaking down the adversarial relationship by enlisting you on "the team." Thousands of "information specialists" and public relations "consultants" in both the government and private sector devote careers to "handling" the media and steering coverage in certain directions (and not always toward the news). Don't mistakenly think this happens only in big league journalism, on the White House lawn; it happens also in the mayor's office, on the school board, in the sheriff's department, all those news beats where you likely will draw your first reporting assignment. Given a bit of experience—and unceasing vigilance—you will have little trouble spotting efforts to manage you and the news.

More difficult to spot is a subtle breakdown in the adversarial relationship that can create grave ethical crises for you. For example, you inevitably will develop friendships among news sources, or grow sympathetic with the efforts of those

---

VIEWPOINT 3-1

AND WHO WILL KEEP SCORE?

"The government always wants the reporters on the team. But if the journalists are on the team, who will report the game?

"...There can't be any freedom of inquiry without irreverence. All presidents seek to capture the press and the two defenses against that are professionalism and independence."

James Deakin commenting on twenty-five years as White House correspondent for the *St. Louis Post-Dispatch*, in *Straight Stuff: The Reporters, the White House and the Truth*, William Morrow & Company, Inc., New York, 1984

you are covering—whether they are trying to win ball games or protect U.S. interests in foreign policy. If you get too friendly, too sympathetic, you'll find the adversary relationship crumbling; you'll find it difficult to write objectively, dispassionately. And, even if you reject friendship or avoid sympathy, you can be vulnerable in another way: you will become dependent on sources for news tips and leads, for spot news developments and background explanation of highly complex matters. Sooner than later, you will find yourself weighing the news value of a story against whether publishing or airing it will embarrass a source and close down an information pipeline important to you.

In sum, adversarialism is far from the perfect technique. It may force you into uncomfortable confrontations, make you feel at times like an unethical inquisitor. Certainly, it can be embarrassing to you and damaging to the media's image if television captures grown men and women shouting at the President of the United States for the sake of the people's right to know, or ambushing unsuspecting innocents and thrusting them with gross insensitivity into the glare of publicity because they, through no fault of their own, have become "news." But adversarialism may be the only way, given the importance of your job of getting the news and the unfortunate tendency of those in power to hide it. Tempered but forceful, courteous but insistent, adversarialism should continue to distinguish American journalists from the captive reporters of authoritarian nations or the willing, active media propagandists in communist societies.

NEWS: MAKING IT OR REPORTING IT?

Whip out your reporter's notebook or point a camera at the world around you and you start *making* news. You become a participant, a catalyst even, in the newsmaking process. Things happen when a reporter arrives on the scene. Therefore, if you want to report a balanced, fair view of what was happening before you arrived and what likely will happen after you depart, you must develop methods of getting the story as unobtrusively as possible. You will not face many greater challenges as you try to construct an ethically sound reportorial technique.

Meg Greenfield, distinguished editorial page editor of the *Washington Post,* puts it this way:

> To the extent that it is working at all, the press is always a participant. Our decisions on where (and where not) to be and what (and what not) to report have enormous impact on the political and governmental life we cover. We are obliged to be selective. We cannot publish the Daily Everything. And so long as this is true—so long as we are making choices that 1) affect what people see concerning their leaders and 2) inevitably therefore cause those leaders to behave in particular ways—we cannot pretend we are not participants.
>
>   But of course we do, or at least some of us do. The "Shucks, I'm just a simple country stenographer, writing it all down as it happens" affectation is still with us, even though most people would agree that reporters (not just editorial writers and political columnists) must make subjective judgments every step of the way and are

not merely walking tape recorders. The question, of course, is how honest, fair and professional those judgments are—and that is what the argument over journalistic participation in our national political life has been about.[7]

Not only in covering politics is being "honest, fair and professional" required. Your story can move financial markets, shake large institutions, cause angry debate; your camera can inspire otherwise normal football fans to leap from their seats, wave their arms, and make insane faces. Your mere presence can make news. Discussed below are elements to watch.

Presence and Numbers

In the chemistry of reporter influence on the newsmaking process, one plus one does not equal two. It equals five. That is, two reporters arriving to cover a story more than doubles the impact of one; if one of the two reporters is from the *New York Times, Washington Post,* or *Wall Street Journal,* the impact widens exponentially, for of all news-gathering organizations in the country, those papers set the tone for coverage. They "legitimatize" a story; they set the national news agenda. A reporter from one of those papers will draw competing special correspondents, TV cameras, and news agency reporters. It's called "herd journalism," and no matter how you try to make independent news judgments or follow your own instincts, you will find it difficult to "go against the flow." Your editor or news director will wonder why you are proceeding in one direction while the *New York Times, Washington Post,* AP, and UPI, plus the networks are moving in another. Then, *you* will begin to wonder why.

The Ego Factor

Nothing in journalism causes more news to be *made* than the ego gratification of getting your byline on a front-page scoop, or doing a standup for the 6 P.M. news in front of city hall. Most truly instinctive reporters are driven by an urge to find and tell, dig and reveal—and win appropriate applause, a prize or two, from peers and public. It is a creative but dangerous thing, this ego factor. More than money, more than anything else, it drives great reporters to uncover important stories. It also can become rampant careerism, which leads weak reporters to manufacture news where none exists, to "hypo" stories with importance they don't deserve, to press for front-page display of stories that are page-20 caliber. Recognizing that you feel such stirrings (and that other reporters do, too) is half the battle of controlling the ego factor. But you'll also feel considerable external pressure to make news (although it will be called "developing an enterprise piece"). If faced with a gaping newshole on a slow news day, your editor will quickly have you on the telephone or out on the beat, initiating interviews, "working up" a feature or two. And that is when you must guard against intruding into the news process and manufacturing the news—particularly if you are proud to be the one reporter in the newsroom who on a slow day can be counted on to come up with a "bell-ringer" for the front page. George V. Higgins of the *Wall Street Journal* describes distortion of the newsmaking process:

> The journalistic tendency to react to a paucity of events amounting to news, by instigating some news, is most pronounced among television reporters and gurus because dead air is exponentially more excruciating for them to endure than dull columns are for us ink-stained wretches. TV journalists are likelier to go around making trouble than are members of the pencil press, not because they are more mischievous but because their need is greater and more urgent. They commence therefore, very gingerly, to reverse the polarity of media and politics, by their analysis prodding the drowsy politicians from their dozes onto their feet to do a little barking. The print media do not find this cruel sport. We troop happily right along behind the television folks, duly perpetuating in the papers the next day the news which is thus made.[8]

Moving Center Stage

A former president of the Associated Press once said being a reporter is to have a front row seat watching history being made.[9] Sometimes, however, reporters move into center stage—or are thrust there—to help *make* history, and that can raise complex ethical questions. For example, few would doubt a reporter or photographer must intrude into the "story" to prevent a deranged person from a suicidal plunge off a bridge. But can suicide be a political statement into which reporters should *not* intrude? That was the judgment of AP reporters who watched—and photographed—a Buddhist monk immolate himself at a busy intersection in downtown Saigon to protest his government's policies during the Vietnam war. The photos had immense impact on world opinion, and created antiwar sentiment in the United States.

Closer to home, but still dealing with life and death, reporters sometimes become involved in police work: prisoners seize guards and insist on making public statements through reporters (it happened at Ossining, New York, prison, and the governor's top aide says television "became a part of the process"); a deranged man seizes hostages in the Washington Monument and demands that a reporter serve as intermediary with police (an AP man does, with considerable courage, but also with concern over being part of the story, not an observer, and with being asked to do police work by getting a description of the man and a detonator-like device he is holding).[10]

The difficulty for mere mortals in judging whether reporters should play such roles is summed up in AP's statement after the Washington Monument incident:

The involvement of our reporter, Steve Komarow, in the siege at the monument brings home again the lesson that terrorist-hostage situations defy the normal journalistic ground rules.

Steve performed bravely, calmly and responsibly. One could not have asked for more from the young AP newsman.

Yet, the whole scene is troublesome. Reporters don't belong in the middle of these situations, as Steve himself observed later in describing his own reaction.

Perhaps all that can be said now of crises like the one at the monument is that as journalists we must judge the circumstances that confront us each time and respond in a way compatible with our professional role.[11] (See Case Study 3-1 for what happened when two Mississippi editors were asked to cooperate with police.)

CASE STUDY 3-1

REPORTERS OR POLICEMEN?

The U.S. Attorney asks to meet secretly with you, managing editor of the city's only daily newspaper, and the general manager of its only television station. The official explains police want to trap a man trying to hire a "hit man" to kill a local cattle farmer. Payment has been promised when the killing is reported in the news.

The U.S. Attorney wants you to publish a false story—he calls it a "deception"—reporting the farmer's bloodstained truck has been found and police are searching for him. Your television competitor agrees. Police fear that if TV carries the report and your paper does not, the "deception" will fail. The U.S. Attorney is more forceful: He tells your publisher he might be responsible for deaths.

Question: Do you cooperate with authorities by actively engaging in the hoax?

When confronted with that question in 1984, Frank Sutherland, managing editor of the *Hattiesburg* (Miss.) *American,* told police they had presented him with three options, "all of them bad": Publish the hoax and damage his newspaper's credibility, expose the officials' secret maneuvering, or write nothing, "which will look funny when people, including the guy you're trying to catch, see something on TV and nothing in the newspaper."

Sutherland and publisher Duane McCallister finally decided to publish a single sentence that was true but wouldn't deceive readers: "Police are seeking information concerning suspected foul play directed toward Oscar Black III [the farmer]."

WDAM-TV broadcast the "victim's" name, and described how his truck was found with apparent bloodstains in it. WDAM carried the false story for several days, but an informant told police the case had been "blown."

Police went public to praise WDAM and condemn the *American.* WDAM general manager Cliff Brown said he had chosen ethics of life over ethics of journalism. In a single two-hour call-in show, 2,000 viewers telephoned about the incident, and WDAM said 80 percent agreed with its action.

Managing editor Sutherland said, "Not many people understand our ethics.... The problem gets confusing if someone thinks we are not being a good citizen. But if we lie to them, they will always be able to wonder—say perhaps the next time we run a police story—are they telling us the truth?"

Publisher McCallister said, "Once you break that bond of trust with the reader, you can never put it back together."

Postscript: Months later, using more traditional methods, police arrested a Hattiesburg man and charged him with trying once more to have the farmer killed. He was sentenced to seventeen years in prison and fined $10,000.

What is a journalist's obligation *as a citizen* in such a case? Did Sutherland and McCallister put their newspaper and its reputation above a man's life?

Stunting

Indefensible involvement in newsmaking comes occasionally from reporters who court arrest or break laws in search of sensational copy. This might be a reporter breaking through guard lines to test security on a military base, who steals to "research" a story on shoplifting, or deals in narcotics on the street for an inside view of the underworld. Such stunting is unethical, probably illegal—and can get you shot.

SOURCES AND YOUR ETHICAL TECHNIQUE

Reporters without news sources are like soldiers without rifles or cowboys without horses; they lack the essential tool of the trade. So important are sources that complex ethical considerations have grown up around their care and feeding, to which successful reporters devote much of their working day.

For the aspiring journalist, ethical considerations divide roughly in two parts: First, the ethics of your relationship with sources themselves and, second, the ethics of what you reveal to your *readers and viewers* about your sources.

In developing sources, you must get close to power centers; you've got to find out where the button is pushed and by whom. The most important sources are those who control money, public or private, who possess political influence, or who can provide you with expert knowledge in one of the highly specialized news categories—law, medicine, science—popping into the news ever more frequently these days. Move upstream, along the flow of money, influence, and expert knowledge, and you will find sources crucial to your success. When you do, be alert. Sources will agree to help you for a variety of motives—not all of them ethical. For example:

• *The fun of the game.* At times, the world seems full of frustrated reporters, people in other lines of work who genuinely want to help get a story on the front page or on the 6 P.M. news, and know they helped you develop it. Treated cautiously, such people can become helpful, ethically sound sources.

• *The public interest.* These are "whistle blowers," who believe they serve a higher cause by leaking news of graft, corruption, and malfeasance. Washington is full of them, and they break a great deal of important news. Your guard should be up with this category of sources because mixed in with true dedication to public interest there often is a heavy component of self-interest.

• *Self-interest.* Individuals, bureaucratic cliques, political parties feverishly leak news to advance their own careers or causes. In Washington, around budget time, when the armed forces scramble for larger shares of the tax dollar, a Navy source will reveal the Soviet fleet in the Mediterranean poses a threat to world peace; an Air Force source will reveal that the *real* threat comes from Moscow's bombers and missiles. And, both will provide irrefutable evidence! The same dynamics will motivate your sources on Main Street; only the scale is different. There is nothing ethically unsound in accepting news tips from partisan sources; just remember precisely where you got the news, and why it was given to you—then make elaborate efforts to report all sides of the story and write a balanced, fair account.

• *Jealousy, hatred, revenge, and other motives not so nice.* Huge ethical problems can be raised by sources who try to strike at enemies by subjecting them to the special agony of twisting slowly in the glare of unfavorable media coverage or, even, by getting them fired or sent to jail through news tips to reporters. For the reporter, the dilemma is acute if the source clearly is acting out of personal jealousy or hatred *but* is leaking a story that just as clearly belongs in the public view. On his first reporting job, the author was tipped by a county treasurer that the sheriff was misusing county cars, a big story in smalltown journalism in Illinois. The treasurer hated the sheriff for personal reasons, waited patiently for years until he made a misstep, and then contacted the reporter. The *treasurer's* motive may have been unethical, but the story— carefully checked and double-checked—indeed was news important to the public. It was published. When a source bares fangs in revealing a story, an ethical reporter will proceed extremely carefully, but always keeping in mind the greater news needs of the readers or viewers.

Often, sources impose "ground rules" for use of information given you. Frankly, much important news enters public view only because reporters agree to restrictions, so sometimes you must go with "informed sources," unnamed "officials," or another of the anonymous labels sources often duck behind to avoid public responsibility for your story. This can raise many ethical issues. For one thing, those sources spurred by hatred or revenge will insist on avoiding, almost without exception, any connection with the story. But also—and more importantly—playing the "informed sources" game opens you to manipulation by sources, and distances you from your basic mission of providing readers and viewers with important, reliable news tightly attributed to authoritative sources by name, rank, and serial number. Your readers and viewers *deserve* to know the source of the information you place before them so they can judge for themselves its reliability.

In dealing with sources, your best stance is that of a reporter who talks openly, above-board with sources, and

---

VIEWPOINT 3-3

INFORMED SOURCES AND OTHER GAMES

"It allows that well-known unknown, the 'informed source' or 'high administration official,' to get his knife into an opponent or float a trial balloon without political danger. It permits a reporter to write a story which proves he is in the know, but protects him from the consequences of error, since he is simply relaying what the person behind the mask has said. And it provides useful reading for all the other participants in the Washington game, since they usually know enough to be able to make out, at least hazily, the identity of the source and the meaning of the message.

"The problem is that the average reader or viewer can't do the same...."

Hodding Carter III, former State Department spokesman, writing in the *Wall Street Journal* on Washington journalists quoting "informed sources," January 20, 1983, p. 25

names them in print or on the air. Don't *offer* to go "off the record." If the source insists on anonymity, you have a dilemma. As we will discuss in the next chapter, you have an ethical responsibility to consult a supervising editor before granting anonymity. You also must decide whether the story's news value seems to warrant departure from your stance as a reporter who tightly attributes news. Is there another way to dig it out? If not, insist on attribution that will reveal to readers or viewers as fully as possible the authoritative credentials of your source and, importantly, make clear the source is in a position to know the accuracy of the information being given you. That is, "deep background," a ground rule against any identification, is least satisfactory. The source is insisting you use the information as your own. So, "informed source" is somewhat better than no source; a "high-ranking administration official" is an improvement; a "top aide in the President's inner circle of advisers, who declined to be identified," is even stronger. Warning:

Be certain you agree explicitly with the source *in advance* on how information is to be attributed. "Deep background" means one thing to some officials, quite something else to others. It is unethical to agree to "protect" sources, then publish descriptions that identify them even if names are not used. A few such betrayals and your sources will vanish. You have a serious problem if, midway through an interview you assume is on the record, the source announces, "Of course, this is all deep background." Your options are: (1) insist on full usage and identification, which will cost you a source or (2) grudgingly agree—and promise yourself never again to start an interview without establishing openly that it is on the record.

Never promise to protect a source's anonymity unless you are prepared to go all the way—to jail, even—to keep your promise. Whatever the *source's* motives, you must be known far and wide as a completely reliable, ethical reporter who stands by a promise. Any number of your journalistic predecessors have gone to jail on contempt of court charges because they refused to identify confidential sources on the grounds that no reporter can work effectively without complete trust from sources. As we will discuss later in this book, such trust is a foundation principle of a free press in a free society.

VIEWPOINT 3-4

JAIL OR CONSCIENCE

"I would be betraying my sources. It's a matter of conscience."

  Loretta Tofani, 31-year-old reporter for the *Washington Post,* when warned she faced six months in prison for refusing to identify her sources in a story on sexual assaults in the Prince Georges, Maryland, county jail, August 16, 1984

THE ETHICS OF "NEWS SLEUTH" TECHNIQUES

The age-old debate over what means are justifiable to reach worthwhile ends is becoming heated for journalists involved in investigative reporting. The equation is complex: Readers and viewers tell pollsters they want newspaper and TV reporters on guard, digging out wrongdoing. But by a wide margin they disapprove of investigative reporters using undercover techniques such as secret tape recorders or cameras.[12] Editors generally don't want reporters acting like undercover sleuths...*unless* a major story of high public importance is at stake and there is no other way to get it.[13]

As you try to sort out your own ethical position, you plainly are left alone to wrestle with your conscience and your supervising editor on a case-by-case basis. Areas of current concern are:

Concealing Identity and Masquerading

Let's say you're a reporter doing a story on the mood of a city. Is it ethical to walk around, talking to people, without identifying yourself as a reporter? No problem, right? Now, let's say you're doing a story on, for example, cost of auto repairs. Is it ethical to take your car to ten garages, without revealing your identity, and write a story comparing cost estimates for an engine overhaul? Still no problem? How about checking into the local hospital's emergency ward, identifying yourself as John (or Mary) Doe, and complaining about a fierce pain in your side—to research a story on medical practices in your town. See any ethical problems yet? Let's take the issue another step: Would you not only conceal your identity, but create another by, say, impersonating a police officer? Would you walk over to a witness after a bank holdup and identify yourself as a detective to obtain an exclusive interview? No? Well, would you talk to that witness and passively deceive the person by letting him or her *assume* you are a detective?

Ethical issues arising from such questions are equalled in number perhaps only by the differing views journalists hold on such conduct. On one extreme is the reporter who impersonated a police officer to interview a prison inmate (an illegal act for which the reporter spent ten days in jail).[14] In the middle are some editors who support undercover techniques if the story being sought is of crucial importance to the public and not available through other, more open means. Some newspapers take firm stands against masquerading, the *New York Times* among them—but the *Times* permits restaurant critics to sample food without alerting the chef in advance. The underlying concern among journalists over "news sleuth" techniques was summed up by J. Russell Wiggins, former editor of the *Washington Post:* "Deceit of this kind may now and then produce a story not otherwise obtained. The more often used the less effective the tactic will be and the greater the public distrust of the press."[15]

Secret Recorders, Hidden Cameras

Conflicting ethical, legal, and logical arguments enter any discussion of whether reporters should use secret recorders.

All reporters take notes during telephone conversations with news sources, and, one might ask, isn't it logical to use a tape recorder to catch those quotes verbatim? Legally, isn't it an excellent defense to have an electronically precise record of the conversation in case of a libel threat? But, as always, the reporter comes back to basics: Is it ethical—honest—to secretly record a conversation?

For once, there generally is unanimity among journalists, readers, and viewers. By large majorities, they disapprove of secret taping.[16] But dissenters ask why replacing pencil with recorder, even secretly, creates an ethical problem. State laws on the question differ (and check yours before proceeding). In some, "participatory" taping—one party using a recorder in a two-party conversation—is legal; wiretapping—a third party listening secretly to two others—may be illegal.

On this issue there is little doubt: Secret taping *is* unethical, and a reporter would do well to routinely never use a recorder unless the other party is advised. For that matter, even when merely taking pencil notes, it is proper to point out the conversation is on the record. (See Case Study 3-2 for a different twist in the on- or off-the-record controversy.)

Using hidden cameras creates different questions. As any foreign correspondent knows, openly photographing on the streets during, say, a riot can lead to cameras—and heads—being smashed. Secretly photographing from a second story window in such cases clearly is not only ethical, but wise. But, let us say you are investigating drug dealing in your town. If you witness drug sales in a playground or park, photographing secretly from a nearby house or parked car would be acceptable. The action is taking place in public and thus is obvious to all who care to look. Many journalists agree, further, it is ethical to use a secret camera if, say, a drug dealer comes to your apartment to offer narcotics. However, secretly photographing an unsuspecting person in *their* private home, where they have the right to privacy, is unacceptable to many. CBS News outlines for its photographers just those distinctions: Use hidden cameras in public or your own home or office. But don't secretly intrude into the private domain of others.[17]

The *Chicago Sun-Times* made the public versus private distinction when it established a tavern—a licensed public place—for use in an investigative reporting series. The tavern became a watering hole for corrupt city employees shaking down local businesses. *Sun-Times* reporters worked as bartenders and overheard conversations; *Sun-Times* pho-

---

VIEWPOINT 3-5

WHEN THE PRESS PRESSES IN

"The Salt Lake City hospital's public relations staff had been overwhelmed by the requests for information by news organizations and, in some cases, by the behavior of journalists. At the Utah hospital, a photographer had leaped out of a laundry hamper where he had been hiding and snapped pictures of the medical team that later appeared in a Japanese newspaper."

Alex S. Jones describing coverage of a human heart transplant, the *New York Times*, April 5, 1983, p. 9

CASE STUDY 3-2

REPORTING OR EAVESDROPPING?

Your network is making technical arrangements for a broadcast by the President of the United States. During a routine microphone test the President says a few words so technicians can adjust sound levels: "My fellow Americans, I am pleased to tell you I just signed legislation which outlaws Russia forever. The bombing begins in five minutes."

Laughter erupts in the studio. Such joviality helps reduce prebroadcast tension. This time, however, the President's remark and the laughter are transmitted—not to the listening public, but to your recording equipment outside the studio.

Question: Should you treat the President's obviously jocular but nevertheless startling remark as news to be reported publicly?

The issue arose in 1984 when that remark by President Reagan was transmitted into CBS recorders. That was on a Saturday. CBS didn't use the tapes until AP broke the story and printed the quotes. CBS then *quoted* the President on its late Sunday news. On Monday, after lengthy internal deliberations, CBS ran the actual recording on Dan Rather's *Evening News.*

Edward Joyce, CBS president, emphasized two points:

First, broadcasting the taped comment offered an explanatory dimension not created by merely quoting from the transcript: "There's a very clear indication of the jocularity around the mike when the laughter comes up. One of the questions we asked was, 'Does this in some way advance, clarify, further develop things?' Because of the jocular tone, and the laughter that developed, we felt it did."

Second, Joyce said CBS and other networks would feel free to use the President's comments if they left the studio.

White House spokesman Larry Speakes furiously charged off-the-record ground rules had been broken. The networks claimed they rejected any ground rules two years earlier when Reagan made a similar off-the-cuff remark before broadcast. That time, he referred to Poland's military government as "a bunch of no-good lousy bums" (which later in the broadcast became "a military dictatorship.") The "bums" remark was widely used.

More questions: Should reporters consider the international implications of such off-the-cuff remarks before using them? Are reporters in effect obliged to protect public figures from repercussions of their casual remarks? Did AP stampede CBS?

After the "bombing" comment stirred international protest, Reagan said: "Isn't it funny? If the press had kept their mouth shut, no one would have known I said it."

---

tographers caught the whole thing from a hidden room. (The paper also invited in CBS's *60 Minutes.*) The *Sun-Times* generally was expected to win a 1979 Pulitzer prize, but two members of the Pulitzer advisory board blocked it— Ben Bradlee, editor of the *Washington Post,* and Eugene Patterson, then managing editor of the *St. Petersburg Times.* They explained honoring the *Sun-Times* would signal journalists across the country that misrepresentation was an acceptable technique.

The Case of the Purloined Documents

Stealing somebody's dining room silver is a crime. So is *receiving* stolen silver. Not many people will defend either.

Yet, recent journalistic experience shows many reporters will obtain and use official or private documents without permission if the resulting story is deemed to serve the public interest in a matter of compelling importance. That is, many reporters will receive and use what technically are stolen goods in order to get a crucial story. But, as in all ethical issues, there are nuances.

It is to be hoped, for example, that few journalists will break into an official's office to obtain a document (although that has been done, and although some reporters might make a questionable distinction between committing a night-time burglary and "entering uninvited" during office hours). Some will read a document on the official's desk if invited in but left alone for a while (that happened in the White House where press aides left documents out that way, and "planted" on a few reporters a minor scoop that turned out to be a major hoax). Many reporters will consider the document a prize catch if they find it, say, after a meeting in an open conference room where the official absentmindedly left it (at one seminar on ethics where this scenario was presented as a case study, the major reservation among attending journalists was only whether to give the official advance word his document would be published).[18] And, finally, as is proven in the newspapers and on the evening newscasts nearly every day, many journalists gleefully will accept the document—or a detailed report on its contents—if it is obtained by a "news source" (and no questions asked about how the source obtained it).

If you've already made up your mind never to use purloined documents (particularly those stamped "secret"), consider the most celebrated instance in which they *were* used. That, of course, was the publication in 1971 of the so-called Pentagon Papers, a massive official analysis of U.S. involvement in the Vietnam War. A former Defense Department analyst leaked them to the *New York Times, Washington Post, St. Louis Post-Dispatch,* and *Boston Globe,* which published them despite vigorous legal efforts by the government to keep them secret. Now, many years later, it is clear the Pentagon Papers were improperly classified secret, that publication of excerpts did not jeopardize national security, that the public had a right to know what was in them, and that the newspapers involved served well the principle of a free press. But none of that disguises the fact that the documents were stolen goods, and that the next time a similar case arises, as it is certain to, massive ethical issues will again be raised.

In such cases, the reporter's dilemma often is compounded because other critically important issues are involved besides whether the documents are stolen goods. In the Pentagon Papers case, for example, journalists had to decide whether national security would be jeopardized by publication of documents classified as secret by government officials purportedly in a position to know. In Juneau, Alaska, in 1985, an unusual twist was given another

---

VIEWPOINT 3-6

MORE TO IT THAN THAT

"The old notion that you 'get the story, and to hell with everything else' has no responsible defenders in American journalism today."

John Hohenberg, *The Professional Journalist,* Holt, Rinehart, Winston, Inc., New York, 1978, p. 320

case, when two reporters searched a courthouse trash can and found copies of a court clerk's notes on grand jury proceedings still under way. Of four papers offered the resulting story, three refused to publish on grounds that the integrity of the grand jury's secret proceedings had to be protected and that, as one editor put it, the story came from a questionable source—the garbage. The editor who published the story said his job was to learn what was happening and tell his readers.

GOOD NEWS VERSUS BAD NEWS

In developing your own ethical guidelines on what is news and what techniques to use in getting it, you will confront a fundamental question: Is news by definition mostly bad, shocking, negative, mankind's *exceptions* to expected behavior? (Certainly, polls show that type news popular with readers and viewers.) Or, is it just as frequently positive, upbeat—the good mankind performs every day in *conforming* to expected behavior? How you answer is central to your personal code because the issue constitutes an important fork in the career path where you must decide which direction to take as a reporter.

There are reporters whose reasoned professional judgment is that news mostly is aberrant behavior—crime, corruption—and the wars, natural disasters, and other calamities that befall the world. But also in the "bad news school" are reporters who intentionally seek out bad news as part of a rampant careerism that feeds off front-page bylines and the top spot on the 6 P.M. news. These reporters know the journalism fraternity rewards its members more frequently for stories on sheriffs who beat prisoners than on sheriffs who patiently, gently try to reform their wards. The rewards are better assignments, promotions, and more pay.

For readers and viewers, the result is an unremitting, overwhelming drumbeat of death, disaster, and doom. And, readers and viewers say they don't like it. One frequent criticism of the media is that they are possessed by a bad news syndrome. In one poll, 66 percent of respondents say newspapers pay too much attention to bad news and not enough to good things; 64 percent say that about TV news. Among blacks and other minority men and women, 75 percent feel that way.[19]

Editors, responding to such polls, strive to present more "good" news. Some newspapers even set aside a "good news page" for all the Boy Scout promotions,

---

VIEWPOINT 3-7

JOURNALISM OF HOPE

"The issue, very simply, is whether the 'old journalism' of despair, the derisive technique of leaving readers discouraged, or sad or indignant, can or should survive in the '80s and '90s. Or whether a 'new journalism' of hope—a technique that chronicles the good, the bad and the otherwise—leaves readers fully informed and equipped to judge what deserves their attention and support can and will prevail in the decades ahead."

Al Neuharth, chairman of Gannett Co., criticizing journalists who "out-bad-news" each other

church dinners, and other nice things that happen. But, is "nice news" news? Good news certainly doesn't play all that well. Readers and viewers, despite what they say, *are* attracted to bad news, and do read or watch it attentively.

For you as a reporter, the dilemma is: If you decide your basic technique will be to emphasize the positive as well as the negative, are you in fact deciding to distort the news in accordance with some personal yardstick on which good and bad are measured? Are you failing in your journalistic responsibility if you set forth intentionally to *find* good news, rather than taking the world as it comes and balancing events—good and bad—to create a discerning, meaningful daily report of what is important?

These questions we will explore in more detail in Chapter 4 as we look at your ethical relationships with your public and your editors or news directors.

CHAPTER SUMMARY

A reporter trying to build a personal code of ethics must consider not only ethical intent, but also the ethics of *technique*. One of the most important influences on reportorial technique is the adversarial relationship, the always cautious, sometimes tense relationship between reporters and the "structure" they cover. Some reporters believe in head-on confrontation with news sources; others passively accept news handouts. It's possible to build, however, a decorous but effective relationship of getting close to sources but never joining their team.

One ethical dilemma for reporters is that their mere presence at a news event can *make* news, involving them in much more than an observer's role. Each reporter must carefully avoid getting involved in a story.

News sources are critically important, and successful reporters spend much of their working day developing them. Complex ethical considerations have grown up around reporter-source relationships. It's important to understand the source's motives in giving you news. Some do so to advance their personal interests, others to damage a foe. To be fair to your readers you must identify your sources, whenever possible. If it's not, you should describe the source's authoritative credentials as fully as possible so the reader or viewer can decide on the reliability of your information.

The ethics of undercover reporting techniques are hotly debated. Readers, viewers, and editors like the *result* of investigative reporting, but disapprove of such techniques as using secret tape recorders or cameras. Editors also increasingly frown on journalists concealing their identity as reporters or masquerading under an assumed identity.

CHAPTER 3

Notes

1 Gallup Opinion Index, 1982.
2 Michael J. O'Neill, speech to American Society of Newspaper Editors, Washington, D.C., May 5, 1982.

3 For a full discussion of this exchange, see "The Adversary Press," a report on an Ethics Center Seminar, p. viii, 1983, Modern Media Institute, 801 Third St. South, St. Petersburg, Fla., 33701.

4 Such horror stories abound, of course, but one particularly fine wrapup is Anthony Marro, "When The Government Tells Lies," *Columbia Journalism Review,* March/April 1985, p. 29.

5 James Reston, "Reagan and the Press," *New York Times,* March 21, 1982, p. 23.

6 Howell Raines, "President Denies Lapses Laid to Him in the Press," *New York Times,* Feb. 19, 1982, p. 16.

7 Meg Greenfield, "When the Press Becomes a Participant," Annual Report 1984, The Washington Post Co., 1150 15th St. N.W., Washington, D.C., 20071, p. 21.

8 George V. Higgins, "TV: The Democratic Oratory Contest," *Wall Street Journal,* July 23, 1984, p. 13.

9 The full quote is, "I would not want to be a newsman at any other time.... Man's aspiration was never higher in reaching for the stars, his material wealth never greater, and his chance for survival in a nuclear age never thinner. And we, in the AP, sit in front row seats to report all this." The quote is from Wes Gallagher and can be found as the introduction to Charles A. Grumich, *Reporting/Writing from Front Row Seats,* Simon & Schuster, Inc., New York, 1971.

10 The burning monk was photographed by Malcome W. Browne, then AP Saigon bureau chief, on June 11, 1963. The photos created a tremendous stir over whether their use was in good taste. For details on the Ossining story, see Jonathan Friendly, "Officials and Newsmen Discuss TV's Ossining Role," *New York Times,* Jan. 15, 1983, p. 16. Steve Komarow describes his role in the Washington Monument incident in "Eyewitnesses to History," *AP Log,* the Associated Press, 50 Rockefeller Plaza, New York, N.Y., 10020, Dec. 13, 1982, p. 1.

11 Lou Boccardi, "A Note of Caution," *AP Log,* op. cit.

12 Reader disapproval of undercover techniques is reported in a number of surveys, in none so clearly as "Newspaper Credibility: Building Reader Trust," research report, 1985, American Society of Newspaper Editors, P.O. Box 17004, Washington, D.C., 20041.

13 Several studies of editor attitudes reveal this ambivalence. Note Guido H. Stempel III, "New Studies Explain Credibility, Secret Taping of Calls," *presstime,* Nov. 1985, p. 55; Ralph S. Izard, "Technique: Certain News Procedures Found to Bother Journalists," a special report on ethics, Associated Press Managing Editors, 50 Rockefeller Plaza, New York, N.Y. 10020; and, "Editors Say Journalists Should Not Use Hidden Recording Devices," research bulletin, Southern Newspaper Publishers Association, P.O. Box 28875, Atlanta, Ga., 30328, June 16, 1983, p. 1.

14 "Reporting Subterfuge," *The APME Red Book 1983,* Associated Press Managing Editors, 50 Rockefeller Plaza, New York, N.Y., 10020.

15 Ibid. Also see Tom Goldstein, "The News at Any Cost," *Washington Journalism Review,* Sept. 1985, p. 48.

16 "Editors Say Journalists Should Not Use Hidden Recording Devices," Southern Newspaper Publishers Association bulletin, op. cit., and "Newspaper Credibility: Building Reader Trust," ASNE research report, op. cit.

17 *CBS News Standards, a policy manual,* CBS Inc., 51 W. 52nd St., New York, N.Y., 10020, April 14, 1976.

18 Seminar in media ethics sponsored by Morris Communications Corp., Savannah, Ga., March 9–11, 1986.

19 "Relating to Readers in the '80s," a survey by Ruth Clark for the American Society of Newspaper Editors, 1984, p. 28.

CHAPTER 4

YOUR PARTNERS IN ETHICS: YOUR PUBLIC AND YOUR EDITOR

Few issues are more personal than your own sense of good and bad. Does anything more intimately reflect the inner you than your concept of right and wrong? This highly personal nature of ethics has been the thrust of our discussion so far.

Yet, we fail if our discussion stops with the individual journalist's responsibility to think deeply about ethical concepts or techniques and fashion a strictly personal code of conduct. For, unlike the lonely artist laboring over attic easel or block of granite, journalists must practice their craft daily in full view of millions, and not simply to express themselves but to serve readers and viewers in a much higher cause. And, journalists must do it quickly, under the discipline of meeting deadlines, in busy newspaper or television newsrooms—not as free-spirited individualists, but as employees, directed by editors, and as part of a much wider, collective effort.

For the individual journalist, then, a concern over ethical concepts and techniques can have professional meaning *only* if cast within the wider context of relationships with others. To conclude Part One of this book, we now turn to that wider context—to ethical relationships between journalist and public, and between reporter and editor or news director.

To be effective, journalists must relate their personal sense of ethics to readers and viewers, to whom goes the reporter's first allegiance, and accomplish that while working within the wider corporate environment of a newspaper or television news operation that has its own very strong business as well as ethical imperatives.

In fashioning effective relationships with the public, any journalist at all sensitive to the historic thrust of the craft must believe the basic mission is to serve the greater good of the people, to collect and disseminate news for the purpose of informing those who need to know on matters of crucial importance to their lives. The ASNE "Statement of Principles" puts it this way:

> The primary purpose of gathering and distributing news and opinion is to serve the general welfare by informing the people and enabling them to make judgments on the issues of the time. Newspaper men and women who abuse the power of their professional role for selfish motives or unworthy purposes are faithless to that public trust.
>
> The American press was made free not just to inform or just to serve as a forum for debate but also to bring an independent scrutiny to bear on the forces of power in the society, including the conduct of official power at all levels of government.[1]

It's a tall order. To be effective professionally, the journalist must serve an external constituency, the public, while working efficiently within the very special relationship that exists between reporter and editor or news director, employee and boss. And, realistically, the journalist must "mesh" in an ethical, as well as businesslike, manner with both. The journalist who doesn't will not be effective in reaching the public, nor long employed.

YOU AND YOUR PUBLIC

In fashioning an ethical relationship with your readers or viewers you must understand, first, they feel newspapers and television news often fail to deliver the information they want and need. And, second, they frequently doubt the motives of journalists in general. It's not a comforting picture:

In studying public attitudes for ASNE, researcher Ruth Clark finds readers question whether newspapers are fair and unbiased, and, also, that they think newspapers try to manipulate them. Fifty-seven percent of respondents do *not* feel newspaper stories are fair; 53 percent do not believe they are accurate; 42 percent feel newspapers try to manipulate them. Many complain about newspaper content (30 percent say journalists are "more interested in Paris and Peking than in their own communities") and sensationalism (52 percent charge this about newspapers, 81 percent about TV news). But that doesn't mean dislike of journalists personally; 56 percent say they want to know more about reporters and editors who put out their local newspapers.[2]

VIEWPOINT 4-1

ANOTHER VIEW OF BIAS

"Could it be that bias sometimes is in the eye of the beholder? Do we sometimes have slanted readers?

"People are so committed, so involved, so agitated in this age of change and controversy and instant communications that many of them look for newspaper accounts of events—from Nicaragua to South Africa—to reinforce and agree with their own views, even their prejudices. If they don't get that, they often feel the press is not credible."

Warren H. Phillips, chairman and chief executive officer, Dow Jones & Co., Inc.

A gap between journalists and their public is found in an Associated Press Managing Editors survey. Although 45 percent of journalists give their papers high credibility ratings, only 32 percent of the public does; 70 percent of journalists feel newspapers are fair, but only 52 percent of the public does; 57 percent of journalists regard newspapers as unbiased, whereas just 36 percent of the public does.[3]

Belden Associates, a noted research firm, finds major criticisms of newspapers are "biased or slanted news, too much bad news, and inaccurate reporting." Gallup finds newspapers rank sixth among ten institutions in which Americans have a "great deal" or "quite a lot" of confidence; television is tenth among ten. Harris pollsters find only 14 percent of U.S. adults have a "great deal" of confidence in the *people* in charge of running the press; for television, it is 24 percent. Roper finds 51 percent of U.S. adults would believe television if they got conflicting or different reports of the same news; 22 percent, newspapers.[4]

A Times Mirror Corp. survey finds 53 percent of respondents feel the press is "often influenced by the powerful," including government, business, advertisers, and special interest groups; only 37 percent consider the press "pretty independent." Times Mirror finds deep belief the press doesn't care about the people it reports on, invades privacy for a story, serves up too much bad news, and is biased.[5]

You may regard the media as surrogate of the people; note how *they* feel: just 36 percent believe newspapers watch out for their interests; and only 31 percent believe TV news does, according to an ASNE study. Only 44 percent feel newspapers or TV care what readers or viewers think; 68 percent believe reporters frequently overdramatize the news.[6]

VIEWPOINT 4-2

LIVING WITH THE CONSEQUENCES

"We see ourselves as driven professionals, informed by good intentions and purposes. Readers see us as moral vigilantes, driven only by the desire to sell newspapers. We protest our meritorious intentions. But the public does not understand. We protest that we bear no responsibility for the consequences of our journalism. It is a world, many of us feel, we never made. We only report.

"Baloney. As human beings, editors and reporters ought to be terribly burdened, haunted, by the very real consequences of our decisions to publish. We ought to live uncomfortably with the fact that our journalism does damage. It can only be redeemed by the knowledge that, on balance, it helped more than it hurt."

Arnold Rosenfeld, then editor of the *Dayton* (Ohio) *Daily News,* writing in the *Washington Post,* April 8, 1979, p. D4

Clearly, Americans find much that is good in newspapers and TV news. Each survey cited above detects considerable support for the media, particularly in fundamental First Amendment rights and as a watchdog of government and other large institutions. And, Americans vote in the marketplace for the media: Nearly 63 million newspapers are purchased daily, more than ever before, and tens of millions watch TV news. Nevertheless, there are disquieting signals in those survey results for any discerning journalist attempting to construct an ethical, effective relationship with readers or viewers. ASNE's "Statement of Principles" outlines the challenge:

"Good faith with the reader is the foundation of good journalism. Every effort must be made to ensure that the news content is accurate, free from bias and in context, and that all sides are presented fairly. Editorials, analytical articles and commentary should be held to the same standards of accuracy with respect to facts as news reports.

"Significant errors of fact, as well as errors of omission, should be corrected promptly and prominently."

Based on thirty years in communications, the author suggests a journalist cannot build an effective relationship of trust with readers or viewers without a professionalism characterized by reporting that is accurate, writing that is honest and open, and by personal self-discipline and courage. Let's look at each in turn.

The Ethics of Accurate Reporting

Accuracy is so fundamental to responsible journalism that it can be argued it shouldn't even be discussed along with ethical issues on which there legitimately can be differing opinions, or nuances of good and bad. Accuracy is good, inaccuracy is bad—and that's that. But, accuracy *must* be discussed, because by definition an inaccurate journalist cannot be ethical. And, certainly, the subject is central to understanding the public perceptions of media ethics in general, because what readers and viewers term unethical conduct by the media often is nothing more than sloppy, inaccurate reporting.

Becoming an accurate reporter, as the first step toward a responsible, ethical relationship with your readers or viewers, is a matter of mindset. It requires accepting, early in your career, that a journalist's responsibility above all is to provide accurate, reliable information. Then, you must fashion reportorial *attitudes* that will produce it. Among the most important:

Respect for the Basics   In our world of stunning complexity, a reporter must dig out the meaning behind the facts, take readers and viewers gently by the hand and lead them, with interpretation and analysis, toward understanding. But the basics of ethical reporting remain balanced, factual representations of the "Five Ws and How," tightly attributed to authoritative sources: Who is involved? What is happening? When? Where? Why? Plus, How is it all coming together? And, importantly, Who says so? For many journalists, the temptation is overwhelming to explain "true meaning" at the expense of reporting the facts. For reporters, that can result in breakdown of the line between reporting and opinion. For readers or viewers, the result is a distinct feeling they are being manipulated. Time and again, they tell pollsters: Report the facts, and we'll decide on meaning and make up our own minds. In her survey for ASNE, Ruth Clark reports readers are saying, "Give us the news—hard news, *real* news, whether it's national, state, regional or local....Tell us the facts about health, science, technology, diet and nutrition, child-rearing—and we'll do the coping ourselves."[7] Like football players concentrating on basics of blocking and tackling, reporters never should overlook the basics of old-fashioned, hard-nose reporting of the facts.

Respect for Detail   There is greater danger, by far, that you will be inaccurate on "little" details more than on "big" ones. It's more likely you will catch accurately the central thrust of the evening speaker's argument than the precise spelling of his name, his age, title, address, corporate affiliation, and the name of the club that sponsored his visit. There is an almost universal tendency among reporters to let down, to get sloppy on the "little" details (libel lawyers, frequently called on to defend the media in lawsuits arising out of "little" inaccuracies, say the same thing). Yet, no detail is unimportant, and if you fail in any of it, you fail as an accurate, reliable reporter. And, each time you misspell the speaker's name or report inaccurately it was "The Garden Club," rather than "The Tree and Shrub Club," you chip away at the bridge of trust you are trying to build to your readers or viewers. Develop the technique of taking time to focus intently on such "housekeeping" details early in your coverage of any event. Soon, it will become automatic.

Recognition of Your Own Weaknesses   No reporter can possess strong background in all sectors of the news, or even more than a couple. Forget what you've heard about fabled general assignment reporters of days bygone who boasted ability to cover fires, floods, or bank failures with equal skill. They covered them all right, but not always well. It is your ethical duty to recognize where your academic preparation or on-the-job training left you short of background required to cover a story properly. Seek out authoritative sources, frankly acknowledge if you don't know the difference between a Federal Reserve Bank and the Federal Reserve System, or why movement in the prime interest rate has an effect on local home construction costs. Large numbers of your readers or viewers, increasingly sophisticated in financial, technical, and scientific matters, *do* know the difference, and your credibility will plunge dramatically if your reporting shows weakness. So, ask someone who knows. *There are no dumb questions—just dumb reporters who fail to ask.* Aside from using authoritative sources on a day-by-day basis, you can cover weaknesses in your background with disciplined reading or night school courses in, say, accounting, statistical analysis, or other highly specialized subjects that will help you cover complex stories in the news these days. It will give your reporting an authoritative note that goes far toward establishing reader or viewer trust in your byline. It will give you a rewarding sense of self-confidence, too.

Healthy Skepticism   It's not that your sources always *want* to mislead you, although some do, of course. Some will lay for you the "Baited Trap," attempting for their own purposes to mislead you with misinformation or disinformation.

But even those who honestly want to give you accurate information sometimes will fail. A busy policeman, a court clerk, or the U.S. Secretary of State easily can err as they talk with you while trying to direct traffic at an accident site, hurry into the judge's chambers, or depart Andrews Air Force Base for Manila. So, check and double-check, pose the same question another way to another source to see if you get the same answer—and whenever possible go to documentation, the public records, a piece of paper, for facts. Facts—precise numbers, lots of names, dates, addresses, exact quotations—are mainstays of accurate reporting. But, a warning about "healthy skepticism": If you're not careful, it can evolve into cynicism, a disbelief in everything and everybody. If *that* becomes apparent in your reporting, you will be unable to bridge the gap with either news sources or your readers or viewers.

VIEWPOINT 4-3

CLOSETS AND CORPSES

"It can be very hard for a journalist who has been knocking around for a couple of decades, or even a couple of weeks on some assignments, to take anything at face value anymore. So the error often comes in raining down sardonic doubt on some assertion that it just does not seem possible is true. We are morally certain that if we just yank open one more closet door the corpse will fall out. And maybe we don't give enough attention to things that are going well."

Meg Greenfield, *Newsweek* columnist

The Adrenalin Factor Get "up" for your reporting assignments, watch the crest of the news story as it develops—anticipate the next direction it will take. Then, prepare. Go to the files, get your housekeeping details straight, check sources, names, dates, places. The more you prepare to cover a story, the more accurate will be your reporting. To move into a story unprepared and at half-speed is to risk being overwhelmed by it. And out of that come errors.

The "No Cop-Out" Attitude There never is enough time in daily journalism to collect all the facts, never enough newshole or air time for an account long enough. Those are realities of your craft. But it is a cop-out to cite them as excuses for less than accurate, fair reporting. To your readers or viewers, there are *no* excuses for anything less than sound, complete, ethical reporting.

The Ethics of Honest Writing

Honest writing is your most important tool in building an effective relationship of trust with readers or viewers. In print, honest writing is the ceremony of transmittal, the reporter's hopeful leap from page toward reader comprehension. In television, it must be the substance behind smile, meaning behind glitter. In either medium, trust is established through sound, honest writing that effectively communicates. Without it, trust vanishes.

Writing rates high on the code of ethical priorities because writing that is dishonest—by design or error—can defeat best attempts to be objective, balanced, and fair in reporting. Accurate, unbiased reporting withers in dishonest writing.

We can treat quickly writing that is dishonest by intent. There is *no* justification for intentionally and covertly slanting a story through choice of language, selective inclusion or omission of facts, improper emphasis, misquotation, or, worse, "creative" use of quotations with prejudice to prove a point. As discussed in Chapter 2, an ethical writer approaches each story as objectively as possible. Writers who are dishonest by intent are propagandists, not journalists.

It is dishonesty by oversight, by error, that must concern us. For it is here, ambushed by carelessness and amateurism, that most of all we fail as honest writers.

The challenge of writing honestly is highly complex. But the fundamental need is simple to state. First, ensure the internal dynamics of each story communicate honestly, dispassionately, and with balance. Second, ensure an open, honest relationship with readers or viewers, leveling with them not only within each story, but also in a wider sense over a period of time. This requires learning to say, "The facts aren't available on this one," rather than trying to pirouette around factual weaknesses with fancy writing. It also requires saying on occasion, "Sorry, but I was wrong."

Let's look at some traps in the path of a writer trying to structure an honest story and some of the ways the writer can avoid those traps.

The Sin of Omission   An intentionally dishonest writer easily can skew a story away from accuracy through sin of *commission*—by including erroneous, unfair, biased material in a story. However, a writer with the most honest intentions just as easily can commit the sin of *omission,* skewing a story by omitting material that should be included. This is a particularly dangerous trap in newspaper and television news writing because time/space constraints are so severe; not *everything* can be shoveled into a story that will get only 6 column inches or forty-five seconds airtime. But if the mayor is charged with official corruption and a noted business leader rushes to his defense, take space, take time to mention they have been friends for thirty years and play golf together on weekends. Excluding those essential details is to commit the sin of omission. Deciding what to include in a story and what to omit can be pure agony for a young writer trying to do an honest job. It may be of little comfort, but seasoned and successful writers wrestle with the same agony of choice on most stories.

The Sin of Disguised Opinion   Our earlier discussion of objectivity covered dangers of letting opinion penetrate the *reporting* process. They will confront you in the *writing* process, too. (Again, we make the distinction between writing *news* copy, where your opinions don't belong, and *advocacy* copy which is openly and honestly labeled, and in which, obviously, your opinions do belong.) In striving for objective and fair news writing, beware of using too many adjectives. Opinions sneak into your writing on their backs. Saul Pett, an Associated Press reporter who won a Pulitzer prize for writing, says the honest writer maneuvers around the adjective trap by leading readers to discovery, not by telling them. For example, don't *tell* your readers there was a "bitter picket line battle." Describe how rocks were thrown, cars overturned. Let readers *discover* the meaning for themselves. In avoiding the sin of opinion disguised in news writing, be particularly alert on two types of stories: Those dealing with issues on which you have strong personal feelings, and those that send you back to the newsroom breathless over the passion, danger, bitterness, and bloodshed you have witnessed. Sit back for a moment, settle down, then do an honest writing job.

The Trap of Selective Quotation   You can write a story almost entirely around direct quotations and still distort what was said—in effect, use the principal's own words to misquote him. If the mayor speaks to the Rotary Club on both the promises and dangers in your town's economic future, and you quote him only on the bright spots ahead, you have been dishonest both with him and your readers or viewers. You even can *reverse* the meaning of what he said through selection of quotations. Beware particularly if you break up a long quotation to paraphrase some of what was said and use only a portion in direct quotes. *Consider:* The mayor tells Rotary, "We're headed into a short-term recession in our economy, but in the distant future are rosy times." You're dishonest in writing, "Mayor Fred Smith said today 'rosy times' are ahead for Our Town." Honestly selecting quotations that truly represent the speaker's position requires that you broadly assess the central thrust of what was said and attempt to identify its meaning. It's a delicate business. When you come to that point in your writing just remember to apply your best reasoned judgment to the process.

The Error of Assuming Too Much   To communicate honestly and effectively, each news story must be self-contained, backgrounding and explaining the news as well as reporting it. A common error among writers is to assume readers or viewers know more than they do, even about stories frequently in the news. Not everyone knows what the foreign trade deficit is; not everyone remembers (or ever knew) the background of U.S. involvement in Nicaragua. Often, a brief paragraph of explanation will bridge the gap between writer and reader or viewer.

"Rumors" to "Reports," "Source" to "Sources"   In a very real sense, the mark of an ethical writer is being open and honest with readers and viewers. The writer must *level* with them. It is patently unethical to write a story in a manner that conceals—or distorts—facts or nuances important to true understanding.
     You're being dishonest if a *rumor* you hear from a secretary in the City Hall's cafeteria escalates, on the evening news or in tomorrow morning's paper, to a

"*report* from City Hall." And, if, in the writing, a single Pentagon briefing officer rises to a tidal wave of "high-ranking sources in the military," more dishonesty is afoot. Obvious, perhaps; yet, writers every day busily escalate rumors to reports, and multiply a source to sources. It's dishonest, unethical—and can be extremely damaging. A rumor of a corporate takeover, perhaps let loose by a single investor who stands to gain, can move mountains of money on Wall Street if elevated to a "report," and if precise identification of the source and his or her motives are lost in the writing.

Watch Those "Press Reports"   The predilection displayed among some writers for quoting other news writers merits, here, its own paragraph of condemnation. It's a dangerous habit, particularly because—plagiarism quite aside—with each retelling by successive writers the rumor from the cafeteria line gains stronger credibility until you, unless careful, will serve up to reader or viewer a glob of baseless gossip disguised as news. If you feel compelled to quote your colleagues, do so with precision, as AP does in this Washington story: "*The Washington Post,* quoting unidentified government sources and citing intelligence documents..." That AP writer was honest with readers that day.[8]

Explain the Holes   If there are holes in your story, if you don't have all the facts pinned down, say so, openly and frankly. Note how AP explains why it must quote "diplomatic sources" and "conflicting reports" in a story on the Afghanistan war: "Accounts were pieced together from reports by Western diplomats in Kabul, Afghans who claimed to witness the disaster, and rebel sources in Pakistan. Independent accounts were impossible to obtain because Afghan authorities sharply restrict foreign reporters."[9]

In a long, moving piece on politics in Honduras, *New York Times* writer Barbara Crossette explains why she quotes an anonymous rancher even though he willingly spoke openly: "...after hearing his tales of corruption and brutality, it seemed prudent to give him anonymity."[10]

Not only do these AP and *New York Times* writers explain holes, they *strengthen* their stories by adding new dimensions of reader understanding of what goes into the news-gathering process.

And, *never* fail to explain even an *apparent* lapse in fairness. If the mayor charges the police chief with corruption and you cannot reach the chief, say so: "The chief did not return four telephone calls to his office." If you get through to him and he still declines comment, write that, too: "The chief, reached at his office, declined to comment."

Setting the Record Straight   Honest writers level with readers or viewers when errors are committed. It hurts, it bruises the ego, but it must be done. *New York Times* writer Tom Wicker tries each year to set the record straight with what he calls a column of confession. Here, under the headline, "Excuse It, Please," is how he starts one piece: "As has long been known, there are lies, damn lies, statistics and reporters' errors. Thus, an annual column of confession, while it may be good neither for the soul nor for the digestion, is necessary to clear the record and answer the mail.''[11]

Wicker follows that with a full column setting the record straight on errors of fact, interpretation, and nuance in his commentaries in the preceding twelve months. It is a refreshingly open, honest technique for leveling with readers, one that bears emulating. Readers and viewers also deserve to have the record kept straight over a period of time, through a series of stories as events develop. The *New York Times* and *Washington Post,* for example, do this with occasional stories explaining how rumors get started in the capital and soon sweep the press corps as ''reports,'' or how briefing officers work, and how ground rules get set up for reporting the news or quoting officials.[12]

Courage and Self-Discipline

When Myron Farber of the *New York Times* promised anonymity to news sources while covering a murder story, he meant it. Farber spent forty days in a New Jersey jail for refusing a judge's order to turn over to investigators his notes. William Farr of the *Los Angeles Herald Examiner* spent forty-seven days in jail for refusing to identify sources in a murder case he covered.[13]

Courage and self-discipline are part of ethical journalism. Along with honest reporting and honest writing, those qualities are essential for any journalist attempting to create a relationship of trust with readers and viewers.

For Farber and Farr, crisis of conscience arose over a principle of ethics fundamental to journalism in a free society—that reporters must be permitted special relationships with news sources, including the right to grant them anonymity, if the free press is to function properly. Their defense of that principle at enormous personal cost brought much of the media to the barricades in their support. Their cases drew national interest.

For you, courageously defending ethical principle may be a lonely affair. Perhaps you will have to make your stand over an issue which, although of compelling importance to you, holds no significance for your media colleagues or interest for the public. Perhaps you will face ethical issues lacking the clarity of those faced by Farber and Farr. And, wrestling with nuances of right and wrong and shades of meaning can leave even you doubting the wisdom of your course.

Defiance of Authority   Few things require more courage than doing what an ethical, responsible journalist must do, if that means defying authority. Even pushing your way into a closed meeting of the school board, which should conduct business in public, takes courage. Push you must, of course—politely, professionally, but very firmly. At other times, a different kind of courage is required because doing what must be done can open you to a wide range of serious risks. As with Farber and Farr, defying a judge's subpoena power, for example, can land you in jail; defying internal authority—your boss, say—can get you fired; refusing to back down before external legal pressure can result in personal exposure in a libel case (we'll discuss bosses and libel cases later). One of the more common forms of confrontation places you in defense of a story against attack by officialdom. Young American correspondents who reported the Vietnam war was not going well repeatedly found themselves defying an unending stream of optimism from the combined authority of the armed forces, Pentagon, State Department, and, more than once, White House. It took courage for those correspondents to stand by the accuracy of their reporting when such formidable authority was arrayed against them (see in Case Study 4-1 how reporters on one White House story faced enormous pressure to "back off").

Maintaining Independent News Judgment   Covering a story in accordance with your own judgment often takes courage. In the early days of the Watergate story, young reporters for the *Washington Post* revealed misdeeds in the Nixon administration while others failed to find such skullduggery or, even, reported all was well. Being exclusive for too long on such a story can put great strain on the courage of an entire news organization, particularly if it is depending, as was the *Post,* on relatively inexperienced reporters. That magnifies the strain on the reporters themselves. Enormous pressure built on the *Post,* both from the Nixon administration and other media which began to doubt the *Post*'s accuracy. *Post* reporters stuck to their story, and, of course, eventually were proved correct. For young reporters, there often is great pressure from many sources to move in a certain direction with a story. In covering school affairs, for example, you will feel it from the board of education, parents, teachers— all of whom want the bond issue passed so a new high school can be built. *Their* news judgment will be that the merits of the issue already have been proved; *yours* should be that the story still must be covered objectively and dispassionately.

Resisting the "Scoop" Mentality   In competitive situations—two newspapers going head-on for circulation, or TV stations fighting for ratings—great pressure builds on reporters to bring in "scoops." Frequently, this drives coverage toward the sensational and trivial, and away from substance. It also can lead to grossly unethical behavior—invasion of privacy, playing loosely with facts, overwriting or "hyping" a story beyond its news merits, all to score a competitive beat. Standing firm against such pressure can require enormous self-discipline. (See Case Study 4-2 for how one journalist faced pressure from many sources during an important investigative story.)

Learning When to Hold 'Em   Picture it: Your editor is calling for the story; your training, your every instinct, is to go with it, get into print, get on the air. Yet, you have a nagging concern that you don't *quite* have it pinned down; there are a couple loose ends, a few facts unsubstantiated, a source or two you haven't had time to check. Whoa! If you have any doubt about the story's accuracy or its honesty, hold it—don't go with it. Going with an inaccurate story is a cardinal sin. Many times, you'll be forced to go with an incomplete story, one that could be improved with more time. But *never* go with one that is inaccurate. Learning when to hold a story takes self-discipline of the first order.

CASE STUDY 4-1

WOULD YOU "BACK OFF"?

You are a Washington reporter on a big story: You learn the White House is directing secret talks with certain elements in Iran, a nation the United States officially terms a "terrorist state." One goal is release of American hostages, including an AP correspondent, being held in Lebanon. A small Mideast publication breaks the story, but the White House nevertheless warns that if you publish details, you could jeopardize hostages. One already freed hostage, the President at his side, tells reporters: "In the name of God, will you please just be responsible and back off. Unreasonable speculation on your part can endanger their lives...."

Question: Will you probe for details and publish a story?

It happened in 1986, and reporters indeed probed and published, eventually forcing President Reagan's administration to reveal the real story was much larger than hostages. Despite pledges he never would negotiate with terrorists, Reagan acknowledged he had approved arms sales to Iran, then at war with Iraq. He said goals were to improve relations with Iran, establish ties with moderates who eventually might govern the country, and end Iran's support for international terrorism, as well as free hostages. Money from Iran was diverted to supply Contra guerrillas in Nicaragua. There was an uproar in Congress, which had not been informed of the arms sales, and among American allies, who had been pressured by the United States not to deal with Iran.

More questions: In these tense times, must reporters consider whether they jeopardize a President's conduct of foreign policy by reporting his secret moves? Would knowing of the Iran deal but *not* publishing make reporters participants in official covert

policies? Did the small Mideast publication, in revealing some details, relieve American reporters of moral responsibility for considering the impact of their stories?

The response among American print and broadcast journalists was to publish as many details as possible.

Ralph Langer, executive editor of the *Dallas Morning News,* said the media could not get enlisted in covert policies; official charges that reporters might endanger lives was "very sobering," but "I'm not sure how reporting something the other side already knows could endanger [hostages]. The only ones who did not know were the American people."

Ben Bradlee, executive editor of the *Washington Post,* said Washington publicly tried to draw European nations into promising not to negotiate with terrorists, but then itself did so. "You can't do it and then tell me I can't report it," Bradlee said.

Warren Hoge, *New York Times* foreign editor, said, "I think our responsibility is to give an accounting to our readers about what the government is doing, especially when it's doing the opposite of what it says it's doing."

President Reagan told *Time* magazine "What is driving me up the wall is that this [foreign policy initiative] wasn't a failure until the press got a tip from that rag in Beirut and began to play it up. I told them that publicity could destroy this, that it could get people killed. They then went right on....This whole thing boils down to a great irresponsibility on the part of the press..."

Were editors, who could not know all the facts in such situations, justified in printing the story? Such reporting can have enormous impact on governments and nations. Does that carry journalists across the line from reporting into policy making?

CASE STUDY 4-2

WHEN BAD NEWS HITS GOOD GUYS

You are editor of a metropolitan daily and have heard rumors a high-ranking officer in a local Salvation Army post, an ordained minister, has been misappropriating donated goods—a car, boat, motorcycle, and other things—for his own use.

Your reporters confirm the rumors, and you tell Salvation Army officials what you have discovered. They are candid and open: It in fact happened. They plead with you not to publish, citing damage that would be done to an institution that itself is innocent, although one of its own has gone astray. They offer to open to you their own internal investigation so you will be satisfied that the wrong has been righted.

The Salvation Army has an outstanding record of public service in your city, is regarded highly by the public, and has a board of directors that is a "Who's Who" of local philanthropic, civic, and business leaders—including the president of the company that owns your paper.

Questions: Do you publish the story? If not, why not? If so, why—and will you give it special handling?

Editor Burl Osborne of the *Dallas Morning News* faced those questions in 1985. He describes what he did:

"We...explained that we had to publish; that not to publish would cause greater damage to the institution since rumors already were about, and that, further, not to publish could be construed as vigilante journalism,

with us in effect going around threatening people with exposure if they don't do what we say....That decision was reached quickly. What was more difficult, at least for me, was deciding *how* to publish the story, doing what needed to be done, without unfairly painting an entire organization as tainted. There also were the standard forces working against the concern: Reporters had invested a lot of time. That circumstance generally produces an overlong story and expectations of second-coming play, whether or not it is merited.

"Here is what we did:

"We ran the story on page one, with a very carefully written headline, not at the top of the page. We made certain that the Army's response was high. We followed up with a story in the same place on the page when corrective action was announced. We wrote an editorial focused on the Salvation Army's value to the city, and trying to insure the problem was viewed in context. And we undoubtedly will find a good Salvation Army Christmas story to tell. This isn't a big-deal event to a newspaper. There is a common view that our responsibility is to get it and get it right. I am not sure responsibility ends there.

"This case *was* a big-deal to the Salvation Army."

When the "good guys"—and everybody knows the Salvation Army is among them—slip up, should reporters look the other way? Was the *Morning News* justified in what it did?

YOU AND YOUR EDITOR

"Meshing" with your editor or news director on ethical matters can be as important as ensuring you have the required reporting and writing skills. If the two of you cannot agree on many of the basic ethical concepts and techniques discussed so far in this book, you will be either a very unhappy employee or unemployed.

Ideally, you can avoid such extremes by selecting in advance a newspaper or television news employer whose ethical standards match yours. If writing a steady stream of murder, rape, and arson isn't quite your thing, don't go to work for the *New York Post;* if your personal code of ethics makes it difficult to report on creatures from the moon landing in the pumpkin patch, avoid some of those papers you find in the supermarkets. Particularly in your early years as a reporter, you may feel compelled to work for smaller papers or stations where editors and news directors themselves may be ill-trained and possessing little if any sense of ethical responsibility. There, however, are many small-town papers and stations that do an excellent job journalistically in a principled, ethical manner. Such considerations should be added to pay, career opportunities, and other factors you assess when deciding where to apply for a job.

But even if you luckily find the perfect employer, tension can arise as you try to relate your personal sense of right and wrong to your editor's ethical views, and, beyond him or her, to the policy stance taken by the corporate entity for which you both work.

Here are factors to consider:

Who's in Charge Here?

You may find your editor more deeply involved than expected in setting standards of conduct and deciding ethical issues once thought properly left to individual reporters. This stems from a widespread feeling among newspaper editors and television news directors that they must take firmer control of what is happening in their own newsrooms.

There were fears, particularly in the late 1970s and early 1980s, that insufficient supervision was permitting some reporters to practice a new style of advocacy journalism where objective reporting once was the goal, or, even worse, get into print and on the air with phony stories. Fears became reality when a reporter, Janet Cooke, managed to slip through the *Washington Post's* editing safeguards with a nationally acclaimed—and phony—story about a child heroin addict. What shook journalists most is that on this hoax, the *Washington Post's* renowned editors simply lost control of a reporter's performance in their own newsroom, and the story got into print.

In a speech that received widespread notice in the news industry, Michael J. O'Neill, then editor of the *New York Daily News,* called for stronger, more vigilant editing:

Editors, he said, "need to be ruthless in ferreting out the subtle biases—cultural, visceral and ideological—that still slip into copy, into political stories, mostly, but also into the coverage of emotional issues like nuclear power and abortion. Lingering traces of advocacy are less obvious than Janet Cooke's fiction but, for that reason, are more worrisome. Editors—myself included—have simply not exercised enough control over subeditors and reporters reared in the age of the new journalism."[14]

Lee Hills, a leading architect of the principled journalism for which Knight-Ridder, Inc., is noted, called on editors to prevent such "journalistic felonies" as the Janet Cooke story from striking their papers:

Be more rigorous on editorial standards and less self-righteous when something goes wrong....Use blind sources sparingly....The editor trusts the reporter but the reporter must also trust his or her top editor and tell them everything....Insist on corroboration. The reporter wants to protect his source. But the editor must protect the very reputation of the newspaper itself. He cannot delegate it. If the *Post* had taken this precaution, or any one of several others, the scandal of the [child addict] story would not have happened. Never forget that our most precious and fragile asset is credibility. In a society running short on trust, we are one of the trustees.

If an editor has given up control of his newsroom to reporters, get it back. If the editor is too weak to insist on carrying that responsibility, get a new editor.[15]

The O'Neill and Hills comments illustrate the effort by many editors to exert firmer administrative control over their newsrooms. For reporters, this can raise ethical issues in several areas.

Those Anonymous Sources Again

In many newsrooms, editors have taken solely to themselves the power to decide whether a news source will be granted anonymity. Reporters who once granted anonymity with relative impunity or made deals with sources now must seek permission.

James D. Squires, editor of the *Chicago Tribune,* claims editors and reporters too long have been "duped and manipulated" by news sources who attack enemies through the press, and who "simply want to cower behind the walls of a reporter's privilege and throw rocks in anonymity." He says his reporters cannot unilaterally agree to protect a source's identity:

[T]he time has long since passed when that pledge by an individual reporter can bind and incapacitate a news organization to the point where it supersedes all other ethical considerations. Readers deserve honesty as much as sources deserve loyalty. And there is no greater editor's responsibility than the life and credibility of the newspaper.[16]

The *Youngstown* (Ohio) *Vindicator* suspended a reporter for three days because he signed an agreement with a news source promising confidentiality in return for exclusive information. The agreement permitted the source to read any news story written from the information *before* it was published, and committed the paper to certain other restraints. An arbitrator rejected the Newspaper Guild's contention that the suspension was without "just cause."[17]

VIEWPOINT 4-4

EDITORS WARNED TO EDIT

"*Post* editors simply failed to do their job. They trusted a gifted liar; a kid from Ohio who had even faked her background to get her job only nine months before. Everyone in our profession was injured some because it gave ammunition to critics who want the press somehow controlled."

Lee Hills, former chairman of Knight-Ridder, Inc., warning company editors to control their newsrooms because of the Janet Cooke hoax on the *Washington Post*

Should editors support such deals made independently by reporters? (See Case Study 4-3.)[18]

When a reporter unilaterally committed the *Athens* (Ga.) *Banner-Herald* to an embargo—not using a story until a time set by the source—the paper's associate editor, Rick Parham, wrote a lengthy signed column for the editorial page, explaining to readers what happened. His lead: "There is a story that you didn't read in today's paper." He wrote that his reporter had to make a quick judgment on whether to accept the embargo, that he didn't agree with her decision, "But we'll keep our promise on the embargo."[19]

CASE STUDY 4-3

WOULD YOU PRINT OR HOLD?

You are a sports editor in a town gone crazy over professional football. It appears the local team can win the league championship.

Then, one of your reporters drops a bombshell on you: He heard rumors of drug problems on the team, but couldn't verify details so he asked the coach. The coach said his players "tested clean," and he hadn't seen drugs affect performance. He agreed to give your reporter background *if* the story were held until after the season. Your reporter agreed, only later informing you and saying he didn't think he could have gotten the story any other way.

Questions: Are you bound by the reporter's deal? Must you consider what revealing even a hint of a drug scandal would do to the team's championship drive? What would your readers, many of them sports fanatics, think if you broke this story with a championship within reach? Your competitors might sniff out the story. Should you break it while it still is exclusive?

It happened at the *Boston Globe* in 1986 when reporter Don Borges made the deal with Coach Raymond Berry of the New England Patriots.

Vincent Doria, *Globe* assistant managing editor for sports, decided breaking the commitment "would have damaged us—our integrity as reporters." He said he worried the story was "potentially libelous.... There was no boosterism involved." Doria said he had thought the Patriots would lose their battle for the league championship, and he then could use the story quite quickly. In fact, they extended the season by going to the Super Bowl, and Doria had to sit on the story much longer than expected, which made him "uncomfortable." After losing in the Super Bowl, Patriot players voted to be the first NFL team with a voluntary drug-testing program.

Boston TV stations learned that and broke the story, scooping the *Globe.* Criticism of the *Globe* was widespread:

Sportscaster Howard Cosell: "I think it raises serious questions about print ethics. The *Globe* had a duty to run the story, and they didn't."

Producer Mark Williams of a call-in show on WRKO Radio in Boston: "Callers wondered if the paper would have held on to the information in other situations, like something involving a politician. And there was a feeling that the reporter knew and the bookies knew and that's why the point spread was so wide."

Publisher Patrick Purcell of the competing *Boston Herald:* "Regardless of whether the story is about politics, business or sports, the paramount concern should be the public's right to know. I believe it was wrong for the *Globe*'s reporter to make a deal to delay the story until after the Super Bowl in return for verification. If the reporter could not get verification of the story through diligence and hard work, so be it. He shouldn't have struck the deal."

Who was right? The *Herald*'s Purcell or *Globe*'s Doria? Was Cosell right in terming the issue one of *print* (and, presumably, not TV) ethics?

In addition to the principle of who is in charge of making such decisions, editors fear a reporter's agreement to protect a source can land the newspaper in big, expensive trouble. For example, a newspaper can be charged with contempt of court, too. Myron Farber's refusal to turn over his notes in the New Jersey murder case, which would have identified sources, was backed all the way by the *New York Times*. The paper paid $286,000 in fines, although the *Times* got $185,000 of that back when pardoned with Farber of criminal contempt four years later.[20]

The *Roanoke* (Va.) *Times & World News* grants anonymity only if (1) a supervising editor determines there is no other way of getting information the public needs, (2) the reader is told as much as possible about the source, without revealing identity, (3) extensive efforts have been made to corroborate the source's information, *and* (4) the editor knows the source's identity.

If asked by your editor or news director to reveal your source's identity, you have a reasonable right to seek assurances that your supervisor—and newspaper or TV station—will protect the source. Your credibility with sources, the main tool of the reporting trade, is at stake. But the right of an editor or news director to demand the identity of your source is clear. Refusing to comply at some newspapers or TV stations will keep your story from being published or aired; at others, it will get you fired.

VIEWPOINT 4-5

YOU, YOUR EDITOR, YOUR SOURCE

"Refusal to tell your editors where you got a story is grounds for dismissal."

   Wayne Sargent, then editor, the *San Bernardino Sun*

"[O]n request, a senior editor must be able to learn the identity. The request is made only intermittently, when a story is sensitive or shocking."

   Allan M. Siegal, news editor, the *New York Times*

"To assure maximum protection for sources who have been guaranteed anonymity, the editor who gives the copy its first reading MAY NOT reveal the identity of the source—even to other editors—without the permission of the author. Consequently, reporters will routinely reveal their sources only to one editor. Sources should be assured their identities will be protected."

   Champaign-Urbana (Ill.) *News-Gazette* policy statement quoted by Frank Caperton, Ethics Committee, American Society of Newspaper Editors 1983–1984 Committee Reports, p. 15

Who Owns Your Byline?

In addition to everything else they do, editors and news directors are paid to supervise you—assign you to stories, edit your copy, and oversee your training. In return, you draw a salary for helping get the paper out or the evening news on the air.

Fair enough, except that on occasion an assignment may offend your sense of ethics—interviewing a grieving widow at graveside may not be your idea of journalistic integrity, for example. Or, your ego will be bruised if your elegant prose is heavily edited—"butchered," you will think—and your personal code of ethics compromised if editing, in your view, changes the meaning of a story.

If given an assignment or edited in a manner that seems to fundamentally contradict your personal code of ethics, consider several factors:

First, maybe—just maybe—that editor or news director knows what he or she is doing. It may be there *is* important, topical news in that assignment, and that by virtue of greater experience in news, your supervisor sees it; it may be you *did* mess up the writing. So, don't automatically blow your ethical top.

Second, assignments must be covered, stories must be written, the newscast must get on the air, the paper must get out—and you *are* paid to help. You are not a free-lancer, after all; you're a member of a news team.

Third, however, you still may see fundamental ethical problems. If so, *negotiate*. A reasonable editor or news director will be sensitive to your crises of conscience. Perhaps the story can be assigned to someone else; perhaps you can convince your supervisor you *do* have a point on the editing. Perhaps your byline can be removed from a story you feel was botched in the editing process. (However, some editors claim the newspaper owns your byline while you are on the payroll and that its usage is at *their* discretion; it generally is agreed the newspaper paid for and owns the story itself.)

Fourth, you may find yourself up against an editor or news director with an inflated sense of self-importance or lack of sensitivity to your ethical dilemma, and you may have no choice but to refuse an assignment on a point of personal integrity. That, of course, can lead quickly to unemployment, a high price to pay for courageous journalism, particularly if you have car payments and college debts to pay off. But it is a price paid by others before you.

VIEWPOINT 4-6

WHEN YOU AND YOUR BOSS DISAGREE

"If your reasons conflict with your firm's objectives, you've got a problem that's a lot deeper than this decision; either your values must change or your job should. Beware if you're frequently rearranging your values to align them with those objectives; you may be learning how to do business in an unfamiliar environment, but you may also be prostituting yourself. You can't be happy if you've surrendered your dignity. That's when it's time to get out."

Peter A. Reinhardt, writing in "Manager's Journal," *Wall Street Journal,* September 9, 1985, p. 24

On behalf of the newsroom employees it represents in about 120 newspapers (out of 1,674 dailies nationwide in 1986), the Newspaper Guild attempts to force publishers to contractually recognize reporters' rights in matters of ethics and integrity. Many publishers refuse, but the Guild issues to each of its newspaper bargaining units very broad "model" contract language to strive for in negotiations:

An employee shall not be required to perform, over the employee's protest, any practice which in the employee's judgment compromises the employee's integrity. An employee shall not be required to use the employee's position as an employee for any purpose other than performing the duties of the employee's position. An employee's byline or credit line shall not be used over the employee's protest. Substantive changes in material submitted shall be brought to the employee's attention before publication. An employee shall not be required to write, process or prepare anything for publication in such a way as to distort any facts or to create an impression which the employee knows to be false. If a question arises as to the accuracy of printed material, no correction or retraction of that material shall be printed without prior consultation with the employee concerned. An employee whose work or person is mentioned in a letter to the editor shall be informed of such letter immediately and shall have the right to respond to such letter simultaneously and adequately on the page on which it is published.[21]

Your Editor's Other Concerns

Editors and news directors have other concerns that influence directly how easily you "mesh" with them on ethical issues. To understand their views, understand these concerns:

Money   Because solvency must be the first goal of any newspaper or television operation, your editor or news director is on a strict budget. And, that means there may not always be enough money to do the job journalistically as you think it should be done. You may feel it irresponsible—unethical, even— if you cannot travel to Hong Kong to round out your reporting on a story. Your supervisor may agree, but simply be unable to afford to get you there. You may feel you need at least 15 column inches or three minutes of air time to do an honest writing job—and be told to do it in nine inches or one minute. A newspaper editor often has no more than 35 to 40 percent of a newspaper's total space for news; in television, your news director may have only thirty minutes, minus time for commercials, to cover the entire world.

The Law   No editor or news director today can make any important decision in the newsroom without considering legal implications. It's called the "chilling effect": Just the cost of defending against a libel suit, let alone losing one, can be stunningly expensive, and, as a result, some stories quite frankly are not covered or, perhaps, are covered in a certain way. If this happens on a story of yours, you may not have to argue that it is irresponsible or unethical to pull punches because of a threatened lawsuit; your supervisor probably will agree. But his or her decision must be whether your story is worth, say, $200,000 in defense lawyer's fees or, perhaps, $2 million in judgments if a jury decides against you. That is the harsh reality in every newsroom today. Even in relationships with you, your editor or news director is severely constrained in what can be done or said. Hours you work, conditions under which you work—all are mandated by law and, perhaps, union agreements, as well. In other words, what to you might be an *ethical* issue, may be to your supervisor an ethical issue in a complex legal wrapping.

The Corporate Imperative   For want of a better catch-all category, this one includes the responsibility your editor or news director has to perform journalistically in keeping with corporate guidelines. News strategists set goals in such things as "tone" and "image" to be achieved with a newspaper or news program. Often, these goals are designed to ensure certain market segments—chosen readers, viewers, or advertisers—are served and that the newspaper or television news operation thus achieves marketplace success. That is why the *New York Times* and other similarly elitist newspapers take one approach to news coverage while, for example, the *New York Post* or *New York Daily News,* both mass appeal newspapers, take quite another. Call it what you will—tone, policy, guidelines—you *and* your supervisor are expected to meet a certain level of performance that could directly influence any discussion between you of ethical issues.

You, the Unknown   Look at yourself as your editor or news director must: young, inexperienced, a hard charger, and, journalistically, an unknown factor. Yet, on any given story the reputation of the newspaper or television news operation—plus your supervisor's own reputation—could depend on how well you perform. One misstep by you could damage corporate image or purse. So, be a bit understanding if your editor or news director suggests you conform to work procedures and ethical guidelines he or she has laid down, rather than the other way around.

In sum, many factors influence the relationship you and your supervisor have on ethical issues and matters of professional conscience. The author does *not* suggest you sacrifice principle because of them, only that you understand the wider context in which today's journalist must consider ethical issues. We now turn, in Part Two of this book, to a more detailed discussion of that wider context.

CHAPTER SUMMARY

Journalists have two partners in ethics: the reading or viewing public, and their editors or news directors. First allegiance goes to serving the greater good of the people with news and information crucial to their lives. The mission must be accomplished within the corporate environment of a newspaper or television news operation which has its own ethical and business imperatives.

To build a bridge of trust to the public, journalists must understand that the public often feels newspapers and television news fail to deliver the information they want and need. Further, surveys show the public doubts the motives of some journalists and fears manipulation by the media.

Accurate reporting is essential to creating trust and is fundamental to responsible journalism. Journalists must get the basic facts and get them accurately, seeking out authoritative sources and quoting them precisely.

Honest writing rates high ethical priority because it is the most important link between journalist and reader or viewer. Marks of the honest writer are careful selection of which facts to include in a story, which to omit, and constant effort against permitting disguised personal opinions to seep into copy. Above all, the honest writer is willing to explain factual holes in a story, to admit error, and to set the record straight.

In "meshing" with your editor or news director on ethical issues be aware he or she is under considerable pressure to exert firm administrative control over the newsroom and what happens there. Breakdowns in editing controls let errors and hoaxes slip into print or a newscast. Many editors and news directors, therefore, are reserving for themselves the sole right to grant anonymity to news sources, and insisting on closer supervision of how their staff members report and write.

CHAPTER 4

Notes

1 "Statement of Principles," American Society of Newspaper Editors, The Newspaper Center, P.O. Box 17004, Washington, D.C., 20041. The statement was adopted by ASNE directors Oct. 23, 1975, and superseded ASNE's "Canons of Journalism," adopted in 1923.
2 "Relating to Readers in the '80s," a 1984 survey conducted by Ruth Clark, president, Clark, Martire & Bartolomeo, Inc.
3 MORI Research, Inc., survey for the Associated Press Managing Editors Association, 50 Rockefeller Plaza, New York, N.Y., 10020, released 1985.
4 Belden Associates, 2900 Turtle Creek Plaza, Dallas, Tex., 75219, released its findings in 1984 and 1986; Harris and Roper results are quoted in "Why Is the Press Disliked?" a paper presented April 3, 1984, in Dallas to the Southern Newspaper Publishers Association, by Deanne Termini, Belden senior vice president, and Sheila Miller, research associate.
5 Gallup organization survey commissioned by the Times Mirror Corp., Times Mirror Square, Los Angeles, Calif., 90053, and released Jan. 15, 1986.
6 "Newspaper Credibility: Building Reader Trust," an ASNE survey conducted by MORI Research, Inc., Minneapolis, 1985.
7 "Relating to Readers in the '80s," op. cit. p. 9.
8 "Leak About CIA Operation Against Khadafy Angers Congress," AP story for morning papers, Nov. 5, 1985, published in *Atlanta Constitution* that day, p. 9A.
9 "2,700 Killed in Afghan Tunnel," AP story for morning papers, Nov. 10, 1982, published that day in *Athens* (Ga.) *Daily News,* p. 1.
10 Barbara Crossette, "On Honduran Coast, A World Apart," *New York Times,* July 2, 1983, p. 2.
11 Tom Wicker, "Excuse It, Please," *New York Times,* Dec. 31, 1982, p. 26.

12 Examples abound, of course, but the author found two particularly pertinent (and amusing): Martin Tolchin, "When Nothing Happens And They Call It News," *New York Times,* March 22, 1985, p. 16; Leslie H. Gelb, "Sounds Like News, Tastes Like News, But Fact?" *New York Times,* Aug. 21, 1984, p. B6.

13 Farber recounts his story in "Somebody Is Lying: The Story of Dr. X," Doubleday, New York, 1982; Farr served 47 days in the Los Angeles County Jail in 1972–73 for refusing to identify sources in the Manson murder case.

14 Michael J. O'Neill, speech to American Society of Newspaper Editors, Chicago, May 5, 1982.

15 Lee Hills, speech April 21, 1981, to annual meeting of shareholders, Knight-Ridder Newspapers, Inc., One Herald Plaza, Miami, Fla., 33101.

16 James D. Squires, "When Confidentiality Itself Is Source of Contention," 1985–86 Journalism Ethics Report, National Ethics Committee, Society of Professional Journalists, Sigma Delta Chi, 53 W. Jackson Blvd., Suite 731, Chicago, Ill., 60604, p. 7.

17 "Arbiter Upholds 3-Day Suspension of Reporter For Signing Agreement With News Source," *presstime,* Nov. 1985, p. 60.

18 Among treatments of this incident see Andrew Radolf, "Boston Globe Tells Why It Held Patriot Drug Use Story," *Editor & Publisher,* Feb. 8, 1986, p. 27, and Gregory Katz, "Paper Denies Boosterism In Holding Story," *USA Today,* Jan. 29, 1986, p. 3C.

19 Rick Parham, "The Story That Isn't—Yet," *Athens* (Ga.) *Banner-Herald,* March 5, 1986, p. 4.

20 Jonathan Friendly, "Byrne Gives Pardon to *Times* and a Reporter for Contempt," *New York Times,* Jan. 19, 1982, p. 9.

21 Article XXII, "Employee Integrity," U.S. Model Contract, The Newspaper Guild (AFL-CIO), 1125 Fifteenth St., N.W., Room 550, Washington, D.C., 20005, July 15, 1984, p. 23.

PART TWO

ETHICS IN PURSUIT OF PROFIT

In Part Two, we switch focus to the corporate entity—the newspaper, or the broadcast company—and its ethical stance as an institution of major economic, political and social influence.

Broadly, our goal is twofold: First, we will discuss the *external* position—the corporate morality—that a newspaper or broadcast company must create in its marketplace to ensure it operates not only with journalistic validity for readers or viewers, but also conducts itself ethically in business relationships with advertisers and community. Second, we will examine the interaction of *internal* operational and ethical imperatives in newspaper and broadcast companies. This will take us into how effective codes of ethics can be established for news, advertising, and other "business-side" departments.

In none of this can we stray far from the underlying theme of Part One—ethics is an intensely personal subject, and the individual, even if wrapped securely in a corporate cocoon, retains ultimate responsibility for (and, really the only meaningful influence over) how newspaper and television journalism is practiced.

In Part Two, we must cover a wide range of subjects central to ethical conduct by print and broadcast companies. We first must examine the concept that corporations in fact have social responsibilities; not everyone believes they do. Then, we must look separately at corporate ethical attitudes in news, advertising, employer-employee relationships, and relations with the public.

5

CORPORATE SOCIAL RESPONSIBILITY

Once, a corporation was considered a good citizen if it sold customers a suitable product at acceptable prices, provided employees with decent wages and working conditions, and ensured fair profit for its shareholders.

Today, that won't guarantee good citizen status for the most obscure manufacturer of nuts and bolts, let alone the highly visible and enormously influential print and broadcast media. There is widespread conviction that corporations have an ethical and moral, as well as operational and legal, character that gives them social responsibilities far beyond making customers happy and improving profits.

The pressure from these societal attitudes was illustrated when Henry Ford II, whose family had pursued personal profit with remarkable dedication for several generations, told the Harvard Business School:

"The terms of the contract between industry and society are changing.... Now we are being asked to serve a wider range of human values and to accept an obligation to members of the public with whom we have no commercial transaction."[1]

But, isn't that simply the idea, already rather well established, that for a *journalist* rights and freedoms are tied to obligations and duties? Yes, but Ford and others argue *corporations* have "social responsibility" and operate within ethical parameters wider than narrow business interests. Not everyone agrees, however, so we must turn, in Chapter 5, to examining whether newspaper and broadcast corporations have such social responsibility. We also must look at how they handle the question of whether precise ethical policies must be laid down to cover corporate affairs.

There never has been unanimity among management theorists on whether corporations in fact have social responsibilities beyond caring for their own customers, employees, and profits.

Well into the 1930s, a traditional or "classicist" view was dominant: A firm is socially responsible if it creates jobs, thus strengthening a community's social structure, and through profits, wages, and bank deposits broadening its economic base. This view still has support, despite rising opinion that corporations must serve wider societal purposes in addition to meeting their own, more narrow goals.

Milton Friedman, a Nobel Prize winner in economics, is a leading proponent of the traditional view that the social responsibility of any business is to increase its profits.[2] This view holds that a profitable corporation by definition is socially responsible. Society evaluates its product or service in the marketplace, consumers judge its value and purchase it, ergo the corporation performs a socially responsible task. The traditional or classicist view holds that a profitable corporation by definition is socially responsible because its profits are invested, one way or another, by the corporation itself or shareholders, in other endeavors aimed at increasing profits. This, in turn, creates new jobs, new products, new demand—and society benefits. For a manager, this traditional measure of success simplifies the task of keeping score. The firm is successful if it maximizes profits and creates new products and jobs, all easily measured. Such easy measurements are denied newspaper and television managers whose yardsticks also must cover progress in wider, far less tangible social sectors. How, for example, does a media manager measure progress toward such socially responsible—but intangible—goals as informing the public on important issues or defending the people's right to know?

Basically, then, critics attack the concept of corporate social responsibility in two broad areas:

1 Business pragmatism   "Business is the business of business." Profit, not social reform, is the goal, so newspapers and television companies should get on with the job of making money. Critics also maintain social responsibility is costly and penalizes shareholders. Consider, for example, professional managers for Knight-Ridder, Inc., or CBS, who donate money to a good cause or invest in operational moves designed to discharge what they view as social responsibilities. Those executives aren't spending personal funds; those dollars belong to the thousands of shareholders who own Knight-Ridder and CBS— and it's unlikely anyone determined *their* views on social responsibility. Anyway, the critics say, charging business with social responsibility

---

VIEWPOINT 5-1

PROFITS AND RESPONSIBILITY

"There is one and only one social responsibility to business—to use its resources and engage in activities designed to increase its profits so long as it stays within the rules of the game..."

Milton Friedman, Nobel laureate in economics

is expecting too much. Managers know they are judged (and rewarded) for business, not social, success. And, that means most managers give only lip service to social responsibility.

2 Journalistic philosophy Some critics argue that if social responsibility is accepted as the measurement of success in journalism, freedom of the media will disappear, along with independent news values and judgments. These critics see social responsibility leading newspapers and television toward bland, consensus journalism that is responsive to public opinion, not its leader. Such critics long for the days of libertarian journalism, when newspapers determined themselves what course to follow in both news and business affairs, rather than trying to sense the public mood and react to it. It is voluntary abrogation by the media of true freedom that some see in acceptance of social responsibility. They fear conformist media merely responding to whatever public mood or political ideology is current, rather than maintaining independent, adversarial attitudes.

VIEWPOINT 5-2

PROFIT VERSUS PUBLIC SERVICE

"Can a newspaper simultaneously be both a business serving its own interests and affect to be a quasi-public institution serving everybody's best interests as defined by the newspaper itself?"

  Leonard Silk, economic correspondent, the *New York Times*

"[A]vailable evidence does not suggest that the most socially responsible firms are the most profitable."

  Jack W. Duncan, *Management,* Random House, Inc., New York, 1983, on the cost of social responsibility

---

However, the American way of life has changed dramatically since such traditionalist views first were laid down.

Are Traditionalists Outdated?

The traditional view that corporations have no wider social responsibilities is outdated by fundamental changes both within individual companies and the society in which they operate. Change is particularly striking in three sectors:

1 Public attitudes change as corporations grow larger, more visible, and are perceived as having enormous impact on daily life. This happens with industrial firms—society no longer asks only whether a chemical company makes a profit, serves customers, and keeps employees happy; it also asks whether the firm pollutes the rivers and skies. Certainly, attitudes toward the media change with bigness. No longer does society make limited demands on a hometown newspaper or TV station when it becomes a multimillion dollar communications conglomerate that influences, not simply observes, how government is run and life lived. Society demands more of a corporation that influences public opinion and affects the lives of millions.

2 Within American corporations there are important changes, too. Social consciousness rises and erodes traditional measurements of corporate success as ownership shifts from private to public status, and as managers are drawn from society, not owning families. Nonfamily managers tend to take a wider view of what a corporation must achieve. Professional managers expanded tremendously the social responsibility horizons of formerly family-owned companies such as Knight-Ridder, Gannett, and others. Workforce attitudes also change. Employees win improved job security and higher living standards, which permit them to switch from preoccupation solely with economic survival to also demonstrating concern over wider social issues. In communications, both factors are operative: The largest most influential newspapers are in multibillion-dollar, publicly owned companies run by professional, not family, managers; television networks and the largest stations are publicly owned. And, for both newspaper and television journalists, wages and job security are improving, permitting social consciousness to become a daily concern.[3]

3 Government attitudes and the law—themselves expressions of society's thinking—evolve in a manner requiring a corporation to take a wider, more meaningful view of social responsibility. As a regulated industry, broadcasting must be alert to letter of the law in such matters; newspapers, though free of direct regulatory supervision, nevertheless also must respond to societal pressure. That pressure is reflected, for example, in libel judgments against newspapers, or moves by special interest groups to influence how the news is covered. Newspapers and television companies must respond carefully to any libel dangers in stories they cover, and build financial and journalistic independence that enables them to resist pressure groups.

So, changes in both the external and internal environments influence heavily all sectors of media management and raise, inevitably, the question: Do corporations in fact have social responsibility? Increasingly, the answer is yes.

VIEWPOINT 5-3

PRESS AND PUBLIC OPINION

''You no longer shape public opinion, you have supplanted it.''

Kurt Luedtke, former executive editor *Detroit Free Press* and later a prize-winning screenwriter, on role of newspapers

---

Social Responsibility: Other Views

The concept of social responsibility not only strongly influences individual American journalists and why and how they cover the news. It is reflected, also, in the *business* of journalism, albeit partially in self-interest.

Those who would extend the concept to business activity argue, furthermore, there is strong reason to institutionalize it, formalize it, as a driving motivation in both newspaper and broadcast operations. They hold:

First, U.S. business history clearly shows that any industry unresponsive to societal demands risks government intervention. It is an argument that society grants legal rights to an industry, and, in turn, expects certain conduct—and government, representing society, will intervene if the industry doesn't perform as expected. Thus, the Equal Employment Opportunity Commission, established to help implement the 1964 Civil Rights Act, is society's response to industries that fail to voluntarily prohibit job discrimination on basis of race, age, sex, religious beliefs, or national origin. Many newspapers and television stations are forced to take affirmative hiring action under the act because they did not move voluntarily on their own. The Occupational Safety and Health Act of 1970 reflects society's demands for improvements in health and safety conditions in the workplace; OSHA inspectors fine newspapers that do not clean up their own production departments.

Second, supporters of social responsibility as central to corporate philosophy see in the concept a way of improving business conditions. Business is in the business of meeting societal demands, so if society demands social responsibility in the media, that's what newspapers and television stations should provide—or so goes the argument.

Third, of course, supporters see social responsibility as the *right* course for a newspaper or television station. It's the *ethical* thing to do, they say.

So, arguments *for* social responsibility in the media have strong support. But it clearly does not come first with newspaper or television corporations.

Whenever publishers or broadcasters meet, due deference is paid the need for media behavior that is socially responsible, for protecting the public's "right to know."

Be it the *New York Times'* slogan, "All the News That's Fit to Print," or CBS's claim that Dan Rather's evening newscast "Keeps America on Top of the World," there runs through the media's self-esteem a theme of public responsibility and service.

Unquestionably, many individual journalists, both in print and broadcast, feel strongly theirs is a craft with a higher calling. Editors are wont to express their desire to sell newspapers in terms of serving the public.

Yet, the concept of social responsibility and, beyond that, ethical behavior, do not get top billing in statements of *corporate* goals. For example:

Tribune Company, a nearly $2 billion communications conglomerate built around the *Chicago Tribune,* other newspapers, and television stations, says in its annual report to shareholders: "[W]e measure success by our ability to attract audiences by informing and entertaining, to produce results for advertisers, and to attain a return on stockholders' investment competitive with that being achieved by other media companies. Tribune Company is in excellent position to fulfill these objectives in the years ahead."[4]

Knight-Ridder, owner of TV stations and some of the nation's most prestigious and journalistically outstanding newspapers, is more balanced in stating its company goals: "The basic operating goals of the company are systematic and orderly profit growth, diversification via acquisition and entrepreneurial startups in the media communications field, and maintenance of the highest standards of professionalism and editorial quality. The company is dedicated to serving the communities where it operates, providing its employees with an opportunity to make their lives more productive and rewarding, and enhancing the investment of the company's shareholders."[5]

Dow Jones, publisher of the *Wall Street Journal,* dailies in 22 communities, and internationally renown high-quality economic and financial news services says that "Dow Jones is a unique blend of the old and the new. Old in the sense that the company is committed to those values on which its success has been built—values that stress high standards of quality, service, ethics and individual achievement. New in that the company, in a constant quest for improvement, embraces the most up-to-date concepts and technology to produce and deliver *The Wall Street Journal* and our other publications and services."[6]

In any statement of their objectives, broadcast corporations must give major billing to conformity with government regulation because they are in a federally regulated industry. For example, in its policy handbook for employees, ABC states: "Broadcasting is...a regulated industry. We operate in a thicket of legal decisions that may not allow the freest rein in news operations. So, while we want to be flexible and imaginative and allow for individual initiative, before you set out on a bold new path, check with someone in the management. Do not set policy on your own. Sometimes there are problems you didn't think of."[7]

Now, all four companies—Tribune, Knight-Ridder, Dow Jones, and ABC—enjoy among newsmen and women strong reputations as socially responsible practitioners of high-quality journalism. But, clearly, service to society is not the No. 1 corporate goal for any of them; service to shareholder is. This is not to suggest the media *should* put social responsibility first, becoming public utilities that put service even at a financial loss ahead of service at a profit. Journalistic success can rise only from financial success, journalistic independence only from financial independence; financially weak newspapers or television stations become easy prey for special interest pressure that distorts the news process.

Nevertheless, despite the need for profits, *some* response to social pressure is required by any newspaper or television station.

Setting Response Levels

In self-interest, any corporation sensitive to social responsibility issues must "audit" influences on its business. This involves determining the source of both external and internal pressure, measuring its intensity, and judging the response level necessary to deal with it.

Externally, important pressure comes from national, state, and local governments and their official agencies and regulatory bodies; special interest groups, and the general public. Company attorneys and regulatory specialists judge government pressure; public opinion surveys are one way of judging public attitudes.

Internally, adjustment must be made to pressure from employees (and unions), customers, suppliers, competitors, and, of course, the profit expectations of owners, whether private or public. Skilled managers spend much time ascertaining employee attitudes, watching customers and suppliers, and analyzing each move by competitors.

The social audit then must evaluate company operations that might draw fire, and determine what the company must do to preempt hostile moves by government or other forces. In most companies, the combined intelligence thus gathered by management goes before a board of directors, which, in turn, establishes policy guidelines for the chief executive officer, the manager responsible for efficient, profitable operation of the company.

For many newspaper and television operations, then, social responsibility attitudes don't just happen; more often, they are established carefully in response to detailed analysis of what the corporate stance should be.

Response levels vary widely:

• *The minimum response*   This is a defensive move to build corporate image, not truly meet any social responsibility. It really is designed to improve business conditions, to create a more favorable climate for sale of newspapers and advertising, or, in the case of television, sell advertising and meet certain requirements from regulatory bodies. Handing out company T-shirts to marathon runners or sponsoring the local soap box derby are minimum response ploys.

• *The good citizen move*   Here, the newspaper or television company escalates its response. Company executives and employees, for example, are given time off to participate in community affairs. This response level is characterized by company commitment of significant resources—time, money, employee effort.

• *Full social responsibility*   This requires high-level commitment to aggressively meet social challenges with the same dedication that business problems are met. This can involve substantive change in corporate structure and direction. In the communications industry, this frequently takes the form of special minority training programs, or the establishment of socially oriented trusts or scholarship funds (of course, self-interest is at work here, too: tax advantages or recruiting benefits flow from all three examples). Difficult dollars-and-cents questions flow from social responsibility. For example, should a newspaper spend heavily to achieve circulation in low-income neighborhoods, whose residents are of only marginal interest to advertisers? The business of newspapers, after all, is selling news to readers who are sold, in turn, to advertisers—and the more affluent the readers, the happier the advertisers. Does the newspaper have a social responsibility to penetrate those poorer neighborhoods with its daily package of uplifting, educational news, even at financial loss? Try finding the elitist *New York Times* for sale on slum street corners in its own city. Should a network television news show maintain its own correspondents in foreign capitals at the cost of hundreds of thousands of dollars each annually? Will covering those cities firsthand attract more viewers? More advertisers? Note the number of network news shows that use "talking head" anchors in New York, reading from AP or UPI dispatches from those capitals. Social responsibility is expensive. Luckily, however, many newspapers and television news operations still accept—at considerable cost—such social responsibilities.

In sum, there are important reasons for newspapers and broadcast companies to respond willingly and affirmatively to pressure for socially responsible behavior.

Externally, it's good for business. A newspaper or television station out of sorts with readers, viewers, or advertisers is headed for financial difficulty. Socially irresponsible conduct in the marketplace adds enormously to the "credibility gap," and that's bad for business. Irresponsible conduct also can attract direct government intervention in corporate affairs, which newspapers—despite their First Amendment protection—cannot risk lightly these days, any more than can television companies.

Internally, enlightened policies can benefit a media employer over the long run. Providing employees with better work environments, creative jobs, and involving them in how things are run can produce more efficient work performance.

Finally, it can be argued that adopting a socially responsible corporate policy is the *right* thing, the ethical thing, to do. But, as we have seen, most response to social pressure is largely in self-interest, and carries us far from ethics, from *corporate* ethics. We must get back on the ethical track, for although the concept of social responsibility has been around a long time, the idea that a corporation can—or should—operate in accordance with precise codes of ethics has won widespread acceptance only relatively recently. Let's look at current thought in the newspaper and television news industry.

CORPORATE ETHICS

It was traditional: Sometime after first walking into the newsroom a new reporter would be introduced to "the way we do things around here." There might be a company handbook on vacation policy and health insurance, or a short session with someone from the personnel department. But the company ethos— its collective characteristics and beliefs—seldom was formalized. It passed haphazardly in bits and pieces to new reporters by word of mouth, in learn-as-you-go fashion. That was an industrywide custom.

Today, however, media executives increasingly are formalizing corporate policy, and often writing precise directives on specific ethical principles that require adherence, especially by reporters, editors, and news directors, as a condition of employment. This trend arises in part from external, societal pressure, but also from growing awareness within journalistic circles that a hap-hazard approach to this crucial issue no longer is sufficient. In 1974, the Associated Press Managing Editors Association surveyed members and found only 9 percent of respondents had written ethical codes; in 1983, a survey for the Society of Professional Journalists, Sigma Delta Chi, found written policies on, at least, outside work and freebies at nearly three-fourths of 902 newspapers and television stations responding.[8]

The trend is not without controversy.

The Controversy over Codes

In discussion of corporate ethics policy, there is general agreement in two areas:

1 A newspaper or broadcast operation must not only ensure its conduct is *legal,* but also that it conforms to accepted ethical principles of right and wrong.

2 It is top management's responsibility to shape and enunciate those principles and ensure they are followed at all levels of corporate activity.

That is, there is agreement ethical considerations are essential to both journalistic and business endeavors, and that to omit them from the training of any employee is an error. But there the general agreement ends, and controversy begins over *which* principles to adopt, *how* to enunciate them, and, indeed, whether formalizing corporate ethical attitudes—in say, a written code—is a legally dangerous form of self-censorship.

Proponents of written codes argue ethics is an issue too important to leave to individual whims and interpretation, and that writing them down is the only way to ensure every employee understands them and conforms to them.

Opponents, who include some of the nation's leading editors, argue against sweeping written codes for a number of reasons:

There is a danger that any definitive and widely accepted code, particularly if endorsed by major newspapers or television operations, could become—in the eyes of judges, legislatures, or the public—a general standard of behavior to be enforced on *all* media. That is, opponents view written codes as a self-inhibiting first step toward licensing the media under a universal standard of conduct.

VIEWPOINT 5-4

"THEY DON'T WORK"

"Everyone, so it seems, has been adopting codes over the past decade or so, ranging from the simplicity of the Ten Commandments to the complexity of a corporate prospectus. All have one thing in common: They don't work.

"A bad person does not become a good person because his newspaper has an ethics code...

"[I]f readers don't like what we're doing, they'll quit buying our papers. The marketplace is the best regulator the press can have."

Michael Gartner, former president of the *Des Moines Register,* and editor of Gannett's *Louisville Courier-Journal* and now co-owner and editor of the *Ames* (Iowa) *Tribune.*

A written code could be used against a newspaper or television station in court. In a libel case, for example, wouldn't a lawyer be well on the way to victory if it could be proven a reporter deviated from written company policy while covering a story? If a code calls for, say, double-checking every fact provided by an anonymous source and a reporter under deadline didn't, would that be damaging evidence the newspaper broke even its own rules? A study by the *Iowa Law Review* for ASNE in 1986 shows four of 106 responding newspapers were asked to turn over written policies during litigation. In no instance were standards actually used against the newspapers. A separate review of case law found five papers had their own written standards used against them in libel cases by lawyers attempting to show the newspapers had breached their own standards. Two of the five newspapers lost their cases.

Often, opponents say, codes simply are insipid window dressing, nothing more than grudging concessions to public anger at the media—and are so regarded by management, staff, and public.

And, opponents of written codes argue, if a code purports to represent the totality of a newsroom's ethical stance, it necessarily will be general to the point of being vague and, therefore, of little use in the daily struggle where countless fine points of journalistic ethics must be decided. (Note the sweeping generalities in the codes, addenda at the end of this book, for the Associated Press Managing Editors Association and Radio-Television News Directors Association.) Also, the argument continues, newsroom values shift, ethical thought evolves, and calling the shots under deadline pressure requires judgment in an editor or news director, not a code hanging on the wall. (Ethical absolutists would counter, of course, that *absolute moral laws* exist, regardless of time or place, and that they can be defined and followed.)

Opponents argue codes generally lack any enforcement provisions and, thus, have no punch. That indeed is true for *industrywide* codes. Unlike those drawn up by physicians, attorneys, and other professional groups, codes adopted by journalism associations lack provisions for expulsion or other discipline. But ethical policies of many individual newspapers and television stations *are* being enforced. An ASNE survey in 1986 revealed that of 226 newspapers responding, forty-eight dismissed employees for ethical violations and thirty had suspended employees for varying periods.[9]

VIEWPOINT 5-5

JOURNALISTIC WIMPS?

"Journalists should actively censure and try to prevent violations of these standards, and they should encourage their observance by all newspeople..."

Code of Ethics, Society of Professional Journalists/Sigma Delta Chi, adopted 1973, revised 1984

"The Society of Professional Journalists has turned wimpish toward its own code of ethical standards..."

Casey Bukro, of the *Chicago Tribune* and the Society's 1985–1986 ethics chairman, commenting on the society's reluctance to strictly enforce its own code of ethics

Most importantly, opponents say, it is management example, not a written document, that changes corporate attitudes in ethical matters. In a real-life work environment, only open, unmistakable corporate commitment to ethical conduct will bring along a newspaper or broadcast staff. And in companies where ethical parameters are being drawn, the distinguishing characteristic is management commitment.

Top-Level Endorsement Vital

Nothing is more important to successful corporate ethical policy, written or unwritten, than emphatic and open endorsement by top-level management.

The "tone" of any company's response to its challenges—journalistic, business, or ethical—is set at the top and transmitted to each employee through a managerial chain of command leading from board chairperson down to lowest first-level supervisor. Over the long run, no newspaper or broadcast station will outperform, in either a journalistic or business sense, expectations of top management. And, no newsroom will develop ethical policies and adhere to them unless management reflects a determination to do so.

The first element of corporate ethical policy, then, must be guidance by management. We saw earlier in this chapter how some of today's leading communications corporations state with varying precision their sense of external social responsibility; statements of internal ethical policy vary widely, too.

Knight-Ridder, explicit in public acceptance of social responsibilities and enormously successful journalistically (its papers were awarded an unprecedented seven Pulitzer Prizes in 1986 alone), is unmistakably clear in statement of ethical policy. Knight-Ridder's flagship, the *Miami Herald,* gives each employee an ethics code ("The *Herald* and You") that opens:

> We strive to attain the highest standards of journalism and to publish a newspaper that is fair, accurate and objective. We try to avoid all conflicts of interest. That, simply, is our goal. It is not a goal easily achieved. It requires from each of us decisions of conscience on matters both professional and personal. Often there are no clear answers or precise precedents.
>
> We ask that you use your own best judgment. We ask that you act in good faith and that you recognize the best interest of The Herald. Whenever in doubt, inquire. Talk to your department head.[10]

The *Herald* code then deals more specifically with ethical concerns such as free-lancing, acceptance of gifts, and improper use by employees of their connection with the newspaper.

Eugene Patterson, chairman and chief executive officer of the *St. Petersburg Times and Evening Independent,* an editor widely known for producing high-quality newspapers, takes a different approach:

> We have no written code of ethics because I can't imagine any manageable code that would be comprehensive enough to cover the ethical judgments that have to be made at a newspaper in the course of a given half-day.

Specific areas of ethical decision are too unpredictable to be covered by any imaginable list of right answers. To try to compose one, therefore, would in my judgment produce much gas but little lift.

Instead we talk about fairness and balance, accuracy and sensitivity, honesty and candor. And we try to teach by example; the reporter who sees the kind of story his editor puts into print, and the kind of story he kicks back as unacceptable, learns our code of ethics over time.[11]

Patterson, however, *does* manage the *Times and Evening Independent* under a forceful "Standards of Operation" drawn from Nelson Poynter, chairman of the papers from 1969 until he died in 1978. The standards state:

Our Mission: To set and maintain the highest standards of excellence in the field of journalism, through independence, enterprise and commitment to the public interest.

Our Strategy: While maintaining a national perspective and reputation, to operate our newspapers in accordance with a philosophy of community involvement and public service. To preserve their independence from conglomerate ownership so as to maintain a direct responsiveness to the needs of the community of which we are a part...to sustain freedom from any pressure that could alter our commitment to service to the nation's citizens through impartial political research and unbiased coverage of the government...

Patterson's statement goes on to charge his staff with "integrity" in news coverage and "sensitive" discharge of community obligations, and concludes: "Our publications' policy is very simple—merely to tell the truth."[12]

The *Chicago Tribune*'s policy makes no sweeping statement of ethical philosophy, opening instead with this proposition: "All professional staff members of the *Tribune* are expected to avoid any compromises of their journalistic integrity. This must include even the appearance of compromise, which can be equally damaging to the credibility of the newspaper." The policy, written by editor Jim Squires, then deals with specific ethical subjects such as free gifts, outside employment, and involvement in public affairs.[13]

William F. Thomas, editor of the *Los Angeles Times,* similarly is broad in a code of ethics he wrote for the *Times*' staff: "[T]o try to avoid embarrassment or conflicts with your responsibilities to *The Times,* and to answer questions which arise from time to time, here are some general guidelines to confirm and clarify our existing practices..."[14]

A completely different approach is voiced by Bob Haring, executive editor of the *Tulsa World:* "I don't have a written code of ethics here. Frankly, it's not been a problem....In general, I tell people to do what they think is right, what they feel comfortable with. *In most cases, they're more restrictive than I would be*" [author's emphasis].[15]

Components of a Policy

Regardless of how it is structured, whether written or not, an ethics policy must address key basic issues if management's corporate philosophy is to be translated effectively into day-to-day operations.

Who Is Covered?   Editor Thomas at the *Los Angeles Times* directs his ethics policy at "editorial staff"; Jim Squires addresses "all professional staff members" at the *Chicago Tribune;* the *Miami Herald* has a code for "newsroom staff members," and the parent corporation, Knight-Ridder, has another for "key executives." The 26,000-circulation *Longview* (Wash.) *Daily News* has written policy guidelines for each department in the newspaper.

What Is Covered?   For newspapers, the essentials are conduct of employees in news, and advertising policy. One way or another, most newspaper managers lay down explicit rules for both. In television, goaded by explicit federal regulation, policy direction is much broader. The networks, for example, issue highly detailed rulebooks covering personnel (and such matters as objectivity, gifts, etc.), production (interview technique, confidential sources, investigative reporting), the law and regulatory practices (Fairness Doctrine, libel, copyright).

Why Ethics?   No policy is complete without explicit explanation of why the policy is necessary. Policies generally bow toward social responsibility, meeting community obligations, serving reader and advertiser—but, above all, in both newspapers or broadcast, they make clear *corporate integrity* is at stake, and that an ethics policy is necessary to protect the commercial position of the newspaper or broadcast station in the marketplace. Though laced with undeniably sincere desire to do what is right, what is ethically correct, most *corporate* ethics policies in communications today clearly are defensive gestures designed to counter external pressures.

Who Is Accountable?   With striking unanimity, newspaper and broadcast ethical policies place squarely on the individual employee full responsibility for conforming to corporate policy—even if policy is not explicitly laid out in writing. Look again at the *Chicago Tribune*'s language: "All professional staff members of the *Tribune* are expected to avoid any compromises of their journalistic integrity." The *Tribune*'s policy, understandably, makes no effort to comment in detail on the hundreds, if not thousands, of challenges to integrity every newsperson meets during a career. Rather, the *Tribune*'s policy states general philosophy, and hits high spots of problem areas in just a page and a half. Repeatedly, ethics policies instruct employees to "talk it over with a supervisor" if unsure how to proceed in questionable circumstances. ABC News cautions employees, "The burden of acting sensibly in most situations rests on each of us."[16] What is questionable, what is sensible, is left to individual interpretation. Clearly, each employee in communications today must possess a highly developed *personal* sense of ethics; *corporate* statements of policy cannot cover all bases.

How Is Policy Enforced?   Here, ethics policies are noticeably silent. For legal reasons, employers find it unwise to spell out precisely how an employee will be disciplined for an ethical breach. Newspapers and broadcast stations *do* fire or suspend employees for policy transgressions, but prefer to handle each case separately and, mostly, quietly. Sometimes, explicit statement of policy is unnecessary. The author recalls an era in the Associated Press when a foreign correspondent could disappear on a toot for a few days (perhaps, even, with the bureau petty cash) and be welcomed back when it was all over, the steam all let off. But by word of mouth, tradition, osmosis—however you want to describe the process—every employee understood instant dismissal was the penalty for compromising the integrity, honesty, objectivity of the news report. Nothing stays simple, however, and today many ethical questions arise in truly gray areas where tradition or osmosis are inadequate in alerting employees to enforcement rules or what is right or wrong, acceptable or unacceptable.

In sum, essential components of an ethics policy are statement of corporate philosophy, guidelines for employee behavior that ensure everyone knows where accountability lies, and a system for judging conduct plus means for enforcing policy.[17]

Implementing Ethics Policy

At corporate level in American media, drafting and implementing ethics policy is considered top management's responsibility. Thus, most policy statements clearly are drafted to protect the corporation's best interests.

But there is some sentiment for involving employees in creating and implementing policy as a means of elevating the dialogue over ethics from unfocused conversation to a focused effort with meaningful impact on how things are run.

John Murphy, executive editor of the *Portland* (Maine) *Press Herald, Evening Express* and *Sunday Express,* recommends editors approach newsroom ethics from several angles:

1 Develop a newsroom policy manual.

2 Discuss ethical problems as they arise with individual employees, then at staff meetings, and finally codify them in a book of ethical standards.

3 Ensure ethics are discussed in orientation programs for new employees.

4 Establish an ethics committee that includes all newsroom departments, the city desk, reporters, the editor, and the publisher.[18]

The Newspaper Guild opposes codes written solely by management on the grounds that they in fact are enforceable work rules designed to protect company interests. The Guild argues codes threaten employee job security and, therefore, should not be imposed unilaterally by management but, rather, should be negotiated with employees and jointly written—as ethical guidelines or ideals, not enforceable codes.

Some management theorists recommend permitting widest possible participation in drafting ethical codes.[19] The theory is that a staff that helps create a code is more likely to follow it. In reality, however, for many publishers and editors that smacks of abrogating managerial responsibility. A group of editors meeting in a Southern Newspaper Publishers Association seminar on standards and the ''credibility gap'' put it this way:

"Solving the credibility problem, everyone reluctantly agreed, is a managerial problem. The people at the top set the tone; to act on this problem we must rediscover ourselves as managers. Perhaps we are too reluctant to be autocratic when necessary as we run our participatory management newsrooms."[20]

CBS makes it clear who originated its TV standards and who is to follow them: "Meetings of senior management to consider the policy and operating questions these new circumstances raised were held, and standards and guidelines to cover them were decided upon and circulated to the appropriate personnel."[21]

The Limitations of Codes

Newsroom codes today aren't much more thoughtful than the few that existed a generation ago; most are limited to pragmatic, situational ethics—what to do if this narrow situation arises, what not to do if that one does. Almost without exception, the central thrust of codes is to delineate guidelines for individual conduct. But the goal is protection of corporate image and marketplace position. Rarely do editors or news directors sketch for their staffs the wider philosophical question of profit versus excellence, or establish an ethical "tone" for a newspaper or TV news show that reflects top management's commitment to excellence. The range of concerns in most written codes is much more narrow.

Here, in a synthesis of some codes in effect across the country, are examples of how some newspapers handle particularly sensitive subjects:

Gifts Codes written by leading newspapers and television news organizations leave the impression that newsrooms are under siege by regiments of special interest pleaders trying to subvert reporters with gifts of everything from free calendars to cases of imported wines—and, further, that reporters are easy prey.

The *Los Angeles Times:* "Shun gifts from news sources or subjects of coverage, except those gifts of insignificant value. Books or records received for review should not be sold to staffers."[22]

Chicago Tribune: "Gifts of significant value should be returned immediately with a courteous explanation that acceptance constitutes a violation of this policy. Gifts of insignificant value such as pencils, key chains and unavoidable surprises such as birthday cakes or anniversary flowers are acceptable. However, even these should be avoided and discouraged whenever possible."[23]

VIEWPOINT 5-6

ACCEPT NO FAVOR WHICH COMPROMISES

"[I]t is not intended that the guidelines inhibit employees to the point of foolishness such as, for example, refusal of a cup of coffee or anything equally insignificant. But the basic concept the guidelines seek to implement is clear: Employees may accept no favor, overt or otherwise, which can compromise their roles as newspersons or give the appearance of doing so."

CBS News Personnel Standards

Junkets, Free Meals, and Tickets   Existing codes show editors regard this area of "freebies" as troublesome, particularly for news organizations that assign writers to frequent travel in covering politics, say, or sports.

The *Miami Herald* provides its staff with detailed guidance:

> As a general rule, we pay our own way. We also act with common sense and good manners....Common sense should prevail in situations where it may be socially awkward or even impossible to pay at the time. In most instances, department heads should make payment arrangements before an event.... Free tickets to movies, plays, sports events and other entertainment attractions for which admission is normally charged shall not be solicited or accepted. There are some exceptions: private screenings or special press showings for which tickets are not sold to the public; registration fees at seminars or conventions attended with specific story coverage in mind; passes to special press box facilities, photo galleries and other areas available exclusively to the press, provided these are used only by those assigned to cover the event. Generally, *The Herald* will pay all transportation expenses incurred on assignment. In certain circumstances, such as use of military transit, a staffer may accept free transportation if it is the only way to effectively complete the assignment. The executive editor should be advised as quickly as possible.[24]

Outside Conduct   The *Miami Herald* puts it bluntly: "Staff members should avoid outside activities that conflict—or appear to conflict—with their jobs." The *Herald* warns employees against endorsing political candidates, or contributing to their campaigns, and, indeed, instructs staffers not to run for office themselves.

Editor Thomas of the *Los Angeles Times* goes into considerably more detail, noting *Times* staffers "are being offered increased opportunities these days to use their expertise for outside publications or the electronic media." He adds: "These offers can bring career enhancement and personal satisfaction, and we do not seek to discourage either." Thomas, however, forbids writing for competing publications or for groups *Times* reporters cover. He also bans paid sports scoring by his reporters (once a favorite means for sports writers to profitably spend time in the pressbox), and "with rare exceptions," paid record or book jacket reviews not published in the *Times*. As for appearing on broadcasts or in other outside events: "All such appearances for pay should be carefully examined from the aspect of possible conflicts and embarrassment to yourself or the newspaper. In general, regularly scheduled appearances or those under any other circumstances which might confuse the staffer's primary identification as a *Times*

VIEWPOINT 5-7

A GUIDELINE, NOT A RULE

"A policy is a guideline, not a rule. A guideline is not an undeviating course that must be followed invariably. This is not to say that deviation from all policies is permissible, but rather to allow the flexibility that is necessary oftentimes to deal sensibly with unusual or unexpected situations."

Longview (Wash.) *Daily News,* "General Policies"

person should be avoided.'' Note this is a statement by the *Times* that it has vested interest in the *professional identity* (not just the byline) that it helps each staffer build.

Other Income   Due to near explosive expansion of news coverage of business and finance, the question of whether reporters should be restricted in outside investments will be a major ethical issue in years ahead. Most newsroom codes cover moonlighting (clear it with your supervisor, do it on your own time, and it's okay), but few wrestle with this central issue: News moves market prices for everything bought or sold in this world, and the temptations for misusing that news are extraordinary. An unethical reporter who uses ''inside'' information—news learned on the job but not yet available to the public—can make a fortune (if not first arrested under federal laws prohibiting such conduct).

Should, say, editor Thomas of the *Los Angeles Times* (1) forbid staffers to invest in all outside companies or (2) somehow otherwise attempt to avoid conflict? Here is how he puts it in the *Times*' code of ethics: ''Staff members with investments or stockholdings in corporations should avoid making news decisions that involve these corporations. If it is impossible to avoid them, these potential conflicts should be disclosed to a supervisor.'' (Thomas also forbids staffers from entering any ''business relationship with their news sources.'')

In the *Chicago Tribune*'s ethics policy, editor Squires doesn't deal directly with stock market investments. His language: ''Outside employment *or compensation* [author's emphasis] is permitted when it is compatible with the newspaper's right to the full time and efficient service of its employees and does not constitute a conflict of interest.'' Squires adds: ''Each year all *Tribune* staffers will be asked to fill out and sign a disclosure statement detailing all civic and political involvement *and identifying the sources of outside income*'' [again, author's emphasis].

As is to be expected, the *Wall Street Journal* pays great attention to outside investments and trading activities by staffers. It is newspaper lore: If a reader could obtain—today—a copy of tomorrow's *Journal*, he could be a millionaire. On occasion, that occurs to staffers, including R. Roster Winans, the *Journal* columnist sentenced to prison for illegally attempting to enrich himself and investor friends who traded on inside information obtained working at the *Journal* (see, again, Case Study 2-1). Possible conflict of interest between reporters' journalistic responsibilities and their right to invest in—and profit from—outside opportunities will be a major issue as newspaper and broadcast companies expand their business coverage. Yet, few newsroom codes even acknowledge that possibility, let alone deal with it in any detail. For that reason, we reproduce at the end of this book pertinent sections of the conflict of interest policy laid down by the *Journal*'s parent company, Dow Jones. The Dow Jones code will not guarantee all staffers live honest, ethical, responsible personal and professional lives. No code will. But the precision language of the Dow Jones code can serve as a model for any editor anxious to explain clearly how conflict of interest must be avoided. It should be noted all Dow Jones staffers are asked to sign statements that they have read and understand the policy, and agree to abide by it. Not abiding by it is cause for dismissal.[25]

Plagiarism   In 1986, ASNE surveyed 225 newspapers and found, to the surprise of many editors, that plagiarism is a major problem. One of every six editors said they discovered instances of plagiarism by staffers in the previous three years. Appropriating as one's own work the language, ideas, and thoughts of another author and "out-and-out fabrication of a story" were among the serious ethical problems that led ASNE to report, "The extent of unethical behavior is disturbing." Responding editors said they dismissed forty-eight staffers and suspended thirty for ethics violations in the three-year period.[26] If ever a rule was part of the journalistic fabric, it is that a reporter should not steal or rewrite another reporter's story. Written codes of ethics don't spell that out. Perhaps they must in the future, particularly because news work can create conditions where reporters unthinkingly can commit plagiarism. The unwary, for example, can dip into a news morgue for background on an event and incorporate into their story another reporter's work. On fast-breaking stories particularly, reporters tend to build on developments revealed by other reporters. The danger is in "advancing" the story by reporting today's developments atop the background of what happened—and was reported by others—yesterday. In some cases, the solution can be tight attribution—giving credit—to what other reporters have done.

So, Are Limited Codes Enough?

So, the question remains: Are the limited codes in effect in newsrooms across the country enough? Aren't they, as written, so painfully obvious, so basic—don't take bribes, don't cheat—as to be useless? And, even with best intentions, can editor Squires of the *Chicago Tribune* more than touch major issues in his ethics policy of one and a half pages? Can editor Thomas of the *Los Angeles Times* in his two and a third pages?

Editors and news directors obviously must set personal examples and use other devices—staff seminars, one-on-one meetings, speeches, periodic memos—to create an environment of ethical, socially responsible journalism. They need to construct—and implement—a checklist for excellence.

Michael J. Davies, publisher of the *Hartford* (Conn.) *Courant,* told an editor's seminar on ethics they should create a newsroom environment that ensures:

Compassionate understanding of readers.

Fair and accurate reporting and writing.

Fast, full correction of errors.

Two-way dialogue with the public and accountability for what is reported (he recommended an ombudsman, or reader representative, be appointed on the staff).

Good and bad news are presented with balance.

The context of events and wider meanings are explained.

The newspaper covers itself and other media just as it covers any other major story.

The newspaper cares about its community.

Activists whose personal views color their copy are weeded out.[27]

Clearly, corporate ethics will continue as the prerogative of management. Some managers seek staff participation in defining ethics or writing codes; all to some extent feel staff pressure on questions of ethics and corporate conscience. But there is no sign of managers in either print or broadcast relinquishing to staff consensus the prerogatives of management, including writing codes of ethics. How management exercises those prerogatives in the newsroom is the subject of our next chapter.

CHAPTER SUMMARY

Management theorists don't agree American corporations have social responsibilities beyond profitably serving customers and employees.

Traditionalists say "business is the business of business," and that social responsibility is too expensive, a disservice to shareholders, and, anyway, not the function of any corporation. Traditionalists fear social responsibility leads to bland, consensus journalism, and the media's voluntary abrogation of independence.

However, times change. Society now demands more of corporations which grow huge and strongly influence everyday life. Professional managers of publicly owned corporations frequently regard social responsibility as important; so do employees when job security and higher living standards permit. Government enters the equation, reflecting societal pressure for certain standards of performance.

Supporters of social responsibility argue corporations face government intervention unless they perform as expected, and, anyway, business is in the business of meeting societal demands. Also, social responsibility is considered the *right* course for newspapers and broadcast stations to follow. But the concept still comes second to service to shareholders.

The concept of social responsibility is old; widespread acceptance of the idea corporations must follow precise ethical policies isn't.

Opponents of written codes argue they could lead to general standards of behavior—licensing, perhaps—for all media. Also, some consider written codes dangerous because they could be used against the media in court if, say, reporters were proved to have broken their own company's policies. Opponents argue codes necessarily are vague window dressing, and that what is needed is an editor or news director with judgment, not a code hanging on a wall.

Whether or not they're written, ethical policies need endorsement by top-level management, and should state explicitly who is covered, which activities are acceptable, and how they will be enforced. Although industrywide codes have no enforcement provisions, individual newspapers and broadcast stations increasingly fire or otherwise discipline employees who compromise the integrity of the corporation.

CHAPTER 5

Notes

1 Thomas Donaldson, *Corporation and Morality,* Prentice-Hall, Englewood Cliffs, N.J., 1982, p. 6.

2 See Milton Friedman, ''The Social Responsibility of Business Is To Increase Its Profits,'' *New York Times Magazine,* Sept. 13, 1970, p. 32.

3 Among commentators on the social responsibility of business, the author found particularly helpful: Michael A. Hitt, R. Dennis Middlemist, Robert C. Mathis, *Effective Management,* West, St. Paul, 1979; W. Jack Duncan, *Management,* Random House, New York, 1983; George A. Steiner and John B. Miner, *Management Policy and Strategy,* Macmillan, New York, 1977; Davis L. Kurtz and Louis E. Boone, *Marketing,* Dryden Press, New York, 1981. Also see Milton Friedman, *Issues in Business and Society,* G. A. Steiner, ed., Random House, New York, 1972, and J.W. McGuire, *Business and Society,* McGraw-Hill, New York, 1963.

4 Annual report to shareholders, Feb. 14, 1986, p. 3, Tribune Company, Tribune Tower, 435 North Michigan Ave., Chicago, Ill., 60611.

5 Annual report to shareholders, Feb. 3, 1986, p. 2, Knight-Ridder, Inc., One Herald Plaza, Miami, Fla., 33101.

6 Annual report to shareholders, March 1, 1986, p. 1., Dow Jones & Company, Inc., World Financial Center, 200 Liberty Street, New York, N.Y., 10281.

7 *ABC News Policy,* an employee handbook, March 10, 1982, preface, American Broadcasting Companies, Inc., ABC News, 7 West 66th Street, New York, N.Y., 10023.

8 The APME 1974 report can be obtained from The Associated Press, 50 Rockefeller Plaza, New York, N.Y., 10020; Dr. Ralph Izard, professor of journalism, E.W. Scripps School of Journalism, Ohio University, Sigma Delta Chi survey, available at 840 N. Lakeshore Dr., Suite 801-W, Chicago, Ill., 60611. For a discussion of trends in the early 1980s, see C. David Rambo, ''Codes of Ethics,'' *presstime,* February 1984, p. 20.

9 John R. Finnegan, senior vice president and editor, the *St. Paul Pioneer Press and Dispatch,* and an ASNE official, in speech at Morris Communications Corp. seminar on ethical issues, Savannah, Ga., March 10, 1986.

10 Richard G. Capen, Jr., chairman and publisher, *Miami Herald,* One Herald Plaza, Miami, Fla., 33101; letter to author, Oct. 2, 1985.

11 Eugene Patterson, chairman and chief executive officer, *St. Petersburg Times and Evening Independent,* P.O. Box 1121, St. Petersburg, Fla., 33731; letter to author, June 11, 1985.

12 Eugene Patterson, "Standards of Operation," June 15, 1979.

13 Jim Squires, editor, *Chicago Tribune,* 435 N. Michigan Ave., Chicago, Ill., 60611, "Ethics Policy," June 24, 1982; and letter to author, Oct. 7, 1985.

14 William F. Thomas, editor, *Los Angeles Times,* Times Mirror Square, Los Angeles, Calif., 90053, "Code of Ethics," Nov. 16, 1982, and letter to author, Feb. 4, 1986.

15 Bob Haring, executive editor, *Tulsa World,* P.O. Box 1770, Tulsa, Okla., 74102; letter to author, Nov. 6, 1985.

16 Roone Arledge, memo to staff on "News Policy," ABC News, 7 West 66th St., New York, N.Y., 10023, March 10, 1982.

17 Ethical issues in business are discussed with skill by Fred Luthans, Richard M. Hodgetts and Kenneth R. Thompson in *Social Issues in Business,* Macmillan, New York, 1984; Thomas Donaldson, *Corporations and Morality,* Prentice-Hall, Englewood Cliffs, N.J., 1982; as well as W. Jack Duncan, *Management,* Random House, op. cit., and David L. Kurtz and Louis E. Boone, *Marketing,* Dryden Press, op. cit.

18 See report of Professional Standards Committee, APME Red Book 1984, The Associated Press Managing Editors Association, 50 Rockefeller Plaza, New York, N.Y. 10020, p. 169.

19 W. Jack Duncan, *Management,* op. cit., comments on this.

20 A report on this seminar, "Closing the Credibility Gap," was written by John Dillon, special assignment editor, *The Richmond Times-Dispatch,* and is available from SNPA, P.O. Box 18875, Atlanta, Ga., 30328.

21 CBS News Standards, memo to personnel, April 14, 1976, CBS Inc., 51 W. 52nd St., New York, N.Y., 10020, p. 2.

22 "Code of Ethics," *Los Angeles Times,* dated Nov. 16, 1982, and letter to author from editor William F. Thomas, Feb. 4, 1986.

23 "Ethics Policy," *Chicago Tribune,* and letter to author from editor James D. Squires, Oct. 7, 1985.

24 "The Herald and You," an ethics code, *Miami Herald,* One Herald Plaza, Miami, Fla., 33101; and letter to author from Richard G. Capen, Jr., chairman and publisher, Oct. 2, 1985.

25 "Conflicts of Interest Policy," Dow Jones & Company, Inc., and letters to author from Lawrence A. Armour, director of corporate relations, Oct. 15, 1985, and Warren H. Phillips, chairman, Oct. 17, 1985.

26 "Newsroom Ethics: How Tough Is Enforcement?" a survey by American Society of Newspaper Editors, P.O. Box 17004, Washington, D.C., 10041, released April, 1985.

27 Michael J. Davies, speech at ethics seminar held in Savannah, Ga., March 9–11, 1986, by Morris Communications Corp., P.O. Box 936, Augusta, Ga., 30913.

CORPORATE PROFITS AND NEWSROOM ETHICS

Profit must be a primary goal of any newspaper or television station. Without profit, talented employees cannot be hired; newsrooms will starve for operating funds to support credible reporting and editing. News organizations scrambling to stay afloat financially cannot shine journalistic light in dark corners. Importantly, unprofitable newspaper or broadcast companies cannot attract investor capital necessary for building for the future. Communications is a capital-intensive industry (a metropolitan daily, for example, easily can spend $50 million to install new presses). So, many companies are forced into the marketplace to attract shareholders who will invest expecting to share increased profits.

All this gives rise in newspaper management to the marketing concept which holds, in part, that each department—advertising, circulation, production, promotion, *and* news—must be integrated in a planned, disciplined drive for financial as well as journalistic success. Newspaper editors and television news directors are expected to construct news strategies within a unified marketing effort aimed at exploiting the economic potential of the marketplace. They must create news and information packages that will lure sufficient numbers of readers or viewers with income and spending habits attractive to the advertisers who foot the bills (advertisers contribute 80 percent of most daily newspapers' total revenue, readers just 20 percent or so; for magazines, 49 to 50 percent of revenue generally comes from advertisers, the rest from reader subscriptions or newsstand purchases; commercial television is free to viewers, of course, so advertisers contribute 100 percent of revenue, although cable-TV viewers contribute subscription fees).

But, can editors or news directors be harnessed to the marketing concept by such success-oriented news strategies and still remain true to the higher ethical standards and social responsibilities of journalism? Can editors hotly pursue affluent readers, often to the neglect of the less affluent, because that's what advertisers want, and still cover the world in accord with the way their news instincts and training dictate it should be covered? Can TV news directors hold true to their journalistic responsibilities, and still pursue the larger numbers of viewers promised by "happy talk" news shows and the other silliness that so often afflicts TV news organizations driving for better ratings?

Indeed, is ethical conflict inherent when the "rising tide of shareholder expectation" surges out of the executive suite, and dashes up against the journalistic imperatives of the newsroom? If shareholders—public or private—push unceasingly for ever more profit, either because they need it or simply because they like it, can ethical, socially responsible journalism flourish? This is the compelling ethical issue facing policy makers in American newsrooms today. So, we must turn to the broader question of how to create in this profit-oriented era a qualitatively strong news product that is ethically sound and socially responsible.

Newspapers properly managed in economically strong markets yield great profit, particularly if they face no competing papers of like size and characteristics. Under the right conditions, small and medium-size newspapers can convert as much as 35 to 40 percent of total advertising and circulation revenue to operating profit. That is, of every dollar received from advertisers and subscribers, 35 to 40 cents goes to pretax profit. Those are conversion ratios envied in many other industries which boast profits only a fraction of that.

Television's profit potential is even greater. A network affiliate in a market such as, say, Richmond can convert 50 percent of gross revenue from advertisers to operating profit. At network level, a thirty-second commercial on NBC's "Today" show sells (at 1986 prices) for $17,000; CBS-TV charged $600,000 for a single thirty-second commercial on its 1987 Super Bowl football broadcast. During network evening news, a single ratings point is worth more than $8.5 million in advertising.[1]

In Wall Street parlance, communications companies are "cash cows." Not surprisingly, all this attracts investor attention. Medium-size newspapers without competition in growing markets can sell for three to five times gross revenue. That is, a newspaper taking in, say, $10 million annually from advertisers and subscribers could sell for $30 million to $50 million. That is a price multiple extraordinarily high in other industries. Major market TV stations sell for hundreds of millions of dollars. Communications companies, particularly those diversified in both print and broadcast, are hot properties on stock exchanges.[2]

Newspapers and broadcast stations are passing with increasing speed from private ownership into large, publicly held communications companies. More than 70 percent of all dailies (and nearly 80 percent of all Sunday papers) are owned by groups. Importantly, groups control over 80 percent of all daily circulation, and nearly 90 percent on Sunday. Inheritance taxes make it impossible for many owning families to pass newspapers or stations to succeeding generations. High profit potential lures groups into offering attractive prices. Tax breaks provided companies that expand through acquisition give groups additional incentive to acquire more and more. For a multiplicity of reasons, then, newspaper families of two, even three or more, generations of journalistic commitment to a community are being succeeded by professional, profit-oriented managers who, in some cases, have no particular allegiance to community or, indeed, journalism itself.

This does *not* mean automatic degradation of journalistic quality; publicly owned groups such as Knight-Ridder, Dow Jones, The New York Times Co., Times Mirror Corp., are producing the finest journalism ever seen in this country. Those companies are as eager as any for improved profitability but, fortunately, commit to journalistic excellence as means of achieving it. Nevertheless, the switch from family to group ownership has brought to top-level management of communications companies a new breed of managers who by training are accountants, lawyers, business school graduates, not the editor-turned-publisher of old who received early training in the newsroom. And some new breed managers are less concerned with covering news on Main Street than with responding to their distant group headquarters and its profit demands on the local "property." For this type manager, it is axiomatic that gaining a dollar in new circulation or advertising revenue through improved news content carries with it certain costs, so only a portion of that dollar will descend to bottom line profit. However, a dollar stripped out of existing operating costs is added almost intact to the bottom line—and thus are born careers devoted not to imaginative, expansive, community-minded journalism of high quality, but, rather, to squeezing a few bucks out of costs here, there, and everywhere—including the newsroom.

Clearly, all this has central importance to any discussion of ethical, socially responsible journalism for it means *newsroom* issues of what is good or bad, right or wrong could be decided for the most part *outside the newsroom.*

GOOD JOURNALISM ISN'T CHEAP

The first move toward ethical, responsible journalism must come not from the newsroom, but, rather, the executive suite. There must be owner commitment to excellence, and that means commitment of money. Good journalism isn't cheap.

Witness three world-class newspapers (all members, incidentally, of profit-oriented, publicly owned communications groups) and their *newsroom* budgets: The *New York Times* reportedly spent $80 million covering the news in 1986; the *Los Angeles Times,* $68.6 million; the *Washington Post,* almost $50 million.[3] Those newspapers, among the prestigious handful that set the news agenda in the United States, demonstrate management commitment to excellence.

By one estimate, the three television networks spend $750 million or more annually on news programming.[4]

The biggest individual newsroom spender in newspapering is the *New York Times*. A. M. Rosenthal, until 1987 executive editor of the *Times,* leaves no doubt about what he regards as the first essential ingredient of ethical, responsible journalism. Commenting on the *Times'* very considerable journalistic achievements under his direction, Rosenthal says:

> This could not have been done without cooperation between the business and the news side, and it most certainly could not have been done well without the participation and encouragement and adventuresomeness of the publisher, (Arthur Ochs) Punch Sulzberger.
>
> As a matter of fact, looking back it seems to me that perhaps the most important single thing in the success of a newspaper is the willingness of a publisher to invest his mind and money to improve the quality of the newspaper. Not just promotion, not just circulation, not just advertising, but quality. When in trouble you can either put more water in the soup or more tomatoes—the *Times'* publishing tradition has been to add tomatoes.[5]

When A. H. Belo Corp. decided in the early 1980s its *Dallas Morning News* would attack Times Mirror Corp.'s *Dallas Times Herald* in all-out war for dominance of the city, Belo's owners recruited talented—and expensive—newsroom managers, writers, and reporters from top-flight newspapers throughout the country. Then, it *doubled* the newsroom's budget in one year. Within three years, the *Morning News* achieved superiority over the *Times Herald,* and won nationwide acclaim for journalistic quality.[6] In 1986, Times Mirror sold out and left town, whipped. Other factors, including a natural advantage to the *News* as a morning paper, contributed to the outcome. But massive amounts of money wisely spent by Belo were key.

Knight-Ridder management repeatedly urges its newspapers toward journalistic quality, then puts money where its slogans are. In 1986 alone, Knight-Ridder won seven Pulitzer Prizes.

Few of the nation's 1,674 daily newspapers (1986 count) spend on news as do the *New York Times* or *Dallas Morning News.* To be fair, not many have the strong economic base offered by New York City or Dallas.[7] And, no newspaper can perform for long above the economic strength of its marketplace; if advertising and circulation revenue isn't there, principled, ethical journalistic quality won't be either.

VIEWPOINT 6-1

GOOD JOURNALISM IS GOOD BUSINESS

"[W]e believe good journalism is good business. As an information company, our success depends on the excellence, reputation and usefulness of that information which is our product. We want our readers and viewers to have the highest possible confidence in what we produce. This is essential to maintaining our credibility and consequently the loyalty and following of our readers and viewers."

Alvah H. Chapman, Jr., chairman of Knight-Ridder, Inc., in 1985 a $1.7 billion company, letter to author

---

Market strength aside, however, American journalism is characterized by enormous variances in management commitment to ethical, responsible news coverage.

MEASURING COMMITMENT TO EXCELLENCE

American newspapers range from world-class journalistic quality to shoddy dogs. For every Knight-Ridder or New York Times Co., there is a company that publishes low-quality (but often highly profitable) newspapers.

Television's performance swings equally wide. For every news special combining space-age communications technology with superb reporting to produce outstanding journalism, there is a silly "happy talk" local anchor team that wouldn't know news if it dropped on its blown-dry coiffures.

In either newspapers or television, which it will be—excellence or shoddy amateurism—is up to top management. One measure of management commitment is the number of employees made available to the newsroom. In newspapers, it varies from 0.7 to 1.04 or more newsroom staffers per 1,000 circulation. In its drive for excellence, the *Dallas Morning News* achieved a newsroom employee ratio of 1.05 per 1,000 circulation.[8] Personnel accounts for generally 46 to 49 percent of a newspaper's total costs and most of a newsroom's costs, so a management that commits people to news is committing substantial money. In television, the choices can be handling news relatively cheaply with a "talking head" in a studio, augmented by a few stringers and heavy reliance on lifting news from local newspapers, or commitment of expensive mobile units and large outside reporting staffs.

One crucial indicator of newspaper management commitment to excellence is newshole—total space given news and information. Almost without exception, newshole is *not* determined by flow of news or newsroom judgments of how news should be covered; rather, newshole is established by amount of advertising sold. Thus, on heavy advertising days—Wednesdays and Sundays in most cities—papers are "fat." (A Newspaper Advertising Bureau study shows the average weekday edition in 1983 was 27.5 pages; on Sundays, 79.2.) If big news breaks on "fat" days, there is a better chance it will be covered in full. Chances aren't so good on "lean" days, such as Mondays, Tuesdays, and Saturdays. With newsprint at $570 per ton (in 1987) and climbing, only managers truly committed to journalistic quality will provide news pages for a big story even without supporting advertising.[9] Done repeatedly, that eats deeply into profits, unappealing to many shareholders and their surrogate managers in publicly owned companies. The *New York Times* managers, and those of a few other great newspapers, routinely make space available for important stories, regardless of advertiser support, to their great credit among serious journalists.

The news-to-advertising ratio within a newspaper is thus an indicator of quality. It varies widely from paper to paper. In some metropolitan dailies on heavy advertising days, news gets as little as 25 percent of total space; in small-town dailies on slow advertising days, 70 percent or more can go to news (or, frequently, meaningless but inexpensive "filler" mailed from a syndicate). A ratio traditionally regarded as about right, 60 percent advertising and 40 percent news, is breaking down under pressure to sell more advertising. If news content over a prolonged period runs substantially *under* 40 percent, readers simply are being cheated. (Of course, if news runs heavily *over* 40 percent for lengthy periods, the newspaper may be starved for advertising, and facing a financial crisis.)

A critical problem is the increasing swing by many advertisers from pages of the newspaper itself into, instead, "preprints," those colorful minicatalogues inserted in many newspapers, particularly on Wednesdays ("food day") and Sundays. This reduces, dramatically in some instances, the number of pages available to news, and there is no discernible widespread trend among newspaper publishers to use profits gained from carrying preprints in supporting a larger number of news pages in the paid circulation paper if advertising support is not forthcoming for them.

In television, there is equivalent tension in the news versus advertising equation. TV's version of newsprint—time—is expensive, too, and there is struggle over who gets it. The plain fact is that although news programming can attract advertising and be profitable, entertainment programming generally is more profitable, and really is what television is all about. For news directors concerned with ethical, responsible journalism, the conflict takes many forms. Most visible is whether news or special events programming, particularly an unexpected fast-breaking news story, can preempt regularly scheduled entertainment programming. At network level, preempting entertainment can cost hundreds of thousands of dollars, millions even; at the local level, it's almost unheard of. Another source of conflict is whether network evening news should be extended from the current half-hour to a full hour. The issue is not whether Dan Rather each evening *needs* more than twenty-two minutes for news (thirty minutes minus commercials). He does; the world simply cannot be covered in any meaningful depth in the time given network news teams. The real issue is that local network affiliated stations sell that extra thirty minutes to local advertisers, often at great profit, and are unwilling to turn it over to Dan Rather or anyone else, whatever the news needs.

In both newspapers and broadcast, an important indicator of management's commitment to excellence is whether the newsroom is forced to rely heavily on external news resources such as news agencies and syndicates.

Bluntly, the cheapest way to put out a newspaper is to fill it with Associated Press or United Press International copy, tucking in around the edges yards of syndicated columns and features. AP, a membership cooperative, is relatively inexpensive because its prices are controlled by the newspaper publishers who pay them; UPI, weakened from decades of struggling in a distant number two position behind AP, often is forced to sell its services for what the marketplace offers, not what they cost. In the 1980s, AP costs were 4 percent of the *Baltimore Sun*'s newsroom (*not* total) budget; AP provided 24 percent of news the

Sun published. The *Phoenix Gazette* and *Arizona Republic* drew 37 percent of their news content from AP and paid AP 4 percent of their newsroom budget. At the *Kansas City Star and Times*, it was 7 percent of newsroom budget for 39 percent of content. Smaller papers and broadcast stations pay AP and, certainly, UPI much less. For both newspapers and broadcast, supplemental news agencies and syndicates are even cheaper.[10]

Now, AP is one of the world's premier news organizations. Much of its news and photo coverage is of outstanding quality. Supplemental agencies such as The New York Times News Service and Los Angeles Times-Washington Post News Service are excellent. And, any editor who makes *discerning* use of AP and leading supplementals to augment local coverage can do the reader a great service. Problems arise, however, when profit-oriented managers of smaller papers realize AP or a supplemental agency can be obtained *for less than the cost of an experienced local reporter or two.* That can lead to newspapers, even of 20,000 to 25,000 circulation, maintaining local reporting staffs of only four or five persons, and stuffing their pages with inexpensive, albeit often high-quality, copy from distant cities on esoteric subjects of little local consequence.

Management's commitment to excellence really is signaled in major part by total dollars allocated to newsrooms. The range is enormous—anywhere from 7 percent of total expense to 20 percent for papers of 20,000 circulation to over 100,000.[11] It is impossible to construct a valid model with widespread application that will predict what total expense will yield "excellence." The nature of local competition, the type market to be covered, owner profit expectation—all vary, as indeed does the definition of "excellence" itself. And, all these variables influence strongly newsroom expenditures.

Now, how can an editor justify larger expenditures for news? It will be difficult to do by simply arguing that heavier spending will achieve journalistic quality which, in turn, will produce greater profit.

QUALITY AND PROFIT: BASIC DILEMMA

Search as they will (and must), editors and news directors concerned with ethical, responsible journalism cannot find *proof* that spending heavily to produce high-quality reporting and writing will assure profitability. No such provable link exists. With business departments and top-management ranks increasingly staffed by accountants, lawyers, and other nonjournalists, the need to cost-justify excellence is no idle exercise, and convincing that type manager to pay for quality becomes crucial to everything else that follows in a newsroom.

Those who believe ethical, responsible, high-quality news coverage is essential to *long-term* financial as well as journalistic success (and the author is among them) can point to much evidence. In newspapering, names jump easily to mind: the *New York Times, Philadelphia Inquirer, Washington Post, Chicago Tribune, Los Angeles Times, Dallas Morning News,* and *Wall Street Journal.* The list is longer. All spend heavily on news, producing ethical, responsible, outstanding newspapers—and, to boot, enjoying immense profits. In television, the networks spend heavily on their evening news shows, and profitably so. CBS's *60 Minutes,* expensive to produce, always is among most-watched and most profitable shows.[12]

However, American newspaper history is filled with examples of first-rate newspapers that withered even in economically good times, then keeled over dead during dislocation in the local or national economy. The *New York Herald Tribune,* "a newspaperman's newspaper," was filled with fine writing and reporting, even when it had a death rattle in its cash register. The *Philadelphia Bulletin, Washington Star, Cleveland Press, Minneapolis Star,* and many others died not because their news products were poor. Rather, they died for complex reasons of economics, competition, changing lifestyles—and mismanagement—that not even outstanding journalism could overcome.

Conversely, there are many examples of low-quality newspapers producing high profits. The Thomson, Ingersoll, Park, and Donrey newspaper groups, among the nation's largest in number of newspapers owned, specialize in small and medium-size newspapers with no direct print competition and which, therefore, can extract maximum economic reward from their markets for minimum investment in journalistic quality. There is some question whether such tactics succeed over the long haul. Disaffected readers seek other sources of news and advertising; competitors slip into the market if a newspaper's circulation and household penetration falter. But particularly in small and medium-size cities which have no alternate sources of local news and advertising, cut-rate journalism can produce enormous profit ratios over lengthy periods.

In television, sheer perversity is at work—a sort of Gresham's Law of Journalism: poor quality, low-cost entertainment shows drive out high-quality, high-cost news programming. First-rate network news shows lose viewers when opposed in the same slot by entertainment such as *Wheel of Fortune.* Superb news specials in the Edward R. Murrow tradition of thoughtful, responsible broadcast journalism vanish before stampedes of cops-and-robbers shows.

Clearly, the newsroom ethicist dedicated to high-quality journalism must be prepared to fight quite outside the newsroom itself, well beyond the limited ethical issues met in the daily struggle to get the newspaper on the street and the evening news on the air. The fight must be carried to higher management in

---

VIEWPOINT 6-2

READ ALL ABOUT THE DOLLARS!

"It is a chain where the proprietor is more interested in what the financial statements say than what the newspapers print."

Richard Behar, commenting in *Forbes* magazine on Donald Worthington Reynolds, sole owner of Donrey Media and its fifty-four daily newspapers, and a man reputedly worth $1 billion, May 19, 1986, p. 144

NEWSPAPERS OR CASH-BOXES?

"Its small-town monopoly papers are, almost without exception, a lacklustre aggregation of cash-boxes."

Canada's Royal Commission on Newspapers, commenting on Thomson Newspapers

terms nonjournalist managers understand—that is, purely and simply, how better, more responsible journalism can assist the newspaper or broadcast station in reaching its overall strategic goals of increased share of reader (or viewer) time and advertiser dollar—the ingredients of eventual financial success.

Learn to Talk Their Language

Editors or news directors seeking top management's commitment of resources necessary for quality journalism can *think* ethics and social responsibility, but upon entering the executive suite it's more productive to *talk* dollars and cents. They must learn to express their journalistic needs in countinghouse language.

Essentially, the *business* imperative for corporate strategists who direct newspapers today is quite simple: on behalf of advertisers, attract (at acceptable cost) readers in sufficient numbers and affluency who live in right places (near advertisers' stores), then help influence them to purchase advertisers' goods and services.

Obviously, many enlightened corporate strategists *also* think ethics and social responsibility; we've mentioned some great newspapers they publish. But when it comes to business, the challenge is to get, hold, and persuade the right kinds of readers who, in turn, are "sold" to advertisers. Most advertisers want their message delivered into homes where more than one reader awaits, especially women aged 18 to 49, the big spenders. So, in addition to attractive "demographics"—income, education, and spending habits—advertisers and, thus, newspaper strategists seek household "penetration." Note the game no longer is simply adding more and more circulation; in fact, circulation among the "wrong" types of readers (the demographically unattractive) in the "wrong" places (distant from advertisers' stores) will not gain advertiser support and thus for the newspaper that type circulation is *not a revenue producer but, rather, a cost factor that drains profits*.

Understanding these basic facts of modern newspaper marketing permits editors to express truthfully their journalistic needs and ethical imperatives in terms of what will yield not only responsible journalism, but also—music to publishers' ears—deeper household penetration and improved demographics. Editors *can* produce newspapers that salve their professional consciences, meet their ethical and social responsibilities—and fit neatly and productively into the corporation's overall marketing concept.

"Attractive" readers by definition want superior news coverage. They are, compared to TV viewers, for example, well educated and sophisticated in news needs, cosmopolitan in news interests; they are affluent and adventuresome in lifestyle and way of thinking. Constructing a newspaper to reach *that* type reader with improved political coverage, strong business news, and thoughtful editorials and commentary can be delightful for editors, and profitable for publishers.

Frankly, this is more difficult to achieve in television news and, consequently, high-quality network journalism faces perilous times. Numbers of viewers—huge, raw, undifferentiated numbers—are the goal of network television. Millions of men who want a close shave, tens of millions who drink more than one beer, and women of all ages and types who use detergents are what the television advertiser wants. Whether they earn $12,000 annually or $120,000, went to college or not, is immaterial—just so they shave, drink beer, or wash dishes. To their despair, responsible television journalists recognize that playful game shows, cheap to stage and easy to watch, sometimes produce larger numbers than thought-provoking (and expensive) news specials on pressing issues of the day; mindless situation comedies can rival in popularity the hard-hitting, award-winning, million-dollar-a-year evening news anchor.

All this bodes ill for network television journalism. It is, after all, strictly an adjunct in an entertainment-oriented medium managed at the top almost exclusively by nonjournalist executives raised in an industry scarcely 40 years old and, compared to newspapers, lacking a long tradition of journalism. At ABC, NBC, and CBS, there have been major cutbacks in their superb news staffs; more likely are ahead. Combined with expansion of local television news, this may mean Dan Rather, Tom Brokaw, Peter Jennings, and other star anchors are among the last who will become household fixtures coast-to-coast. If there occurs fractionalization of television—and growth of CNN, Fox, and other independent networks indicates it will—each network's slice of the viewer and advertising pies will get smaller. And that will mean less money available for the high-quality news produced for so many years by the major networks.

The reality, then, is that profit as a motivational factor in modern communications corporations has fundamental importance to the practice of ethical, responsible newspaper and television journalism. Yet, many editors and news directors resist the thought that they are involved in a "business" manufacturing a "product" that must compete and win in the marketplace just like any other product.

Editors and Business: Conflicting Ethics?

For thirty-two years, in good times and bad, Charles W. Bailey worked for the *Minneapolis Star and Tribune*. He was editor when bad times arrived in the early 1980s. The morning and afternoon papers, in serious financial difficulty, were merged and the principal owner, John Cowles, Jr., ordered a 15 percent staff cut.

Bailey, whose reputation as an ethical, principled journalist extended far beyond his upper midwest base, resigned in protest with a public statement that spoke the sentiments of many editors concerned over intrusion of business considerations and marketing concepts into their domains:

> I think there are some new threats to the independence and public utility of newspaper editors. One is the growing tendency to encourage, in fact, to require, editors to become businessmen—to be part of a "management team," to concentrate on things that involve business rather than journalism.
>
> An editor has to know where the money comes from, and it is currently fashionable to talk about "the total newspaper," but speaking from personal experience, I don't think most editors are especially qualified in matters of business and finance.

And even if they were, I do not think they should spend most of their time and energy on such matters.

They have more important things to do. There will always be people around to tell a publisher how he can do things more cheaply, more profitably, less controversially. He needs someone to explain, from time to time, why things have to be done more expensively, less profitably, and in ways that create rather than avoid controversy.

For some editors, conflicting demands of newsroom and countinghouse create major job tension. An Associated Press Managing Editors Association survey of 902 editors found most stimulated by the journalistic challenges of their jobs, but suffering emotional stress when their publishers imposed profit-oriented policies that compromised newsroom integrity or denied resources necessary for high-quality journalism.

Robert H. Giles, then editor of Gannett's Rochester, N.Y., newspapers, and now editor of the *Detroit News,* directed the survey. He explained:

> Fifteen years ago, editors were editors. Today, they are editor-managers. They direct the editing of the newspaper with one hand and, with the other, they are deeply involved in business management.
>
> The editor is expected to carry on in the best traditions of journalistic excellence, but also is expected to share the responsibility for the newspaper as a "profit center." Many editors discovered that this dual obligation created unfamiliar stresses, stresses born of a conflict between the need to be good and the need to be lean.

Whether editors and news directors *should* be inducted into the integrated management team can long be argued; in fact, many *are*—and, along with other department heads, assume responsibility for the marketplace success of their newspapers or television news shows. Their performance is measured in businesslike terms: whether they expand circulation properly and achieve deeper household penetration or, in TV, pull in more viewers. And, while doing it they must learn how to carefully draw expense budgets and stick to them.

Corporate cross-pollination—making editors responsible, in part, for marketing the product as well as creating it—is reflected in the increasing number who also carry corporate titles. "Vice president and editor" is a favorite combination, and it very clearly signals dual responsibilities. Alex S. Jones, *New York Times* perceptive media reporter, noted in 1986 the top four officers of the American Society of Newspaper Editors, *which officially won't even admit publishers to membership* (some

---

VIEWPOINT 6-3

THE INTEGRATED EDITOR

"[N]ewsroom strategy must be integrated with the strategy of the entire newspaper. The editor and the publisher and the marketing director and the operations manager must be a team.... The day is gone when the editor can be going in one direction while the marketing director is going in another and the operations director in a third."

Michael Gartner, then president and editorial chairman, *Des Moines Register and Tribune,* letter to author.

---

in fact are members), carried corporate, as well as newsroom, titles, or once served
as publishers. In a Washington dispatch, Jones wrote:

> Many of the nation's newspaper editors, gathered in record numbers here this week
> for an annual convention, grumbled in hotel corridors with the sophistication of pub-
> lishers about flat advertising revenues that threaten to squeeze news budgets.
>
> In the modern newspaper, top editors who once shunned business concerns have
> had to become knowledgeable about corporate finance as well as news coverage,
> and the American Society of Newspaper Editors reflects that change...[13]

Just a year earlier, at the Society's 1985 convention, Jones reported:

> [T]he job of being a newspaper editor has changed so dramatically in the last decade
> that the society is no longer sure precisely what a newspaper editor is or should be....One
> of the traditional pleasures of being a newspaper editor has been the role of defending
> the sanctity of the paper's news operation from encroachment by the business side of
> the paper, represented by the publisher. At conventions in past years, editors would
> often grumble about their publishers and bask in the sense of muscular brotherhood that
> made the society almost an executive-level labor union.
>
> But that adversarial atmosphere has almost completely disappeared from the society's
> annual meeting.
>
> As newspapers have been consolidated into chains and the chains have grown
> into communications conglomerates, editors have increasingly become key execu-
> tives in a corporate structure whose product is news, and there are fewer single-
> minded, hard-bitten editors of newspapers. For instance, editors now frequently use
> the jargon of publishers to describe their newspapers; what was "a good newspa-
> per" a few years ago is now described by editors as a "quality product."
>
> [E]ditors expressed concern that they now spend too much time pondering bud-
> gets and the company's bottom line and are distracted from their duties as editors.
>
> The editor's role now often includes participating in such corporate functions as
> strategic planning and marketing. Many editors have assumed corporate titles that
> suggest relatively little of their time is spent editing.[14]

Rather than sullenly resisting their inevitable induction into corporate affairs,
newspaper editors should use such cross-pollination as opportunity to battle
meaningfully and where it counts—in the publisher's office—for ethical, socially responsible journalism. If editors don a "vice president" hat at the planning table, they can fight for the resources—people, money, time, newshole—
they need as "editor" to produce that kind of journalism.

As we have noted, many editors and news directors already accept the importance of close interaction between their news and corporate business responsibilities. They see the need for producing newspapers or TV news shows
that succeed financially, as well as journalistically. They accept organizational
responsibilities extending beyond the newsroom.

Yet, curiously, few write newsroom codes reflecting this fact. Few deal effectively, for their staffs, with the wider question of profit versus excellence.
Few attempt to present newsroom and corporate imperatives as synergistic—
not conflicting—forces. However, it *is* done effectively in the small lumbering
town of Longview, Washington.

From 1923, when founded, until 1985, when sold to a group, the *Longview* (Wash.) *Daily News* was published by John M. McClelland or his son, John, Jr. They were of a rapidly vanishing breed of owners who lived where they published the *Daily News* and other nearby community papers, and felt personally responsible for the newspapers' business *and* journalistic direction.

In a policy statement first written in 1948, then revised five times, the McClellands address the troublesome question of how to create a managerial ''tone'' that properly balances the twin objectives of journalistic excellence and profit. It reads:

> Our newspapers' only license to publish is the freedom of the press clause in the Constitution. As such, their first obligation is to publish the news, to broadcast the truth, to keep the people informed. Their primary obligation is to serve the readers.
>
> Secondly, they are business and manufacturing enterprises depending on the sale of their products for the financial success which enables them to continue publishing the news. That success is necessary to provide compensation for employees, to furnish reserves for improvements in productive capacity, to provide for the payment of taxes necessary to maintain the government, and to allow the shareholders whose capital has made the business possible a reasonable return on their investment.
>
> To assure this success, it is essential to produce newspapers that are as good as we are capable of producing, to increase continually our family of readers and to provide, through well planned advertising, a means of serving effectively the sales objectives of our customers.
>
> Talented, truthful, energetic journalism; well prepared advertising and the finest printing our employees and machines are capable of producing—these shall be our objectives.[15]

Such sentiments effectively link business success with journalistic performance. But important change is being forced by such linkage.

CORPORATE PROFITS AND JOURNALISTIC ELITISM

Implicit in American journalistic tradition—and, certainly, in the concept of social responsibility—is a sense of communications media serving to inform and educate, to *uplift*.

Newspapers claim special societal (as well as constitutional) status on grounds they inform and enlighten, which, in turn, strengthens our society. Because of this sense of mission, many types of preferential treatment, such as favorable postal rates for newspapers, are justified by publishers and editors alike.

Yet, as we noted earlier in this chapter, newspapers are *positioning themselves journalistically in a manner best suited to yield profit*, and that requires a marketing scheme aimed at attracting well-educated, highly affluent readers.

But, how about the less-well-educated, not-so-affluent citizenry? Who exists to inform and uplift them?

The Elitist Newspaper

Marketing directors at many leading newspapers throughout the country would panic if large numbers of low-income, poorly educated readers began subscribing to their newspapers. Such newcomers would "dilute" the "purity" of reader demographics upon which high advertising rates are based.

How pure? Dow Jones boasts of the elitist audience attracted to its *Wall Street Journal:*

"The quality of the *Journal* audience...remains unsurpassed among major publications," says a Dow Jones promotional ad directed at advertisers. "Household income of the *average* [author's emphasis] *Journal* subscriber is $107,800 and average net worth exceeds $750,000. The typical *Journal* subscriber is in the ranks of top or middle management, with diverse job responsibilities in key areas. He or she also is an active investor, with an average personal portfolio of more than $600,000."[16]

Well, one might say, the *Wall Street Journal* is a special case, a publication aiming at the carriage trade audience. So, obviously, is the *New York Times:*

Walter E. Mattson, president and chief operating officer of the *New York Times,* tells securities analysts his paper's national edition "...is aimed really at maintaining the position of *The New York Times* in the marketplace as a newspaper of national and worldwide influence and as a newspaper that delivers to its advertisers an influential and affluent market."[17] The *Times,* too, aims at upper-income, well-educated professional and managerial executives—seeking perhaps the top 1 percent, in demographic terms, of the nation's population.

The *Los Angeles Times* boasts households taking its daily paper are "84 percent more likely" than non-*Times* households to "serve wine/champagne once a week or more"; on Sundays, the figure is 98 percent.[18] The *Boston Globe* claims, on behalf of the entire newspaper industry, that "Better-educated, higher-income consumers are above-average readers of newspapers. On the average weekday a newspaper is read by 78 percent of those with $40,000 or more incomes...and by 78 percent of college graduates."[19]

In Dallas, the *Morning News* claims it is read by "the right people....People advertisers are most interested in reaching . . . more families with household incomes of $50,000+ and $35,000+, more professionals and more people with a college degree."[20] The *Washington Post* claims its Sunday magazine reaches 265,000 households with incomes of more than $50,000.[21]

What's all this talk about serving the champagne crowd, the rich, the "right people"? Across the country, in city after city, the pattern is the same: On behalf of the all-important advertiser, newspaper strategists are striving to attract the affluent, and editors are developing special approaches to the news that will help. It's nice to be a journalistic servant of the people; it's nicer to serve the rich.

Some leading big-city newspapers, those on everybody's list of the "best" fifteen or so, are moving upscale so rapidly in search of more affluent readers that they are leaving behind great sectors of their publics. Serious questions of social responsibility are raised.

For most metropolitan papers, the *business* necessity today is to leapfrog out of the socioeconomic deterioration of their core cities, and develop new circulation and advertising possibilities in affluent suburban areas. The 1980 census takers found 44.5 percent of all Americans live in the suburbs, and, of course, they by wide measure are the most affluent so highly desired by advertisers.

Left behind in the center city are many low-income families, blacks and Hispanics—in whom advertisers have less interest, and for whom upscale newspapers have little relevance.

Evidence of this upscale shift is found in the very shallow household penetration major newspapers achieve in their own home counties. The *New York Times* penetrates just 12.7 percent of households in its city's five boroughs. (It achieves 13 percent in Connecticut's affluent Fairfield County, 10 percent in New Jersey's rich Bergen County.) The *Los Angeles Times* penetrates just 24.8 percent of households in its home county; the *Chicago Tribune,* 25.2 percent; the *Dallas Morning News,* 32.4 percent. The *Miami Herald,* one of the nation's finest papers, penetrates just 38.9 percent in its home county, Dade, which now has a great many Spanish-speaking residents. An exception to this metropolitan newspaper pattern is the *Washington Post,* which scores 63.2 percent penetration in the District of Columbia. However, detailed analysis of circulation within the district would show the *Post* achieves only shallow penetration in large pockets of low-income areas.[22]

Nationwide, newspaper circulation in the fifty largest cities dropped 13 percent from 1961 to 1981; households grew 41 percent. Lee Dirks, a Detroit-based newspaper analyst, reported tracking circulation performance by 364 dailies of more than 10,000 circulation and finding that in 1984 they averaged 55 percent household penetration in their primary markets—down 12 percent since 1973.

In adjusting circulation patterns to meet advertiser demands—and to reduce their own costs—newspapers eliminate "inefficient" circulation, and withdraw from distant areas of no interest to home-base advertisers. Thus, the *Atlanta Journal and Constitution, Minneapolis Star and Tribune, Miami Herald,* and other newspapers that once circulated statewide now are pulling back closer to home. The *Boston Globe,* which once circulated widely throughout New England, now identifies an area within 50 miles of downtown as its primary circulation target.[23]

Clearly, then, editors of the nation's best newspapers have joined the marketing team and are employing news strategies designed to attract—in the "right" places—highly affluent readers appealing to advertisers. Thus, the *New York Times'* editors create a journalistic tone appealing to readers who buy fur, not cloth, coats; those who vacation in the Caribbean, not Coney Island. That means covering se-

---

VIEWPOINT 6-4

COVERING UPSCALE MURDERS

"I remember being trained as a green police reporter to understand, through repetition, that a murder on Park Avenue was big news and a murder on Dean Street in Brooklyn wasn't worth interrupting the card game for."

Sydney H. Schanberg, then a *New York Times* columnist

rious books, music, and drama and in other ways positioning the entire paper for the $50,000+ audience.

When advertisers demand—as many do—that 90 percent or more of all households in a market be reached, most newspapers provide "Total Market Coverage" vehicles (usually, direct mail services or free-circulation shoppers) to do the job. They avoid "diluting" content of the newspaper itself or positioning it downscale.

In small towns, newspapers often achieve deep penetration with their paid circulation—80 percent or 85 percent is not unusual. They serve settled, long-time residents for whom reading the paper often is a second- or third-generation habit. And, importantly, those small towns often are, relative to large cities, demographically homogeneous, and there is no advertiser pressure to move upscale and leave large portions of the public behind.

In sum, American newspapers today sell roughly 77 copies per 100 households. In 1950, it was *124* copies for each 100 households. Who isn't being reached? Mostly, it is the low-income and minority sectors. Leo Bogart, executive vice president of the Newspaper Advertising Bureau and one of the industry's leading researchers, finds that in 1979, 72 percent of whites polled had read a newspaper the previous day; 59 percent of blacks had. Most big-city newspapers do not try to construct a news strategy that delivers *both* the affluent suburban audience and low-income, city-core residents. For most, the strategy is *not* to reach down, in a journalistic sense, but rather to wait until the less affluent achieve middle-class education and income—and become attractive to advertisers. At that point, the elitist newspaper, in content and tone, becomes relevant.

VIEWPOINT 6-5

THE MINORITY VIEW

"Blacks are loyal readers of newspapers. They *are* reading the newspaper. They should be rewarded with fair coverage of minority groups ... lack of education and poverty, not race, are the big obstacles to newspaper reading. ... Minority groups have some doubts about newspaper style and substance and the people who produce it. With blacks, it's a matter of distrusting a predominantly white establishment; with some Hispanics, it's a matter of the tone and emotional level of content."

Lee Stinnett, executive director of American Society of Newspaper Editors, summarizing 1986 study of minority views of the media

EDITORS WHO DON'T BELIEVE

"It's going to take us 20 or 30 years to fully integrate our newsrooms. There are a lot of editors who just don't believe in it because of their own bias or because they say, 'I don't have any minority readers, why should I have any minority staff members?'"

Robert P. Clark, vice president ASNE and vice president for news, Harte-Hanks Newspapers, quoted in the *New York Times,* April 12, 1985, p. 9

Fashioning mass appeal, "downscale" newspapers made fortunes for the Hearsts and other press barons fifty years ago; there is considerable evidence that editors who try that today are headed for financial disaster. Incapable of competing against the *New York Times* for the elitist audience, both the *New York Daily News* and *New York Post* position themselves downscale in content and marketing strategies. The *News* is barely profitable; the *Post* is losing a reported $1 million *monthly*. The *Boston Herald*, fighting the dominant *Boston Globe*, fits itself into a somewhat downscale market niche, and it, too, is financially precarious. Newspaper failures stem from complex causes, but unquestionably their inability to attract the affluent audiences desired by advertisers contributed strongly to the deaths of the *Cleveland Press, Chicago American, Baltimore News-American,* and other "blue-collar" papers.

But if an elitist paper dominates its upscale market and enjoys financial strength, does its editor have an ethical responsibility to reach out to the downscale audience, to strive for better balanced content, a news and information offering that appeals to all sectors of the public?

A Checklist for Balance

An editor or news director intent on doing an ethical, socially responsible job must strive for balanced coverage and presentation of the news. The newspaper or newscast must represent, in "good" as well as "bad" news, the various constituencies of its market.

This does not suggest such silliness as "yardstick editing"—allocating, say, 12 percent of newshole or airtime for news about blacks, because blacks are 12 percent of the local population. But over a prolonged period, news strategy must ensure all sectors of the community are covered.

Many editors are experienced in seeking balance in the sense of fairness—reporting all sides of a controversy. Ensuring geographic balance by covering all areas of a market, country as well as city, is second nature. Producing balance through subject diversity—covering science as well as politics, economics as well as sports—for many is almost instinctive.

However, even casual study of many American newspapers reveals editors don't do as well covering the poor along with the rich, minorities as well as the majority, elderly as well as the young.

Christy L. Bulkeley, longtime Gannett publisher and executive, counsels editors to take strong action in a number of areas, not just news selection, to insure against bias. The following checklist is adapted from her work with ASNE's Minorities Committee (it serves as good guidance, also, for TV news directors):

Hire minorities; inform existing minority staffers of openings so they can get word out on the minority grapevine.

Develop minority community news contacts, including churches, schools, civic clubs, business, and labor groups. Actively seek help from the minority community in opening news contacts for staff; specifically, develop ministers and funeral directors as sources of news on minority engagements, weddings, funerals, and other community news.

Evaluate news content regularly to ensure "nontraditional" organizations such as minority fraternal or civic organizations are fairly covered and given appropriate newshole; regularly monitor photographic coverage to ensure it reflects population mix. Does usage of wire copy reflect needs of all sectors of the community? In monitoring news content, "check handling elsewhere"— that is, in competing media—"when you suspect traditional values interfered with broader understanding and handling of events or issues stories."

Watch for "patterns of unconscious bias" among supervisors, such as favoring one type of employee over another, giving one group most overtime pay, "taking complaints more seriously from traditional groups or neighborhoods than from others..."

Use advisory boards, coffee klatches, and other representative groups drawn from all sectors of the community because they "help broaden perspectives."

Bulkeley also cautions publishers to evaluate *their* activities, ensuring appearances in public reflect a cross-section of the community, that corporate donations and involvement in community affairs are even-handed—and, importantly, that their office doors are open to all groups.[24]

CHAPTER SUMMARY

Operating profitably is essential for any newspaper or broadcast station. Without profit, no news organization can sustain itself. But can ethical, socially responsible journalism flourish in any organization whose owners—whether a private individual or thousands of shareholders of publicly owned corporations— push unceasingly for ever more profit? This is the compelling ethical issue facing policy makers in American newsrooms today.

Growth of large, publicly owned communications conglomerates does not mean automatic degradation of journalistic quality. Some of the nation's finest journalism is produced by groups. But group ownership has brought many non-journalists into key management positions, and journalists interested in ethical, responsible reporting must learn their language. For good journalism is not cheap, and editors and news directors must convince top management to make the first step toward excellence by committing sufficient resources—money, newshole (or air time), and personnel.

A basic problem is that high-quality, responsible journalism does not guarantee financial success. Indeed, some newspaper managers press for higher profits, at least over the short term, by intentionally holding down costs and, thus, journalistic quality.

Many editors are assuming corporate titles in an integrated marketing scheme that makes them responsible in part for not only creating the news product, but, in a sense, also selling it. Though seemingly inevitable, this expansion of editors' roles is highly controversial. Some editors feel corporate titles and duties detract from their function as editors.

Newspapers claim special societal—and constitutional—status because they inform, educate, and uplift. But to meet advertiser demands for more affluent readers, many newspapers are moving "upscale" in journalistic tone and market positioning. These newspapers boast of well-educated, high-income readers. But who serves the poor along with the rich, the elderly along with the young, the minorities as well as the majority? Serious questions of ethics and social responsibility are created because less-attractive readers are left behind by elitist newspapers.

CHAPTER 6

Notes

1 Insightful comments on network news and the value of commercial time are made by Desmond Smith in his, "Is the Sun Setting on Network Nightly News?" *Washington Journalism Review,* January 1986, p. 30. Also see Peter J. Boyer, "After Tie, News Race Heats Up," *New York Times,* April 14, 1986, p. 17. The Richmond figure is from the author's personal experience.

2 From author's personal experience, which includes three years in newspaper acquisitions.

3 Figures for 1986 are from David Shaw, "Foreign Correspondents: It's On-the-job Training," *Los Angeles Times,* July 2, 1986, p. 7. For comparison, executive editor Ben Bradlee of the *Washington Post* stated in a July 11, 1983, letter to the author that his newsroom budget that year was $38 million. The *Los Angeles Times* 1982 newsroom budget was put at $45 million in "Coast Paper Feeling Pinch of Recession," the *New York Times,* Aug. 15, 1982, p. 13. In 1980, the *New York Times* spent $53 million covering the news.

4 Desmond Smith, "Is the Sun Setting on Network Nightly News?" op. cit.

5 A. M. Rosenthal, letter to author, March 28, 1983.

6 Dallas insights were developed by author from a variety of sources, notably extended correspondence and conversations with Burl Osborne, president and editor of the *Dallas Morning News,* 1984–1986.

7 The count on daily (and weekly) newspapers in the United States fluctuates constantly; the author uses *Facts About Newspapers, '86,* American Newspaper Publishers Association, The Newspaper Center, Box 17407, Dulles Airport, Washington, D.C., 20041.

8 A very helpful look at various staff-to-circulation ratios is in "Newsroom Management Committee Report, 1979, Continuing Studies," Associated Press Managing Editors Association, 50 Rockefeller Plaza, New York, N.Y., 10020.

9 Newsprint prices escalated from $179 per metric ton in 1970 to $535 in early 1986; see *Facts About Newspapers, '86,* op. cit., for year-by-year price changes.

10 These figures on AP costs were developed in 1985–1986 by the Associated Press, 50 Rockefeller Plaza, New York, N.Y., 10020, to show the cost-benefit ratio for AP membership.

11 For excellent background see "Editors Need Larger Role in Budgeting Practices, INCFO Told," *Southern Newspaper Publishers Association Bulletin,* July 7, 1983, p. 3, and C. David Rambo, "Excellence," *presstime* November 1984, p. 15.

12 Desmond Smith, "Is the Sun Setting on Network Nightly News?" op. cit., quotes Don Hewitt, "the $1.5 million-a-year executive producer of '60 Minutes,'" as saying the show's profit for CBS in 1985 was $70 million.

13 Alex S. Jones, "Stagnant Revenue Worrying Editors," *New York Times,* April 14, 1986, p. 13.

14 Alex S. Jones, "Newspaper Editors on Business Role," *New York Times,* April 14, 1985, p. 11.

15 *General Policies,* a handbook, Longview Publishing Co., P.O. Box 189, Longview, Wash., 98632.

16 Annual Report 1984, Dow Jones and Company, Inc., World Financial Center, 200 Liberty Street, New York, N.Y., 10281.

17 Walter E. Mattson, Morton Newspaper Forum, Montreal, May 3, 1984.

18 "Our Readers Have Big Appetites For Spending," *Los Angeles Times,* advertisement, *Advertising Age,* May 9, 1983, p. M-15.

19 "Newspapers. Everybody You Want to Reach Reads One," *Boston Globe* advertisement, *Advertising Age,* Jan. 23, 1984.

20 "Fact Is, The People With Money and Influence In Dallas Read *The Morning News,*" advertisement, *Advertising Age,* Aug. 15, 1983, p. 30.

21 "'Post' Time For Revamped Sunday Book," *Advertising Age,* April 21, 1986, p. 35.

22 Penetration figures from "Circulation '84/'85," published by American Newspaper Markets, Inc., P.O. Box 994/22619, Pacific Coast Highway, Malibu, Calif., 90265.

23 Tom Winship, then editor, *Boston Globe,* letter to author, March 11, 1983.

24 Adapted from presentation by Christy C. Bulkeley to New York State Publishers Association, Saratoga Springs, N.Y., Aug. 26, 1980.

7

ETHICS IN THE COUNTINGHOUSE

It is advertising revenue that ranks the U.S. newspaper and television industries among the nation's largest and most profitable. The statistics are impressive: Advertisers spend over $1 billion annually to inform, persuade, and sway; to sell products, services, candidates, ideas, viewpoints, and opinions. Of that amount, daily newspapers get 26.8 percent, or $25.4 billion; television, 21.7 percent, or $20.6 billion. The largest 100 media companies had in 1986 over $52.7 billion in media revenues, plus $37.5 billion more from diverse other businesses.

Individual television and newspaper companies are financial empires. American Broadcasting Co., for example, hit $3.6 billion in media revenue before being absorbed by Capital Cities Communications, a diversified newspaper and broadcast company with $939.7 million revenue of its own. CBS had $4.6 billion in sales, assets of $3.5 billion, and a market value of about $2.7 billion. Gannett, the largest owner of newspapers but also diversified in other businesses, had $2.2 billion in sales and a market value of $4.9 billion.[1]

Predictably, advertising and other business considerations involved in running such wealthy companies can create highly complex ethical questions for the media and, indeed, all of society. As noted in Chapter 6, the primary business imperative of any newspaper or TV operation is to succeed financially, and there are times in the real world of media management when economic self-interest conflicts with wider societal responsibilities and journalistic aims.

So, our examination of *news* ethics must turn to closer scrutiny of advertising and other related *business* sectors—and that we do here in Chapter 7, "Ethics in the Countinghouse."

Because of its enormous financial importance, advertising will be examined first. Then, we will turn to ethical considerations in other corners of the countinghouse—the office of publisher or station manager, plus the personnel ("human resources") and production departments. Each pulls together with news under the integrated marketing concept that focuses a media company's total resources toward reaching common goals. And, each influences newsroom operations, so that relationship must be examined.

Under the integrated marketing concept, advertising's importance to the financial success of any newspaper or television operation creates tight—almost synergistic—linkage between newsroom and advertising department, between editor or news director and sales director. The need to achieve common corporate goals, starting with financial viability, requires editors and news directors to fashion news, information, and entertainment packages that attract readers or viewers who, for their affluence or other attributes, are designated by advertising strategists as important.

Often this is only implicitly agreed between news directors or editors and advertising executives. It is considered very bad form at most newspapers and television networks for the advertising department to explicitly suggest how journalists should treat a story or create the news product. But, as editors and news directors join integrated management teams, *willing cooperation* often develops between departments in joint design of marketing strategy for, among other things, news content, journalistic tone, and audience segments sought.

Nevertheless, there are occasions—and every newsperson knows of some—when advertising considerations overtly intrude into, distort even, the news process. So, let's turn to advertising's role in newspaper and television ethics. We will start with the most basic ethical question: Are the consumer and society truly served by advertising or, as some argue, is advertising wasteful, unnecessary, and simply devoid of any redeeming social value?

ETHICS IN ADVERTISING

Advertising's defenders—newspaper and television executives among them, naturally—argue it is a form of communication that permits consumers to make intelligent choices by providing them with valuable information on products and services. They see advertising as creating consumer desire that stimulates consumption which, in turn, permits the free enterprise system and mass production with all its efficiencies and lower prices.[2] Without advertising, its defenders say, business, commerce, and industry would slow, and the consumption-oriented American economy—the richest in the world—would falter.

Importantly, advertising revenue gives American newspapers and television the *financial* independence from government or political groups that is essential to their *journalistic* independence. Of course, this can create dependence on advertisers and expose newspapers and television operations, particularly those marginally profitable, to economic pressure. The pressure sometimes is intense because in most cities only a few advertisers provide the bulk of a newspaper's revenue. The *New York Daily News,* only narrowly profitable despite its 1.3 million circulation, lost $11 million in annual revenue when just *two* companies, Gimbels and Ohrbachs, closed department stores in New York City in 1986. The paper immediately laid off scores of employees. (Publisher James F. Hoge said, "Survival is at stake and there is no time to lose.") Television networks often have multimillion-dollar contracts with individual—and influential— national advertisers. The importance of this was illustrated in 1987 when Chrysler Corp. objected to the content of an ABC miniseries, *Amerika,* which depicted a Soviet takeover of the United States. Chrysler pulled $7 million worth of commercials from the program, which cost $40 million to produce. However, despite the dependence on advertisers thus created, being able to avoid government or political subsidies gives the American media extraordinary freedom compared to the state-supported (or state-dominated) media of many other countries. The advantages to American society as a whole are far from inconsequential.

Advertising's critics argue:

Advertising adds enormously to "selling costs," eventually paid by the consumers, without adding actual value to goods or services produced.

Advertising, particularly on television, doesn't fill an information need because its often sketchy slogans and thirty-second jingles (such as Coca-Cola's, "It's the real thing") don't truly inform consumers about a product; advertising, in fact, is designed only to sell, not inform, critics say.

Advertising doesn't create consumer desire; rather, it simply shifts desire from one product to another. And this, critics say, negates claims that advertising engenders mass consumption and its resultant benefits to society.

Advertising creates unnecessary materialistic consumer desires psychological in origin and, thus, advertising is manipulative and wasteful. Economist John Kenneth Galbraith claims, for example, an individual's physical needs, such as food and shelter, are finite and quickly met, so much advertising is aimed at creating expandable desire for such things as social acceptability, sexual attractiveness, or personal beauty.[3]

Advertising permits large, financially strong firms to dominate an industry because only they can afford the high cost of advertising. With small firms thus effectively barred from an influential role, the oligopolistic few can raise prices at will, critics say.

Debate over these issues is lengthy but inconclusive, and neither supporters of advertising nor its critics can prove its true *social effect.* Some argue, for example, advertising *helps* small firms enter the market against larger competitors. And, far from clear is whether advertising creates societal values or merely reflects them. Nor is it possible to measure with complete accuracy advertising's impact on *consumer desires.* Some products and services flourish without formal advertising (illicit drugs and prostitution are two).

However, it is possible to get a firmer grasp on *consumer perceptions* of advertising. They include the belief it raises costs, which consumers must pay; that it creates unnecessary demand; and sometimes is untruthful, misleading and often insultingly strident, intrusive, unpleasant, and simplistic. Further, the perception persists that advertisers can influence news coverage in unethical ways. Researcher Ruth Clark finds, "A majority (57 percent) of men and women believe that news coverage is often influenced by advertisers or other business interests. Only 30 percent disagree, and 13 percent are not sure."[4] Television gets even lower marks, consistently ranking behind newspapers in such things as "believability" of advertising (68 percent of respondents in one poll found newspaper advertising "believable and very believable"; only 34 percent so voted for television).[5]

Other evidence of societal concern over advertising erupted in 1986 and 1987 when a civil rights group pressured the *Washington Post* to insist its advertisers show minorities in real estate display ads. The Lawyers' Committee for Civil Rights Under Law said minorities were shown in fewer than 2 percent of the *Post*'s real estate ads from January 1985 to April 1986; the *Post* wrote advertisers they had to show blacks in at least 25 percent of display ads and prominently feature the equal housing logo.

For media executives, all this raises important questions of how to improve public perception of the media, protect corporate self-interest, guard advertising's huge revenues—and still operate in an ethical, socially responsible manner.

ETHICS AND CORPORATE SELF-INTEREST

In advertising departments, more so than in newsrooms, it often is difficult to isolate for examination how newspaper and television executives truly regard many ethical issues. Corporate self-interest has become so intertwined with advertising ethics that it is nearly impossible to tell where ethics begin and self-interest ends.

The primary reason for this linkage, of course, is the enormous financial importance of advertising. But other factors enter the linkage, too.

First, many media executives feel advertising is a significant portion of the total information service provided to readers or viewers. They feel public perception of their newspaper or television operation depends on the accuracy, reliability, tone, and, yes, ethical quality of advertising content, as well as on the quality of the news content. Newspaper executives know, for example, substantial circulation is with readers who buy the paper as much for advertising as news; classified advertising ranks as popular reading material in some community papers. So, many statements of ethical principle in newspaper and television advertising really are part of an image-building public relations or marketing effort.

Second, executives in community newspapering or broadcasting feel advertising contributes heavily to local economic activity, introducing buyer to seller and energizing, if not creating, business and commerce. And that more than subtly changes their view of social responsibility. Although a news executive may see the mission of a newspaper or TV station as *observing* from the side-lines and commenting with disinterested detachment, advertising executives often see it as one of *participating*. In both print and broadcast media, this tends to pull advertising executives and other managers into close cooperation with business and industry, into community "boosterism" ("What's good for this town is good for my newspaper"). In some newsrooms, that would be seen as unprincipled fawning before economic interests, if not an outright sellout. (But, boosterism is not always bad; we'll discuss it later in more detail.)

Third, this is an unprecedentedly litigious era for the American media, and extremely important legal considerations surround advertising activity. So, statements of ethical principle tend to reflect the need for avoiding lawsuits as much as resolving any underlying ethical issues. Also, crucial questions of First Amendment rights arise with increasing frequency in advertising, and, as in the growing controversy over whether tobacco advertising should be made illegal, many statements of ethical principle actually are designed to protect in the advertising department the right to publish that is so important in the news department.

Note the blend of ethical principle and self-interest in these statements:

CBS Television, in the introduction to its highly detailed "Advertising Guidelines," states, "CBS believes that advertising is an important element of the information presented to broadcast audiences. In this connection, CBS recognizes its responsibility to review—for truth, taste and legal requirements—all advertising submitted for broadcast."[6]

The *St. Petersburg* (Fla.) *Times and Evening Independent,* introduces its "Advertising Standards of Acceptability," by stating, "The intent of these standards is to encourage and preserve believability in advertising, to multiply its impact and effectiveness, and to promote accountability in sales and marketing throughout the Suncoast market area. The Times Publishing Company advertising columns are open to competition of all legitimate advertisers."[7]

Robert P. Smith, longtime head of the *New York Times* Advertising Acceptability Department and a thoughtful commentator on principled advertising policies, is more specific:

VIEWPOINT 7-1

ADVERTISING AND THE FIRST AMENDMENT

"[A]dvertisers and agencies...have come to prize the freedom of speech that you and your editors have protected for us for so long. So, believe with me. Act with me. Defend with me, when I say that the freedom of expression belongs to the advocates as well as the observers. Know that any limitation on the freedom to advertise is a direct obstacle to your freedom to cover a trial, write an editorial or publish a political column."

Louis T. Hagopian, chairman of N W Ayer, Inc., the oldest U.S. advertising agency, in speech to American Newspaper Publishers Association, April 22, 1986, San Francisco

The character of a newspaper is determined not only by its news and editorial content, but also by the advertising it publishes. Those that accept inaccurate, misleading, deceptive, or offensive advertising, or that tolerate slipshod performance by advertisers run the risk of demeaning their most valuable asset—their credibility. That's just plain bad business.

Don't get me wrong. It's gratifying to be on "the side of the angels" for its own sake. But nowhere is it written that concern for the welfare of the reader and sound business practice are mutually exclusive. On the contrary, self-regulation and discipline with regard to the acceptance of advertising is about as good an example as you will find to illustrate the profitability of principle.[8]

Against that general background, let's look at how newspapers and television police their own advertising content.

Three Areas of Ethical Screening

Many newspapers and television operations attempt to protect the sanctity of their advertising as zealously as they guard the ethical character of their news content. They do so with codes of acceptability that screen advertising activity in all three broad aspects of communication:

First, codes address *the originator or authors of advertising,* attempting to prevent deception by the manufacturer of a product, its advertising agency, or anyone else involved in creating an ad. NBC says "ultimate responsibility for advertising rests with the advertiser," and that advertising agencies "should consult the Broadcast Standards Department in advance of production." It adds, "NBC accepts advertising only after securing satisfactory evidence of the integrity of the advertiser...." ABC reserves the "right to investigate the advertiser and the accuracy of all statements and claims made in commercial copy." Codes insist advertisers not only avoid outright falsehood, but also deception through misleading ads.[9]

Second, however, codes by their very nature—and, sometimes, explicitly—commit the newspaper or network, as *the medium of advertising,* to accept responsibility for truth, good taste, and legality. The *St. Petersburg* (Fla.) *Times and Evening Independent* says in its acceptability code that it "does not, and will not, knowingly accept any advertisement that may be misleading, deceptive, fraudulent, unlawful, is immorally suggestive or in bad taste. Any advertising which tends to destroy the confidence of our readers is unacceptable. In order to fully serve the advertiser, the Times

---

VIEWPOINT 7-2

GOOD TASTE, TIME, AND AUDIENCE

"All advertising messages should be prepared with proper consideration of the type of product being advertised, the time of broadcast, and the audience to whom the advertising is directed. Good taste must always govern the content, placement, and presentation of announcements."

ABC Advertising Standards and Guidelines

Publishing Company must have the full confidence of its readers. Truth and good taste must prevail.''[10] Paul Ruffin, classified ad manager of the *Eugene* (Ore.) *Register-Guard,* says he applies to advertising the same standards of truth applied to news: "What it comes right down to is a person delivering wood and shorting some 85-year-old widow woman. She calls me....I find out what happened....If [the advertisers] do not make it up or give her money back, I will not accept their advertising anymore.''[11]

Third, codes address the *audience for advertising.* Essentially, most codes consider advertising's acceptability within the context of the audience at which it is aimed. Television network codes clearly state, for example, that advertising acceptable for an adult audience might not be acceptable for an audience of children unable to filter out hyperbole or misleading nuances easily recognized by adults. CBS's code states, "CBS recognizes the special obligations it has as a responsible broadcaster to insure that commercial announcements directed to children are not misleading in any way.''[12]

The Price Tag on Ethics

None of this works, of course, unless management is willing to make financial sacrifice for ethical principle. Substantial revenue can be lost if ads are rejected on ethical grounds or the newsroom proceeds with coverage offensive to a major advertiser. Newspaper and television lore is burdened with examples of managers who caved in before that harsh reality. But many stand firm on principle, even at considerable cost.

The *Wall Street Journal,* for example, diligently reported on Mobil Corp., and business activities of its executives and their families despite clear signs this would cause trouble. In 1984, citing "five years of problems," Mobil announced it would not give the *Journal* any information on its corporate affairs, wouldn't grant interviews to *Journal* reporters, and would cancel its advertising in the newspaper. That cost the *Journal* advertising worth $500,000 annually, a significant but hardly fatal loss for the hugely successful *Journal* ($670 million total revenue, $185 million operating profit in 1985).[13] Lawrence Armour, *Journal* corporate relations director said, "The point is, we're not in the business of acting as cheerleaders for corporate America and sometimes this offends certain people. But they seem to understand and they seem to quickly get over their immediate annoyances....''

The *Journal* tangled in 1954 with powerful General Motors Corp., the nation's largest corporation in sales and always one of the biggest spenders on advertising. A *Journal* reporter obtained details of new cars GM planned for the following year, a tightly guarded secret. Furious GM executives canceled all advertising in the *Journal.* The boycott lasted just one month, and years later it became apparent there had been an unexpected bonus in the affair for the *Journal.* In 1985, vice chairman Donald Macdonald of the *Journal* commented, "It put us on the map. GM's actions were on radio and in newspapers all over the country. It gave us credibility. It said you couldn't buy the *Wall Street Jour-*

nal's news columns.'' Said executive editor Frederick Taylor: ''Millions of people who hadn't heard of us and the millions who had knew we weren't patsies for business. It turned out to be the best thing that could have happened.''[14]

Despite its importance, Mobil and GM advertising represented just a fraction of the *Journal*'s total revenue. How about smaller newspapers operating closer to the thin line between profit and loss and which, consequently, might jeopardize their very financial viability in a dispute with advertisers? This question surfaced in a convention of newspaper publishers and editors. Katharine Graham, chairman of the *Washington Post* ($426 million ad revenue in 1985), acknowledged small-town editors and publishers have ''a particularly tough job because they cannot afford to run the risk of lost advertising or a costly libel suit.'' Publisher Virgil Fassio of the *Seattle Post-Intelligencer* said metro dailies can ''let the chips fall where they may but small-town publishers have to look businessmen in the eye every day. They don't have our anonymity.'' Robert Phelps, vice president of Affiliated Publications, owner of the *Boston Globe,* said, ''The most ethical newspapers are the richest and most powerful. They can withstand economic buffeting.''[15]

Nevertheless, some small-town newspapers can take ethical stands because they gain strength against advertiser pressure when acquired by larger groups. The 36,000-circulation *Jackson* (Tenn.) *Sun* was boycotted in 1985 by auto dealers, among the largest local retail advertisers for any community newspaper, because it published articles on how car buyers can negotiate lower prices. Behind the *Sun* were the huge resources of its group owner, Gannett Co., which owns nearly 100 dailies with more than 6 million total circulation. Publisher Michael Craft said Gannett was ''supportive'' of his stand that the auto dealers had made ''an unwise business decision.''[16]

Independently owned newspapers must stand alone on matters of principle in advertising acceptability. But sometimes they find the cost of ethical conduct not as high as expected. The *St. Joseph* (Mo.) *Gazette and News-Press,* 45,000 morning circulation and 15,000 afternoon, instituted an advertising screening code and calculated its loss from rejected ads was less than 1 percent, of annual revenue. Larger newspapers, television stations, and networks don't reveal how much revenue they turn away in rejected ads. But it should be noted that 1 percent of the *Wall Street Journal*'s $670 million 1985 revenue would have been, of course, $6.7 million. That figure undoubtedly is far below what the *Journal* actually spurned; it will accept only ads ''not offensive to good taste or public decency,'' and unacceptable categories include some of the most heavily advertised services and products—investment advisory services, lingerie, plus any drugs, cosmetics or other substances applied to the skin, and firearms.[17] At the *Washington Post* in 1985, 1 percent of advertising revenue would have been $4.2 million. To illustrate the impact on smaller papers, a 75,000-circulation daily could have about $14 million to $15 million ad revenue annually, and, of course, 1 percent of that would be $140,000 to $150,000.[18]

Precise dollar figures did emerge from one smaller newspaper's loss of advertising due to news coverage. In Albany, New York, a county official angered over the *Albany Times-Union*'s account of the Democratic patronage system withdrew from the 87,000-circulation paper legal advertising worth $60,000 annually.[19]

Ethics in advertising can carry a stiff price tag, obviously. For some media executives, the price is worth paying.[20] At the *New York Times,* Robert Smith said of his acceptability program, "Top management must make a commitment to be selective and realize that this will lead to a loss of some ad revenue. You can't have it both ways: all the lineage that's offered *and* a selective policy on ad acceptance."[21]

WHAT'S ACCEPTABLE AND WHAT ISN'T

Broad unanimity is emerging among newspapers on which types of advertising will be accepted and which won't. Many products and services are taboo, and others are deemed suitable for advertising only under certain conditions. Television is developing even stronger consensus and, particularly at the network level, has extremely detailed codes.

In its "Advertising Policy Manual" for employees, the *Miami Herald* states, "A newspaper is an invited guest in the home. Therefore, in order to maintain an atmosphere of good taste and believability for both readers and advertisers, The Miami Herald Publishing Company holds to the following restrictions." It lists thirteen categories of unacceptable advertising and twenty-two acceptable "subject to restrictions."[22]

The *St. Petersburg* (Fla.) *Times and Evening Independent*—like many newspapers—sets a moral tone for its "Advertising Standards of Acceptability": "No advertising is acceptable which, in the publisher's judgment, will irritate the sensibilities of, or result in harm or insult to, any segment of the Times Publishing Company's wide readership. Any advertising that casts unfavorable reflection, directly or indirectly, upon any individual, group, race, creed, religion, organization, institution, competitive merchandise, business or profession is likewise unacceptable." The code rules out advertising "that may be misleading, deceptive, fraudulent, unlawful, is immorally suggestive or in bad taste. Any advertising which tends to destroy the confidence of our readers is unacceptable."[23]

Inevitably, setting themselves up as guardians against "immorally suggestive" advertising can make censors of the media. In 1986, newspapers and television stations around the country refused to accept advertising on a film titled, *Sexual Perversity in Chicago.* The film was renamed, *About Last Night....*

For years, the media rejected condom advertising on the grounds that condoms were birth control devices considered immoral by some or, simply, because the product dealt with an "indelicate" subject offensive to many. However, in view of increasingly explicit news coverage of sex and sexually transmitted diseases, an advertising policy change was easy for many newspapers and TV stations in 1987, when health officials called for condom advertising as a means of combatting the spread of AIDS. For many advertising directors, condom ads stressing disease control were acceptable—if they didn't mention birth control. Condom companies quickly seized on the difference and soon began producing ad copy featuring, for example, a young woman saying, "I'll do a lot for love. But I'm not ready to die for it." (On March 4, 1987, with its advertising department starting to accept condom ads, the *New York Times* newsroom broke new journalistic ground with a lengthy article by health writer Jane Brody describing in explicit detail how heterosexuals and homosexuals alike could use condoms to avoid sexually transmitted diseases.)

Broadly, newspaper codes reject advertising which:

Violates any law (including, importantly, libel) or encourages violation. Many, for example, refuse ads for devices motorists use to detect police radar.

Is untruthful, misleading, indecent, offensive, or in poor taste. In every case, the publisher retains the right to interpret the impact or meaning of advertising or, indeed, whether to run it at all.

Begs, offers matrimony, escort services, or suspect "companionship." (*Newsday,* Times Mirror Corporation's 600,000-circulation daily on Long Island, publishes many "personals" but rejects any deemed "flaky" or "kinky.") Adult bookstore ads are rejected. The *St. Petersburg Times and Evening Independent* accept no amusement ads "that state or imply conduct that is considered morally or socially unacceptable." X-rated movie ads "can be no larger than 1 column by 1 inch in size and cannot contain illustrations." The newspapers reserve the right to change X-rated film titles considered suggestive.

Offers get-rich-quick schemes or something of value for nothing.

Employs "bait and switch" tactics under which the plan is not to sell the advertised product at the price listed—or at all—but, rather, to entice customers and then offer another product or service (sometimes this can be illegal as well as unethical).

Promotes a lottery—a scheme involving a price, a chance, or a consideration—which is prohibited from the U.S. Mail.

Offers mail-order weapons, bust developers, baldness remedies, diet pills, contraceptives, or, in the words of the *Miami Herald,* ads "injurious to the health or morals of a reader." (The *New York Times* also tries to do its bit in protecting the health of endangered species of animals; it won't accept ads for fur or leather products made from their hides.)

Is intended as a joke or hoax.

Among advertising accepted only under certain conditions:

Employment advertising must actually offer employment and state conditions. Most papers reject any that even implies religious, nationality, sex, race, or age preferences.

Political advertising usually carries many restrictions, including prohibitions against political charges made so close to an election they cannot be answered. (Without exception, newspapers require that politicians pay in advance.)

Religious advertising must not attack other religions or imply "faith healing."

Business opportunity advertising undergoes detailed scrutiny. Many newspapers require advertisers to submit detailed verification of claims made in ad copy along with proof they conform to relevant state and local laws. The aim is to weed out fraudulent ''pie-in-the-sky'' offers.

Service advertising is severely restricted. The *Tampa* (Fla.) *Tribune,* for example, requires building contractors to include in any advertising the number of their competency license issued by the city. This policy also was established at the St. Petersburg papers after their own reporters found 25 percent of their home improvement advertisers lacked the necessary licensing. Many newspapers require proof of license from insurance companies, new car dealers, investment advisors, and real estate brokers.

It's not known how many newspapers have written codes of acceptance or subscribe to the acceptability provisions of the Advertising Code of American Business (see addenda at end of this book). However, the American Newspaper Publishers Association counted in 1985 more than 300 refusing at least one type of advertising. About 100, mostly small dailies, refuse liquor ads.[24]

For the entire industry, a major question is advertising of another controversial product—tobacco.

Tobacco Ads: The Controversy Grows

On their front pages, American newspapers report the latest study linking use of tobacco to cancer.

On their editorial pages, American newspapers sound the alarm, calling for massive research into cancer and its causes.

Throughout their pages, American newspapers publish advertisements for tobacco products, including cigarettes, which, according to no less than the Surgeon General of the United States, are a deadly product.

A moral contradiction? Are newspapers failing in their ethical and social responsibility by helping promote a product which, much of medical science says, *kills when used as intended*? Or, is tobacco advertising legitimate exercise of commercial free speech? Should advertising be illegal for a product that is legally manufactured and sold? Forces on both sides of the issue are gathering for a fight.

The influential American Medical Association and American Cancer Society have joined the rising demand for a total ban on tobacco advertising. In 1986, the Supreme Court upheld legislation in Puerto Rico restricting advertising by gambling casinos and thus held state legislatures can restrict advertising of even legal activities or products if they are considered undesirable. Antismoking forces see that ruling as a step toward banning all forms of tobacco advertising.

Resisting a ban are the American Newspaper Publishers Association, American Civil Liberties Union, and others who see in it a threat against commercial free speech and, thus, against the First Amendment. ANPA, which packs its own public relations wallop in that it represents 1,393 newspapers with 90 percent of U.S. daily newspaper circulation, links all forms of advertising to the wider constitutional right: "Commercial speech also is protected under the First Amendment...legal products and services should be legal to advertise...governmental restrictions on advertising content often infringe unnecessarily upon commercial speech...."[25] In pursuing the First Amendment argument, ANPA also argues against expanding laws dictating the type of health warnings that tobacco products and advertisements must carry.

It will be some time before First Amendment implications of the controversy are clarified. A few months after the Supreme Court ruling, an administrative law judge in Washington ruled for dismissal of a Federal Trade Commission complaint that R.J. Reynolds Tobacco Co., engaged in "false or misleading" advertising in connection with tobacco products. Judge Montgomery K. Hyun said the ad was "an editorial" which enjoyed First Amendment protection, not commercial speech which has "limited protection" and is subject to government regulation. The judge said the ad "does not name any brand or list prices or discuss desirable attributes of a product or show where the product may be purchased" but, rather, expressed Reynolds' views in the argument about smoking and health. Hyun's ruling was taken by many in the media to affirm First Amendment rights of businesses and set an important precedent against government regulation of advertising that advocates controversial arguments.

Antismoking forces were quick to argue the Constitution's framers never intended it should protect such things as tobacco advertising. Joe B. Tye, president of an antismoking group, wrote for the *Wall Street Journal:* "Cigarette makers like to frame the issue as one of freedom of speech. Any attempt to restrict their efforts to promote smoking is portrayed as a violation of First Amendment rights and the first step toward mass censorship of commercial speech. In fact, no other industry has abused freedom of speech so egregiously. For 60 years, cigarette firms have used unfounded health claims to encourage people to smoke despite the risk of harm."

Tobacco generally is the third most lucrative national advertising category for newspapers (behind transportation/travel and automotive). In 1984, it yielded $236 million, but that was just 1 percent of all newspaper advertising that year. About $40,000 annually was lost by two newspapers that voluntarily dropped tobacco advertising in 1985—the *Salina* (Kan.) *Journal* and the *Whig-Standard* of Kingston, Ontario, Canada. It cost the *Saturday Evening Post* much more—about $400,000—to take that step in 1983.

Television's Ethical Consensus

Television's approach to ethics and social responsibility in advertising is one of strong consensus established primarily by the three major networks in a relatively brief period when the infant medium was subject to sharply focused external pressures.

The detailed advertising guidelines published by ABC, NBC, and CBS are strikingly similar in content, and clearly reflect pressures on television since its development as a commercial medium—really beginning, we should remember, only in the 1950s. Newspapers, by contrast, have had many decades to develop their ethical consensus. Four sources of pressure are instrumental in shaping television's stance:

1 The law. The Federal Communications Commission can lift broadcast licenses (though it rarely does) for rules infractions, and along with other federal agencies strongly influences advertising practices. To some extent, close federal scrutiny prevents the television industry from effectively regulating its own activities. For example, the National Association of Broadcasters in 1982 dropped its code suggesting limits on number and length of commercials after a federal court found the guidelines violated the Sherman Antitrust Act. The powerful Federal Trade Commission also is particularly watchful of television advertising.

The point is that no executive in broadcast ever can forget the federal presence. It can be argued that for many in television conforming to *legal* requirements has become an end in itself that, in fact, has stunted individual or corporate development of *ethical* thinking in advertising (as well as news). Television, unlike newspapers, for example, faces no ethical dilemma over cigarette advertising; the federal government kicked it off the airways. Certainly, network guidelines in advertising are heavily weighted to ensure legal and regulatory—as distinct from ethical—requirements are met.

2 Special interest groups. The law is a reflection of societal attitudes, of course, so regulatory surveillance of television can be regarded as societal pressure. But there is more to it than that. Because of its amazing ubiquity—over 98 percent of all American homes have sets and the average TV is on (in 1985) a little more than seven hours daily—society in general and special interest groups in particular have policed television with an intensity that causes every advertising executive to place pleasing them second only to conforming to the law. Ralph Nader and the consumerism of the 1960s, for example, focused strongly on television advertising content, truthfulness, accuracy, and impact on audiences, particularly children. Such pressure, again, can stunt purely *ethical* development in television advertising either by individuals or corporate entities. Placating the Federal Trade Commission *and* consumer advocates can be a full-time job for anyone. Importantly, such strong societal pressure can lead television to steps that might appear to be self-restraining ethical volunteerism, but which really are designed to fend off special interest or legal pressure. For example, the networks reject liquor advertising and tightly restrict beer and wine commercials (ever see one of those happy guys actually *drink* a beer in a TV commercial?). With beer and wine commercials worth (in 1985) more than $900 million annually, the networks want to preempt growing societal pressure for a total ban on *any* advertising of alcoholic beverages on the airways. Because most stations are owned by or affiliated with a network, the Big Three set the consensus for the entire industry.

3 Money.   For any advertising medium, money is pressure. And television advertising represents money, lots of it. As one example, NBC charged $350,000 to $400,000 for each thirty-second commercial on *The Cosby Show* in 1986 and 1987. That situation comedy was worth nearly $3 million *per episode* to NBC. How severe must an ethical crisis be to permit tinkering with nearly $3 million? Very severe, is the answer. In March 1987, NBC preempted Cosby to carry the first press conference President Reagan held during four and a half months of the Iran/Contra affair. Other networks also shoved aside entertainment programming that night. But the networks made clear they would do so only relatively few times, and only to clear the way for truly major news stories. One NBC executive told the *Washington Journalism Review* that the network's news department interrupted entertainment scheduling forty to fifty times annually, at a cost of $20,000 to $750,000 in lost revenue. When President Reagan requested prime time for a television report to the American people following his Geneva summit in 1985 with Soviet Premier Mikhail S. Gorbachev, NBC had to reschedule *Night Court* at a cost of more than $500,000. However, in 1986, all three networks refused Reagan's request for airtime to explain why he was asking Congress to vote $100 million in aid to Contra rebels fighting in Nicaragua. It was a compelling news story, for the next day Congress approved the aid and moved the United States perceptibly deeper into the Central American conflict. The networks explained Reagan had nothing new to say. Regularly scheduled (and lucrative) entertainment shows were broadcast. To the law and societal pressure, obviously, we must add dollar signs as instrumental in influencing ethical development in television advertising.

4 Competition.   There is a fierce fight for TV advertising at both the national and local levels. Nationally, the three major networks, joined recently by Cable News Network, battle not only newspapers, magazines, direct mail, and other competitors, but, particularly, each other. Conversely, until new technology recently permitted the *Wall Street Journal,* the *New York Times,* and *USA Today* to launch truly national editions, there was no newspaper competition at that level. And, whereas most cities long ago were reduced to one newspaper, direct, head-on competition in television is fierce at the local level. Most cities have three network affiliates, an independent or two, public broadcasting, and a plethora of cable channels—all fighting for the same ad dollar. Thus, the struggle for audience is all-consuming. Whoever—*or whatever*—pulls in most viewers wins because the higher the ratings, the higher the ad rates. Now, if Cosby attracts well over 50 million viewers to NBC of a Thursday evening, as he did in 1986, will CBS or ABC that night feature newsy public service programming? Of course not; that would surrender the *entire* evening to NBC. At the local level, if one station's news achieves higher ratings with a jazzy set, handsome young anchors, the happiest chatter in town—and a decided soft pedal on serious, deep-dig journalism—will its competitors counter with craggy, decidedly unhandsome, but truly experienced reporters who go for serious news? Of course not, again. Thus is consensus established in local TV news programming and attitudes. Except for a relatively few stations that "counterprogram" to be different, the drive for ratings, which translate into advertising dollars, frequently leads to "formula" journalism that is easy to watch and acceptable to the widest possible audience. And if that means an "Action News" format of blown-dry anchors, helicopters in the sky, and ambush interviews down here, so be it.

Leveling with Reader and Viewer

An important ethical consideration in advertising is whether newspapers or television truly inform readers and viewers about what is being placed before them. Neither medium is above letting advertisers slip one over on the audience, now and then.

Networks, for example, ban commercials that attempt to lend products respectability or authenticity by using pseudo reporters, fake physicians, or phony scientists to do the pitch. Gone is the distinguished gentleman wearing a doctor's white coat and standing in a "laboratory" while pitching aspirin. Yet, television permits commercials implying the way to happiness with friends is to drink beer, that buying a new car will get a fellow a beautiful woman, that eating *this* cereal, not *that* one, promises health and good times. It's in the very nature of sight-and-sound advertising that gullible viewers are thus bamboozled—and television lets it happen.

Many newspapers permit a con job on readers with "advertorials," advertisements made up to look like news copy, or an advertising insert that looks for all the world like a special news supplement. Ad executives love advertising that looks like news because, as one put it, "people are five times more likely to read editorial as ads."[26] The ethical way to handle such copy is to clearly label it as advertising and set it in type distinctly different from type used in news columns. Special inserts should carry editor's notes informing readers the copy is advertising, *and* stating whether the copy was prepared by qualified newspersons, advertising employees, or outsiders such as stringers or ad agency writers.

The *New York Times* did that with an insert on condominiums. It attached the notice: "Advertising Supplement to *The New York Times*" and each page was labeled "advertisement." The insert carried this notice: "This advertising supplement is sponsored by participating advertisers. The promotional material was prepared under the direction of Ernest Dickinson and did not involve *The Times* reporting or editing staff."[27]

Leveling with readers and viewers in financial advertising got a big boost—but more from federal truth-in-lending laws than the collective conscience of the advertising world. It's now possible to read or view some advertising and figure out, for example, the true annual percentage rate you'll pay on a loan or time purchase. But it's also possible to see almost nightly a salesman banging on a car hood and shouting at the camera, "Only $100 a month"—and neglecting to say whether that is monthly for nearly a lifetime.

For broadcasting, conscience and the law clashed for decades over "advocacy" or controversial issue advertising. For 38 years, the FCC's "fairness doctrine" required broadcasting to permit opposing sides to respond to *news* coverage of controversial issues, a principle held to apply also to advertising. Thus, the networks and most television stations rejected issue advertising. This, of course, put television in the position of denying access by proponents of controversial ideas and denied viewers the opportunity to see or hear them. The FCC abolished the "fairness doctrine" as unconstitutional in 1987. Newspapers vigorously defend their right to reject any advertisement, but most open their pages to issue advertising. Says the *New York Times* Smith: "We've published opinion advertisements representing a wide range of public discourse—from the John Birch Society to the Communist Party. In our view, the First Amendment does not only guarantee a newspaper's right to disseminate news or publish editorials and commercial messages but it also guarantees the public's right to enter into open discussion in the realm of ideas."[28] In 1986, the *Times* opened its op-ed page for a lengthy article written by J. Peter Grace, chairman of W. R. Grace and Company, and his attorney, Joseph A. Califano, Jr., complaining that the networks rejected a commercial the company made on the danger of a growing federal budget deficit. The article said in part:

> [A]ll three networks said in essence that the advertisement deals with a controversial issue of public importance that should be dealt with only through the process of journalism by news professionals. We find that position indefensible in a free and democratic society.
>
> One of this country's guiding principles has been the view that it is essential to have more debate on public issues, not less. By closing down this kind of commercial advertising, the networks arbitrarily limit an important and vital avenue for debate.... The networks sell commercial time to advertise soap, deodorants, cars, hamburgers, beer and wine. Can it really be argued that allowing the same time to be used at the same rates to convey facts or ideas on important public issues will be detrimental to the interests of the country or the three networks?[29]

The *Times* used its news pages to level with readers when it, along with other newspapers, was hoaxed by a bogus advertisement. A lengthy article explained why the *Times* didn't properly check the origin of the ad that "seemed to attribute anti-Israel sentiments to six relief organizations [which] later disavowed any connection with it." The ad was signed by a group that gave an address later found to be false. What it boiled down to, the *Times* informed its readers, was that checking such things prior to publication "was impeded by the fact that many advertising executives, advertisers and executives of newspapers held differing views as to whose job it was."[30]

That may not have made readers any happier, but it *did* level with them on what went wrong. A similarly responsible explanation was published by the *Athens* (Ga.) *Banner-Herald and Daily News* when a reader wrote complaining about content. Executive editor Hank Johnson told his readers in a Sunday column:

> She cancelled her subscription, in part she said, "because of our disgust at the lack of objectivity of your 'Dining Out' column. Every week, the column gushes over a

different restaurant. It appears that the restaurants must pay to have this column run, since we have yet to see a complaint about food/service—quite unrealistic. This is typical small-town "good boy" reporting and we do not wish to support it through subscription."

The letter writer had stumbled on a flagrant violation of advertising ethics. "Dining Out" was an advertorial, cleverly written and laid out to appear as news copy. Johnson's explanation to readers continued:

> Well, as a matter of fact, the "Dining Out" column...is a paid advertisement. The restaurants whose ads appear on the page sign a contract to advertise on that page. In addition to the ad which runs every week each restaurant is periodically allowed to tell its own story.
>
> Given those circumstances, it is easy to understand why the letter writer had never seen a complaint in the "Dining Out" column. Our mistake was in assuming that it would be obvious to readers that the description of the restaurant, its food and service, was not objective and clearly was not a straight news story or legitimate review.
>
> Steps have been taken to correct that.
>
> While we're clearing up misunderstandings, I should point out that the "Business Review" page that runs in both Monday papers is done the same way as "Dining Out."[31]

That's leveling with readers, and it is the way newspapers should deal with the deplorably unethical advertorial.

ETHICS IN OTHER CORNERS OF THE COUNTINGHOUSE

Discussing ethics in all departments of a newspaper or television network is beyond this book's scope. Nevertheless, some business activities, in addition to advertising, strongly influence what happens in a newsroom, and we should look at them.

It is important to emphasize that newspapers and, certainly, television are not in the news and advertising business only. Both deal in entertainment, and newspapers are in the "manufacturing" and transportation business as well. So, we must take a wider view to understand why newsrooms come under pressure from other departments, and why publishers and network executives sometimes act more like business than news executives.

Note these characteristics of the newspaper and television industries:

Both are managed mostly by *profit-oriented* individuals whose professional success depends on their ability to extract maximum economic reward from their markets. This sometimes leads managers to identify more closely with outside sources of revenue and community than their own newsrooms.

Both are *high-cost* industries. ABC's production costs alone were $140 million for the 1984 winter and summer Olympics.[32] One hour of entertainment programming can cost $1 million, a miniseries more. Newspapers' basic raw material, newsprint, is over $570 per metric ton, and dailies alone use more than 8.8 million tons annually.[33]

Both industries are *personnel-intensive*. Newspapers employ more than 453,000 persons.[34] CBS in 1986 had 1,300 in its news division alone.[35] And, there is no way to automate a reporter on the beat, or an editor on the desk.

Newspapers face the enormous challenge of *"manufacturing" and distributing* 62.7 million copies of newspapers daily, 58.8 million on Sundays. Circulation of weeklies is 47.5 million. Millions of free circulation papers and "shoppers" are churned out.

Both industries are *high profile,* exposed daily to public critique, subject to market and societal pressure, and thus are image-conscious.

Let's look more closely at the implications in all this for conduct in the newsroom.

Ethics in the Executive Suite

Media managers today must perform efficiently and profitably in their business responsibilities or soon be unemployed. The "rising tide of shareholder expectation" and other imperatives of successful business leadership force many newspaper and television managers to put profit first; everything else is second— sometimes including ethical, socially responsible journalism.

Exceptions are those lucky managers whose organizations are enlightened (and profitable) enough to follow good, sound journalism as a route to financial success. But even they must keep their business priorities straight. It was *important* for Alvah Chapman, chairman of Knight-Ridder, to be able to inform his shareholders that company newspapers won seven Pulitzer Prizes in 1986. It was *imperative* that he announce corporate profits were up. (Chapman, an extremely successful executive, of course consistently had victories in both sectors.)

Because of the huge profits involved and the sheer business complexity in the media today, a process of executive selection, under way since communications companies began going public in the mid-1960s, has pushed nonnews executives into the top ranks of almost all major communications firms. The perceived need is for executives skilled in finance, accounting, long-range planning, assets deployment, advertising strategy—and, it would be nice if they know something about news or at least are interested in it. If there is a network or major television station headed by a career newsperson, the author doesn't know of it.

And, note the career backgrounds of those managing major publicly owned companies built primarily around newspaper properties: two (Washington Post Co. and the Times Mirror Co.) are led by men trained as lawyers; two (the New York Times Co. and the Tribune Co.) by executives who came up through production; three (Affiliated, Belo, and Media General) by executives trained on the business side, mostly at family-owned newspapers. Two major companies—Dow Jones and Gannett—are led by executives with substantial careers in news. Knight-Ridder has a president trained in news, although its chairman came up through the business side.

Rising mostly from nonnews origins and forced into profit-minded, high-profile roles, top managers often assume community responsibilities that make it difficult for them to simultaneously serve as objective, dispassionate news executives. Publishers and station managers serve the Boy Scouts, United Way, and many other civic organizations, and problems can arise. One survey showed 49 percent of responding publishers acknowledge their involvement in local community groups poses conflicts of interest (42 percent said items published in their newspapers caused them "professional embarrassment" with the groups they joined). But that doesn't hold them back: 90 percent said they were involved with local business or professional organizations, 76 percent with charitable groups. Half believed their sales managers should be *required* to join local business organizations; fewer made that demand on editors, circulation managers, or production chiefs.[36]

The dilemma: Even if assured free rein, do reporters feel completely free to investigate a charity organization headed by their boss? Do editorial writers criticize with impunity a city planning board chaired by their publisher? Importantly, *does the public perceive* reporters and editorial writers capable of fair, dispassionate coverage of activities involving the publisher? (See Case Study 7-1 for how one editor handled a story involving his boss.)

VIEWPOINT 7-3

'TWAS ALWAYS THUS?

"One of the basic troubles with radio and television news is that both instruments have grown up as an incompatible combination of show business, advertising and news.... The top management of the networks, with few notable exceptions, has been trained in advertising, research, or show business.... They also make the final and crucial decisions having to do with news and public affairs. Frequently, they have neither the time nor the competence to do this. There is no suggestion here that networks or individual stations should operate as philanthropies. But I can find nothing in the Bill of Rights or the Communications Act which says they must increase their net profits each year, lest the Republic collapse."

Edward R. Murrow, CBS's famed correspondent, in a 1958 speech to the Radio-Television News Directors Association

---

Some newspaper publishers try to carry the concurrent title of editor; television managers often read station editorials. Michael Craft, both publisher and editor of Gannett's *Jackson* (Tenn.) *Sun,* warns against this:

> Involvement with the business community and government cause some of the most difficult ethical and soul-wrenching problems. Instincts as a newspaperman tell you that there are stories involved with your activities as publisher. An editor would jump at some of the stories or tips, sending reporters immediately on the trail of a good story.

CASE STUDY 7-1

WHEN BAD NEWS STRIKES HOME

You are managing editor of a daily newspaper whose owner is a prominent local real estate developer. His wife is publisher. Your reporters investigate rumors of wrongdoing on the town's planning and zoning commission. Officials eventually uncover what they describe as a bribery conspiracy aimed at getting zoning laws changed so developers can construct an apartment complex.

One person arrested is owner of your newspaper. He is charged with conspiracy to commit bribery and released on $2,500 bond.

Questions: Do you publish the story? If not, why not? If so, how prominently? Would you mention the link between your newspaper and one of the persons charged?

Chris Powell, managing editor of the 44,000-circulation *Enfield* (Conn.) *Journal Inquirer,* confronted those issues head-on in 1986 when it happened in his town. He broke the story with a front-page headline and a lengthy page-3 story. The second paragraph pointed out that one

of the men charged was the newspaper's owner. The next day, Powell published a follow-up story on page 5—with a page-1 box directing readers to the story.

Powell told a *New York Times* reporter his paper "has pursued the story aggressively and will continue to do so.... I suspect to an outsider it may look like a bigger deal to us than it really is. We've been covering our owner's business interests for many years. His instructions to us always have been to play it straight, and we always have."

Powell said the owner issued no instructions on how to handle the story, adding: "He didn't start this newspaper as a moneymaker. He started it because he had a certain view of the world and wanted to raise hell."

What do you think? In this context, was the owner's connection with the paper *really* significant to readers? Did Powell overreact and in fact create doubt about his paper through handling of this story?

But the editor-publisher is torn by 1) his involvement in the first place in something that might be secret or confidential and 2) his inner cravings and title as a newspaper editor to get cracking on a possibly good story.

Editors-publishers must ask whether their ethics will permit having both jobs and then how they will perform when conflicts do arise.

For him, Craft said, "editor" is a "title without substance."[37]

Richard Buzbee, both editor and publisher of the *Hutchinson* (Kan.) *News,* said, "To be sure, there is danger of conflicts of interest. There's a certain challenge in writing an editorial reaming the mayor, and then [as publisher] sitting across the dinner table from him at Rotary that day."[38] The *real* challenge under such circumstances, of course, is to write the editorial as the facts dictate without even subconsciously pulling punches—and convince the public that you are—regardless of who the dinner companions will be. (Note in Case Study 7-2 how a sense of community obligation created a serious ethical problem for publisher Richard G. Capen, Jr., of the *Miami Herald.*[39])

Active involvement by managers in politics creates ethical conflict. Warren Lerude, longtime Gannett executive and journalism professor, said the main questions are: Firstly, "How newspaper publishers, who elect to work openly for one candidate or another, will keep the gate open for opposition points of view, fullness of reporting, editorial page comment, letters to the editor and columnists' analysis, so as to protect the strong tradition of the American press

CASE STUDY 7-2

ARROGANT OR A WIMP?

You are publisher of a major daily, and thus responsible for its business operations, news columns, and editorial pages. You strongly feel your paper should endorse the Republican candidate for President. Your Pulitzer Prize–winning editorial board of fifteen men and women, carefully selected as representative of your community, votes to endorse the Democrat.

Questions: What are your obligations to your readers, your editorial board, and your own sense of duty? Should you accept the board's decision or override it? Either way, should your differences with your board be kept private or revealed to readers?

Publisher Richard Capen, Jr., of the *Miami Herald* rejected his editorial board's vote to endorse Democrat Walter Mondale in 1984, and ordered endorsement of Ronald Reagan. But *first,* he spent five days explaining his views to board members and seeking theirs. Then, he wrote a column telling readers why he thought Reagan was the best choice ("I must consider what's best for this newspaper and South Florida —and I must live with my own conscience," he wrote.) Capen said not all his associates agreed—and that editor Jim Hampton would present his objections in a column in the same issue.

Hampton wrote, "On behalf of the substantial majority of this newspaper's editorial board, I respectfully but strenuously dissent from today's recommendation.... This recommendation represents publisher Dick Capen's exercising his authority to override the board's collegial decisions. None of us questions or begrudges him that authority. As publisher, he

must have it—just as I as editor must be able to overrule everyone but him.... My first, visceral reaction was to resign irrevocably.... My resignation-in-principle would have triggered others.... I could not do that to this newspaper, to my staff, to Dick, to all those who trust in us—and in me personally—to be fair and honest and caring. My conscience wouldn't let me be so selfish."

Hampton said he did write a one-sentence resignation letter so Capen could bring in an editor "whose views were more consonant with his." Capen tore it up.

Why did Capen handle the affair this way? He says:

"I felt a responsibility to defend our presidential endorsement. While most readers would already have arrived at their own selection, there was a principle involved in terms of my need to agree with the ultimate choice.

"I felt the readers were entitled to know of the divisions that occurred and the reasoning behind the editor's choice as well as my own. The ethics of credibility in our profession are critically important indeed.

"In the end, the newspaper received high marks for credibility, with many readers divided into two camps—one group that felt the publisher should be fired for his arrogance in overruling a majority, and another that felt I was a wimp because I failed to fire those who opposed me."

Was Capen justified in overriding his board? Why have a board if its advice isn't followed? Should Hampton have quit?

in getting to the readers all the information the electorate need." And, secondly, "How publishers so involved will proceed to ensure their readers and critics of a full and balanced story..."[40]

Many newspapers prohibit *any* staff member from personal involvement in politics. A survey of thirty-four newspapers in the northwest, for example, revealed 51 percent had written ethics codes and 90 percent of those prohibited both top management and newsroom employees from active involvement in politics.[41]

Because their newspapers or television stations are among any community's

VIEWPOINT 7-4

EDITORS AND PUBLISHERS: FAIR GAME

"Newspaper editors and publishers are fair game, and we should expect our lives to be as open to public scrutiny as the public officials we scrutinize. We're not elected officials but we write about issues in the public domain and we, therefore, are in the public domain."

Gene Roberts, president and editor, *Philadelphia Inquirer*

most important institutions, media managers often are as open to public scrutiny fully as penetrating as that afforded elected officials. Such was the fate of Darrow ("Duke") Tully, publisher of the *Phoenix Republic and Gazette*. An Arizona politician, angered over coverage of his affairs, revealed Tully, a colorful and powerful man in the state power structure, had fabricated his background as a war hero. Tully often appeared in public wearing war decorations on an Air Force colonel's uniform. But when it was revealed he never had been in the military, he resigned and left town.

VIEWPOINT 7-5

BOOSTERISM: THREE VIEWS

"One of the biggest chasms between editors and readers today is differing concepts of what is boosterism. Boosting the opening of a new store or a shopping center can be news. To many readers, having a new place to shop is more important—and more interesting—than what is going on at city hall or with the school board or the local politicos."

Rey Hertel, managing editor, *Joliet* (Ill.) *Herald-News*

"Because a newspaper is usually a vital part of any community, the publisher is often asked to take an active civic role. It seems perfectly appropriate that he or she do so providing no pressure is exerted on the editorial department."

Kenneth J. Botty, vice president and editor, *Worcester* (Mass.) *Telegram and Evening Gazette*

"We don't join and we don't boost."

John K. Murphy, executive editor, *Portland* (Me.) *Press Herald*, "The Ethics Report," Associated Press Managing Editors, 1984

For some media managers, the temptation is to influence news coverage of individual advertisers on which rests the economic future of any newspaper or television station.

Such an issue caused wholesale resignations in the newsroom of the *Trenton* (N.J.) *Times* in 1982 and drew attention from Jonathan Friendly, media reporter for the *New York Times*. He reported "[T]he paper's owners have moved to increase the business office's control over what had been a money-losing operation....The journalists say the business office has interfered with news operations and allowed advertisers to dictate what goes into the news columns. They noted, for example, the dismissal of a business reporter who, according to officials for the paper, wrote too comprehensively about the financial troubles of a major local advertiser." The paper's owner denied undue advertiser influence, but by that time one-quarter of his news staff had resigned.[42]

Covering a local business story in accordance with its editors' news instincts caused the *Fort Worth* (Tex.) *Star-Telegram* considerable grief. The paper re-

---

---

vealed Bell Helicopter Textron had a safety problem with Huey and Cobra helicopters manufactured in Fort Worth. The Bell Office Workers Union organized a campaign that led to 1,200 subscriptions being cancelled. The company prevented the newspaper from servicing its vending machines at the plant. (One consolation: The story won a Pulitzer Prize for the *Star-Telegram*.)

Many media executives see nothing wrong in boosterism if it involves the wider economic interests of a community (as contrasted with, say, favoritism for an individual advertiser.) For example, looking back on its first 100 years, Times Mirror Co., unashamedly reported the "relentless boosterism" of its *Los Angeles Times,* which "undoubtedly lured multitudes of Easterners and Midwesterners to the City of Angels."[43]

Ethics in the Personnel Department

In establishing the character or "tone" of a newspaper or television operation, no department is more important than personnel. This department assembles the staff that creates the news product—and 46 to 48 percent of most newspapers' total costs. In television, personnel recruits those million-dollar anchors and others for the nightly news. Two ethical questions arise from all this that are central to our study of countinghouse influences on newsroom ethics:

First, are the newspaper and television industries doing the best job possible of recruiting and then properly training and motivating the finest available talent to produce ethical, socially responsible journalism? The quick answer: probably not, but things are improving.

Second, are the media building ethnically diverse newsroom staffs truly representative of the communities they cover (or *should* cover)? Definitely not.

Most young men and women entering newspaper or television news today come from journalism schools, which compete on campus for talented students against other courses of study, particularly business. In recent years, business has been a "hot" course of study for many. Conversely, the newspaper industry has been perceived by many young people as offering low pay, hard work, anonymity, and a limited future. Although the industry in fact never has been stronger, many young people arrive on campus already turned off by the spectacle of once-great newspapers failing—the *Philadelphia Bulletin, Washington*

Star, Cleveland Press, and *Baltimore News-American,* for example. As a result, journalism school enrollments universally are lower than in business, and within journalism schools, enrollments in newspaper writing and editing courses are down, some dramatically. Television's entertainment orientation attracts many students for whom the substance of responsible journalism is less important than the "show biz" possibilities of being a happy-chatter anchor. Many journalism schools require no courses in ethics, although instructors often touch on ethics in reporting, writing, and management courses.

When they graduate, here is where journalism students go:

	Graduates (1985)	% of Total
Newspapers/news services	3,162	15.5
Radio/TV	1,653	8.1
Public relations	2,407	11.8
Advertising	2,142	10.5
Magazines	286	1.4
Other media	1,626	8.0
Total media hire	11,275	55.3%
Graduate study	1,346	6.6
Nonmedia	5,324	26.1
Unemployed	2,454	12.0
Total graduates	20,400	100.0%

Source: Dow Jones Newspaper Fund, Inc.

Although improved in recent years, newspaper and television starting salaries still are too low for many talented students who can fare better in other industries (see table below, left).

Things don't improve much for working newspaper and television journalists. Two Indiana University researchers, David H. Weaver and C. Cleveland Wilhoit, surveyed 1,001 journalists in 1982 to 1983 and found these median salaries (see table below, right):

MEDIAN ENTRY-LEVEL SALARIES FOR JOURNALISM GRADUATES, 1985

Public relations	$14,560
Advertising	13,780
Newspapers	13,520
Radio/TV	11,180

Source: Dow Jones Newspaper Fund, Inc.

MEDIAN SALARIES, 1982–1983

Weekly newspapers	$13,999
Radio	14,999
Television	17,031
Daily newspapers	20,999
News services	24,100
Newsmagazines	34,750

So, what type person is attracted to industries offering such salaries (albeit, it must be acknowledged, the very considerable excitement and sense of involvement that comes with working in news)? The Indiana research draws this profile of American journalists:

70 percent are college graduates.

96 percent are white, 66 percent are male.

57.5 percent claim to be middle-of-the-road politically; 22.1 percent position themselves to the left, 17.9 percent to the right.

The "typical" journalist is 32 years old, Protestant, married, and earning $19,000 annually.[44]

At the top, salaries are better. Arthur Ochs Sulzberger was paid $949,991 in salary and incentives in 1985 as chairman and chief executive officer of the diversified New York Times Co. The president, Walter Mattson, was paid $715,413. At Dow Jones, chairman Warren H. Phillips's total compensation was $1,107,252; his president, Ray Shaw, received $784,036.[45]

Editors' salaries ranged widely—averaging $22,366 annually for the top editors of newspapers under 5,000 circulation to $165,539 for papers over 250,000 circulation, according to a 1986 survey by ASNE.

In terms of how the public is served by newspaper and television journalism, perhaps the most important ethical question arising from all this is why newsrooms haven't done a better job of recruiting minorities. In the past, with advertisers demanding demographically attractive readers, newspapers felt little *economic* pressure to reach low-income black or Hispanic neighborhoods, and thus had no need to actively recruit minorities to cover those neighborhoods. However, with rising *societal* pressure, reflected in the 1964 Civil Rights Act, the media had to recruit minorities—and found themselves in vigorous competition with other, high-paying industries, all responding belatedly to changing times, and all trying to preempt trouble from the Equal Employment Opportunity Commission, charged under Title VII of the act with enforcing equal job opportunity. Newspapers have fallen far short of what society now demands in minority hiring. ASNE surveyed 996 daily newspapers, 62 percent of the total, and found that of a newsroom work force of 53,985 in 1986, 3,402—6.3 percent—were black, Hispanic, Asian, or Native American. There was rejoicing in some quarters because minority employment was up 50 percent since 1978, but the 6.3 percent still compared poorly to the total minority population, which was 20 percent of the total U.S. population in the 1980 Census. And, 57 percent of daily newspapers employed no minorities; 89 percent had no minority news executives.

VIEWPOINT 7-7

HIRING MINORITIES IS SMART

"Promoting and practicing equal opportunity is not only the right thing to do, it's the smart thing to do.... No newspaper can cover all of the community unless it employs all the community."

Al Neuharth, chairman of Gannett Co., and industry leader in minority hiring

Though increasingly successful in newsrooms and middle management, women have not yet been widely accepted in top executive positions. An American Newspaper Publishers Association study showed in 1987 just 7 percent of U.S. daily newspaper publishers and general managers were women.

In television, women and minorities often fare well as reporters or on-camera talent. The Radio and Television News Directors Association found in 1982 that 92 percent of TV stations had women anchors; women made up 36 percent of all anchors on the air. But the industry's *policymaking* structure is nearly all male and lily-white. It wasn't until 1986, for example, that a black was appointed general manager of a television station owned and operated by a network. He was Jonathan Rodgers, sent by CBS to WBBM-TV in Chicago—a station then under boycott by black civil rights activists who were demanding more jobs for blacks.[46]

In sum, to fashion a staff dedicated to ethical, socially responsible journalism an editor must travel far beyond the newsroom—to the classroom, where today's editors must recruit tomorrow's reporters and writers from talented, committed, responsible students, and to minority communities, where editors must seek the ethnic balance from which alone can come coverage truly representative of audiences that must be served.

Looming ahead for personnel managers is a new dimension of ethical problems involving an employee's right to privacy and an employer's rights to penetrate that privacy either in corporate self-interest or on behalf of other employees' interests. For example, is it proper for an employer to require testing for drug usage or acquired immune deficiency syndrome—AIDS—as a condition of employment? Since the early 1970s, drug testing has been routine for job applicants at the *New York Times,* and other papers now are testing. The *Birmingham* (Ala.) *News* began requiring AIDS testing in 1986 as a condition of employment (Publisher Victor H. Hanson 2d said, "We don't want knowingly to get involved with somebody who has a debilitating illness that would be very costly to us.") Societal attitudes have evolved in a manner that permits employers to lay down rules governing employee behavior in two areas once thought no business of any employer—sexual harassment and smoking. Sexual harassment is illegal, of course, and many newspaper and television employers take steps against it in the workplace. And, some forbid smoking or set aside certain areas for smokers and nonsmokers.

VIEWPOINT 7-8

TALK BUT ALSO DO

"While the expressed commitment to equal opportunity from within the newspaper industry has been great, the demonstrated commitment has been far less. What is at stake here is, ultimately, our relevance to our customers. Unless we can make real progress, and at a faster rate than heretofore, the price we pay will be fewer customers."

David Lawrence, Jr., publisher and chairman, *Detroit Free Press*

Ethics and the Tyranny of Production

Few forces shape the character of news reporting and writing more than production deadlines. Newspaper and television journalists spend their working lives trying to meet them and still get into print or on the air with stories that are complete, balanced, accurate, fair. Complete or not, balanced or not, news copy *must* meet deadlines.

In newspapering, newsroom deadlines are set not by editors but, rather, by the production and circulation departments. Newspapers must be gotten off the press and into delivery trucks in time to meet trains, buses, motor delivery drivers, and 15-year-olds on bicycles—none of whom wait for late deliveries. In television, of course, the camera's red light blinks on immediately following the commercial and complete or not, balanced or not, the evening news is on the air—now, not two or three minutes from now. More than the general public realizes, such purely mechanical considerations dictate how newspaper and television journalists perform.

From the earliest days of movable type, newspapers were production oriented. The entire effort revolved around the costly, laborious task of printing the paper on time. "Ye olde country editor" of lore was a printer, not truly an editor; larger papers were tied to huge presses and schedules set by printers. Only in recent years, with introduction of electronic editing devices and computer-controlled production processes, have editors gained some breathing room. Still, however, deadlines aren't set in response to news and the way it flows. To explain: Everyone involved in newspaper production sets deadlines that work backward from readers and optimum times for delivery to them. For morning papers, that is about 6 A.M.—before breakfast and in time to assist in the news orientation of those who have slept through the night and now need to quickly catch up on the world as they prepare for the day ahead. For afternoon papers, it's 4 P.M.—in time for leisurely reading after work, before dinner and, importantly, before evening television.

Editors of morning papers have better opportunity to meet their responsibility of producing a sound, newsy, more up-to-date newspaper. Their "cycle" covers news that breaks throughout the day and late into the night. They can have deadlines of midnight or later and the paper can be printed and distributed in predawn hours. For these reasons, and because readers want that early morning "reorientation," morning papers often emphasize late, "hard" news, and are perceived as being fact-filled and informative.

The news cycle for afternoon editors includes predawn and morning hours. For metropolitan afternoon editors, a first-edition deadline of 9 A.M. or 9:30 A.M. is not unusual; for editors of small papers, a news deadline of 10:30 A.M., and press time of noon is routine—and how much "today" news can an editor scrape up locally by 9 A.M. or 10:30 A.M.? Also, research indicates afternoon readers want the "reward" of easy reading after a day's work, not the challenge of news reorientation. Therefore, for purely mechanical reasons, a great many afternoon papers are warmed-over versions of morning papers; many

emphasize ''soft'' feature writing, columns, and behind-the-scenes analytical writing.

Anyone outside the media trying to influence how the news is reported is a
giant step toward success if they understand newspaper and television production. Demagogue Joe McCarthy, a Wisconsin Republican senator, understood
it in the 1950s, and he played the media like a fiddle. For newspapers, he broke
''news'' (often completely undocumented charges of communist infiltration into
government) just before deadlines. Repeatedly, newspapers rushed into print
without time to double-check. For television, McCarthy would wave a sheaf of
paper and declare he had in his hand a list of communists in high places—thus
providing the dramatic video and ''sound bite'' around which so many TV news
stories revolve.

Today, government officials, politicians, and public relations executives also
understand all this. For example, they schedule committee hearings, press conferences, and ''media events'' for midafternoon—just in time for evening TV
news but too late for afternoon papers and too early to be exclusive in morning
papers. It's a tactic highly favored by those with an idea they would rather
deliver directly to the public, through the tube, than through the analytical reporting and interpretive writing of a print journalist.

The enormous costs involved in newspaper and television production add to
the ''tyranny of production.'' For a 50,000-circulation daily, production and
newsprint alone soak up about 33 percent of total costs; circulation, 13 percent
or so. Those two departments, representing at least 46 percent of total costs,
have great clout at the planning table. (At this size paper, news represents about
13 percent of total cost; advertising, 8 percent; general/administrative, 33 percent.) Television news production is costly, too, particularly in the field. For
example, whereas a newspaper can maintain a foreign correspondent for
$200,000 to $250,000 annually, ABC calculates its cost for a bureau at $1 mil-
lion minimum.

What's an editor to do?

First, newspaper editors should fight to gain for newsroom purposes every
minute saved by new technology. Electronic editing already has speeded the
production process. Electronic pagination, the computerized layout of full pages,
will speed it even more. Time saved should go to extend the period the newsroom has for thoughtful, sound, responsible journalism. Particularly for afternoon papers, later deadlines would help tremendously.

Second, new technology transfers to the newsroom many tasks formerly performed in production and permits staff reductions in production. Editors must
demand more staff. The countinghouse tendency will be to add tasks but not
bodies, thus subtracting substantially from the time and personnel resources
editors have to do the *news* job.

Third, and we say it again: editors, both in print and television, must learn
countinghouse language and ways. They must learn to justify, in terms advertising and circulation strategists understand, adding that $200,000 foreign cor-
respondent or $1 million news bureau. Neither will be approved on a ''nice-

to-have'' basis; both will be if editors can translate the newsroom's needs into improved circulation and prestige with advertisers—results the countinghouse understands.

Ethics in Circulation

Many reporters and editors seldom, if ever, visit the circulation department, where the press run ends and distribution begins. They should, for out of circulation can come serious ethical questions affecting the newsroom.

First, circulation considerations swing increasing weight in any upper management strategy session. Simply put, advertising executives want the paper in the hands of certain people attractive to advertisers. Circulation executives must get it there—but can do so only if editors create a product essential or at least tempting to those certain people. And there, at that point in the integrated marketing concept, is where the newsroom is pressured to pull in tandem with the advertising and circulation departments. In television, of course, the parallel is pressure from the advertising sales department to produce programming—including news—that wins higher ratings, which, in turn, makes it easier to sell commercial time at higher rates.

Second, there is ongoing debate in both the newspaper and television industries over not only how circulation numbers (or ratings) are achieved, but also how they are counted or measured, publicly reported, and promoted.

In bygone, perhaps simpler times, newspaper editors pretty much covered the news as they saw it. The circulation department sold the resultant product to as many readers as possible; who they were and where they lived were not as important as total numbers. Using those total numbers as bait, the advertising department then ''sold space'' in the paper to advertisers. Some papers pushed their circulation out to distant horizons, covering many states and in some cases becoming regional powerhouses. The *Atlanta Journal,* for example, sallied forth with the promise that it ''Covers Dixie Like the Dew.'' But times changed.

Advertisers won't pay ad rates based on circulation hundreds of miles distant from their retail outlets. Atlanta retailers no longer are interested in circulation in south Georgia where they have no shoppers. Meanwhile, newsprint costs have risen dramatically, along with gasoline prices and other costs of distant circulation. The Atlanta paper has retreated toward its home market—all in response to *circulation,* not *news,* considerations. Any societal responsibility Atlanta editors feel to get their papers into every small town in Georgia fades before the circulation department's argument that they cannot afford to do that. Editors proud of achieving widespread circulation now hear advertising salespeople say they cannot sell that distant circulation to downtown department stores and that it therefore is a *cost* factor, not a generator of profit.

In sum, editors who once viewed news in terms of its importance to a general, widely scattered audience now have new marching orders: create a product precisely tailored to specific *geographic* and *demographic* targets selected to meet advertiser needs. It's called "zoning" or "target marketing," and it has revolutionized newspaper strategy, yielding new, undreamed profit opportunities—and, make no mistake, *it requires editors to edit in response to business considerations.* In its bluntest form, circulation pressure on the newsroom can be a memo from on high stating that subscription sales crews will be working suburb X next month, and would the newsroom please get out there right away and cover the territory to give them something to sell? In that context, whether there is anything truly newsworthy in suburb X is immaterial. Thus do editors, in a world of war, famine, and disaster, show sudden interest in handshaking Rotarians in suburb X and large pumpkins grown by householders there. (Of course, given resources and time, editors can produce meaningful coverage in such areas even when reacting to circulation department pressure rather than their own news instincts; many metropolitan newspapers have high-quality suburban coverage developed over the past decade.)

In its worst form, circulation pressure on the newsroom can create sensationalistic, profoundly unethical and irresponsible journalism. Newspapers and television alike have their sinners. The *New York Post,* with its daily diet of rape, murder, and arson, serves as an example of circulation-driven newspaper editors pandering to the most ignoble instincts of their street audience simply to push a few more copies at thirty-five cents each. In television, with its desperate need of more numbers, the inexorable pressure is toward news fare palatable to the widest possible audience, if not particularly enlightening or uplifting.

Because their financial future depends on winning readers or viewers, then "selling" them to advertisers, counting the numbers has ethical implications for both newspapers and television, too.

Newspaper circulation figures historically were so chaotic—not to say intentionally inflated—that the industry *and* advertisers created in 1914 a nonprofit cooperative, the Audit Bureau of Circulations, to do the counting. Today, paid circulation figures for 1,344 daily newspapers and 521 weeklies in the United States and Canada (along with hundreds of magazines) are checked by 76 full-time ABC auditors. Newspaper promotion aimed at advertisers is built around those ABC numbers. Non-ABC papers promote numbers they have sworn are accurate in statements submitted to U.S. Postal Service officials. Generally, these numbers are far less reliable than ABC numbers.

Television measures its numbers primarily through two companies, Nielsen and Arbitron, which use meters wired to television sets and, until 1987, diaries filled out by viewers to report what they watched and when. Clearly, the meters measure many sets on but not watched; diaries often were filled out from memory and were incomplete and inaccurate. By some estimates, television audiences are overstated by as much as 10 to 15 percent—which could mean the three major networks, with annual billings of $3 billion, are overbilling national advertisers by as much as $300 million to $450 million.[47]

With so much money riding on the numbers, outright falsification of circulation or audience is not unknown in the media. But fudging takes other forms—

newspapers giving away prizes to entice subscribers just before an ABC audit, or television pumping up its offerings just before audience surveys. Sometimes, competing claims get heated. In one celebrated flap in 1986, for example, the *Wall Street Journal* refused to run an ad in which *USA Today* claimed second-largest circulation in the country. The *Journal* (which at nearly 2 million circulation is the nation's largest paper) said *USA Today*'s numbers included "bulk sales" of about 250,000 copies—those sold to, say, hotels for free distribution to guests—and thus compared "apples to oranges" when laid alongside circulation of other newspapers mentioned in the ad. The *New York Times* printed the ad, saying an asterisk and footnote adequately explained the difference.

CHAPTER SUMMARY

Any study of newsroom ethics must pay special attention also to ethics in the "countinghouse"—developments in other departments of a newspaper or television operation that influence why and how news is covered. Because of its enormous financial importance, advertising is particularly influential. There is debate over whether advertising has true societal value or is a wasteful, costly endeavor that creates unnecessary materialistic consumer desire.

For American media, advertising creates the financial independence from government or political groups that permits extraordinary journalistic independence. There is danger, however, of economic dependence on a relatively few large advertisers who exert undue influence on news coverage.

Newspapers and television networks go to elaborate lengths to screen advertising for acceptability and, in fact, most protect the sanctity of their advertising columns or airtime just as editors try to protect the ethical character of the news. Screening codes prohibit the originators or authors of advertising from placing deceptive ads, and commit a newspaper or network, as the medium of advertising, to ensuring trust, good taste, and legality. Because this can involve turning away unacceptable advertising, there is a price tag attached to advertising ethics.

Media managers must protect the business interests of their newspaper or television operation, must perform efficiently and profitably—and simultaneously administer news operations that cover many of the individuals and industries on which those business interests depend. Many managers report conflicts of interest in that equation.

In personnel, the challenge is to hire and train a talented staff committed to ethical, socially responsible journalism, and to build an ethnically diverse staff truly representative of the community it covers (or *should* cover). Results are mixed.

Many production factors influence the character of news reporting and writing. Newspaper and television journalists spend their working lives trying to meet production deadlines and still get into print or on the air with stories that are complete, balanced, accurate, and fair. More than the general public realizes, the purely mechanical factors in production—and the cost—influence news coverage.

In circulation, ethical questions arise because of the influence circulation executives have on the geographic and demographic targets editors are given to cover. Many editors today edit in response to business, not news, considerations. There also is ongoing debate over how circulation (or ratings) figures are achieved, measured, and promoted.

CHAPTER 7

Notes

1 Excellent sources of financial information on leading companies are *Advertising Age,* which in June of each year treats in detail the nation's top 100 media companies, and *Forbes,* which in April publishes its "Forbes 500 Annual Directory." For superb analysis, see the *Newspaper Newsletter* issued monthly by John Morton of Lynch, Jones & Ryan, a brokerage house at 1037 Thirtieth Street, N.W., Washington, D.C., 20007. Information on the newspaper industry is summarized in "Facts about Newspapers '86," American Newspaper Publishers Association, The Newspaper Center, Box 17407, Dulles Airport, Washington, D.C., 20041.

2 Advertising ethics are discussed particularly well within a wider context by Manuel G. Velasquez in *Business Ethics,* Prentice-Hall, Englewood Cliffs, N.J., 1982.

3 John Kenneth Galbraith, *The Affluent Society,* Houghton Mifflin, Boston, 1958.

4 Note particularly Ruth Clark, "Relating to Readers in the '80s," a 1984 opinion study done for ASNE, P.O. Box 17004, Washington, D.C., 20041. Also, a 1986 study done by Times Mirror Corp., Times Mirror Square, Los Angeles, Calif., 90053, found 53 percent of all Americans regard the press as "...too often influenced by powerful interests and institutions."

5 Helpful is a national survey in 1981 by Opinion Research Corp., for the Newspaper Advertising Bureau, 1180 Avenue of the Americas, New York, N.Y., 10036.

6 "CBS Television Network Advertising Guidelines," CBS Inc., 51 W. 52nd St., New York, N.Y., 10020.

7 "Advertising Standards of Acceptability," The Times Publishing Company, 490 First Avenue South, St. Petersburg, Fla., 33701.

8 Robert P. Smith, "Advertising Acceptability Policies Protect Newspaper's Credibility," *INAME News,* June 1984, p. 11.

9 "Advertising Standards and Guidelines," American Broadcasting Co., 1330 Avenue of the Americas, New York, N.Y., 10019; and, "CBS Television Network Advertising Guidelines," op. cit.

10 "Advertising Standards of Acceptability," op. cit.

11 Marcia Ruth, "Taboo Ads," *presstime,* October 1985, p. 34.

12 "CBS Television Network Advertising Guidelines," op. cit.

13 Details of this incident are available in Alex S. Jones, "Effects of Mobil's Journal Ban," *New York Times,* Dec. 5, 1984, p. 36; William F. Gloede, "Mobil's Still Mad," *Advertising Age,* April 8, 1985, p. 6; "Boycott Big Business," *Editor & Publisher,* Dec. 15, 1984, p. 10.

14 A detailed review of this incident is in "A Helluva Bureau," an historical look at

Dow Jones' Detroit bureau, in *What's News,* Dow Jones employee publication, Spring 1985, p. 1.

15 Comments made at the Dec. 5, 1984, meeting in Tacoma, Wash., of Allied Daily Newspapers, a group of papers in Washington, Oregon, Idaho, Montana, and Alaska.

16 This boycott is reported in, "Car Dealers Boycott Tennessee Daily," *Editor & Publisher,* Oct. 12, 1985, p. 22.

17 Marcia Ruth, "Taboo Ads," op. cit.

18 Every newspaper faces many variables such as competition, market strength, and journalistic quality, so there is no "typical" newspaper. But a detailed and, in the author's opinion, accurate picture of the finances of a 75,000-circulation paper is drawn in "The Business of Newspapers: An Essay for Investors," by C. Patrick O'Donnell, Jr., senior publishing analyst, EF Hutton & Co., Inc., Feb. 12, 1982.

19 Jonathan Friendly, "Albany Paper Irks Official, Loses Ads," *New York Times,* Feb. 16, 1984, p. 15.

20 "Newspapers Ponder Advertising Codes," *presstime,* August 1984, p. 43.

21 Robert P. Smith, "Advertising Acceptability Policies Protect Newspaper's Credibility," op. cit.

22 "Advertising Policy Manual," *Miami Herald,* One Herald Plaza, Miami, Fla., 33101.

23 "Advertising Standards of Acceptability," op. cit.

24 Marcia Ruth, "Taboo Ads," op. cit.

25 "An Overview of Current Issues," policy statement by American Newspaper Publishers Association, The Newspaper Center, Box 17407, Dulles Airport, Washington, D.C., 20041.

26 Stuart J. Elliott, "Advertorials: Straddling a Fine Line in Print," *Advertising Age,* April 30, 1984, p. 3.

27 *New York Times,* Oct. 10, 1982.

28 Robert P. Smith, "Advertising Acceptability Policies Protect Newspaper's Credibility," op. cit.

29 J. Peter Grace and Joseph A. Califano, Jr., "Networks vs. Free Speech," *New York Times,* June 12, 1986, p. A31.

30 Eric Pace, "Whose Fault Is Bogus Ad?" *New York Times,* July 30, 1982, p. 16.

31 Hank Johnson, "What's Going on at One/Press Place," *Athens* (Ga.) *Banner-Herald and Daily News,* May 12, 1985, p. D2.

32 Randi G. Murray, "Investment Research Analysis, ABC," Goldman Sachs, Oct. 31, 1984, p. 10.

33 "Facts About Newspapers '86," op. cit.

34 "Facts About Newspapers '86," op. cit.

35 "CBS News Abolishes 25 Jobs, Citing Costs, Closes 2 Foreign Bureaus," *Wall Street Journal,* Dec. 1, 1982, p. 33, and "Facts about Newspapers '86," op. cit.

36 Survey by John Reddy, vice president/editorial, Suburban Communications Corp., Livonia, Mich., of 207 suburban publishers; reported in *Research Bulletin,* Southern Newspaper Publishers Association, P.O. Box 28875, Atlanta, Ga., 30328.

37 ASNE survey, "Editors and Publisher: Wearing Two Hats Comfortably," *ASNE Bulletin,* October 1985, p. 4.

38 Ibid.

39 Richard G. Capen, Jr., letter to author, Mar. 17, 1986, and "Publisher's Perspective," *Miami Herald,* Oct. 28, 1984, p. 3E.

40 M. K. Guzda, "Ethnically Speaking," *Editor & Publisher,* Sept. 29, 1984, p. 11.

41 Survey by Allied Daily Newspapers and reported by M. L. Stein, "Survey of Free-bies," *Editor & Publisher,* May 31, 1986, p. 11.

42 Jonathan Friendly, "*Trenton Times* Journalists Quit Over New Policies," *New York Times,* Feb. 21, 1982, p. 39; also see, John Helyar, "Reporter Finds That Writing News Means Following Company Line," *Wall Street Journal,* Feb. 19, 1982, p. 32.

43 "Annual Report, 1984," Times Mirror Co., Times Mirror Square, Los Angeles, Calif., 90053, p. 10.

44 David H. Weaver and G. Cleveland Wilhoit, *The American Journalist: A Portrait of U.S. News People and Their Work,* Indiana University Press, Bloomington, 1986.

45 Notice of 1986 Annual Meeting and Proxy Statement, The New York Times Co., 229 West 43rd St., New York, N.Y., 10036, and Dow Jones and Company, Inc., 200 Liberty Street, New York, N.Y., 10281.

46 For a detailed, fascinating account see Steve Daley, "Chicago Assignment," *Washington Journalism Review,* July 1986, p. 27.

47 For a penetrating examination of this issue see Jeffrey A. Trachtenberg, "Anybody Home Out There?" *Forbes,* May 19, 1986, p. 169.

THE CHANGING FACE
OF THE MEDIA

We discuss in this chapter a fundamental restructuring under way in the character, ownership, and management of American newspaper and television companies. Most significant is the concentration of enormous nation-wide media influence and economic power by a relative handful of conglomerates. Privately owned newspapers are disappearing into groups with increasing speed. As of 1986, 1,186 daily newspapers—71 percent of the total—were group-owned.

Does a community suffer when control of its single most important communications medium, the local newspaper, passes from hands-on, home-town owners to distant group executives? Should society be concerned about such concentration of media power?

Television long ago became big business and its extraordinary profit potential led groups to snap up almost any local station of consequence, often for whatever price the owner felt emboldened to demand. Newspapers also sell for extremely high prices—and paying high prices often forces profit-oriented groups to cut costs to make the new property "pay." What impact is that likely to have on the future of high-quality journalism (which necessarily is high-cost)?

With corporate treasuries swelling—twenty-five groups each have over $500 million in annual sales, sixteen over $1 billion—an entirely new layer of media management is being created. It is composed of accountants, lawyers, and others skilled in handling money and expert in pure management science. Many are nonjournalists removed both geographically and psychologically not only from the communities their newspapers and television stations serve, but, indeed, from news work itself. What are the societal implications of concentrated media power in absentee hands?

Expansion is the game plan for media groups. The rush to corporate bigness will continue. Society already limits the number of broadcast stations any individual owner can hold to twelve TV, twelve AM, and twelve FM radio licenses. Should it similarly limit newspaper owners before groups start devouring groups? If so, how would that square with the First Amendment guarantee of a free press?

Diversification is part of the plan, too, and companies that started as newspaper or television operations will tuck strange bedfellows beneath their ''communications'' roofs. Already there, for example, are the Chicago Cubs, owned by Tribune Company, and Grand Ole Opry, owned by Oklahoma Publishing.[1] Should communications companies own other companies their reporters cover?

In pages ahead, we will touch on the tremendous fortunes being made in both media ownership and management. Note how the policy-setting apparatus of some large media companies is controlled by a relatively few wealthy families and individuals. Some have interlocking relationships with other media firms that expands considerably their influence (for example, an executive of Gannett, the country's largest group in terms of newspapers owned, also serves as chairman of The Associated Press, the world's largest general news agency). Should society demand such media giants have boards of directors or management truly representative of the communities they serve? Should it insist, for example, on ethnic, gender, or racial balance in the policy-setting apparatus of any company so influential in how this country is run?

Now, the author does *not* suggest ''big is bad'' automatically in media ownership or that ''profit'' is a dirty word in journalism. To the contrary. Even the media's most severe critics must acknowledge the best American journalism—and some of it is superb—is produced by large, profit-oriented corporations. Nostalgia for the days of privately owned ''mom-and-pop'' news organizations is, in this sense, largely misplaced. Mom and pop simply had neither the vision nor financial strength to produce newspaper or TV journalism of the quality routinely produced daily by Knight-Ridder, the New York Times Co., Times Mirror, or other similarly enlightened conglomerates. The author *does* suggest, however, that when there is such concentration of media ownership and power this book's examination of journalistic ethics and social responsibility must push beyond whether a sports writer should accept a Christmas bottle of whiskey, whether a small-town publisher should get into community ''boosterism,'' or whether a local television station manager should monkey with how the news is covered just to improve ratings. We must survey the character and structure of America's leading newspaper and broadcast companies, moving upstream along the power flow and into the boardrooms of those conglomerates to see who really runs the media empires, who really creates operating policy for that sports writer, the small-town publisher, and the station manager.

So, we'll open a new dimension of our discussion by looking, here in Chapter 8, at the ''Changing Face of the Media.''

It was April 21, 1986, and Robert Erburu, chairman of Times Mirror Co., was summing up for his annual meeting of shareholders the stunning growth that had transformed a single newspaper, the *Los Angeles Times,* into a diversified corporation of enormous size. Company revenues in 1985 from newspapers, television, and many other interests hit $2.96 *billion,* he reported, up from $112.6 *million* in 1960. Net income of $237 million was *more than fifty times greater* than 1960's $4.6 million. One share of Times Mirror common stock worth $25 in 1960 and paying dividends of slightly more than 38 cents annually would have grown through dividends and stock splits to nine shares worth more than $500 and paying $12.50.[2]

A few days later, in Miami, chairman Alvah Chapman told Knight-Ridder shareholders their company's revenue nearly tripled in ten years, rising to $1.7 billion from $593 million. Dividends in that period grew at a compound annual rate of 19.3 percent.[3]

At the New York Times Co., annual meeting, chairman Arthur Ochs Sulzberger reported revenues of $1.3 billion in 1985, up from $444 million in 1976. A marginally profitable company based primarily on the *New York Times* had become a widely diversified—and hugely profitable—conglomerate with fifty-two subsidiary companies and holdings in seventeen states, the United Kingdom, Canada, and France.[4]

For network television's annual meetings, the news was megabucks growth—to nearly $9 billion total media revenue for ABC, NBC, and CBS—and acquisition moves of almost bewildering dimensions. ABC ($3.6 billion in sales) was bought by Capital Cities ($939.7 million), and the resultant giant was the nation's largest media conglomerate. NBC went along with its parent RCA Corp., when it was merged with General Electric Co., and, shareholders were told, now represents about 7 percent of the total $38 billion revenue of the newly enlarged company. CBS told its annual meeting it fought off four takeover attempts, but had to take on hundreds of millions of dollars in debt to do it.

The annual meeting: that ritualistic celebration of media power, go-go expansion, takeovers and antitakeovers, talk of money—lots of money—and plans to make more, lots more.

How did it get this way? How were a group of newspaper people at the *New York Times* succeeded by MBA-types and hard-charging acquisition specialists who grabbed up properties in seventeen states, the United Kingdom, Canada, and France? How did the grand old *Los Angeles Times* get a top man who was educated as a lawyer and who talks like a banker? What were those guys thinking at the Tribune Tower in downtown Chicago when they bought a *baseball* team?

WHY THEY EXPAND AND DIVERSIFY

If you suspect some sort of modern-day Citizen Kanes are putting together these media conglomerates so they can grab power and influence the minds of America, join the crowd. Some media vigilantes and social commentators fear

Hearstian manipulation of news by media magnates ruling newspaper and television empires and pulling strings that lead to newsrooms across the nation. But, simply put, it is not ideology or proselytism that motivates the empire building. Rather, it's a highly complex combination of profit-oriented business factors and the compelling need of certain aggressive, ego-driven managers to build, to succeed, to be bigger than anyone else.

There, of course, *is* conservatism in newspaper and television management, as in management of most businesses, and there *is* feeling in the countinghouse that business is the business of business. But most groups studiously avoid even the suggestion of a "company line" news editors must follow, and rare indeed is the corporate hierarchy that permits itself to become publicly identified with a politician or narrowly partisan cause—not in this era of nationwide corporate strategies designed to operate profitably in areas diverse geographically, economically, socially, and politically. Following each presidential election surveys will show, as always, that Republican candidates gain more support on *editorial* pages than Democratic hopefuls and that conservative ideas win wider endorsement than liberal ideas. But ever since the media turned so profitable and got organized as *businesses,* critics have been hard pressed to show any significant manipulation of news and editorial pages by the corporate boardroom. In fact, the trend increasingly is to avoid editorial endorsement of *any* party or candidate. *USA Today,* the epitome of the market-oriented group newspaper, a paper methodically constructed to appeal to a wide audience, avoids endorsing any political candidates. Its owner, Gannett, promotes its $2.2 billion, nationwide media network and nearly 100 newspapers as a "world of different voices."

If any charge strikes home against the groups it is *not* that they wrongly intervene in the newsrooms of their distant satellites to set news policy, but, rather, that they don't pay them enough attention and don't care what their news pages or newscasts look like, as long as the profits roll in. The complaint, in fact, often is that groups *don't* intervene to insist on journalistic quality, that they *don't* cart in money and expertise to improve a local substandard journalistic product. And, that they don't force profitable operations elsewhere in the group to subsidize a level of journalistic quality in a newspaper or television station whose market isn't strong enough—or demanding enough—to support improvement, or whose readers or advertisers aren't willing to pay for it. After thirty years of participating in and observing the growth of communications companies, the author sees danger *not* in

---

VIEWPOINT 8-1

"CHAIN" OWNER AND LOCAL LOYALTY

"A 'chain' owner cannot do justice to local publications or radio stations. His devotion and loyalty to any one area is bound to be diluted or divided if he has other ownerships and interests."

Nelson Poynter, late owner of *St. Petersburg Times* who severely criticized in 1947 growth of chains and whose successor managers at the *Times* by 1986 had built a multistate group of high-quality periodicals

---

nonjournalist managers descending into the unfamiliar terrain of the newsroom and trying to run things, but, rather, that untrained in news and insensitive to its complexities or importance, they *ignore* the newsrooms. Many are the publishers who don't carefully read their own news columns or the station managers who don't watch their own newscasts. This is managerial failure through *non*involvement, and it can be remedied only with appointment of experienced, well-trained, highly motivated editors who *do* care and, furthermore, who are capable of fighting in the countinghouse for the resources needed to produce sound, ethical, and responsible journalism.

However you look at it, the groups have come a long way since yesteryear's journalistic barons sat in the splendid isolation of their castlelike estates and hurled ''must run'' telegrams dictating to cowed editors across the land what, on pain of firing, the next day's front pages must carry. Any businessperson— and that's what today's media baron is—would be crazy to even think of doing such a thing. It would queer the whole glorious, moneymaking arrangement.

No, group expansion and diversification are fueled by factors much more easily explained. A manager's first responsibility to shareholders is to create profit, to increase their return on investment (ROI). You'll hear about ROI wherever the mighty meet because it is a fundamental principle embodied in business tradition as ''fiduciary responsibility,'' and carved on MBA diplomas. But, just as importantly, ROI is how you score the game, how you measure your success, how you win the highest salary on the block plus the limo, the private jet, and other ''perks.'' And, expansion and diversification broaden, sometimes exponentially, the revenue base on which improved profit margins and increased ROI can be built. Here is how:

Diversifying geographically protects a company against economic dislocation in a single region. When the New York Times Co., went on an acquisition binge in 1979 to 1985, most of the twenty-eight companies it swept up were newspapers scattered throughout the ''Sun Belt,'' which was faring much better economically than the northeast or midwest.

Diversifying into cities with different industrial bases also provides corporate insurance. Big city groups diversify into small towns; groups based primarily on, say, smokestack industrial towns seek other types of markets as protection against severe economic dislocation in the steel or auto industries.

Diversifying into different media (newspaper companies buying, say, television stations or vice versa) provides corporate balance and reduces the danger of relying on a single source of revenue. Companies traditionally based in newspapers are scouring the land for attractive television and radio stations, outdoor advertising firms, mobile radio-telephone companies—and nonmedia enterprises for protection against dislocation among advertising-supported businesses.

Diversification permits secondary use of existing staff and resources in profitable synergism. For example, paid circulation newspapers develop new revenue (and launch a new competitive vehicle in the market) by producing free circulation shoppers in the same plant with the same staff. And, Tribune Company can buy the Chicago Cubs baseball team, not only for the profits it produces but, most importantly, for attractive television programming Tribune's WGN-TV can sell.

Tax laws can make it financially irresponsible *not* to expand. In the go-go days of the 1970s and early 1980s, when today's media empires largely gained momentum, as much as a twenty-five to forty-five cent tax advantage came with every $1 invested in acquisitions, thus the irresistible temptation to gather profits from far-flung outposts of the empire and buy yet more newspapers or TV stations.

But, finally, expanding a company and building megabuck profits is heady, ego-gratifying stuff. It's *fun* to zoom into town in a private jet, make a multimillion dollar deal, watch the local minions snap to attention, and be known on the industry circuit as someone who makes things happen.

So, although there certainly is sufficient *business* reason for expansion and diversification, *ego* factors have played a large role in all of it, too. Anyone who doubts this should attend a convention of the American Newspaper Publishers Association or a broadcasters' group and watch the wheeler-dealers at work and play. They measure each other's profit levels like gunfighters studying quick-draw techniques.

Of course, all the *buyer* motivation in the world won't change the face of the American media if *sellers* are not willing. Why are they?

High prices paid by groups are one reason. The groups, enormously profitable, have surplus they must invest or give to Uncle Sam as tax on retained earnings. And, smart group executives can improve the profitability of most privately owned (and, often, inefficiently run) newspapers and television stations. So, paying even extraordinarily high prices is justified as a means of achieving greater profit later. Groups often pay three to four times gross revenue or thirty to forty times annual earnings for a newspaper (ten to twelve times earnings is a handsome price multiple in many other industries; for most of 1986, you could buy General Motors stock for a price about seven times earnings). Television stations, many with profit margins even greater than those of newspapers, command higher multiples.

But the greatest single reason for the increasingly rapid disappearance of the family-owned newspaper or broadcast station is federal estate tax. When the principal owner dies, many families are forced to buy their newspaper or station a second time—this time from the Internal Revenue Service—if they want the property passed to heirs. If the heirs don't have sufficient cash for taxes, they must call in a buyer. These same circumstances confront families

---

VIEWPOINT 8-2

TAKING FROM PETER TO PAY PAUL

"The most harmful effect of chain formation may be that profits made in a community paper are not reinvested in that paper. The community daily has become a source of capital to be invested elsewhere."

Ben H. Bagdikian, author, educator, and at times severe media critic, *The Information Machines,* Harper & Row

that own gas stations, farms, or other businesses, of course, *except* for one crucial factor: Estate taxes are based on "fair market value" of the property—what a willing buyer will pay a willing seller—and for reasons already outlined, newspapers and television stations have extremely high market values. Taxes based on those values frequently are more than owners can finance out of their operation.

VIEWPOINT 8-3

TAXED INTO SELLING

"Times change...costs of materials and equipment mount inexorably. The future requirements of journalism, both print and electronic, are difficult to predict. Meanwhile, tax policies make it increasingly hard for family-held corporations to maintain control from one generation to another."

Barry Bingham, Sr., announcing the family-owned *Louisville Courier-Journal* and *Times* were being sold to Gannett Co., for $305 million

---

Even when quarrels in the owning family seem to inspire sales—as in 1986 with the *Louisville Courier-Journal* and *Times*—there often are family members who want to assume full control from relatives but cannot afford to.

It's ironic. We hear so much about the evils of group ownership, how family-owned newspapers or broadcast stations are scooped up by group executives run wild in their empire building, or betrayed and sold by greedy owners who simply want to pick up a huge bundle of cash. But the real villains are not so much in corporate boardrooms as in the lawmakers' chambers. Well, then, what types of media companies come from all this? Who are the big players? Let's look.

THE FIFTEEN LARGEST GROUPS

Most media companies today are highly complex, with not one corporate face, but several. The measurements of distinction are many. To judge Times Mirror would require assessing its performance in newspapers, television, radio, magazines, cable, outdoor advertising, book publishing, real estate, forest and paper products, and other areas—many beyond the scope of our study. So, let's objectively rank the 15 largest firms according to total media revenue (see Table 8-1), then touch on their newspaper and television operations, making a few subjective observations along the way, but not pretending to treat all their corporate affairs comprehensively.[5] Such an appreciation is central to our study of ethics and social responsibility in the media and, certainly, to the media's role in society.

No. 1. Capital Cities/ABC   Holdings include ABC radio and television networks, TV stations in eight major cities, radio stations in nine, plus cable television; eight daily newspapers in seven states, nondailies in eight, and a huge stable of consumer magazines ranging from *High Fidelity* and *Hardware Age* to *Motor Age* and *Skin & Allergy News*. ABC, long an innovator in television

TABLE 8-1
THE FIFTEEN LARGEST MEDIA COMPANIES (1985)

	Media revenue	Total revenue	Net income
1. Capital Cities/ABC	$3.8 billion	$4.3 billion	$301 million
2. CBS	3.1	4.7	27
3. Time Inc.	2.8	3.4	200
4. RCA (NBC)	2.6	8.9	369
5. Times Mirror	2.17	2.9	237
6. Gannett	2.15	2.2	253
7. Advance Publications*	2.0	NA	NA
8. Dun & Bradstreet	1.7	2.7	295
9. Tribune Co.	1.68	1.9	124
10. Knight-Ridder	1.67	1.7	133
11. Hearst*	1.5	NA	NA
12. New York Times	1.39	1.39	116
13. Cox*	1.32	1.37	NA
14. Westinghouse	1.06	10.7	605
15. Washington Post	1.03	1.07	102

*Privately owned.
Source: Advertising Age

news and sports coverage, is in for tight times. Capital Cities is known for extremely high profit margins produced by cutting costs to the bone.

No. 2. CBS   In addition to television and radio networks, CBS owns stations in major cities across the country. In 1986 and 1987, it sold companies dealing in consumer magazines, book publishing, records, music, and video. Starting with Edward R. Murrow during World War II and continuing through Walter Cronkite and Dan Rather, CBS built a reputation for journalism that is solid, responsible, and profitable as well. Numerous outside attempts to take over CBS forced management into extremely expensive defensive moves. By 1986, CBS was carrying more than $1 billion in debt—and was slashing costs in its news division to help pay it off. Its reported 1985 news budget was $188.7 million for covering "hard news" and *West 57th Street;* $7.1 million for "special and unscheduled events" such as natural disasters; $5.1 million for political coverage; $10.9 million for "by-products" such as worldwide distribution of shows; and $30.9 million for staff and executives not charged against specific programs.[6]

No. 3. Time Inc.   After costly attempts to enter the newspaper business (it lost $85 million failing to resuscitate the *Washington Star*), Time returned to what it does best—operating magazines and cable television. By 1985, its media revenue was divided between magazines ($1.5 billion) and cable ($1.4 billion).

No. 4. NBC   NBC is part of RCA, which has been owned by General Electric Co. since June 1986, and thus is just one arm of a giant $38 billion conglomerate, the nation's eleventh largest. NBC's media revenue earns it No. 4 ranking on our list. NBC-TV has more than 200 affiliates throughout the country, and operates its own television and radio stations in many major cities. Although its television entertainment frequently trailed both ABC and CBS in ratings, NBC's "Nightly News With Tom Brokaw" challenged CBS's long dominance in the evening.

No. 5. Times Mirror Corp.   One of the nation's truly distinguished media companies—it is professionally managed, highly profitable, and a producer of high-quality, responsible journalism with its *Los Angeles Times, Newsday, Baltimore Sun,* and other newspapers. After decades of nearly unbroken success and expansion, Times Mirror failed in a big way when its *Dallas Times Herald* was unable to overtake A. H. Belo Corp.'s *Dallas Morning News.* Times Mirror sold the paper in 1986. It has another problem with its *Denver Post,* which is unable to conquer its crosstown rival, Scripps-Howard's *Rocky Mountain News.*

No. 6. Gannett Co.   In number of newspapers owned (ninety-nine in 1986) and newspaper revenue, Gannett is the largest. In twenty years, the company exploded from a handful of upstate New York dailies into an international giant in television, radio, outdoor advertising, and many other media-related areas, in addition to newspapers. The guiding genius who took Gannett into public ownership and set its course for almost two decades was chairman Paul Miller. He acquired small and medium-size newspapers without head-on competition from other papers, a recipe for maximum profits. His successor, Al Neuharth, in the 1980s moved the company into an entirely new level of media activity with acquisition of big-city newspapers—such as the *Des Moines Register & Tribune, Detroit News,* and the *Louisville Courier-Journal* and *Times*— and by launching *USA Today,* a highly innovative national newspaper, but huge money loser. Gannett is known for solid but unspectacular journalism carefully tuned to produce sound community newspapers and high profits.

No. 7. Advance Publications   The nation's largest privately owned media company, tightly-held by an almost secretive Newhouse family and run by S. I. Newhouse, Jr., and Donald Newhouse, sons of founder S. I. Newhouse. Company revenue is estimated substantially in excess of $2 billion annually from daily newspapers in ten states (largest, at 482,000 circulation, is the *Cleveland Plain Dealer*), magazines (*Mademoiselle, House & Garden, Bride's, Glamour, New Yorker, Parade,* and others), extensive cable TV operations, book publishing (Random House, Alfred A. Knopf, Ballantine, Vintage, and Modern Library), and other holdings. The company sold all television holdings in the early 1980s, a clear signal the Newhouses felt network-affiliated TV stations had seen their most profitable days and that cable is the wave of the electronic future. The IRS claims the family owes $914 million in inheritance taxes and penalties from the death of the elder Newhouse; the family puts tax liability at $47 million. The group's newspapers are profit-oriented and generally undistinguished journalistically, although its *Plain Dealer, Newark* (N.J.) *Star-Ledger* (433,000 circulation), and *Portland Oregonian* (288,000) occasionally rise above modest heights.

No. 8. Dun & Bradstreet   Strong in specialty magazines (*American Journal of Medicine, Dun's Business Monthly,* and others); but most of its media revenue is from narrowly focused business and financial information services outside the scope of our study of newspaper and television ethics.

No. 9. Tribune Co.   One of the nation's premier communications companies in journalistic excellence and profit. Two papers—the *Chicago Tribune* and *Orlando Sentinel*—are on most lists of the ten best dailies. Tribune's WGN-TV in Chicago is first-rate. Tribune illustrates how widely diversified modern communications conglomerates have become. Holdings include the *New York Daily News* (the largest, at 1.3 million, general circulation daily in the country), six dailies in California, Virginia, and Florida; weeklies in Illinois, Florida, and Oklahoma; television stations in Illinois, New York, Colorado, Louisiana, Georgia, and California; radio stations in Illinois, New York, Connecticut, and California; a cable television company based in New Jersey; a nationwide news and feature syndicate with headquarters in Florida; a marketing company operating out of Chicago; newsprint mills and forest products holdings in four Canadian towns, plus 60 percent of a power company in Quebec; Tribune Entertainment Company; an independent TV news network (INN) emanating from New York City—and, of course, the Chicago Cubs.

No. 10. Knight-Ridder, Inc.   No company consistently produces more first-rate journalism in as many parts of the United States than Knight-Ridder (thirty-nine Pulitzer Prizes for group newspapers by 1986). Chairman Alvah Chapman seldom mentions profit and growth without insisting high-quality journalism and community service are the way to achieve them. That spirit pervades the company, notably at the highly respected *Philadelphia Inquirer, Miami Herald, Detroit Free Press,* and *San Jose* (Calif.) *Mercury News.* A businessman by training, Chapman brought along as president and No. 2 in the company a career journalist, James K. Batten, and promoted other highly regarded news executives, thus ensuring continued commitment in top ranks to journalistic quality. With 90 percent of its revenue eggs in the newspaper basket alone, Knight-Ridder is attempting to diversify. It now owns seven television stations, extensive cable operations, plus commodity and business news information services for private subscribers. An electronic delivery system of general news and information for homes proved a $50 million flop.

No. 11. Hearst Corp.   This 100-year-old private company, whose holdings include gold mines and other commercial activities, never publishes its financial figures. The media division is thought (1986) to have about $1.5 billion revenue (46 percent from magazines; 23 percent from newspapers; and 16 percent from TV, radio, and cable). In journalistic impact, the company is just a shadow of the company William Randolph Hearst put together. His strategy of operating big-city newspapers, a winner at the time, proved disastrous when socioeconomic decline in core cities caused affluent residents to flee to the suburbs. One by one, the influential (but never great) Hearst papers died. In 1986, the company closed its *Baltimore News-American,* and in metro markets now has only the *Los Angeles Herald-Examiner,* a distant No. 10 in a two-newspaper market, behind the mighty *Los Angeles Times;* Hearst's *San Francisco Examiner* and *Seattle Post-Intelligencer,* are both No. 2 papers in their markets. The company owns five major market television stations, radio stations, cable, magazines (*Cosmopolitan, Good Housekeeping, Harper's Bazaar,* and many others), book publishing (Arbor House, Avon, William Morrow, and others), and one of the country's leading syndicates, King. Hearst is trying to acquire medium-size newspapers, which yield high profit margins, but in national influence, Hearst newspapers are out of the ball game.

No. 12. New York Times Co. In a pure management sense, this company's turnaround is classic. Though its *New York Times* was the single most influential paper in the country and, at the time, best journalistically by a wide margin, the company itself was in trouble in the 1960s. Profits were marginal, and the company's most important—virtually its only—market, New York City, was in financial and social decline. While maintaining—in fact, enhancing—the journalistic quality of the *Times,* company executives under chairman Arthur Ochs ("Punch") Sulzberger launched the expansion/diversification effort which made the company a nationwide media powerhouse. To the *Times'* circulation of over 1 million daily (1.6 million on Sundays), the company added community papers with (in 1986) more than 750,000 circulation in nine "Sun Belt" states, television and radio stations, magazines (*Family Circle, Golf Digest,* and others), and a large cable TV operation. For thousands of those most important in government, finance, commerce, and industry throughout the world, the *Times* is *the* source of important news and informed opinion. Further, for many editors—in newspapers and TV alike—news becomes news when the *Times* says it's news. The paper thus has substantial influence on worldwide news-gathering habits beyond its own pages.

No. 13. Cox Enterprises Of the largest media companies, none has expanded so widely while remaining so unknown to the public and so without influence in journalistic circles. This privately owned company has (in 1986) properties in twenty-one states and over $1.3 billion in annual revenue (46.8 percent from twenty-one daily and twenty-two weekly newspapers, 30.5 percent from cable, and 18.9 percent from broadcast). Yet, many students of the media would be hard pressed to name any Cox holdings. The flagship is the *Atlanta Journal and Constitution,* financially strong and journalistically competent but without influence much beyond Georgia. Other papers include the *Dayton* (Ohio) *Daily News and Journal Herald, Austin* (Tex.) *American-Statesman,* and smaller community papers. For years, the company's management hierarchy was in musical-chairs turmoil. In 1985, Cox family members, who controlled privately held Cox Enterprises, spent more than $1.2 billion to acquire publicly held shares of Cox Communications. Merging them created overnight the thirteenth largest—and private—media conglomerate.

No. 14. Westinghouse Electric Corp.   Media sales from TV and radio are only 9 percent of total sales—but that still is more than $1 billion and enough to rank Westinghouse among the nation's biggies. Westinghouse sold its cable operations in 1986—for $2.1 billion.

No. 15. Washington Post Co.   After years of producing great journalism at the *Washington Post* and turning out a pretty good magazine, *Newsweek,* this company in the early 1980s got its management act in order and, like its peer companies, began expanding and diversifying. It now is a $1 billion-plus conglomerate, drawing 55.6 percent of its revenue from newspapers, 32.6 percent from magazines. In 1986, it paid $350 million for fifty-three cable systems owned by Capital Cities/ABC. Unlike *USA Today,* the *New York Times,* and *Wall Street Journal,* the *Washington Post* has not attempted significant national *circulation* expansion. It prefers to profitably dominate the Washington market. But in *journalistic influence,* the *Post* is second only to the *Times* nationally, and in covering politics and government, second to none. In Washington, the *Post* sets the news agenda.

Now, ranking media companies by revenue *does* objectively provide some guidance to a company's likely impact on the way Americans think and live, but doesn't really reveal what we need to know about ethics and social responsibility. And the list of fifteen doesn't include some of the country's most influential newspaper and television companies. So, let's quickly look at a few others:

No. 17. Dow Jones & Co.   One of the world's truly great and most influential media companies. Its *Wall Street Journal* (about 2 million circulation), *Barron's Weekly,* and financial and economic news services for private subscribers have enormous impact in business, and in political and government circles. The *Journal,* arguably the nation's best written and edited newspaper, is the flagship of this $1 billion company, perennially ranked among the best managed and most profitable. And, the company is run by executives who first won their spurs in news, then learned management technique. Through its Ottaway Newspapers, a group of community papers, Dow Jones extends its influence into small towns in eleven states. It reaches overseas with European and Asian editions of the *Journal,* local news weeklies, and wire-delivered private subscriber services.

No. 18. Scripps Howard   This company name evokes memory of strong, nationally influential newspapers of yesteryear. But, as with Hearst, it's only a memory. Scripps Howard is privately held, with a publicly held broadcasting arm. It owns properties nationwide, but has comparatively little journalistic impact. The company has turned to more local, more profitable enterprises. It stepped down from the national stage when it sold United Press International, a money loser for decades, in 1982.

No. 21. News America Publishing   This widely diversified company is controlled by Australian-born Rupert Murdoch, who cut a swath through the media world Down Under before he was 40, turned Britain's Fleet Street on its ear, then set course for the New World and its media riches. In just a few years, aggressive acquisitions and low-brow newspapering firmly established News America as a $600 million company. Murdoch's strategy was to produce sensationalistic newspapers for readers left behind by elitist papers driving upscale in search of affluent subscribers. He produced huge circulations in a hurry—as high as 960,000 for the *New York Post,* 630,000 for the *Chicago Sun-Times,* and 360,000 for the *Boston Herald.* But Murdoch's readers were unattractive to advertisers, and the *Post* for years lost an estimated $1 million monthly; the *Herald* swam in red; and the *Sun-Times* didn't flourish. By 1986, Murdoch had sold out in Chicago, was looking for a buyer in New York—and was redeploying assets into television, magazines, and movies. His goal clearly is a new television network. In 1985, Murdoch became a naturalized American, which enabled him to meet federal regulations that only citizens may own more than 25 percent of a television station.

No. (?) Thomson   Only an accountant equipped with inside information could assess this Canadian-based company's U.S. operations. But its newspaper and magazine revenues alone easily top $1 billion. Thomson owns small papers— 96 U.S. dailies, 4 weeklies by 1986—and pulls down profit margins among the industry's highest by serving up journalistic junk food. Donrey Media (forty-eighth largest in revenue) and Park Communications (ninety-first) employ similar tactics. Between them, the three profit-oriented groups operate 179 dailies and 82 weeklies.

No. 27. A. H. Belo   This company is noteworthy because (1) its *Dallas Morning News* is one of the nation's finest newspapers and (2) it is led by young, talented managers brimming with enthusiasm and expansionist ideas. For now, mark Belo as a practitioner of first-rate journalism that may yet move across the national stage in both print and television (it already owns five major market TV stations and four radio stations).

No. 34. Turner Broadcasting   A go-go outfit spurred ahead by gregarious, fast-talking Ted Turner (''The Mouth of the South'') who expanded from his Atlanta base to nationwide impact on television journalism. Turner started an all-news network, CNN, which though struggling financially, is a high-quality, service-minded twenty-four-hour network. Turner, whose holdings include the Atlanta Braves baseball team and Atlanta Hawks basketball team, tried to take over CBS, then snagged MGM/UA Entertainment for $1.5 billion. In 1987, a group of outside cable companies provided $550 million in financing for 35 percent of Turner's company. He was left with 51 percent.

About 100 media companies each have over $100 million revenue annually, or close to it, and we must move on to crucial questions arising from all this: In whose hands rest the business and journalistic fortunes of these companies? Who are the owners and managers of these companies serving, for better or worse, tens of millions of readers and viewers?

THE GREAT MEDIA FORTUNES

Many people have made—and are making—a great deal of money from the companies we've been discussing. Media fortunes put at least 79 men and women on *Forbes* magazine's list of the ''400 Richest People in America.'' To get on that list you must be worth a *minimum* $150 million.

Forbes says three billionaires come from media ranks: S.I. Newhouse Jr., and his brother Donald, who run Advance Publications and are said to share $2.2 billion, and John Kluge, TV entrepreneur (Metromedia), said to be worth $1 billion. A fourth billionaire, Warren Buffett, a stock market investor from Omaha, made much of his fortune in media stocks, notably Washington Post Co., and Capital Cities/ABC. Among those counted personally worth $500 million or more, at least nine made fortunes in the media—or, more usually, had parents who did.

Many of America's great family fortunes were built on media interests: Bancroft (Dow Jones), Block (*Toledo Blade, Pittsburgh Post-Gazette,* TV and cable), Chandler (Times Mirror), Gardner Cowles family (*Des Moines Register and Tribune, Minneapolis Star and Tribune,* and others), William Cowles family (*Chicago Tribune, Spokane Spokesman-Review and Chronicle*), de Young (*San Francisco Chronicle*), Hoiles (Freedom Newspapers), McClatchy (Fresno, Sacramento, Modesto, Calif., *Bee* Newspapers), McGraw (McGraw-Hill, mostly magazines, books), Pulitzer (*St. Louis Post-Dispatch* and other properties), E. W. Scripps (newspapers, television), J. E. Scripps (*Detroit News,* now owned by Gannett, and other papers, television), Sulzberger (*New York Times*), Wolfe (*Columbus Dispatch* and others).[7]

Some might suspect that through that ocean of media money there run currents of political power and societal influence that, if mixed with manipulation of the news, could bode ill for the future of the republic. Such *potential* may exist to some degree—but not much. Most media fortunes are dispersed among many heirs not actively involved in the newspaper, magazine, or broadcast properties that yielded their wealth. *Forbes,* for example, found about thirty descendants sharing the de Young fortune of $450 million. None is named deYoung; one, Richard Thieriot, runs the *San Francisco Chronicle*. However, some media-owning family members still are involved in management—Katharine Graham (worth $350 million, *Forbes* says) at Washington Post Co., and Sulzberger family members ($450 million) at New York Times Co., are examples.

Most significant family companies—including Washington Post Co., and New York Times Co.—long ago went public. Although family members may hold controlling stock, the companies are managed on a day-to-day basis by professionals, chosen not for blood line but for ability to expand, diversify, operate efficiently, and improve profits—for everyone, third-generation heir basking in the Bahamas *and* Mr. and Mrs. Average Investor who take a $1,000 or so fling on media stocks. Of our fifteen leading companies, twelve are publicly traded on the New York Stock Exchange or American Stock Exchange and are owned by thousands of shareholders. In 1986, for example, Knight-Ridder counted 9,468 shareholders in all fifty states holding its 56 million shares.[8] Obviously, not all shareholders are equal. Some are banks and other "institutional" investors or individuals with major holdings. James Knight owns about 10 percent of Knight-Ridder, a company he and his late brother, Jack, helped put together. Otis Chandler, principal Times Mirror heir and architect of its growth to greatness, votes 35.4 percent of the company's common stock.

Now, 10 percent of Knight-Ridder or 35.4 percent of Times Mirror speak louder in company affairs than the $1,000 worth held by Mr. and Mrs. Average Investor. However, we generally don't encounter wealthy family members managing things, certainly not day-to-day in the newsroom. For example, neither Knight nor Chandler holds operating titles in companies they helped build.

No, there are two layers of control other than owners we must examine—boards of directors for setting policy and professional managers for running things.

VIEWPOINT 8-4

MEDIA SIZE AND SUCCESS

"The public . . . is occasionally alienated by the sheer size and financial success of the communications media today. To many, we appear to be a rather rich, monolithic, forbidding institution. Our motives become suspect. Are we in business to serve the public or increase our profits? Are they, in fact, contradictory?"

Katharine Graham, chairman, Washington Post Co.

THE POLICY-SETTING APPARATUS

In theory, the policymaking apparatus of any publicly owned media company is a board of directors composed of experts of one sort or another from both inside and outside corporate ranks with the mission of guiding management and representing shareholders' interests. And, again in theory, the owner of even a single share can rise at the company's annual meeting, open by law to all share-holders, to nominate someone to the board or ask questions or demand action and thus influence company affairs.

In fact, of course, those who own the shares have the votes, so directors often are selected to include holders of large numbers of shares (even if they possess no particular expertise) or individuals they nominate. The selection process itself and policy guidelines eventually issued by the board are influenced heavily by the very men and women they are meant to direct—the professional managers.

A professional manager can have strong influence—control, even—over the board. How much relates directly to his or her track record and strength of personality. Al Neuharth, who each year boosts Gannett's profits to new heights and who is an extremely dominant personality, has enormous clout with his board (he got the chairmanship initially by threatening, while president, to quit, and the board caved in). Chairman Chapman pretty much gets his way at Knight-Ridder; so does Robert Erburu at Times Mirror. Note all three are professionals without blood ties to the original owning families. Executives of their proven abilities are scarce, and boards go to extraordinary lengths to keep them happy.

So, the key to who really runs the nation's largest media companies—and how—lies in the relationship between boards of directors and professional managers. There is no "typical" board of directors, no "typical" flow of policy-making authority. But the men and women who make policy for hundreds of newspapers and television stations and, thus, for millions of readers and viewers clearly are drawn from predictable sources: "inside" managers and family members with large stock holdings, and "outside" members of what, for lack of a better word, can be called the "establishment." Let's look, for example, at Knight-Ridder's board (1986):

Outside directors: Clark Clifford, 69, lawyer, former U.S. secretary of defense and a director of Phillips Petroleum; C. Peter McColough, 63, chairman of Xerox Corp.; Barbara Barnes Hauptfuhrer, 57, (board's only woman), director of several other public companies; John L. Weinberg, 61, senior partner and chairman of Goldman, Sachs & Co., investment firm; Thomas L. Phillips, 61, chairman and chief executive officer, Raytheon Co.; and Jesse Hill, Jr., 59, (board's only black), president of Atlanta Life Insurance Co.

Inside directors: Alvah H. Chapman, Jr., 64, Knight-Ridder chairman and chief executive officer, trained on the business side of newspapering; Byron Harless, 69, retired senior vice president/personnel; Robert Singleton, 55, senior vice president/finance; Peyton Anderson, 78, who sold *Macon, (Ga.) Telegraph and News,* to Knight-Ridder; James Knight, 76, former chairman; James Batten, 50, president and an editor by training; Lee Hills, 79, former chairman and editor of national reputation; Bernard H. Ridder, Jr., 69, former chairman who brought Ridder Newspapers into merger with Knight in 1967; Eric Ridder, 67, former publisher of Ridder's *Journal of Commerce;* Walter Ridder, 68, Ridder's former national editor.

Knight-Ridder's board, then, is drawn heavily from Knight and Ridder family shareholders and company executives. Of sixteen directors, only six are from outside, and they very much are "establishment" types. The directors' average age is 65.3.

New York Times Co., has two classes of directors—"class A," with limited voting power, and "class B," who really call the tune. Average age of Times directors is 61.4, and the powerful class B votes are controlled by members of the Sulzberger family or company officers. Just two class B directors are from outside company or family ranks.

No career journalists are on the board of the nation's ninth largest media corporation, Tribune Co. Five of thirteen directors (1986) are from inside—the company president (engineer by training), the *Chicago Tribune*'s publisher (accountant by early education), the president of the company's broadcasting unit, the head of its Ontario Paper Company Limited, and the company's executive vice president (whose background is finance.) Outside directors are one woman and seven men with widely diverse business connections—officers or directors of companies such as Borg-Warner, Abbott Laboratories, National Can, First National Bank of Chicago, Commonwealth Edison, Corning Glass Works, and United Airlines.

Now, by selecting these examples the author does not suggest it is wrong for media companies to take policy direction from present or former engineers, lawyers, bankers, accountants, or the chairman of Commonwealth Edison and a director of Corning Glass. Indeed, whatever the backgrounds and interests of their directors, the three companies produce some of the finest journalism in the land. The author *does* suggest, however, that with the "credibility gap" and growing public cynicism about the media, society may one day demand more representative balance in the policymaking hierarchies of companies that are among the nation's most influential and important institutions.

Gannett shows awareness of this possibility. Al Neuharth often is uncanny in anticipating social issues, including societal pressure to hire women and minorities, and positioning his company accordingly. His board (1986) obviously is handpicked for societal as well as professional balance. His eighteen directors include four women (none of family connections), one black, an Hawaiian financier of Chinese extraction, a broadcaster (Julian Goodman, former NBC chairman), a politician (former U.S. Senate majority leader Howard Baker of Tennessee, who later resigned to become President Reagan's chief of staff), and an educator (Edward Bassett, dean of Northwestern University's Medill School of Journalism). Eight directors have extensive news background. Average age of directors is 55.9, considerably younger than on most boards.[9]

Outside directors on media company boards often are selected for their legal and financial expertise. Legally vulnerable to libel action and highly complex in corporate organization, media companies do need lawyers. And, as capital-intensive companies, they need access to outside capital, thus the many directors drawn from banks, investment firms, and insurance companies. But boards are constructed also to give media companies *political connections*—access to Washington power corridors.

In addition to former Senator Baker on the Republican side, Gannett in 1986 had Rosalyn Carter, the former first lady with a pipeline into Democratic circles. One director, Andrew Brimmer, was a former member of the Federal Reserve's board of directors and former assistant secretary of commerce. Times Mirror had a former chairman of the powerful Securities and Exchange Commission in Washington; Knight-Ridder, a former secretary of defense; and New York Times, a former secretary of state, and a former ambassador/governor. Washington Post Co., whose chairman Katharine Graham had more clout in Washington than any of them, had on its board Robert McNamara, former U.S. secretary of defense and World Bank president, and Nicholas deB. Katzenbach, former U.S. attorney general and under secretary of state.[10]

So, that's a look at policymaking boards. But who are the professional managers important in that policy? Where, how—by whom—is media policy actually executed?

THE TRUE "POWER CLIQUE"

The true "power clique" in American media companies is in the elite ranks of top management, in the "executive committee" or "management committee" chaired by the chief executive officer. Here, at a level just below the board of directors, are made truly crucial decisions on how the nation's newspapers and television stations will be operated.

Large shareholder interests and family fortunes often are represented on these operating committees, but they largely are composed of men and women who fought to the top by proving they were better managers than others in a key sector such as advertising, circulation, production, business/finance, personnel, or news.

Important responsibilities come with promotion to operating committee level. At Knight-Ridder, for example, a nine-member executive committee makes daily decisions affecting 22,000 company employees, and readers and viewers of the company's news products throughout the world. Readers of the *Grand Forks* (N.D.) *Herald, Milledgeville (Ga.) Union-Recorder,* and other Knight-Ridder newspapers see—or don't see—news winnowed and sifted in great part in accordance with standards laid down by one Larry Jinks—hardly a household name in any of those cities, but very important at Knight-Ridder headquarters in Miami. Jinks is group senior vice president/news and operations, and a member of the executive committee. Daniel Gold is important if you watch television in Flint, Michigan; Nashville; Providence, Rhode Island; Albany, New York; Norfolk, Virginia; Tucson, Arizona; Oklahoma City; or Mobile, Alabama. Gold is president of Knight-Ridder Broadcasting, Inc., which operates TV stations in those cities, and one of sixteen corporate officers who, in addition to the nine-member executive committee, run the company from Miami. As at many companies, there is careful cross-pollination between Knight-Ridder's powerful nine-member executive committee and its board of directors and principal owning families. Of the nine, five are (1986) directors.

At Tribune Co., corporate officers number twelve men and two women responsible for legal, financial, planning, and personnel functions. There is at this level in the company no career newsperson.

New York Times Co., has twelve corporate officers plus twelve other executives who serve as general counsel, directors of planning and corporate affairs, taxes, and so forth. Not until we descend to yet another layer of company management do we find full-time editors—"Operating Group Officers and Executives," who include the executive editor and other departmental chiefs of the *New York Times,* plus directors of company broadcasting, magazines, regional newspapers, and cable TV.

Gannett's powerful eleven-person management committee includes six professional managers who also serve on the board of directors. Seventeen others are designated as principal executive officers. Uniquely, Gannett draws to its top ranks, sometimes on a rotating basis, operating executives from newspapers, television stations, and other units scattered throughout the country. (Because of its huge size, Gannett has organized in national and regional units to facilitate management; each is represented in policy coordination at corporate headquarters in Arlington, Virginia.)

The Source of True Power

But what gives these relatively few top managers such power over their farflung media empires, such influence over what American news consumers see and read? It flows principally from two sources:

First, these executives appoint local managers and editors, the men and women who decide what will be on the front pages tomorrow or the 6 P.M. news tonight in the Flints, Grand Forks, and Milledgevilles. And, if those men and women aren't what the Larry Jinkses and Daniel Golds of corporate hierarchies think editors and managers should be, they are out.

Second, more indirectly but just as importantly, these top executives approve or disapprove financial budgets and operating plans submitted to the group by newspaper and station managers. It is quite possible that in this process a local executive's best intentions to, say, improve journalistic quality or pay higher salaries to attract better talent will wither before the corporate demand for better profit margins.

Most top group executives would bristle at any suggestion they promote those junior managers closest to their own personalities and operating styles, or that they use budgets and operating plans to force conformity at group newspapers or television stations. But the plain fact is that executives all hired nationwide in accordance with the same corporate specifications, all trained at the same company seminars, all guided by the same top-level corporate philosophy, all following identical budget procedures tend to talk the same, think the same, and act the same.

The author detects in none of this any sinister, centrally directed plot to distort or manage the news and sway the hearts and minds of millions of readers or viewers. But, unquestionably, a great deal of dull, look-alike journalism flows from it. It *is* possible to pick up many group newspapers and be struck by how similar they are to those in the last town visited. It *is* possible to switch on a local newscast and see the handiwork of a group "TV news doctor" sent in to boost ratings with the "Action News" format of screaming sirens and whirling red lights, just like the sirens and red lights last night, in another town. And you probably can believe top executives of the Thomson, Donrey or Park groups who swear they don't interfere in local news coverage. But you can also believe they slashed the budget of any local manager who dared propose spending above group-approved levels to achieve journalistic excellence.

In a rare public break with industry colleagues, one group executive charged in 1987 that group ownership was dragging down the journalistic quality of many newspapers. James H. Ottaway, Jr., president of Ottaway Newspapers, Inc., and a vice president of its parent, Dow Jones, said in a series of speeches that semiprivate Thomson and private Donrey were companies with "some of the highest profit-margin, lowest-quality newspapers in America today." He said it was "materialistic management philosophy, not public stockholder pressure, that pushes the men who manage these groups to run their newspapers for maximum short-term profit." Ottaway, whose family built a nationwide group before merging with Dow Jones, said group ownership does not always mean reduction in quality. He added:

"Many well-run groups greatly improve the newspapers they buy. I think we have. But too often in recent years, some groups, public and private, have paid prices that were so high, with multiples of revenue or net profits that were so high that severe cost-cutting, gradual or immediate reductions of staff, newshole, local coverage, news quality and reader service, have been required for the purchaser to make a reasonable return on such expensive investments."

The New Wealthy Elite

Life at the top in the media world is tough, highly competitive, and fast-moving. More than one executive has sacrificed much—including health and marriage—in reaching for the golden ring. And, it *can* be golden. A new class of wealthy elite has developed out of the men and women who run the largest media companies.

Al Neuharth, who started as an impoverished Associated Press reporter in the Dakotas, is paid $1 million annually plus bonus under a multiyear contract. In 1985, his cash compensation was $1,333,333. A deferred compensation agreement will give him $16,666 *per month for life* after retirement and, until 1999, he will be paid $100,000 annually and be given benefits "commensurate to his role and generally comparable to those he received prior to his retirement" for serving as a consultant. Neuharth, who went through two marriages and is a workaholic, has highly paid assistants: president John Curley (cash compensation alone), 1985, $685,000; vice chairman Douglas McCorkindale, $648,333; and vice president/news John Quinn, $518,333. Neuharth owned, in 1986, 68,871 shares of Gannett stock worth about $5.3 million. Curley's stockholdings were worth $3 million; McCorkindale's, $5.3 million; and Quinn's, $4.3 million. None of Gannett's new wealthy elite entered the company through family connections; all worked their way up through the ranks.[11]

At Tribune Co., the *average* cash compensation in 1985 for the top three management executives was $503,516. For the top *fifteen,* it was $258,156.40.[12]

It could be argued a person's income and wealth are of no concern to the public—or authors. This author would agree if the person involved were, say, manager of a nuts and bolts factory or a wheat farmer. But we deal here with men and women enormously influential in every sector of our society, executives who run some of the most important institutions in America. Is the power inherent in that a strong argument for closer public examination of media executives as, say, presidential candidates are examined? Should men and women who direct a company of nearly 100 newspapers or a nationwide broadcast conglomerate be forced to disclose, as presidents are, their most intimate personal and financial backgrounds?

VIEWPOINT 8-5

THE DOUBLE STANDARD ON DISCLOSURE

"The double standard—the press's claimed rights to examine everything and everyone in the public eye, and its own resistance to having its own work and conduct placed under equal scrutiny—is one of the root causes of the huge loss of journalism's credibility with its audiences."

Norman E. Isaacs, editor, educator, media critic, in *Untended Gates,* Columbia University Press

Should individuals with power to influence tens of millions of readers or viewers or to sway the affairs of state, live fully public lives, with their personal ideologies and thought processes open to public scrutiny?

The Changes Ahead

Important changes will occur by the early 1990s in management ranks of influential newspaper companies. Normal retirements alone will move new faces to the top of the policymaking apparatus at several. There probably will not be radical change, however, in the character of those companies or style of leadership. Almost without exception, current media leaders have carefully laid down long-term strategic planning that will guide their companies for years, if not decades. And, importantly, they have moved in behind themselves, in line for succession, executives out of their own mold.

In network television, momentous changes are certain in the next decade, not so much because individual executives will come and go (and they will, frequently), but, rather, because fundamental shifts are under way in the nature of broadcasting. Rapid development of cable TV and independent networks threatens the dominance in news enjoyed for so long by ABC, NBC, and CBS. Also, local news in many cities is so profitable that local stations will resist any network attempt to expand national news to one hour—and, indeed, may try in increasing numbers to get along without Rather, Jennings, Brokaw, or other star network anchors. Inevitably, this will put cost-cutting pressure on network news departments, and the strong international presence of ABC, NBC, and CBS news may weaken.

Signs of changing times at the networks already are appearing. At ABC, the man to reckon with is John Sias, longtime Capital Cities print executive who made his reputation by slashing costs and producing profit margins among the highest in the business before becoming president of ABC. Any ABC editor who wants a new bureau abroad at a cost of $1 million-plus annually or who plans expensive documentaries will face tough times with Sias.

NBC, probably will take years to sort out the precise shape of its future as part of GE. Who leads NBC and NBC News probably will be less important to their future than the proliferation of competing media and how this news and entertainment company will operate inside the $38-billion giant that is GE.

CBS also has problems larger than personalities: First, how to handle the $1-billion debt load assumed to avoid corporate takeovers and, second, how to avoid more takeover attempts in the future. Both forced deep cuts in news department spending in 1987, drawing vigorous public protests from, among others, anchorman Dan Rather. More cuts are certain, and the news division and its journalistic quality will suffer.

Amid the change will be one constant: large groups will get larger, competing even more fiercely for remaining independent newspaper and broadcast operations—then, when they are all gone, trying to swallow each other.

There is strong incentive for the large to get much larger. For shareholders addicted to huge leaps forward, incremental addition of, say, a nice little community newspaper with $10 million revenue or so, or a TV station with $12 million, won't do it anymore. It takes big—really big—acquisitions to add dramatically to the bottom line that must be displayed to shareholders at each annual meeting. And, importantly, for executives who built Gannett, Washington Post Co., Tribune Co., New York Times Co., and the others piece by piece there now is the thrill of chasing a *really* big one. How big? Well, for example, Gannett, at $2.1 billion annual revenue, talked to both Time, Inc., $2.8 billion, and CBS, $3.1 billion, about a merger. One that size would catapult Gannett to the No. 1 spot on the list of the largest. Many of the largest fifteen companies are strongly financed and are positioning themselves for megabuck deals. Washington Post Co., for example, estimated in 1985 that ''over the next few years'' it would have roughly $100 million *annually* available for acquisitions.[13]

It will be increasingly difficult to pull off big coups through *hostile* takeover of another company—that is, by buying stock on the open market, then walking into corporate headquarters one day and introducing yourself as the new boss. That is a tactic used in other industries by raiders who sometimes are serious about taking over a company, but often are practicing "greenmail"—buying enough stock to frighten management, then offering the stock back to the company for, of course, a ridiculously exorbitant price amounting to extortion. Media companies busily erect defenses against such tactics. They take on debt to make themselves unattractive to outside raiders, or stagger terms of their directors so no raider easily can create a power base on the board, regardless of number of shares owned. Or, they change their bylaws to force raiders to buy *all* outstanding shares at the same price, which makes takeover simply too expensive.

Such antitakeover measures, though of course entirely legal, raise philosophical questions central to our discussion of who really controls these huge, influential newspaper and television companies, and in whose interest they are operated. To explain:

Antitakeover measures always are instituted in the name of good and right. Dow Jones and New York Times Co., for example, announced theirs as designed to ensure control remains in the hands of enlightened founding families and managers who supervised the growth to greatness of both companies. And it is true that in both cases socially responsible family members invested heavily in journalistic quality. For decades, the Sulzberger family insisted the *Times* maintain its quality even if that drained profits.

However, some antitakeover measures are ramrodded through by professional managers anxious to protect their own cushy jobs and prerogatives. Any manager who permits takeover by Capital Cities, Newhouse, or other similarly profit-minded companies can kiss good-bye the private jet and limo.

VIEWPOINT 8-6

PROFITS AND THE PUBLIC TRUST

"The Bancroft family, which owns 56 percent of Dow Jones and has controlled the company since 1902, has for generations regarded the *(Wall Street) Journal* as a quasi-public trust and has encouraged journalistic independence and investment for the long term...Our economic success hinges on that."

Chairman Warren Phillips, explaining Dow Jones Co., was instituting antitakeover steps to ensure continued Bancroft control of company

---

Now, all this is of considerable importance to Mr. and Mrs. Average investor with their $1,000 worth of stock. In any hostile takeover attempt bidding for stock can drive up the per-share value 40 percent, 50 percent, or more, and that $1,000 suddenly can grow into the price of a new car or Caribbean vacation. Such hostile bidding contests, which can create wealth for thousands of shareholders in publicly traded media companies, are precluded by antitakeover measures.

Antitakeover measures can solidify in the hands of a relative few complete control of even those media companies whose stock is widely held. The Securities and Exchange Commission signaled on Dec. 16, 1986, it feels one antitakeover measure—issuing stock with different classes of voting rights—undermines "corporate democracy" by placing inordinate economic power in the hands of a few persons. Regarding takeover defenses erected in many industries, not only communications, an SEC spokesperson said, "If we abandon one-share, one vote, to whom will management be accountable for its actions?"

One tactic certain to be used increasingly in years ahead is taking private companies public by selling shares on the open market—selling just enough to raise substantial capital for expansion, but *not* enough to force the owner to relinquish control to anyone. Park Communications did this in 1983 by selling a shade over 10 percent of its stock. The rest—along with complete control of the company— stayed where it was, in the hands of Roy H. Park, founder of the company, and, according to *Forbes,* a man worth at least $350 million from newspapers and broadcast stations in twenty-two states. Using this tactic, small companies unknown nationally today to the reading or viewing public will move into view as media growth companies in the next decade. And, the men and women who own and run them will assume new importance in American society.

Now, we must look at how some media companies and executives expand— greatly—their influence through active participation in the affairs of news agencies.

The Agencies and Who Runs Them

If we ranked media organizations by influence on the flow of news, both The Associated Press and United Press International would rank high. But in total revenue, even AP—twice UPI's size—would rank as only the fifty-eighth largest media company. In profit, both are no-shows. AP is a nonprofit cooperative by design. UPI is nonprofit by accident of journalistic history; it has been a money loser for most of the past several decades.

The strong influence of these agencies stems not from their profit-and-loss statements, but, rather, from their worldwide news collection and distribution networks serving newspapers, television stations, and radio stations which, in turn, serve hundreds of millions of readers, viewers and listeners. AP alone has 1,600 journalists covering the world for (1986) 1,351 U.S. newspapers and 5,600 broadcast stations, plus thousands overseas. Many rely exclusively on AP, the world's dominant general news agency, for all but local coverage. It's a sad commentary on the craft of local editing, but a great many front pages and newscasts are put together in accord with what AP says is news. UPI, subsidized for decades by Scripps-Howard but sold in 1982, has hemorrhaged clients—due partly to ownership and financial problems, but primarily because newspaper editors increasingly take AP as a basic service, and use the money saved in dropping UPI to add a supplemental service from the *New York Times, Washington Post,* and *Los Angeles Times,* Knight-Ridder, or other large media company. UPI's revenues are about half AP's ($201 million in 1985).

AP's policymaking apparatus is a twenty-two-person board of directors—in 1986, eighteen men elected by newspaper members throughout the nation and four men (no women that year) appointed by newspaper directors to represent broadcast members (television and radio stations have nonvoting, "associate member" status in AP).

Cross-pollination with the largest media companies is extremely thorough. In 1986, AP's directors included top officials from Gannett, Times Mirror, Knight-Ridder, Dow Jones, and other newspaper and television groups. Under AP by-laws, at least two board seats go to representatives of newspapers in cities under 50,000 population. Broadcast appointees normally include representatives of networks or major market television stations plus two from small cities.

Policy decisions are passed to the staff through a president and general manager. Because they control the dollars, the media executives on AP's board have ultimate say in its journalistic accomplishments. Try as they might, AP's generally excellent, if largely anonymous, staff cannot for long outperform the financial support it receives for salaries and cost of news coverage. And, the directors who approve those costs represent news organizations that pay them, so the inevitable tendency is toward fiscal conservatism that at times leaves AP short of the money it needs to cover the world as it should.

In twenty-one years with AP, including seven in close contact with the board, the author never saw a director attempt to misuse his or her position by trying to slant how AP covers the news. The organization's tradition of playing the news as straight, dispassionately, and objectively as possible soon overwhelms even the most egocentric small-town publisher who makes it to a coveted seat on the board. However, there have been bush league efforts to keep AP out of certain business activities. One director, for example, opined that he would hate to see AP get into consumer research and market surveying (he had his own research firm). AP dutifully shelved the project. And, AP never has added newspaper critics to those who report on television, movies, art, books, and so forth. How would AP critique, say, the *New York Times,* from which it receives more than $1 million annually, or Gannett, whose representative currently chairs AP's board of directors? Both are *owners* of AP. Although this removes AP from effective media coverage (sorely needed, as we will discuss later), and although AP's form of ownership tends to magnify the importance of the already important Gannetts, Knight-Ridders, and others, the organization does a remarkably sound, responsible job.

UPI is privately owned, principally by a Mexican publisher, Mario Vazques Rana, but it too takes direction from American media companies. First, like AP, UPI must create news and photo services which, in addition to being valid journalistically, are saleable. Their news instincts aside, then, agency editors must cover the news in a manner responsive to the needs and desires of newspapers and stations. Second, UPI has tried to adopt AP-like business methods and has a "board of advisors" (not directors) from which it seriously seeks journalistic and business guidance (and, naturally, financial support). In its current dire circumstances, UPI quickly will see the merits of a suggestion from, say, a major client who feels a new bureau should be opened nearby.

There are, then, interlocking relationships in many forms running through the media world. From oak-paneled boardrooms, where big business reigns, to hotel corridors of publisher and station manager conventions, a relatively few men and women with often common interests have enormous influence over media corporations. In Part Three of this book—"The Media and Society"— we will turn to some wider societal implications of this.

CHAPTER SUMMARY

American newspaper and television companies are being restructured in character, ownership, and management. Widely diversified groups own 71 percent of all daily newspapers and most attractive television stations. The trend toward bigness will continue. It's corporate profit and personal prestige, not ideology or proselytism, that motivate media empire builders. On the sellers' part, extraordinarily high inheritance taxes on media properties force many sales.

Of the fifteen largest media companies, measured in total revenue, three are privately owned—Advance Publications, Hearst Corp., and Cox Enterprises. Among those publicly held, Times Mirror, Gannett, Tribune Co., Knight-Ridder, New York Times Co., and Washington Post Co., are strongly positioned to grow even larger in the 1990s, perhaps through megabuck takeovers of other large communications firms.

Great fortunes have been built in the media. *Forbes* magazine counts three billionaires in media ranks; a fourth made millions buying and selling media stocks. At least nine men and women worth $500 million or more made their fortunes in the media—or had parents who did.

The policy-setting apparatus of any publicly owned media company is its board of directors. Boards sometimes are controlled by heirs of founding families or strong-willed professional managers who get their way because they increase profits.

"Power cliques" in media companies are the elite ranks of top management in the "executive committee" that makes daily operating decisions. Their power flows from the ability to appoint—or fire—local managers and editors of group newspapers and TV stations throughout the country, and in their absolute control at group level of operating plans and budgets drawn up by local managers.

Huge salaries—sometimes over $1 million annually—are paid key media managers, some of whom consequently have become a wealthy new elite in the media world. Normal retirement alone will remove many top media personalities, in the decades ahead, but the operating philosophy of the most influential media conglomerates likely will not change. Many are instituting antitakeover measures to solidify control in the hands of leading shareholders or carefully selected professional managers as insurance against such change.

CHAPTER 8

Notes

1 "Annual Report 1985," Tribune Company, 435 North Michigan Ave., Chicago, Ill., 60611.
2 "Annual Report 1986," Times Mirror Co., Times Mirror Square, Los Angeles, Calif., 90053.

3 "First Quarter 1986 Report," Knight-Ridder, Inc., One Herald Plaza, Miami, Fla., 33101.

4 "Annual Report For Year Ended Dec. 31, 1985," the New York Times Co., 229 West 43rd. St., New York, N.Y., 10036.

5 A variety of sources yield insights into individual companies. Annual and quarterly reports plus letters to shareholders, obtainable from the secretary of each corporation, are prime sources, as are 10-K Reports, also obtainable from corporate secretaries or the Securities and Exchange Commission. Among trade publications, *Advertising Age* does superb wrapups on media activity. Its annual, "100 Leading Media Companies," is highly informative. The author finds one investment analyst particularly insightful—John Morton of Lynch, Jones & Ryan, 1037 Thirtieth St., N.W., Washington, D.C. 20007. In broadcast analysis, Ellen Berland Gibbs, president of Communications Resources, Inc., New York, N.Y., is an excellent analyst. *Forbes* magazine gives valuable details on revenues and profits.

6 Mary Anne Ostrom, "$10.8 Million Overrun: The Way It Is at CBS," *Manhattan, Inc.,* January 1986, p. 12.

7 "The *Forbes* Four Hundred," *Forbes* Special Edition, 1985.

8 "Annual Report 1985," Knight-Ridder, Inc., op. cit.

9 "1985 Annual Report," Gannett Co., Inc., 1100 Wilson Blvd., Arlington, Va., 22209.

10 Makeup of boards is available, of course, in annual reports and accompanying annual letters to shareholders for respective companies. Author analyzed those for 1985 and 1986.

11 Gannett's April 1, 1986, "Annual Letter to Shareholders."

12 "Notice of 1986 Annual Meeting and Proxy Statement," Tribune Co., 435 North Michigan Ave., Chicago, Ill., 60611.

13 Ross F. Hamachek, vice president/planning and development, Washington Post Co., Annual Report, 1985, p. 14.

PART THREE

THE MEDIA AND SOCIETY

We concentrated first in this book on the individual journalist and matters of personal ethics, then on the modern corporate entity—the newspaper, broadcast network, media group—as an institution of major societal influence. Now, in Part Three, we broaden our view to society's relationship with the media as a whole. We will do this in four chapters.

First, we will discuss whether society might feel compelled to change the status accorded media companies as they evolve from traditional activities—news, advertising, and entertainment—into the widely diversified conglomerates described in Chapter 8. Do societal and constitutional ground rules laid down long ago, under quite different circumstances, still apply in the same way? And, who watches the watchdog? An old question, still unanswered, still valid, and we must look at it.

Second, we must examine some critical problems in news coverage certain to bear on how society judges the media in the future. Of great importance are societal attitudes toward media cooperation with officialdom in this era of terrorism and serious national security issues. We'll look also at a house divided— the quarrel between print and television.

Third, we will examine ethics and matters of conscience in the public relations industry, a multibillion dollar endeavor with enormous impact on news and information reaching American media and, thus, readers and viewers.

Fourth, we'll look ahead at freedom of information, official censorship, and the law as they concern the role of the media in American society in the 1990s.

NEW CORPORATE CHARACTER, NEW SOCIAL STATUS?

Shifting societal attitudes and circumstances force change on many American institutions. Big Government, Big Business, Big Church—all must evolve as their institutional character changes, and as they rise or fall in public esteem and trust. Big Government power shifts to the executive branch with rise of a dynamic, charismatic President; absent strength—or ethical conduct—in the White House, congressional power increases. Big Business is forced increasingly to reveal its innermost secrets—not only what profits were made, but *how* they were made, whether skies were polluted in the making of steel or foreign generals bribed in the selling of airplanes. Big Church, whether of Rome or an evangelistic television studio in the Bible Belt, now must endure outsiders pawing through its financial affairs with iconoclastic fervor.

Add Big Media to the list of institutions undergoing critical examination.

As we have seen, newspaper and television companies rank high among all institutions in impact on the national economy as well as societal attitudes and thinking. Most are diversified far beyond news and advertising activities that in many cases were their total preoccupation in yesteryear, when societal attitudes and laws governing their conduct were laid down. We must ask, here in Chapter 9, whether the new corporate character of these companies, and the changed environments and circumstances in which they operate, will lead society to reexamine the special status they were granted in previous incarnations, in those bygone times.

In the beginning, the newspaper won special status in America because of the reverence our predecessors had for free dissemination of information. They held free speech essential in our democracy, and for 200 years a special niche in our society has been granted those who deal in ideas, news, and opinion.

Gradually, however, the print media edged many of their *commercial* as well as *news* activities into that protective niche, and now, for example, argue that commercial speech—tobacco advertising, say—merits the same constitutional protection given other forms of free speech, or that the First Amendment guarantees the right to put a newspaper coin box on a public sidewalk, even if it does block pedestrians. Then came invention of the television money machine and rapid consolidation of broadcast and newspapers into huge diversified institutions of corporate character and philosophy far removed from the venerated political pamphleteer of revolutionary lore.[1]

This inevitably blurs whatever distinction existed between newspaper and television companies and, say, banks, railroads, steel companies, or any other similarly profit-driven firms. And, it can lead to society demanding that media companies now submit to public examination on how responsibly they use their mammoth economic throw-weight, as well as how they meet society's expectations in disseminating ideas or how well they serve the marketplace as advertising vehicles.

Certainly, new questions are injected into the public dialogue by Big Media's character change. For example:

Can profit-oriented companies widely diversified in nonmedia enterprises still expect to position themselves in society as *newspaper and television* companies? Should Tribune Company, owner of the Chicago Cubs and a power company in Ontario, classify itself as a "diversified media company," as it does? Should "media" status, with all its special societal meaning, accrue to these conglomerates? Is Oklahoma Publishing, owner of the Grand Ole Opry, as well as newspapers and broadcast stations, a "media" company? How about NBC News, now a relatively small division of RCA, which, in turn, is a subsidiary of $38-billion General Electric Co., maker of refrigerators and jet engines? Should the special exemption from antitrust laws extended some unprofitable newspapers be claimed, as it is for some of their papers, by enormously profitable Gannett or Knight-Ridder?

Simply put, are the media giants in danger of expanding and diversifying themselves right out from beneath the First Amendment tent, where, as strictly communications companies, they sat so comfortably for so long, enjoying special legal benefits and protection and societal status?

Opinion surveys reveal growing public unease—perhaps not deep comprehension of these corporate changes but definite feeling among readers and viewers that the media's size and power call for new ground rules, and raise new dangers undreamed by the Founding Fathers. Recall our earlier discussion of

---

VIEWPOINT 9-1

THE PRESS AND SUSPICION OF POWER

"...Americans are suspicious of power wherever they see it. The press believes, in my view correctly, that whatever power it has is necessary to combat a government that has grown incomparably more powerful. But the public evidently sees big press corporations as among the social institutions that have to be kept in check."

Anthony Lewis, veteran columnist, *New York Times*

---

seemingly contradictory public attitudes: a fundamental belief in free speech and even appreciation of the media's watchdog role, but, just as clearly, a fear that the media are too big, too powerful, an irreverent, irresponsible cannon loose on a pitching deck that must be snubbed down before it punches a hole in the ship of state.[2]

Does it all portend escalating attacks on the media and their special status? Hard to say. For their part, however, newspapers and television have marshaled powerful forces to protect their interests.

THE MEDIA LOBBY GATHERS STRENGTH

Not many newspaper readers or TV viewers are much concerned with ANPA or NAB. Their congressmen in Washington are, though. ANPA—American Newspaper Publishers Association—represents 1,393 (1986) newspapers with more than 90 percent of all U.S. daily circulation. NAB—National Association of Broadcasters—represents the networks, 900 television stations, 90 percent of the total, and 5,000 radio stations, half of all on the air.[3] And that—speaking for virtually all significant newspapers and broadcast stations in the country— is what brings ANPA and NAB to the alert attention of every politician in Washington. They are special interest groups whose lobbyists have clout and know how to employ it skillfully.

ANPA and NAB are only two of many effective pressure groups the media have organized. There are national groups for weekly publishers, suburban newspapers, the black press, circulation executives, marketing executives, personnel executives, and others. There are powerful regional publishers associations, including the Inland Daily Press Association, Southern Newspaper Publishers Association, New England Daily Newspaper Association, plus groups representing newspapers in each state. Behind NAB are the Television Information Bureau, Radio Advertising Bureau, and regional and state broadcaster groups. These deal primarily with the media's *business* interests. Each industry also has national and state groups dealing with news matters, among them the influential ASNE, Associated Press Managing Editors, and Radio-TV News Directors Association.

There is extremely close cross-pollination between these groups and the newspaper, TV, and cable conglomerates discussed in Chapter 8. For example, ANPA's board of directors in 1986 included executives from nine of the nation's fifteen largest media companies—Knight-Ridder (whose chairman, Alvah Chapman, also chaired ANPA), the New York Times Co., Cox, Hearst, Tribune Co., Gannett, Times-Mirror, Scripps-Howard, and Advance (Newhouse). Also on the board were executives from A. H. Belo (*Dallas Morning News*); the influential *Houston Chronicle;* and representatives of Lee Enterprises, a $184 million, publicly owned newspaper and television group based in Davenport, Iowa; and eight smaller newspapers across the nation. (One Canadian director represented ANPA member papers in his country.)[4]

Not everything done by these industry groups is aimed at influencing public policy, of course. ANPA, for example, broadly states that its primary mission is "...to advance the cause of a free press, and to ensure that newspapers maintain the economic strength essential to serve the American people."[5] ANPA does highly regarded research in equipment, newsprint, circulation, advertising, and other operating sectors essential to a newspaper's business success. NAB provides advisory services crucial to television and radio operations.

But neither industry is reluctant to don the lobbyist gloves in Washington, and when they do, it's not always the First Amendment they're out to protect or the people's right to know—it's often naked self-interest.

NAB lobbies hard for three broad goals: generally reducing federal regulation of broadcasting, resisting federal or state intervention in advertising (fighting bans on beer and wine commercials is a major effort), and gaining full First Amendment rights for radio and TV. NAB has ANPA backing in fighting for relaxation of Federal Communications Commission regulation of broadcast.[6] ANPA members, of course, include broadcast owners. Under the Reagan administration, the two groups made considerable progress. In 1981, for example, the FCC dropped requirements that AM radio stations devote 8 percent of airtime (and FM stations 6 percent) to nonentertainment. Also dropped were restrictions on the number of minutes that could be devoted to commercials in an hour and a requirement that stations keep detailed program logs open to public inspection.

NAB mustered huge support in pressuring the FCC to require cable television systems to carry local TV stations. With nearly half of U.S. television homes wired for cable, TV station owners fear they will lose audience unless their signals are carried on cable. NAB president Edward Fritts says he recruited about 1,000 broadcasters to press members of Congress for action; Fritts estimates 120 Congress members then wrote the FCC supporting "must-carry" rules forcing cable operators to carry local TV stations.[7] NAB also claims its lobbying beat back in Congress an effort to impose mandatory warnings in broadcast advertising that aspirin might trigger in children a serious illness called Reye's syndrome.[8]

In a victory for Big Media that wants to get bigger, the FCC in 1985 raised limits on number of broadcast licenses any single owner can hold, from seven AM radio, seven FM, and seven television to twelve, twelve, twelve. And, broad-

---

VIEWPOINT 9-2

PORK BELLIES VERSUS PUBLIC SERVICE

"Are TV and radio stations becoming, like pork bellies, a commodity to be bought and sold by fast-moving traders? Does the licensee's fitness to serve the public have any meaning today, or are stations to be sold to the highest bidder? Are the public's airwaves to be used as tax shelters for the wealthy? Is there a future for the more responsible station owners—those with a sense of tradition and pride in being assigned those rights—in such a setting?"

Advertising Age, editorial attacking "fast-buck artists" who ignore public service responsibilities of broadcast ownership

casters no longer must own stations for three years before reselling—great news for many who deal in radio and TV properties as they would any commodity, buying and reselling for often enormous short-term capital gain without the slightest concern for serving the public interest in communities where they made those gains.

A significant win came in 1985 with an FCC statement that the "fairness doctrine" is contrary to public interest. In 1987, the FCC said the doctrine no longer was FCC policy. Since 1949, this doctrine had required broadcasters to give opposing sides in any controversy reasonable opportunity to respond—but under such cumbersome, time-consuming conditions that broadcast journalists often simply avoid controversial issues.[9]

In general, the NAB and ANPA slowly are winning their point that new technology, particularly cable TV, militates for relaxed regulatory policy. The FCC's founding principle was that airwaves were finite, were public property, and that the relative scarcity of broadcast opportunities required regulation and licensing of the entire industry in the public interest. In these days of proliferating cable TV and other broadcast options, less is heard about the need for government watching over public interests in broadcast; now the NAB and ANPA argue diversity in a competitive marketplace will work it all out.

Letting marketplace forces rule in broadcasting clearly is a turn toward laissez-faire, a principle venerated if not always followed in American business circles. But neither NAB nor ANPA has the temerity to suggest it will yield for the American viewer or listener higher quality, more principled news or entertainment programming.

In seeking preferential treatment for the business of newspapering, ANPA influences policy with several lobbying efforts that merit our examination.

A Free Press Fights Free Competition

Although favoring a competitive broadcasting marketplace open to all, ANPA is far less charitable when it comes to, say, a telephone company offering information services that might threaten newspapers. Here, naked self-interest has triumphed over laissez-faire in a revealing illustration of how a free press supposedly dedicated to free exchange of ideas can forget all that when money is at stake. To explain:

For decades, bringing in raw newsprint by the expensive ton, then sending it out as finished newspapers for delivery, in part by 15-year-olds on bicycles, caused many publishers to wonder if there was a better way. That same wonder led other communications experts, notably at telephone companies, to develop technology that electronically can deliver huge amounts of information to individual homes. AT&T, for example, found existing—or planned—telephone circuits speedily could deliver shopping information, household hints, banking services, and scores of other information services. Newspapers, expensive to produce and cumbersome to deliver, came under obvious threat: news *and* advertising services could flow over those circuits and into desktop terminals in kitchens or dens all over America for use by increasingly computer-skilled householders. Publishers get upset just *thinking* about electronic Yellow Pages with prices updated minute by minute, or electronic classified advertising.

Newspapers reacted by launching their own electronic systems, using cable TV or telephone company facilities in an effort to profitably exploit the new technology. Some, including Washington Post Co., even got into the telephone business, investing heavily in cellular, or mobile systems in large cities. Simultaneously, ANPA was unleashed for unprecedentedly vigorous lobbying to keep telephone companies out of information services. ANPA lobbyists, including Katharine Graham, then chairman of both the Washington Post Co., and ANPA, hurried to Congress with the argument, somewhat embarrassing even to publishers in the rereading, that telephone companies must be kept out of the information business—but that this is not, gracious, as it must seem, anticompetitive. It in fact is a *defense of the First Amendment,* ANPA said, because if telephone companies are permitted to both generate and transmit information they might be able to use their enormous resources to gain monopoly control over the free flow of information. Said Barry Bingham, then publisher of the *Louisville Courier-Journal:* "I break ranks with the publishers' group when they say in the name of the First Amendment they're going to abbreviate Bell's right to publish."[10] (By 1986, Washington Post Company's telephone business was flourishing—"fulfilling the optimistic expectations we held upon entering this new field," Katharine Graham said in her annual report to shareholders; telephone companies, on the other hand, still were not in the information business.)

VIEWPOINT 9-3

FREE PRESS FAT CATS

"It was a disaster, a complete disaster... we come on as fat-cat heavies trying to protect our turf."

Scott Low, publisher of the *Quincy* (Mass.) *Patriot-Ledger,* recalling ANPA lobbying efforts in Congress against telephone company services that compete with newspapers

---

Newspapers generally found consumers not eager for electronic services they launched by themselves. Knight-Ridder and Times Mirror each lost tens of millions of dollars before scrapping efforts to sell electronic delivery systems to householders. However, the computer-driven technology worked brilliantly, raising the possibility—or, depending on your view, the specter—of telephone companies one day throwing their resources, which dwarf those of even the largest media companies, into serving advertisers with new electronic ways of reaching desired household targets.

The issue is unresolved. Newspapers fail to sell their own electronic home delivery systems on a widespread basis, but they'll fight to prevent telephone companies from trying. It remains ANPA dogma: "A telephone company that provides a conduit for information as a common carrier should not also be a competing information carrier over the same lines or conduits which the carrier controls."[11]

ANPA vigorously fights another competitor, also in defense of newspaper advertising revenue: direct-mail companies. Lacking need for expensive news-gathering staffs, these competitors offer advertisers relatively low-cost service. And, importantly, they do with relative ease two things paid circulation news-papers can accomplish only at high costs and with operational difficulty—reach all, or nearly all, households in a market or, alternatively, single out for target marketing groups geographically or demographically attractive to advertisers. For example, direct-mail companies can reach all households in a certain sub-urb, or just the physicians in a county, or individuals in a city with, say, $50,000 or more annual income.

Direct-mail companies depend on efficient, speedy and affordable perfor-mance by the U.S. Postal Service—and that is where ANPA focuses its attack on them. This requires delicate handling, of course, because (1) newspapers themselves from colonial days have enjoyed highly preferential postal rates, and (2) many today operate their own direct-mail services, either mailing free circulation "shoppers" or circulars and other purely advertising matter.

ANPA's tactic is to lobby for low-est possible second class rates, under which newspapers are mailed, to de-mand expeditious handling of matter mailed by newspapers—and to attack vigorously, in public and before the U.S. Postal Rate Commission, the slightest hint of favoritism for direct mailers. Direct mailers are heavy us-ers of third class rates, and ANPA claims those rates are subsidized by first class rates, unfairly pegged up to nine times higher. Repeatedly, ANPA publishes test results from across the country revealing subsidized "junk mail" is delivered nearly as rapidly as first class despite the rate disparity. Jack Valentine, president of Advo-Systems, Inc., the nation's largest direct-mail company, responded in a speech to ANPA: "People are not being fooled by canned editorials about junk mail and subsidized rates...you really are only seeking higher rates in order to protect your monopolies in local print advertising."[12]

VIEWPOINT 9-4

COMPANY EARNINGS VERSUS
EDITORIAL OPENNESS

"We investigate conflict of interest on the part of public officials. Yet too many me-dia executives are reluctant to acknowl-edge their own conflict of interest when they take editorial positions on legislation or community projects that can affect their own company's earnings.... Until we are as open as we expect others to be, the pub-lic will continue to regard us as one pow-erful institution doing battle with other powerful institutions—and also as having a dubious advantage because of our unique Constitutional protections."

Tom Johnson, publisher, *Los Angeles Times*

A Safety Net for Rich and Poor

As far back as the 1930s, Congress helped maintain separate editorial voices in some cities by granting financially ailing newspapers immunity from certain antitrust laws. In 1970, this became the Newspaper Preservation Act, a safety net into which some of the largest, most profitable media conglomerates have pushed a few of their failures.

In sum, if a newspaper is provably failing financially and in danger of being shut down, it can combine with another, stronger paper in all but news functions and, with the U.S. attorney general's approval, do so free of antitrust restrictions. That permits combining all production and business activities in a "joint operating agreement," housing both newspapers in the same building, selling advertising and circulation with the same sales crew, and using the same accounting, transportation, production staffs. In any other industry, even a hint that two competing companies were discussing such a combination would arouse the Justice Department's antitrust division. The rationale behind the Newspaper Preservation Act, of course, is that greater societal good is served if newspapers, separate in at least news and editorial functions, survive in cities where they otherwise would fail.

Significantly, in light of their subsequent growth into huge, highly profitable conglomerates, groups taking advantage of the safety net outnumber independent newspapers twenty-four to eighteen. (See Table 9-1.)

Note in Table 9-1 that Gannett (1985 sales of $2.2 billion and net income of $253 million) has six newspapers securely wrapped in JOAs; Knight-Ridder ($1.7 billion in sales, $133 million net) has two. Privately held Scripps-Howard, which can keep secret its profits but not its troubles in running newspapers, has seven JOAs. In 1986, Gannett and Knight-Ridder—the nation's sixth and tenth largest media companies, respectively—applied for permission to create in Detroit another JOA. Knight-Ridder said its *Free Press* lost $35 million in the previous five years; Gannett put losses at its *Detroit News* at about $20 million in that period.[13] Gannett published—and thus tacitly endorsed—an estimate by securities analyst John Morton that under a JOA the papers would turn around quickly, showing operating profits of $23.5 million the first year, $40 million the second, and $57 million the third.[14] Gannett's share of profits would be 55 percent in the first year, decreasing on a sliding scale over five years to 50 percent. For the agreement's remaining 95 years, profits would be split fifty-fifty.[15]

JOAs draw heavy criticism. Some advertisers complain they create monopolies under which ad rates can be forced to artificial and unfair heights. Competitors—including television, radio, and suburban newspapers—claim JOAs create an artificially low cost base for the participating papers, giving them unfair advantage over other advertising media. Unions complain they permit newspapers to unfairly fire large numbers of employees displaced when production and business departments are merged. Some argue readers suffer. Detroit's Mayor Coleman Young, noting the *Free Press* was selling for twenty cents, the *News* for fifteen, commented: "They're creating a monopoly...and I'll bet you twenty-four hours after they approve that JOA the...papers cost thirty cents each. If they would do that right now, they wouldn't need a JOA, because the *Free Press* couldn't say they were losing money. They'd both be making money."[16]

TABLE 9-1
JOINT OPERATING AGREEMENTS*

City	Year Began	Partners
Albuquerque	1933	Scripps, independent
El Paso	1936	Scripps, Gannett
Nashville	1937	Gannett, independent
Evansville, Ind.	1938	Scripps, independent
Tucson	1940	Pulitzer, Gannett
Tulsa	1941	Two independents
Chattanooga (dissolved 1966, renewed 1980)	1942	Two independents
Madison, Wis.	1948	Lee, independent
Fort Wayne, Ind.	1950	Knight-Ridder, independent
Birmingham, Ala.	1950	Scripps, Newhouse
Lincoln, Neb.	1950	Lee, independent
Salt Lake City	1952	Two independents
Shreveport	1953	Gannett, independent
Knoxville	1957	Scripps, independent
Charleston, W. Va.	1958	Thomson, independent
Pittsburgh	1961	Scripps, Block
Honolulu	1962	Gannett, independent
San Francisco	1965	Hearst, independent
Miami	1966	Knight-Ridder, Cox
Cincinnati	1979	Scripps, Gannett
Seattle	1983	Hearst, independent
Detroit	Pending	Gannett, Knight-Ridder

*Cities in which two newspapers share all but news and editorial facilities under Joint Operating Agreements. The U.S. Justice Department permits such arrangements free of antitrust considerations if one of the cooperating newspapers can prove it otherwise would fail financially.

Other objections to JOAs arise from structural changes in the media companies involved. For example, Congress's intent clearly was to protect diversity of *news* and *editorial* voices. Yet, JOA partners today engage in many *nonnews* activities, such as publishing free circulation shoppers with no news, or conducting direct-mail operations that hardly add to the diversity of voices and opinions.

Clearly, the alternative to JOAs is a rising number of dead newspapers. The reality is that for complex reasons of newspaper economics only a few cities today support two or more competing metro dailies of like size and characteristics. And, pressed by the rising tide of shareholder expectation, managers of publicly owned media companies will not—cannot—pump unlimited funds into a losing newspaper to subsidize it indefinitely. Gannett's Al Neuharth: "The fact is that the Detroit newspaper issue is very simple. Shall there be one daily newspaper or two?"[17]

However, questions remain:

When, in 1933, it began to succor failing newspapers, Congress didn't have to worry that television competitors would suffer if core city metros were aid-ed. TV hadn't been launched yet. There was virtually no significant radio or suburban newspaper competition, either. Has the newspaper competitive environment changed so radically that the end result of Congress's good intentions is changed?

Did Congress envisage huge, highly profitable groups eventually enjoying JOAs? When, in 1937, it permitted the *Nashville Banner* and the *Tennessean*—both then independently owned—to form a JOA, did Congress intend to create a situation that in 1985 would add handsomely to the coffers of $2.2 billion Gannett?

In many other areas of business activity the media rely on special treatment due to their unique status in our society. ANPA, for example, resists—most often successfully—attempts to tax newsprint and ink purchases, or institute sales tax on circulation and advertising sales. ANPA even resists proposals that would deny tax deductions to companies for their advertising expenditures; it says "valid commercial speech concerns" are raised by such proposals. ANPA also supports the "historic principle of duty-free importation of newsprint"— an historic principle importers of most other commodities would search for in vain.[18] Newspapers seek Labor Department recognition for reporters as "professionals," which would eliminate a Fair Labor Standards Act requirement that they be paid overtime for hours worked beyond a normal workweek.[19] For generations, newspapers have enjoyed special relief from child labor laws covering use of boys and girls as carriers. They are called "Little Merchants," which has a constructive, educational ring to it, and perodically newspapers remind society that presidents, judges, and business tycoons started their careers by peddling newspapers.

So, the media stand revealed as Big Business and preoccupied with profit and self-interest, as are other businesses. But, after all, is that a damning indictment? And, really, who has a better alternative to free-enterprise media that are uniquely independent financially as well as constitutionally?[20]

Viable alternatives are extremely limited:

Narrowly partisan journalism, with political, economic, religious, or other groups owning and operating the media for the purpose of controlling news coverage and editorial opinion. Aside from being incredibly anachronistic in contemporary American society, newspapers and other media owned mostly by railroads, labor unions, or other special interest groups would be impossible in an economic sense. There isn't enough special interest funding to support today's $100-million metro dailies, the multibillion dollar broadcasting industry or, even, the hundreds of small-town papers scattered across the nation.

Creation of widescale nonprofit journalism. Absent the tradition of Britain's independent, nonprofit (but government-supported) British Broadcasting Corp., U.S. publicly supported, nonprofit radio and television have unending financial problems even though they operate on a comparatively limited scale. Public broadcasting in America, like its free enterprise brethren, increasingly seeks commercial support from business and industry.

VIEWPOINT 9-5

THE PRIVATE ENTERPRISE MEDIA

"Private enterprise [media] will not only be with us for a long time, but so far as most of us can see, it will be the best system for producing the general run of news and views.

"Once we have acknowledged that a business enterprise, organized to make a profit, is the optimum basis for our news institutions, we need not ignore serious problems within that system. Keeping our news as honest and as competent as possible is not a luxury; it is not merely the simple elegance of purity. In our society, it is closely related to the survival of democracy."

Ben H. Bagdikian, editor, media critic, teacher

Acceptance of government sponsorship (plus its concomitant control). Even a casual survey of authoritarian systems around the world reveals disasters that befall any society submitting to government control of the media. This alternative is unacceptable in our society.

Is it, then, to be continuation of newspaper and broadcast ownership under a free enterprise system, with its inherent weaknesses and dangers, as well as strengths? Even in those opinion polls revealing public unease about the media, the answer overwhelmingly is yes, that there is no acceptable alternative. Yet, media supporters as well as critics see problems developing between the free-enterprise newspaper and broadcasting industries and society at large, and the problems likely will become more severe due to changes under way in corporate character and philosophy and in societal attitudes. But, if there are to be changes, what shall they be and who shall make them? On those questions, even the media are split.

The Media Bloc That Isn't

In the McCarthy era, an entire ethical "Dark Age" for both American politics and journalism compressed mostly into one decade, the 1950s, there arose the "media conspiracy" theory. For a journalist, the price of attendance at a cocktail party could be the question, "Who *really* tells you what to write?" For media owners, the times gave rise to a suspicion, later refined in the Nixon-Agnew era, when ethical lights went out again for a time in some halls of government, that somewhere, somehow a small but sinister band, often characterized as eastern intellectuals, were conspiring over what news the nation would, and wouldn't, read or view.

It left the author, for one, slightly bemused—laboring in frenetic newsrooms where clearly *nobody* was remotely capable of efficiently handling, let alone controlling, the unending torrent of news, then hearing the suspicion that *somebody* must be telling everybody else how to slant it. Newsrooms in fact were not overburdened with easterners or, certainly, intellectuals of the think-alike type or any other kind. The point was—and is—undeniable: The media are big, powerful, and do hold certain philosophical and business interests in common, and are organized to lobby to protect them. But, there is no "the media"—if that connotes group-think on the media's role in society, if it means united response to external criticism, or that newspaper and television executives are moving lock-step toward jointly creating a new relationship with society. Journalists cannot even agree on whether newspapers and television truly have a serious problem with society, let alone what to do if there is one.

One group within the media is gloomily pessimistic. Norman Isaacs, following a distinguished if peripatetic career as editor at some of the nation's great newspapers, sees a "gathering storm" ahead. He warns in his excellent *Untended Gate* (Columbia University Press, 1986) of "...the next ten to twenty years as possibly being the most crucial for journalism to survive as a free-standing entity." Isaacs fears enemies of free speech undermining the First Amendment—perhaps in a constitutional convention—by using as leverage the public's currently low esteem for the media. Isaacs and others warn that the media have let slip their journalistic quality, their dedication to accuracy, balance, fairness, compassion, and ethical performance. There is call for "accountability"—to a sense of professionalism and to the public—and all under some type of formalized auditing or monitoring, preferably by an independent, nongovernment body.

A second media group—loosely, the Ben Bradlee School—sees the "credibility gap" simply as another in an unending cycle of ups and downs in public esteem that journalists must endure. The *Washington Post* executive editor counsels his colleagues to just do the best journalistic job possible and not worry about being "liked." This group, which includes some of the country's most influential editors and publishers, strongly resists any formalized monitoring of the media, either from within the newspaper and television industries or by outside critics.

A third group we have discussed: journalists of self-doubt, practicing ethical-reactive journalism, displaying Pavlovian response to whatever the latest poll indicates the public wants on the front page or on the evening news.

It's a far cry from "media conspiracy." Indeed, opinions within the media are so deeply divided that newspapers and television operate free of any effective monitoring from within their industries, and generally unite only to reject any systematic outside appraisal other than that of the individual reader or viewer making the daily marketplace decision on what to read and what to view.

The News Council and Other Failures

The most ambitious effort to independently monitor newspaper and television performance was made by the National News Council. It struggled eleven years for support, then died in 1984, generally unknown to the public and mostly ignored or actively resisted by the media.

The council was sponsored by the Twentieth Century Fund (but independently financed), and took the mission of investigating public complaints about media performance and publishing its findings. Participation by newspapers and broadcast organizations was voluntary, and the council had no enforcement powers. The council considered 242 complaints against the media, found 120 unwarranted, 64 warranted, 18 partially warranted, and dismissed 37. Three were withdrawn. Council presidents included a former chief justice of the California Supreme Court, a former chief judge of the New York State Court of Appeals, Norman Isaacs, Edward Barrett (former dean of Columbia University's Graduate School of Journalism), and Richard Salant (former president of CBS News).[21]

That is, the council was not antimedia; in fact, it found for the media more than against them. And, council members generally were widely respected. Why, then, did the council fail? Postmortems reveal not only why the council failed, but also why similar efforts to monitor the media fail at state as well as national levels.

First, the council did not establish a public constituency. It did not convince the media it critiqued to publish or broadcast its findings, or devise public relations means of end-running the media and reaching the public directly to build support or, even, public awareness.

Second, the council failed to win support from some of the nation's most influential newspapers and journalists. For example, publisher Arthur Ochs Sulzberger announced early that the *New York Times* opposed the concept and would not respond to council findings. As in many matters journalistic, the *Times* and a few other similarly prestigious newspapers were watched for guidance by hundreds of newspaper and television journalists.

Third, and most importantly, the council failed to quiet the fears of many responsible, respected journalists that the council could be the first step toward compulsory auditing or, even, licensing by government. These critics feared any widespread support for the council could turn into demands for government control of the media. At minimum, they saw the council lending credence to special interest pressure groups trying to influence how the news is covered.

For roughly the same reasons, the media generally ignore or resist other outside efforts to judge their performance. Even groups allied with the industry are ineffective in critiquing the media and

---

VIEWPOINT 9-6

NATIONAL NEWS COUNCIL: THREE VIEWS

''A lot of people should miss it and nobody does.''

Richard Salant, last president of now-defunct National News Council

''Basically, a newspaper is responsible to its readers and not to a bunch of self-appointed busybodies with time on their hands. Beyond that, it's dangerous in that it creates the notion in some minds that there is such a thing as a code or standards you can edit newspapers by and anybody who deviates from those is not playing by the rules.''

Creed Black, publisher of the *Lexington* (Ky.) *Herald-Leader*

''The death of the National News Council should not mean the death of the concept. Failure to renew these efforts may exacerbate our perilous state. If we don't do it someone may do it for us.''

Peter Stone, vice president and general counsel of Dow Jones' Ottaway Newspapers subsidiary

getting the right people to listen. That includes most journalism schools and journalists' fraternities and associations. The Society of Professional Journalists, Sigma Delta Chi, for example, flirted with encouraging its chapters nationwide to judge local media performance and even talked of expelling ethical transgressors from the fraternity. The idea didn't catch on. In 1985, the Kentucky Press Association voted against establishing a state news council, leaving Minnesota as the only state with its own council. A substantial number of partisan political, economic, and religious groups monitor the media, and a few watch over business interests. None, however, has widespread public support.[22]

So, you still ask, who watches the watchdog? Well, this watchdog reserves the right to watch itself. But, does it *bark* at itself, too?

THE STORY THAT'S COVERED EVER SO GENTLY

If there is a foul-up in U.S. foreign policy, it will be on the news tonight and front pages tomorrow. Business writers will leap all over falling profits at IBM or GM. If the city council flubs a zoning decision or a quarterback goofs on a crucial play, readers or viewers know where to turn for penetrating, no-holds-barred details.

But where do they turn if interested, for example, in whether local TV covered the zoning debate fairly, or how accurately the local paper covered the football game? And, if interested in media investments, where do they turn for detailed information on how well Knight-Ridder, say, or Gannett are being run?

The plain fact is that when *that* kind of behind-the-scenes information about the media is desired, Americans cannot turn with confidence to their newspapers or television. The media story is a story covered ever so gently, without the hard-hitting, methodical regularity that characterizes coverage of nonmedia stories. There are exceptions. About five newspapers have at least one staffer who produces excellent media coverage—the *New York Times, Los Angeles Times, Newsday,* the *Washington Post,* and the *Wall Street Journal.* And, of course, any self-respecting newspaper has a critic regularly slamming away at TV *entertainment* programming. Network TV offers, albeit rarely, some media coverage.

But, anyone seriously interested in investment information on media companies turns to brokers and Wall Street analysts, not newspapers or television. And, for those interested in how accurately or fairly the local newspaper or TV station is performing, there is no readily available third-party source of objective, dispassionate information.

It is not enough to say, as some do, that proliferating information sources—magazines, cable TV, and suburban weeklies—serve as counterbalance, offering wider coverage and alternate views so readers or viewers somehow can assemble the facts and put them together in an understandable, accurate fashion. That simply won't wash. First, general circulation magazines, cable TV, and weeklies don't cover the media establishment with any kind of perceptive regularity, particularly on a local level. Second, the average reader or viewer doesn't have the reportorial training, time, or inclination to go much beyond the twenty-six minutes or so devoted on average to reading a single daily paper, or the twenty-two minutes (thirty minutes minus commercials) allocated for watching an evening anchor.

It comes down to whether the newspaper or television industry barks at itself—whether it honestly, fairly levels with readers or viewers on how well it is doing its job. There are splendid examples of honest newspapers overcoming the understandable instinct to hide their own mistakes—the *Washington Post* agonizing in a published explanation to readers of how it was hoaxed by a staffer who wrote a phony story about a nonexistent child heroin addict (see Case Study 9-1); the *New York Times* using both its front and editorial pages to explain (under the headline, "A Lie in the *Times*") how it was hoaxed by a free-lance writer who never visited Cambodia, about which he wrote a first-person account; the *Wall Street Journal* eviscerating itself in print because a columnist betrayed newspaper and reader alike by misusing inside information.[23] But every journalist knows pride and the instinct for survival are powerful forces preventing newspapers and television universally from being fully frank on their shortcomings as well as triumphs

---

CASE STUDY 9-1

COMING CLEAN WITH YOUR READERS

You are editor of a top newspaper known for hard-hitting, investigative reporting, and you've scored again!

A new young reporter (her resume lists Vassar, magna cum laude; University of Toledo, master's degree; studies at the Sorbonne in Paris; four languages) has developed, while working alone, a terrific series on "Jimmy," an 8-year-old heroin addict "turned on" by his mother's lover.

Police want to rescue the child but your reporter warns her life will be endangered if she identifies "Jimmy," even to you. The story gets national attention.

Then comes a coveted Pulitzer Prize—and startling revelations: The reporter's resume is full of lies, and there is no 8-year-old heroin addict. The story is a fake.

What do you do? Ben Bradlee, executive editor of the *Washington Post,* where it happened, returned the Pulitzer and directed his ombudsman, Bill Green, to tell all to *Post* readers. Green wrote that there was a "complete systems failure" in the high-

tension *Post* newsroom, and not only by Janet Cooke, who wrote "this journalistic felony." Cooke had been hired without background check. Bradlee and other editors failed to control her work and ask tough questions about her story, which simply was too dramatic to be believed. "This business of trusting reporters absolutely goes too far," Green said.

Impatient young reporters already are too anxious for more Watergate exposes, and pressuring them to break big stories "is a high-risk undertaking." "The scramble for journalistic prizes is poisonous."

"If the reporter can't support the integrity of his story by revealing the [source's] name to his editor, the story shouldn't be published."

Another issue: Shouldn't each journalist who saw the "Jimmy" story in preparation—or competing media who saw the published version—have immediately dropped everything and rushed to rescue the child? Wasn't the human failure to do that the *first* ethical breakdown at the *Post*?

(compare the number of full-page ads you've seen recently in which newspapers apologize for errors or unfair coverage as contrasted with those boasting about Pulitzer Prizes or exclusive stories).

WHAT CAN BE DONE?

Given the media's demonstrated refusal to submit to outside judgment or monitoring—and society's reluctance so far to subject them to it—what can be done to build a bridge of trust between the media and society? We return to where we started in this book: to the importance of individual journalists exercising their personal sense of ethics and social responsibility to influence the conduct of their newspapers and television news operations.

This, of course, is highly unsatisfactory to those critics firmly convinced the media must be brought to heel and made more responsive. Even critics of milder persuasion see self-improvement pledges as depending, in the final analysis, on the honesty and ethical character of individual journalists and leaving the media as one of the very few major institutions in the nation without some sort of external control or formal counterbalancing mechanism. If the media do not respond to problems perceived by the public, there is real danger of society becoming impatient and using other means to achieve change—through government intervention or the courts, much as libel law is used today by many who are offended by the media and feel they have no other recourse.

But for anyone seriously interested in protecting free speech in America there seems no alternative to leaving responsibility for change with the media themselves, with reader and viewer free to exert pressure by deciding in the marketplace what is good or bad, right or wrong about how newspapers and television conduct themselves.

David Shaw, widely respected media reporter for the *Los Angeles Times,* says he frequently is asked, "Who watches the watchers?" His response: "No one. We have a free press in this country. That's the way the First Amendment says it should be, and that's the way it is." Shaw, however, acknowledges he has "never been altogether comfortable with that answer," adding:

"If, as we frequently argue, a free, vigilant press helps keep our other institutions honest, just what does keep *us* honest? Our professionalism? Our sense of duty? Our innate goodness? Does the decision to become a journalist automatically render one immune to such otherwise human failings as carelessness, irresponsibility, avarice and egotism? Obviously not. The First Amendment gives us a special privilege and a special responsibility, but it does not guarantee us infallibility...."[24]

Many editors and publishers share Shaw's uncomfortable feeling that society requires—and quickly—answers to questions about the media. These broad avenues are available for a response:

First, the media should cover the media story. Newspaper and television journalists should take off the gloves and cover each other just as critically as they cover any other story. This should include day-by-day examination of how news is covered and, importantly, how the huge media conglomerates dominating the industry conduct their business, financial, and shareholder affairs. Media coverage today is spotty, offering none of the continuity required for true comprehension. Coverage should be straight and hard-hitting, without the undercurrent of personal feuding that characterizes some coverage today—Ben Bradlee's *Washington Post* taking a poke at the *New York Times*, whose former executive editor, A. M. Rosenthal, isn't one of his favorites; or, *Times* and *Wall Street Journal* editorial writers undercutting each other in terms so subtle that only fraternal insiders catch the message. Whether measured in terms of economic impact or the role their information, news, and comment play in our free society, the media are an important story. To see them covered penetratingly would reassure many readers and viewers who now feel the media are essentially free to do as they please without fear of meaningful criticism.

VIEWPOINT 9-7

MEDIA: JUDGE YOURSELVES

"It is very seldom that I read in any of your papers... 'Our colleagues over there on that other sheet are talking nonsense. The real truth is the following'... In my judgment as a citizen, you have an obligation to monitor each other, to debate each other, directly and forthrightly, if the American people are going to be the full beneficiaries of this precious right called the freedom of the press. I do not think I am in favor of codes of ethics in the field of journalism. I do not like rules which tend to inhibit the unrestricted freedom of opinion through the written media."

Dean Rusk, former U.S. secretary of state, in speech to American Society of Newspaper Editors

---

Second, newspapers and television should create a compact of openness with readers and viewers. Done correctly, this is agonizing for editors, publishers, and station managers for it requires brutal, ego-damaging frankness—a journalistic version of a surgeon acknowledging there was a slight slip of the scalpel back there in the operating room, or a lawyer admitting it was his fault as the client heads for prison (and, how often have you heard anything resembling that?). A few newspapers—only about thirty-five—employ full-time reader advocates or "ombudsmen" to go into print regularly on behalf of readers and critique newsroom performance. But, and indicative of the media's general reluctance to take criticism, many editors are uncomfortable with the thought of unleashing even a staff member to barge around behind the scenes, then tell all.

Some editors say it's their duty to do that, and periodically write a column explaining how—and why—the news is covered. But no Pulitzer Prizes have been handed out to editors for hard-hitting, investigative reporting on themselves. As limited as it is, print journalism's self-examination is unmatched in television. Neither at network nor local level does television spend much time dissecting its own performance. In recent years, newspapers have become much more open about publishing corrections or explanations of what appeared in print. Many newspapers regularly position—"anchor"—corrections in the same spot each day. There also is a noticeable increase in efforts by newspapers to explain within the body of stories any special circumstances or background affecting coverage—why they granted anonymity to sources or why an individual mentioned in the story was unavailable for comment.

Making letters columns and op-ed pages easily accessible to readers, or guest editorial spots open to viewers, are other ways links are established with the public. On the local level, newspapers and television stations can do much more to invite the public for tours and get-acquainted chats with newsroom staffers. Newspapers should run house ads describing the people who write and edit the news (public opinion surveys repeatedly show readers want to know who puts out the papers—and that they don't fully trust people they don't know).[25] Just answering the mail quickly and the telephone politely would help remove that patina of cold, distant arrogance that covers so many things journalistic.

Third, however, the media simply must do better in explaining to the public how a great many sincerely dedicated journalists and media managers try very hard to do an honest, ethical, socially responsible job. The media have a much better story in that respect than they tell. Few industries spend so much time in severely critical self-examination as do newspapers and television. In news, highly professional, hard-hitting critiques are run by ASNE, Associated Press Managing Editors Association, and the Radio and Television News Directors Association. But it's all done for insiders, people essentially already in the know, and not the bemused (or befuddled) public watching from the outside. Journalism reviews and professional magazines sometimes do excellent critiques, but they play to extremely small, insider audiences. *Presstime,* the American Newspaper Publishers Association's excellent industry magazine, has (1986) just 10,700 circulation—and charges nonmembers $100 for a year's

---

VIEWPOINT 9-8

SECOND THOUGHTS ON OMBUDSMEN

"For years, I argued that to hire an ombudsman would be to abdicate the editor's responsibility and, in fact, to diminish the responsibility of all the people who work for us. Fundamental to my philosophy—then, and now—is the strong sense that everyone who works for us is a 'reader's representative'...that the way an assistant editor handles the phone can leave a permanent impression—positive or negative—with a reader...that how a circulator handles a complaint can make all the difference in the world as to how the customer feels about us, or even whether we have that customer any more...that our credibility is directly related to every contact we have with readers and potential readers...that no one should get in the way of a collective and individual effort to build real relationships with readers.

"But maybe I have been missing something important—perhaps an ombudsman could complement, and contribute to, our total efforts toward a newspaper of heightened credibility."

David Lawrence Jr., publisher, chairman and former editor, *Detroit Free Press*

subscription. Yes, this is an industry that charges a member of the public, on whose goodwill the whole edifice stands, $100 to read its story.

Too often, when the media story is told it is cloaked in so much self-promotional hocus-pocus that the story is lost, and the public turned off. Times Mirror blossomed forth nationwide in 1986 with an expensive series of full-page advertisements on a significant study it commissioned of public attitudes toward the media, but devoted only a couple paragraphs to the study and the rest to naked promotion of Times Mirror as a company. Television often is just embarrassing in its shallow promotion, stressing not its worldwide news-gathering bureaus, splendid technology, or reporting, but, rather, the cult of personality—bush jackets and palm trees for the newest expert in foreign news, and the White House lawn for political analysts. The media, particularly through industry associations, must reach the public with meaningful, high-quality promotion. Suggested themes for starters:

The First Amendment belongs to the people and we, the media, are defending *your* rights when we stand up for *ours*.

We offer hard news, the facts, on health, science, technology, diet and nutrition, child-rearing—all the subjects you must know to cope with daily life. And, we offer it at bargain prices—free on television, about thirty to thirty-five cents on newsprint.

Every effort is made to present fair and unbiased news and to allocate space and time to all our constituents.

Our job is reporting news and presenting informed opinion, not manipulating you, the reader or viewer.

(Each suggested promotional theme responds directly to negative views of the media uncovered by researcher Ruth Clark in a study of public attitudes commissioned by ASNE in 1984.)[26]

Obviously, it's simplistic to suggest the media can construct a new relationship with society just by answering the telephone more politely or cranking off a few promotional ads. And, the author doesn't suggest that. Indeed, he suggests there are fundamentally serious roadblocks between media and society and that unless the media can remove them, there may be, as Norman Isaacs warns, a "gathering storm" ahead. We'll look at those roadblocks in Chapter 10.

CHAPTER SUMMARY

Big Media must submit to critical examination by society as do Big Government, Big Business, and the Big Church. One question is whether the changing corporate character of the media, from essentially vehicles of news and advertising to diversified conglomerates, will lead society to reassess the media as just another profit-oriented industry. After all, can Tribune Co., for example, position itself before society as a newspaper and television company now that it owns the Chicago Cubs baseball team and a power company in Ontario?

To defend their business as well as news interests, newspapers and television have organized giant lobbying efforts with strong clout in Washington. Television fights for less government regulation, less interference in advertising, and other changes likely to enhance its business interests. Newspapers lobby strongly against competitors and for special exemption from antitrust laws and some taxes.

Despite obvious problems stemming from the profit-oriented, free enterprise nature of our media, anyone seriously interested in protecting free speech in America will be hard pressed to suggest viable alternatives. A journalism owned and operated by narrowly partisan groups is unattractive (and probably unworkable), there is no tradition (and little chance of one developing) for nonprofit journalism (as with Britain's BBC), and government-sponsored (and, thus controlled) journalism is unacceptable in any free society.

There is no "media bloc" when it comes to improving or changing the media to construct a bridge of trust with society. The media don't cover their own industry at all well, and strongly resist outside judgment or monitoring. To change things, the media should cover each other just as penetratingly as they cover other stories. Newspapers and television must create a compact of openness with readers and viewers. And, the industry as a whole must better explain to the public just how hard it tries to do the job well.

At the end of Chapter 9 we are where this book started—with a need for each journalist to help create honest, ethical, and socially responsible journalism at his or her newspaper or television station.

CHAPTER 9

Notes

1 American Newspaper Publishers Association, The Newspaper Center, Box 17407, Dulles Airport, Washington, D.C., 20041, illustrates an expanded view of First Amendment and newspaper rights in two documents: "An Overview of Current Issues," a March 1986 publication, and "ANPA Highlights '86," a summary of association activities.

2 Particularly revealing surveys include, "Relating To Readers In The '80s," commissioned by ASNE and conducted by Clark, Martire & Bartolomeo, Inc., May 1984; "Changing Needs of Changing Readers," sponsored by ASNE in 1978; "Credibility," a 1984 survey by Associated Press Managing Editors Association; "The People & The Press," a 1986 study sponsored by Times Mirror Corp. Major work in reader attitudes has been done also by Belden Associates, 2900 Turtle Creek Plaza, Dallas, Tex., 74219.

3 National Association of Broadcasters, 1771 N Street, N.W., Washington, D.C., 20036.

4 ANPA's board is listed in *presstime*, the association's monthly magazine, an outstanding source for students of the media. Address is 11600 Sunrise Valley Drive, Reston, Va., 22091.

5 ANPA's "Overview of Current Issues," op. cit.

6 NAB discusses each year's lobbying efforts in its annual report, issued to association members from the Washington headquarters.

7 Bob Davis, "Cable TV Operators May Be Required To Carry Some Local Broadcast Stations," *Wall Street Journal,* July 23, 1986, p. 4.

8 NAB "Annual Report 1985," p. 2–3.

9 NAB "Annual Report 1985," ibid.

10 Margaret Garrard Warner, "Newspaper Publishers Lobby to Keep AT&T From Role They Covet," *Wall Street Journal,* July 9, 1982, p. 1.

11 ANPA, "An Overview of Current Issues," op. cit.

12 Andrew Radolf, "Detached Labeler Fights Back," *Editor & Publisher,* June 16, 1984, p. 9; also see, "Valentine: ANPA Trying to Kill Advo," *presstime,* June 1984, p. 35.

13 "First Quarter 1986 Report," Gannett Co., Inc., 1100 Wilson Blvd., Arlington, Va., 22209, p. 3.

14 Ibid.

15 These and other details were revealed by chairman Al Neuharth of Gannett in a number of ways, including "First Quarter 1986 Report," op. cit. Note his speech to the Detroit Chamber of Commerce Legislative Agenda Conference, Mackinac Island, Mich., May 30, 1986, and "Mackinac Straight Talk: How Dailies Survive," *Detroit News,* June 1, 1986, p. 23A.

16 Mark Fitzgerald, "Detroit JOA Sparks Protests, Request For Hearing," *Editor & Publisher,* June 7, 1986, p. 20.

17 "Mackinac Straight Talk: How Dailies Survive," *Detroit News,* op. cit.

18 ANPA, "An Overview of Current Issues," op. cit.

19 A superb treatment of this issue is, "Suit Studies The Wages of Journalism," *New York Times,* July 20, 1986, p. 26.

20 Ben H. Bagdikian, editor, media critic, and teacher, is thoughtful on this. See particularly his *The Information Machines,* Harper & Row, New York, 1971, and his speech to the University of Minnesota Journalism Center, March 3, 1984, reproduced in *Readings in Mass Communications,* by Michael Emery and Ted Curtis Smythe, Wm. C. Brown Publishers, Dubuque, Iowa, 1986.

21 See particularly Richard P. Cunningham's report on his work with the council, "Why The News Council Failed," in "1984–85 Journalism Ethics Report," Society of Professional Journalists, Sigma Delta Chi, p. 4; also, Marcia Ruth, "Does Anyone Miss the News Council?" *presstime,* March 1985, p. 32.

22 For penetrating observations on the wider issues of business and social responsibility and licensing in the free enterprise system see Milton Friedman, *Capitalism and Freedom,* University of Chicago Press, 1962.

23 "A Lie in the *Times,*" an editorial, *New York Times,* Feb. 23, 1982, p. A22.

24 David Shaw, "Watching The Watchers," *The Quill,* December '81, p. 12.

25 See particularly Ruth Clark's "Relating to Readers in The '80s," a study commissioned in 1984 by ASNE.

26 Ibid.

SPECIAL PROBLEM AREAS

Relationships with their readers and viewers preoccupy the media conglomerates we have studied. As profit-oriented businesses, they sample their marketplaces with repeated surveys that, despite their substantial cost and impressively sophisticated methodology, really are designed to answer only a couple of simple questions: "Do you like us? And, if not, how can we change so you will read (or view) us more?"

But our discussion cannot stop there, for the issue of the media and their place in society is much larger than whether as businesses newspapers and television move thusly to protect their economic position. Most businesses do that. We must look beyond such marketplace factors, at institutional relationships between the huge and powerful media and other important forces in our society. Serious problems in some of these relationships create roadblocks to understanding between media and public.

Here in Chapter 10, then, we turn to the media's relationship with officialdom in matters of terrorism, and with the increasingly powerful intelligence and military communities on stories involving national security and war reporting. The institutional relationship between the media and Washington political power centers is a book (or books) in itself, far beyond the scope of our discussion. But we'll look at the media and the most important of those power centers, the presidency. Then, we'll discuss the media and business, and conclude by focusing on an increasingly divisive quarrel within the media, between print and television journalists.

As do many institutions, American media frequently look to their past for a guide to what role they should play in American society of today and the future. Perhaps more than most, journalists tend to idealize their legends and heroes of bygone eras. However, journalism has changed and, certainly, so has the world in which it is practiced—so much so that for many crucial questions the media face today, the past provides no answers.

Item: For generations, it was axiomatic that ethical and responsible journalists provide equal access to the media for all participants in a controversy. But what if some participants kidnap and kill for the *sole purpose* of gaining such access? Which legend, which hero, provides helpful precedent when a terrorist waves pistol and grenade over hostage men, women, and children cowering in a hijacked airliner and demands, in return for their lives, front-page space or a live television interview?

Item: Any aspiring war correspondent wants to be where the action is, just like those of World War II, Korea, and Vietnam who slogged forward with the troops and filed dispatches for tomorrow or the next day. But what if *hundreds* of aspirants show up, some equipped with communications capable of broadcasting live from the battlefield to the world—including the enemy—a blow-by-blow eyewitness account?

Item: It's in the American journalistic fiber—force open the closed doors, let sunshine into bureaucratic files, find the story, and, whatever it is, tell it to the people who, after all, have a right to know. But what if the story, in this age of big-power confrontation and intercontinental ballistic missiles, is how U.S. forces deploy antimissile defenses or break Soviet codes?

Item: President Franklin Delano Roosevelt twice weekly let reporters into his office where they stood around his desk and asked questions; Harry S. Truman took them on jaunty walks around Washington. Will news-coverage techniques developed in those simpler days work today?

All to say things aren't as simple as when Ernie Pyle slogged across France with his World War II GI buddies and filed human interest stories for papers back home weeks later. And time, technology, and circumstances have changed news coverage in ways unforeseen by Edward R. Murrow when he stood atop London rooftops and broadcast live by radio as German bombers approached. So great are the changes that considerable confusion exists within the media, as well as out, about how journalists can adapt, how they can use their new space-age communications capabilities ethically and responsibly, and how the powerful conglomerate media should relate to other institutions in society.

TERRORISM AND THE MEDIA

On June 14, 1985, Arab terrorists found weaknesses in the way that twentieth-century electronic marvel, television, is used. For the next sixteen days, they manipulated the medium in many parts of the world, particularly the United States, as if they owned it.[1]

It all started when two terrorists armed with pistols and grenades hijacked TWA Flight 847 from Athens and forced the pilot to land in Beirut. One American serviceman in the plane was slain. The world was watching the terrorists and the high drama they produced. Television journalists jumped on the story, showing up with lights, cameras, and sound crews each time the terrorists paraded their frightened hostages, each time they shouted yet another demand, each time they created another gun-waving spectacle. Television produced saturation coverage around the clock. Network programming in the United States was interrupted repeatedly with the latest tidbit from Beirut (CBS announced at one point the copilot had an infected spider bite); star anchors interrogated news sources live 5,000 miles from their New York City studios; news shows were given over to the story almost without reservation.

The terrorists thus were given opportunity to tell their story directly to the American people, which of course was the object of the whole exercise. Heretofore unknown Arabs, espousing slogans and causes not entirely clear even to this day, gained an unprecedented international forum and exerted enormous pressure on the White House. In effect, they used network anchors as intermediaries to open public negotiations with the U.S. government, which at the time was trying to sort out things privately, and behind the scenes.

Manipulating the media didn't start with Arab terrorism, of course. It's been tried since the invention of movable type. But the Beirut incident showed that anyone shrewd—and brutal—enough could exploit television's need for a visual story (the more dramatic the better) and the scoop mentality that entices competing networks to rush stories on the air without adequate explanatory background or editing. Above all, Beirut showed television's sense of journalistic caution and discipline could break down and give a handful of screaming gunmen instantaneous links via satellite to living rooms throughout the world. Beirut showed that television's extraordinary technology and its ability to span the world with live broadcasts could outrun its masters' ability to use it ethically and responsibly when they strive for even the slightest competitive advantage over other networks and media.

Intense criticism followed. British Prime Minister Margaret Thatcher told the American Bar Association, "We must try to find ways to starve the terrorists and the hijacker of the oxygen of publicity on which they depend." U.S. Attorney General Edwin Meese III floated the idea of the Justice Department asking the media to adopt voluntary guidelines on covering terrorism. Predictably, there were calls for government regulation of news during any hostage situation. Just as predictably, the media united in opposition to even voluntary guidelines, let alone any imposed by the government. John Corry, the *New York Times'* respected television critic, said a voluntary code wouldn't work, and "it is chilling" to think of the government enforcing one.

VIEWPOINT 10-1

NETWORKS WAR OVER NEWS

"It's trench warfare. There's everything out there but mustard gas."

Van Gordon Sauter, describing news competition between networks when he was president of CBS News

---

Corry said the problem in Beirut was that television asserted "journalism's prerogatives without meeting its responsibilities" and "surrendered journalistic sovereignty by showing whatever it could whenever it could.... Valid criticism of television would disappear if it practiced responsible journalism in the first place."[2]

A few months later, terrorists hijacked the Italian liner *Achille Lauro* in the Mediterranean, killed an American tourist, and again seized the headlines. But because the liner was at sea, beyond reach of cameras, television played a much more subdued role in coverage. Some antiterrorist experts are convinced the incident would have been prolonged had the terrorists gained access to television.

NBC stirred intense controversy in 1986 by interviewing Mohammed Abul Abbas Zaidan, then being hunted on a charge of plotting the *Achille Lauro*'s hijacking. NBC got a three-and-a-half-minute interview by agreeing not to disclose Abbas' whereabouts. The U.S. State Department declared "terrorism thrives on this kind of publicity," and said NBC's refusal to reveal where it interviewed Abbas was "reprehensible." It said the network in effect was his "accomplice." Some media experts felt NBC had scored a newsworthy scoop; others were critical, including editor James Squires of the *Chicago Tribune*. Squires said the news was, "Where is Abbas?" And that news, he pointed out, NBC denied its viewers.[3]

Television isn't alone in its vulnerability to manipulation by terrorists. The gunmen established the news agenda for American newspapers as well as television during the Beirut and *Achille Lauro* incidents. Front-page makeup editors and headline writers responded to gun and grenade as did TV editors. But there is a difference. It relates to television's technical capabilities, its immediacy, its tendency to run stories for visual effect without tight editorial control and editing—thus offering terrorists direct access to the audience they seek. It is television's sight-and-sound high drama the terrorists want to employ. And the sight of a gun held to the head of a hostage, or the sound of one being fired, can create such public sympathy for individual victims that governments have difficulty pursuing broader policies such as refusing to negotiate with terrorists. Once the public sees the frightened, trembling hostages, and hears them plead for their lives, governments lose the option of any military rescue attempt that might further endanger lives. Lesley Stahl of CBS News said, "We are an instrument for the hostages. We force the administration to put their lives above policy." It may have been coincidental, but shortly after all three networks reported the U.S. Army's Delta Force antiterrorist force had left the United States for the Middle East, Flight 847's hijackers dispersed their hostages throughout Beirut, making rescue impossible. Edwin Diamond, New York University commentator on the media, said that "Once TV fleshed out the terse bulletins with human faces and endowed the crisis with everyday emotions, Delta Force and all military options were dead."[4]

All this was widely discussed within the media and by outside critics but, in sum, nobody came up with any definitive guidelines or agreement on how to cover the next terrorist incident. Once again, the individual journalist, each

---

VIEWPOINT 10-2

TERRORISM LIVE AND UNEDITED

"Three miracles—the jet airplane, the television and the satellite—have made it possible for a few anarchists or murderers to take the laws of civilization and the attention of the world into their own hands. When they succeed, we are all hostages, not just the passengers on the jet, but all of us and especially the President of the United States and television. And, it is the television spotlight that is the real ransom the terrorists demand and get....Live interviews—unedited—with terrorists is unconscionable. It is like handing over the front page to one side and saying, 'Fill in the headline.'"

Fred Friendly, former CBS News executive

"[I] hear that TV has become the terrorists' ultimate tool. This is a daffy and irresponsible charge. The competitive zeal with which the networks chased after the story of the [TWA Flight 847 hostages in Beirut in 1985] should be celebrated as an example of what's right about the democratic system, not what's wrong with it. There were, to be sure, some unruly and odious excesses. But I believe that such indiscretions are a worthwhile price to pay for a precious freedom that does not exist for more than 80 percent of the world's citizens."

Morton Dean, former CBS correspondent and, later, Independent Network News anchor

"TV news cameras and political agitators have had a much-discussed symbiotic relationship from the very beginning of TV. TV producers like action and the agitators like attention. But political atrocities did not begin with the television age, any careful reading of the exploits of Joe Stalin, Adolf Hitler or Genghis Khan will attest. Today's political extremists may enjoy the camera's attention, but they do not necessarily 'thrive' on it."

Wall Street Journal editorial arguing against even voluntary codes for television coverage in hostage situations

---

network, and each newspaper was left with deciding how to proceed ethically and responsibly on such stories. Some lessons, however, emerged crystal clear:

• The media, including television, *should* cover terrorist incidents. But they must cover the news, not indiscriminately provide terrorists with a platform and audience. Each journalist must do everything possible to avoid giving terrorists incentive to seek more exposure by striking again.

• The media must reexamine their definition of "objectivity." It is foolishness, not objectivity, to treat as equals both the hijackers and hijacked. By any civilized standard, it is wrong for a person to hold a gun at the head of an innocent. It also is wrong for a journalist to describe such an act as a justifiable political statement.

• TV cameras did not cause the hijackings. But their presence is what the hijackers wanted. Television journalists could take guidance from ABC News' internal guidelines: avoid sensationalizing any terrorist act, do nothing to jeopardize hostages' lives or interfere with authorities' efforts to gain their release, broadcast no incident live except in the most compelling circumstances, and report terrorists' demands but only with explanatory background. NBC warns its reporters to keep a low profile, limit use of lights, and to locate cameras and mikes as inconspicuously as possible.[5]

• The media must avoid participating in negotiations with terrorists. Television anchors in New York City in effect bargained directly with terrorists 5,000 miles away, asking—with the court of American public opinion watching—what their demands were and whether they had any word for President Reagan. That was an impressive display of technological prowess, but it amounted to journalistic stunting, not reporting. Calm, professional editing must be inserted between the sight and sound of terrorism and what hits the screen or front page.

• The media must avoid publishing information that might preempt military or police action to free hostages. For example, the *Atlanta Constitution,* covering the hijacking of an EgyptAir jet in 1985, reported on its front page "[T]he pilot punched the button of the emergency transponder, silently notifying the Athens tower that a hijacking had begun." That undoubtedly revealed to a great many people, prospective terrorists included, there was such a thing as an "emergency transponder."[6]

• The media should not make news or pay for it. After the Flight 847 hijack, some families of hostages were flown to Europe by television crews anxious for exclusive coverage of the story's next stage, release of the hostages.

Then, there is the highly controversial question of whether the media ever should give authorities information collected by reporters but not published. Some say absolutely not, that reporters are not cops and never should cross the line between them. Others take a different view, particularly in stories involving national security or lives of hostages. Katharine Graham, chairman of Washington Post Co., said, "When the media obtain especially sensitive information, we *are* willing to tell the authorities what we have learned and what we plan to report. And while reserving the right to make the final decision ourselves, we are anxious to listen to arguments about why information should not be aired."[7]

In March 1987, it was revealed that ABC television correspondent Barbara Walters had privately passed to the White House two documents with information on the Iran/Contra affair she received in interviews with an Iranian arms dealer. Michael Gartner, then editor of the *Louisville* (Ky.) *Courier-Journal* and president of ASNE, criticized Walters, saying, "She found out something she didn't tell her viewers....[she] let herself be used as a conduit. I don't think what she did was right or should have been done, but the greater sin is knowing something and not telling her viewers." In a statement, ABC said Walters' "transmission of her information to the President was in violation of a literal interpretation of news policy. ABC policy expressly limits journalists cooperating with government agencies unless threats to human lives are involved. Ms. Walters believed that to be the case."

(Polls find journalists generally divided over assisting authorities in such direct ways as providing photographs taken of a crime being committed; one survey found 54 percent would provide such assistance. Much higher percentages— 70, 80 or more—generally are found willing to cooperate by, say, withholding details of a kidnapping to protect the lives of victims.[8] Look at Case Study 10-1. Are *you* willing to cooperate?)

CASE STUDY 10-1

QUICK! YOU DECIDE

You are news director of an ABC television affiliate. A convict being treated at a local hospital escapes, obtains a gun, and holds hostages in the hospital. He warns he will kill his prisoners unless his grievances are broadcast by television. Police want you to broadcast the statement verbatim. Obviously concerned that the killing could start momentarily, police ask you to decide immediately.

ABC News policy gives you this guidance:

"We must guard against efforts by terrorists to use or manipulate us for their own ends...no such incident should be broadcast live except in the most compelling circumstances....Demands of the terrorist should be reported as an essential ingredient of the story. But we must avoid becoming a platform for propaganda and rhetoric. In most cases, this means we will condense, edit or paraphrase the demands and explain the background against which they were made."

Confronted by this problem, WABC-TV, New York City, agreed to broadcast a gunman's statement. Said the station's Cliff Abromats: "We didn't have time to sit down and debate the philosophic and ethical aspects of the request. We had two minutes."

Afterward, the *New York Daily News* commented in an editorial:

"There's something wrong when a guy who was just a number in Attica [a New York State prison] a few days ago can commandeer the spotlight like that. We in the news business must draw the line against being twisted so easily."

Was WABC-TV right to assist police, turning over its facilities to a gunman? Did the station let a criminal "commandeer the spotlight," as the *Daily News* charged?

(*Postscript:* The incident ended without bloodshed.)

SPIES, NATIONAL SECURITY, AND THE MEDIA

It was none other than the President of the United States, Ronald Reagan, on the telephone. He was calling Katharine Graham of the *Washington Post* for what she later described as a "very civilized, low-key conversation" about a story the *Post* planned to publish.[9]

Meanwhile, the then CIA director, the late William J. Casey, in language similarly civilized but unmistakably ominous, was warning the *Post* it risked prosecution under an obscure thirty-six-year-old statute if it published the story.

It was May 10, 1986, and the one-two federal punch brought into sharp focus tension long building between the media and some of the most powerful institutions in Washington—the U.S. intelligence and military communities. The core issue: What happens when the media dig up stories the government claims should be suppressed to protect national security?

In this case, the *Post* had a story on Ronald Pelton, a former employee of the top-secret National Security Agency convicted of spying for the Soviet Union. Reagan told Graham the story was of the highest security importance and that he would support Casey's warning about prosecution. Casey's club: Section 798 of Title 18 of the U.S. Code. The law, passed in 1950, makes it a crime punishable by up to ten years in prison and a $10,000 fine to disclose information about U.S. communications intelligence, secret codes, and technical devices and methods used by spy agencies. Casey was swinging Section 798 at more than the *Post*. He said the *New York Times, Washington Times, Newsweek,* and *Time* also had violated it.

This chapter of the CIA versus media controversy, however, actually was kicked off by NBC, which reported during Pelton's trial that he "apparently gave away one of the NSA's most sensitive secrets—a project with the code name Ivy Bells, believed to be a top-secret underwater eavesdropping operation by American submarines inside Russian harbors."[10] Presumably, the *Post* had even more sensitive details than NBC; "presumably" because we shall never know. After agreeing with Reagan and Casey to delay publication, the *Post* finally published its story stripped of information U.S. intelligence experts said would compromise secrets.

The incident vividly illustrated the tension that has existed between the media and government since the nation's earliest days. On one hand is the journalistic imperative to find and tell, to let the people know, the suspicion that government cannot be trusted, and that bureaucrats manipulate news for their own interests; on the other, the government's insistence that it alone has the resources, the overall view necessary for judging when national security is jeopardized, and that it alone is equipped to decide what should be published—or not published—about some stories.

(Caspar Weinberger, U.S. secretary of defense, once put it this way: "The government's need for secrecy arose not long after the Constitution was adopted. In 1792, President Washington refused to provide Congress with information about the defeat of General St. Clair's forces by the Ohio indians.")

Executive editor Ben Bradlee of the *Washington Post* wrote in an article for his own readers that he and other *Post* executives had been consulting administration officials on many stories they thought sensitive, and in fact had withheld information from more than a dozen published earlier that year. He said *Post* reporters learned details of Operation Ivy Bells even before they knew of Pelton and his betrayal to the Russians. Said Bradlee, "We thought we had the highest national security secret any of us had ever heard. *There was never any thought of publishing any of this information* [author's emphasis]."[11] With Pelton's conviction, however, the *Post* began more than five months of meetings with officials and "tried to frame a story that would tell the American people what the Russians already knew.... We were determined not to violate the legitimate security of the nation, but we were equally determined not to be browbeaten by the administration." At each meeting, intelligence officials said the different versions the *Post* had written would jeopardize national security if published. They argued no one could be certain exactly how much information Pelton had given the Soviets and, in any event, a detailed story in the *Post* could serve to confirm for the Soviets any information he did give them.

When the *Post* finally published a sanitized version, Bradlee said, "In my heart, I think the Russians already know what we kept out of the story. But I'm not absolutely sure of it."

"Not absolutely sure..." That's what bothers conscientious editors in such cases. Lacking all the information sources, all the background of a president or CIA director, they cannot be sure whether they are compromising national security. Two things, however, are certain: (1) under the cloak of "national security," governments from the beginning sometimes have hidden, disguised, and manipulated the truth for purposes having absolutely nothing to do with the fate of the nation, and (2) many of the stories that upset Reagan and Casey were leaked from within their own administration.

At the *New York Times,* the then executive editor, A. M. Rosenthal, pitched in: "The public has the idea that the press is constantly breaking secrets. The reality is that it is the U.S. government and U.S. officials who are releasing information to serve their own political, bureaucratic or governmental ends."[12]

Bradlee wrote that *Post* executives discussed whether to tell the President what their reporters had learned on their own about Ivy Bells. "While the administration was beating the press upside the head for run-of-the-mill leaks, truly important national security information was floating around town." Magnified tremendously by the national security implications involved, the issue was precisely that faced by many reporters on the city hall or police beat: Should the *Post* volunteer to officialdom information it was withholding from its readers? It was decided seeking a meeting with the President would "appear as too self-serving and grandstanding," Bradlee said. He summed up the *Post*'s position:

"In moments of stress between government and the press—and these moments have come and gone since Thomas Jefferson—the government looks for ways to control the press, to eliminate or minimize the press as an obstacle in the implementation of policy, or the solution of problems.

"In these moments, especially, the press must continue its mission of publishing information that it—and it alone—determines to be in the public interest in a useful, timely and responsible manner—serving society, not government."[13]

Still...doubts linger. Yes, Rosenthal is correct. Most leaks come from official sources, and the government does manipulate news. Bradlee is correct, too. It indeed has been so since Jefferson. Still...can editors, whatever their cautious professionalism, whatever their principled intent, in good conscience declare it is not the President nor the CIA who must decide what is in the public interest, but, rather, the press—"and it alone"? How can editors know what truly jeopardizes national security, what really is happening in the shadowy world of espionage? In the gigantic struggle between world powers which employ every possible means, including information and disinformation, editors cannot know all that, of course.

VIEWPOINT 10-3

LEAKS FROM THE TOP

"The executive branch is the only known vessel that leaks from the top. It leaks the baloney it thinks people will swallow, and threatens to sue anybody who publishes information it wants to suppress."

James Reston, *New York Times* columnist, commenting on Reagan administration attempts to halt news leaks in its own ranks

---

Clearly, much sensitive material finds its way into the media. (The author once met a Soviet diplomat who, in a moment of vodka-induced candor, said his embassy faced major problems in finding time to read all the many American newspapers and magazines reporting on defense affairs and then collate the huge amount of information thus gained.) Whether media coverage truly jeopardizes national security is problematical for all but a few top officials really in the know. Judging from official reaction, the government is most concerned about coverage that reveals the names of secret agents or divulges technical details of code-breaking or surveillance procedures. In the early 1980s, at least two magazines made it a practice to uncover and print names of CIA operatives in the field. Congress subsequently made that illegal.[14]

In the *Washington Post* incident, the CIA was not terribly concerned about holding secret the fact that it spies; but it was openly concerned that there be no public discussion of *how* it spies. Should the media make such a distinction, covering national security issues but avoiding publishing names and technical details? The CIA seemed hopeful it could limit coverage in that manner when, strongly criticized following its tangle with the *Post,* it soft-pedaled threats to prosecute under Section 798 (the law has yet to be used against any journalist). The CIA instead offered "cooperation," saying it wanted to "work with" journalists reporting potentially sensitive stories. But such is the institutionalized suspicion in the media that the offer was met with immediate distrust. Michael G. Gartner, a Gannett executive serving as president of ASNE, commented, "I think it's fine that they will be available for comment, but if they're talking about clearance, that's a completely different matter and that's totally objectionable."[15]

Some journalists speculated the whole affair was simply a smokescreen for a larger, more threatening move by the Reagan administration and Casey against official leakers. *New York Times* columnist William Safire said leaks had developed among the 200 or so top officials in Washington who get the CIA's super-secret National Intelligence Daily six mornings weekly. "That's it," Safire wrote. "That's the reason Mr. Casey is having fits, losing sight of the freedoms we hired him to protect: the NID is leaking."[16] Daniel Schorr, longtime Washington commentator, said the *Washington Post* had no new information on Operation Ivy Bells, that details had been known generally for years, even by the Soviets. He suggested the Reagan administration was trying to force the media into self-censorship "...to make the press itself the guardian of secrecy—starting with its successful chilling of the *Washington Post.*"[17]

Few issues are more grave for the media today than the national security

---

VIEWPOINT 10-4

WHO'S LYING NOW?

"The number of newspapers that lie and know they are lying you can count on one hand, but to say that the number of cases of lying in government is bigger is a considerable understatement."

  Ben Bradlee, executive editor, *Washington Post*

implications of such stories as Operation Ivy Bells, nor few threats to freedom of information more insidious than censorship efforts launched indiscriminately under guise of protecting national security. As in so many areas of journalistic ethics and responsibility there are no clear-cut answers. The media must continue their resistance of nearly two centuries to bureaucratic attempts to shut down the flow of information which American citizens have a legitimate right to know; at the same time, the media must reach an accommodation with the fact that their power to reveal all, instantly and on a worldwide basis, is a dangerous mixture when combined with the destructive military technology of the nuclear age. For journalists dealing in sensitive national security issues, the best guidance probably lies in the pattern developed by Graham and Bradlee of the *Washington Post:* retain the ultimate right—and responsibility—of deciding what is news and how it might serve the public interest, but first consult the proper officials on any hidden dangers to national security. The *Atlanta Journal and Constitution* did this on a story it developed about the top-secret Trident nuclear submarines. It informed readers in an editor's note that "By prior agreement, this story was reviewed by the Navy before publication and certain technical descriptions were altered at its request."

MEDIA GO—OR DON'T GO—TO WAR

One sweltering night in 1962, deep in the humid backwaters of South Vietnam's Mekong Delta, the author, then an Associated Press correspondent, learned that within a few hours events would begin unfolding that would result in men being killed and wounded. At dawn, a Vietnamese battalion supported by U.S. advisors would attack Viet Cong units nearby, and in a military/media tradition dating back through the Korean war and World War II, the author was briefed in advance on the entire "game plan." Into the reporter's notebook went precise details on how the attack would be executed. It was information priceless to the enemy commander who, as he was to learn when the sun rose, would have to defend or flee in a hurry. But, in keeping with that military/media tradition, the reporter's notebook stayed shut; the secrets were kept. There was unspoken agreement: The reporter would go in with the troops, would be fully informed—and there would be no attempt to "file" a story, no effort to get word out until after the action. Indeed, there was no alternative. Few battlefields have telephones for story dictation, and this one was no exception; Saigon and its cable links with the home office in New York City were distant, and the only available transportation was military.

For decades, that type military/media relationship was commonplace in American journalism. Now, roll ahead to a new scenario:

It is October 25, 1983, and thousands of U.S. troops are invading the Caribbean nation of Grenada by helicopter and landing craft. The Reagan administration had spotted what it regarded as threatening communist influence on the island, and was determined there would not be another Cuba on America's southern doorstep. Again, there was no leak by the media of the impending attack or, indeed, any coverage that would threaten military security once it was under way. Only, this time the reason for the tight lid was that for the first time in memory, reporters were not informed in advance of the operation or permitted to accompany assault troops. For two days, the U.S. government prevented eyewitness coverage of the operation, and for two more permitted only guided tours of the island. Howls of protest went up from the media.[18]

What happened to the military/media relationship in the two decades between the Mekong Delta and Grenada? How could a democratic government decide, in the case of Grenada, that its people did not have a right to know or, at least, had a right only to know what military and civilian bureaucrats thought they should know?

Such an enormously complicated—and important—turn in the relationship between the media and our government defies easy explanation. One critical factor is that the United States failed to win the Vietnam war, and many U.S. military officers and civilian officials came away convinced the media, in major part, were responsible.

Military officers point out that American units never were defeated in a major battlefield engagement throughout the long war (which a politically astute North Vietnamese officer is reported to have said was irrelevant; for him, the battlefield was world public opinion). Many American officials feel—rightly or wrongly—that excessively negative reporting from Vietnam eroded American public support for the war effort, and that this cannot be allowed to happen again. Vietnam-era officials now are senior policymakers in the Pentagon and Defense Department, and when it comes to media relations their memories of Vietnam are sharp. Here is how Defense Secretary Caspar Weinberger puts it:

> In the past, the news media [were] very supportive of our troops engaged in combat. They were always with the troops on the front lines. A natural camaraderie always existed between combat troops and combat reporters. Recently, however, we have begun to see elements of the news media's desire to second-guess the government creep into this relationship. Even in combat, the media [want] to decide for itself [sic] whether the fight is just. They want to interview the enemy, give equal time to the enemy, weigh the enemy's arguments against ours, and report the enemy's point of view to the American people.
>
> While I do not see how this can ever be helpful, I must again acknowledge that their motives are probably pure enough. This situation results, to a large degree, from many in the media's feeling that they are judges and owe a duty of impartiality to the enemy.
>
> I have to confess that the more extreme examples of this feeling remind me of [former British Prime Minister Winston] Churchill's statement that some felt they had to maintain an objective neutrality even as between the fireman and the fire.[19]

A second factor contributing to change in the military/media relationship is that some reporters *did* commit excesses in Vietnam and other military actions. Coming from an era when it was fashionable to picket the ROTC building, not attend classes there, many young reporters were totally inexperienced in mil-

---

VIEWPOINT 10-5

THREE WARRIORS VIEW THE MEDIA

"The reporters used to be on our side. Now it seems they are always trying to find a way to screw things up."

   U.S. Secretary of State George Shultz contrasting reporter attitudes during U.S. invasion of Grenada in 1983 with those of World War II

"I worry about the propensity of the American press to publish classified information which destroys and jeopardizes intelligence sources and methods.... There's been a vast divulging of sensitive information.... We've seen it destroy our ability to follow terrorists in specific instances. We've seen very

important capabilities to understand and follow Soviet military plans and the development of their weapons jeopardized and diminished. It seems to be happening more frequently, more quickly and at an increasing tempo and is doing more damage than we can tolerate."

   William Casey, then CIA director, in 1986 interview with *Washington Journalism Review*

"Vietnam was the first war ever fought without any censorship. Without censorship, things can get terribly confused in the public mind. Television is an instrument that can paralyze this country."

   Gen. William C. Westmoreland, commander, U.S. forces in Vietnam

---

itary affairs; they learned to cover war on the job. Even experienced reporters, reacting to news manipulation, not to say outright lying by officialdom, lost their professional balance and let tendentious adversarialism run rampant. Some reporters arrived in Vietnam with preconceived—and aggressive—notions of how the story should be covered. So great was the suspicion between media and officialdom that daily military briefings in Saigon were nicknamed "Five O'Clock Follies" by reporters, and frequently dissolved into outright baiting of briefing officers. Jerry Friedheim, executive vice president of the American Newspaper Publishers Association and a former U.S. assistant secretary of defense (for information), speaks to the point:

> [I] was a captain of artillery before I was an editor; and an assistant secretary of defense before returning to newspapering at ANPA.
> Few of today's journalists have served in, or know much about, the military.
> They know even less about wartime military operations and about how to accurately and safely report those operations—without putting in jeopardy the lives of soldiers or compromising the operation.
> Even more importantly, few U.S. military officers or troops know much about how newspapers work. They've met only rarely with a reporter. Newspapermen worry them a lot. Television people scare them almost to death!
> The point is: there is a generation gap.
> We somewhat-older newspaper folks, and our somewhat-older military officers know about each other's role in a free society—we even appreciate our joint indispensibility to the preservation of strong democracies.
> But a lot of younger people in each of our institutions neither understand nor particularly appreciate each other.[20]

The technology of journalism today convinces many in the military there cannot be a return to military/media relationships of World War II, when reporters roamed battlefields virtually at will. During public hearings into how news of the Grenada invasion was handled, one senior Pentagon officer testified television networks wanted to send an airplane to the island with a ground station capable of transmitting live broadcasts from the battlefield.[21] To some in the military, this conjured up images of "see Johnny die" via live broadcasts at dinnertime back home and, more importantly, the real possibility of security lapses that conceivably could result in many Johnnies dying needlessly. Officials who blacked out news of the Grenada invasion recalled that American media published aerial photographs of the U.S. Marine base at Khe Sanh, Vietnam, while it was under attack by North Vietnamese forces, and that American newspapers and television published, in 1984, the location of U.S. artillery spotters in Lebanon.[22] The then head of U.S. Navy information said:

"The reporters and their editors were not sensitive to the safety of those Marines [in Lebanon]. Those same positions came under fire the day after the stories ran and a Navy man was wounded in the bombardment...we all must insist upon a proper balance between mission security and the flow of information."[23]

Media response was quick and equally emphatic. Testifying at the Grenada hearings, John Seigenthaler, a Gannett executive and representative of the Society of Professional Journalists, Sigma Delta Chi, said, "History demonstrates that the American press can keep secrets, honor justifiable news embargoes and help protect the safety of our soldiers...your concern may be larger than the reality makes it." George Watson, ABC News vice president, said even those television journalists equipped with ground station transmitters would be subject to military control and, if necessary, jamming.[24]

Importantly, Grenada was a testing ground for senior Washington officials with no love for the media who, because of President Reagan's own feelings about reporters, felt emboldened to "take on" the media. Reagan, the "Great Communicator," always kept the media at arm's length.[25] Thus, the decision was to manage the news and hope for a quick, relatively bloodless victory in Grenada with no nosey reporters around if something went wrong (and, as subsequent studies showed, plenty did go wrong militarily; the Grenada invasion was not a well-run operation).

Initial public reaction stunned journalists. The triumph over a ragtag mob of Cuban and Grenadian defenders drew cheers for the military and almost no complaints that the media—and, thus, the public—were kept in the dark. At first, the public bought the administration's explanation: Hundreds of reporters would have wanted to go to Grenada, and the military could not transport them; taking reporters could have jeopardized security, and, anyway, some might have gotten hurt. After every leading journalistic organization in the country complained—and after the real meaning of the blackout sank in—public opinion reversed itself. Just two months after the invasion, a Louis Harris poll found

Americans convinced 65 to 32 percent that the Reagan administration was wrong in not letting reporters accompany the troops. Nevertheless, the Harris poll and other surveys detected more than slight feeling that in such cases the President was in the best position to judge.[26] Clearly, a precedent of sorts had been set. And, sure enough, in 1986, journalists were not informed of fighting—in fact, were steered away from it—when the U.S. fleet in the Mediterranean launched punitive strikes against Libyan forces said to be supporting terrorist groups throughout the world. There was no public outcry over that and, strangely, only muted protests by the media.

What course should the media follow in reporting military affairs? A few observations:

War is serious business. And, that's why the media never should relax efforts to fully inform the American public each time their government decides to wage it. Reporters, at their own risk, should accompany U.S. troops.

However, the media must recognize war is never so serious as for those who must fight it—and hundreds of noncombatant journalists, some sadly inexperienced in battle, can get in the way of those charged with winning it. There is a tried-and-true technique of using "pool" reporters, a few who accompany combat troops and then share dispatches with those forced to remain behind. Increased use of this technique might be necessary, and pool ground rules must be followed. In the past, the Pentagon has put together pools under tight security as a test—and word promptly leaked out and was published and broadcast. That hardly built confidence among military officers that they ever could get along with the media and still ensure the security of a mission or the lives of their soldiers. A danger, of course, is that the military will favor journalists who regard the military in kindly light. Or, that it will insist on an accreditation program that involves training in military affairs or some other qualification. That's a first step toward licensing, and the media must reject it, retaining the right to decide who is qualified to report war, just as they pick political writers and court reporters.

The media must recognize there will be times when they cannot use new technology that permits broadcasts live from battlefield to satellite to network office to living rooms all over the world. War cannot be covered the way ABC's *Wide World of Sports* covers football; the media must practice self-restraint in what—and how—they report from the battlefield. Another issue: Two commercial satellites already provide the media with photos from space—the American Landsat which (1986) charges as little as $50 for images of objects larger than 100 feet taken from 438 miles up, and the French SPOT. Both supplied photos of the Chernobyl nuclear disaster in the Soviet Union in 1986. There is talk of American news media launching their own satellite. Presumably, the Soviet Union or any other technologically advanced enemy of the United States could obtain satellite photos, too, but there are suggestions media-owned satellites could present a new threat to national security.[27]

Finally, if the media are to retain their ability to cover military affairs they must do more to obtain public support. It isn't enough to simply shout "First Amendment" or "people's right to know" and expect the public to automatically agree. There must be patient efforts over the long haul to explain why reporters should be with the troops. This could best be done through the American Newspaper Publishers Association, National Association of Broadcasters, American Society of Newspaper Editors, Radio-TV News Directors Association, and other industry groups. Only when the public insists it has a right to know and that the media must be its surrogates in combat zones will the current trend toward restriction and exclusion be reversed. For, as we shall discuss next, public opinion is what counts among policymakers in Washington.

THE MEDIA AND THE PRESIDENCY

In summer 1985, the biggest news in Washington was a polyp in President Reagan's colon and a pimple on his nose. Reporters struggled mightily for details in what to outsiders was a bewildering, if not demeaning, trivialization of what news is all about. In fact, it was yet another in the unending, but fundamentally very important, conflicts between two of this democracy's most important institutions, the media and White House news managers.

At issue in the White House, basically, was the public image of the President as a healthy, vigorous chief executive, despite his being 73 years old. Image makers who spent years carefully crafting virtually his every public move had a major problem: both polyp and pimple were cancerous. At best, word of that could severely damage the image of health and vitality; at worst, it could throw a scare into the American people, embolden the President's political enemies, weaken his influence over other Washington power blocs, particularly Congress, and even cause concern abroad. From the White House's view, the image and political implications could be enormous.

For the White House media, the scent of big news was in the air. Powerful influences began to brew, from the individual reporter's ego drive to break an important story to the wider media belief that the President's health is important to the nation—to the world—and must be covered.

Much excitement and heat, if little light, were generated before precise medical information reached the public (who took it all in stride; the news turned out not too ominous). White House reporters shouted at White House aides about a coverup; White House aides shouted back that they did not either lie or mislead. The aides said that there is such a thing as a person's privacy, even if he is President, and that the relationship between patient and physician is confidential.

"Why did you handle it that way?" Helen Thomas, UPI's longtime White House correspondent, demanded of Larry Speakes, until 1987 the President's chief spokesman.

"Well, I don't think that's any of your business," Speakes replied.

Interjected ABC's Sam Donaldson: "It is our business."

Speakes: "And I think if you had two grains of salt for sense, you could figure it out."

Donaldson: "We have to rely on you for information. It is our business why you leave things out."[28]

Much ado about nothing? Not at all. James Reston, the *New York Times'* senior Washington correspondent, who has known more presidents than most reporters, weighed in:

> The President is back at the White House, to everyone's relief, but his aides are still sore at the press for asking all those questions about his medical record. They say it's "distasteful" to intrude into the private relations between a doctor and his patient.
>
> Maybe so. The only trouble is that this is precisely what the White House said when they were covering up the illnesses of Woodrow Wilson and Franklin Roosevelt.
>
> All would be well, they said. Besides, the questions were not only "distasteful" but painful. Since then, the historians, with good reason, have condemned the press for misleading the people.
>
> The intention here is not to suggest that President Reagan's illness is as serious as Wilson's in 1919 or Roosevelt's in 1944, but merely to question the popular idea that the confidential relationship between doctor and patient also applies when the patient is the President of the United States.
>
> The health of a President is not merely a private but a public concern. . . . [29]

The incident was a classic in the struggle between the media and the presidency, two institutions that dominate the shape and tone of news emanating from Washington, the world's most important power center. It was a struggle over the President's single most important political concern, his relationship with the public. It was a question of who would establish the character of his public image. (In 1987, Reagan underwent surgery for an enlarged prostate. This time, Speakes released full details, and the media handled the affair much more calmly.)

Arrayed against a handful of presidential image makers at any given time are about 10,000 reporters, editors, writers, columnists, correspondents, freelancers, and others who make up the "Washington Press Corps" (4,300 are accredited to Congress, 1,600 to the White House).[30] Despite the lack of parity in opposing numbers, the contest inevitably is weighted in favor of the image makers. They, after all, control what Reagan advisor Michael Deaver called the "talent." But, of course, the media are the main conduits any president must use to reach the public. So, the contest is not only spirited, but almost Machiavellian in its complexity.

For example, to properly market their "talent," the image makers must control not only what the President says, but how is it said, where, when, and under what conditions. Deaver, for years Reagan's top advisor in such matters, worried about the smallest details, even the color of curtains draping windows behind the President as he spoke on television. For Reagan, television was *the* public relations tool. If he could use it under tightly controlled circumstances (that is, without any of those bothersome questions from pushy reporters), the "Great Communicator" was at his best. Few politicians equalled his ability to effectively use television to cajole and convince. For Reagan, it was not even necessary to *speak* on television. His aides learned, for example, that by staging "photo opportunities" involving Reagan visiting schools or talking with children, they could create the image of a man dedicated to education—even though in fiscal policy the Reagan administration was cutting back assistance to education. Reagan held fewer live televised news conferences than any of his predecessors, and generally avoided close contact with reporters.[31] Reagan, in sum, was presented masterfully, at his smiling best and without much harassment from questioning reporters. ABC's Donaldson said of the administration: "They are happy to see cameras but not questions."

For the media, the frustrations were mountainous. Seasoned White House correspondents were denied frequent access to the President, and often kept almost beyond shouting distance. (They, in fact, sometimes were physically restrained behind what they came to call the "shout line.") The daily routine often was limited to sparring with Speakes and other press office aides and accepting news handouts. Deaver later revealed he and other top officials agreed with the President on what single important story would be released each day to achieve major impact from the administration's viewpoint. Some of the President's visitors were whisked away from the press corps; others, presumably more trustworthy, upon leaving were "fed" to reporters anxious to learn, even secondhand, if necessary, what kind of a day the President of the United States was having.

At times, as noted in Case Study 3-1, Reagan slipped the public relations leash and created for the media the ethical dilemma of whether to quote what

---

VIEWPOINT 10-6

OLDEST GAME IN TOWN

"Managing the news, of course, is the oldest game in town [Washington]. Franklin Roosevelt was a master at it. The leaders of all institutions try to manage the news in the sense of emphasizing their virtues and minimizing or suppressing their failures. Even newspaper owners have been known to fiddle with the facts."

James Reston, the *New York Times* columnist

"All presidents seek to manage the news and all are successful to a degree."

George Ready, White House press secretary for President Lyndon Johnson, 1964–65

"[L]et's face it. Presidents want the press to be their press agents."

Helen Thomas, longtime UPI White House correspondent

"I need your help...[But] if you want to play it the other way...I know how to cut off the flow of news except in handouts....If you help me, I'll help you. I'll make you-all big men in your profession."

President Johnson to reporters in 1964

obviously were his inadvertent remarks—that Poland's military leaders were "bums" and, with reference to the Soviet Union, "The bombing begins in five minutes." Such was the strain between media and White House that the comments were both broadcast and published, despite official protests.[32]

Under the Deaver/Speakes technique, the President on occasion went directly to the public with what he said were media distortions in covering his administration's policies. He always chose a forum certain to be friendly. For example, Reagan traveled to a New Orleans convention of the Veterans of Foreign Wars to accuse the media of putting out "discouraging hype and hoopla" about his policies in Central America.[33] He was strongly applauded.

The Reagan approach is described here in detail not to indicate it was particularly unique in manipulation of the White House press corps. All presidents have tried to do the same thing.

Well into his second term, long after most presidents begin to lose public favor, Reagan was scoring his highest ever in popularity polls. Then in 1986 and 1987 came a public relations disaster—revelations that despite public pledges it never would deal with "terrorist states," the Reagan administration in fact had been secretly selling arms to Iran, officially designated a terrorist state, and funneling proceeds to Contra rebels fighting to overthrow the Nicaraguan government.

As the media began prying out details of official coverup, not to say outright lying, the President's popularity plummeted—and the balance of power between President and media shifted dramatically. It was proof again that it is a president's public popularity that establishes the relationship between media and the White House. In times of relatively weak presidents, when lack of substantive policy and open leadership become apparent, the media assume a strong hand; confronted by a president shrewd in image building and strong in the polls, the media's influence wanes.

For their own purposes, the media *invite* some control of the news flow. George Reedy, White House press secretary under President Lyndon Johnson in 1964 to 1965, says reporters know there would be "chaos" if there were an end to daily press briefings, pools, prearranged travel, and other physical arrangements in place since Roosevelt's day. Reedy recalls President Johnson unexpectedly holding Saturday morning news conferences—and Washington bureau chiefs pleading the practice be stopped. Printers had to be called in to work at overtime rates, and everybody's work week simply was being disrupted. Says Reedy:

> This may well account for the indifference of the public to the periodic campaigns [by the media] against news management. Even to an unsophisticated audience it is apparent that journalists are not objecting to news management per se but only to the kind of news management that makes their professional lives more difficult. However it may look in Washington, at a distance the issue appears as a dispute over control of the news for the convenience of the President or for the convenience of the press. In such a situation, Americans tend to come down on the side of the President. Of course, if the President is caught in an outright lie—a lie about something in which the public is really concerned—the public will mobilize against him swiftly.

But many charges of news management are directed at statements that Americans do not regard as outright lies. Americans have become too accustomed to the kind of exaggeration and misleading facts that are used to sell products on nightly television that a little White House puffery seems quite natural.[34]

For reporters who want to enjoy an uninterrupted meal, White House press aides will announce, "The lid is on." That means no news will be released until mealtime is over. When Reagan imposed a news blackout on his 1985 summit meeting with Soviet leader Mikhail Gorbachev in Geneva, some reporters applauded. Robert Timberg of the *Baltimore Sun* says the blackout applied to not only formal briefings, but also private background sessions through which administration officials regularly leaked information to favored reporters, particularly those of the *New York Times* and *Washington Post*. Timberg says it "sounds like heresy" but the blackout worked to the benefit of reporters from other papers who otherwise would have been scooped.[35]

THE MEDIA AND BUSINESS

It's almost a given in business, industry, and commerce: reporters are anti-business, don't know anything about covering it, and the media in general give biased, inadequate news treatment to anyone who tries to make a buck. For decades, research into business executive attitudes has identified those beliefs.[36]

Much of the public also sees bias in business coverage. Only, the public often can't decide whether it's a bias for or against. One survey showed 60.6 percent of all respondents perceived bias; of them, 50.2 percent found the media biased *for* business, 49.8 percent biased *against* it.[37]

In studies of *reporter* attitudes, researchers tend to slip into subjective considerations and extrapolate broadly—to state, for example, that political liberals don't like business, and many reporters hold liberal attitudes, therefore reporters don't like business. Yet, as we have seen, newspapers and television themselves have become Big Business. Can men and women who manage billion-dollar media conglomerates be antibusiness? Do they spend increasing millions to cover business and still perpetuate institutionalized antibusiness bias? Are highly paid, profit-oriented media executives harboring in their newsrooms journalists who are free to indulge in antibusiness vendettas?

Or, as the author suggests, does business suspicion of the media really trace back to quite different origins: 1) many years of, frankly, superficial and sometimes inaccurate coverage by media that accorded business news low priority and didn't train their staffs properly in how to report and write it, and 2) the business world's misunderstanding of the news selection process, and an egocentric belief that it *must* be antibusiness bias that goads reporters to ask tough questions at corporate annual meetings, or to cover bad business news as well as good news.

Whatever the origins, the media and business have problems with each other. An early researcher, Dr. Joseph R. Dominick, found unusual metaphors being used to describe the uneasiness of the business-journalism association

---

VIEWPOINT 10-7

"WE KNOW YOU'RE A CROOK"

"As a frequent interviewee, I have been struck by the inexperience of many reporters and by their lack of preparation, their ignorance of basic economic principles, and what often seems an unnecessarily hostile adversarial attitude. In fact, at the outset of certain interviews I have had the feeling that the interviewer's attitude was one of: 'We know you're a crook, and I'm here to find out how and why.'"

John E. Swearingen, chairman, Standard Oil (Indiana)

"It's almost like they prefer it if the executive wasn't able to answer the question. They prefer the executive stuttering and looking like he had something to hide."

Jerry Sloan, public relations vice president, American Motors Corp., on television business news coverage

---

such as "two strange dogs circling one another," "two scorpions in a bottle," "cowboys and indians," and "lions and Christians." Dorothy Lorant, a reporter (*Boston Herald-Traveler* and *Boston Herald-American*) who became public relations vice president for Greyhound Corp., said that "A serious rift exists between the press and the private sector today, reinforced by businessmen who frequently approach an interview with a newspaper or television reporter with all the enthusiasm of a missionary asked to dine with cannibals."[38] *Fortune* magazine published in 1987 a survey of 107 senior executives randomly selected from the nation's 1,000 largest companies and revealed 59 percent complained journalists do not know enough about the subjects they report on; and 35 percent charged journalists with "distortion," meaning sensationalism, incomplete information, or misquoting (but 54 percent also said executives are not effective in dealing with the press and 42 percent agreed the press has good reason to be wary of business).

Herbert Schmertz, public affairs vice president of Mobil Oil Corp., wrote for *Washington Journalism Review*:

Why is the journalist viewed as the bum of the ball? Maybe because when the executive turns on the seven o'clock news, he sees that the two-hour interview he taped earlier that day has been boiled down to twenty seconds. Worse, the editing has turned him into a blunt, crude, stereotype of a business executive, something akin to the money-grubbing, cardboard figures on *Quincy*.

An exaggeration? Sadly, no. Many executives have been burned this way after granting interviews to television reporters. The problems lies partly with the medium, which both massages and mangles. By contrast, the print media on occasion mislead, even distort the news through the word-editing process, but these are mostly errors of omission. Print reporters usually have the space to develop complex stories and to produce substantive in-depth interviews. TV journalists edit film, a process that by its very nature is highly subjective, and when content is chopped into twenty-five-second bites, the latitude of error and distortion is great.

There is another, even more important difference: Newspapers and newsmagazines do not edit to transmit viewpoint. That is left, as it should be, to the editorial pages. Network television news all too often seems to edit, by inclusion or omission, for point of view, and it has no electronic counterpart to the editorial pages. So, if the corporate executive has been harmfully misquoted, or edited in such a way that his or her reputation is damaged, the only recourse is to sue.[39]

Note: In 1982, Mobil insured 100 of its top executives to cover $10 million in legal costs should any sue for libel. Mobil also carried an aggressive public relations campaign directly to the public by, among other things, buying advertising space on op-ed pages to criticize what it termed unfair coverage.

Schmertz says television is the prime offender because "the show-biz tail wags the news content dog" and TV editors do not police the ethics of their reporters. "The pandering to the all-important Nielsen rating is probably the major culprit."[40]

Lorant, on the other hand, says business executives themselves are much to blame. Many executives, she says, treat the media "with barely concealed hauteur." Many bankers, executives, and industrialists running publicly traded corporations don't own them, are using other people's money—yet cannot get used to being asked unwelcome questions, and sometimes tell reporters to "Mind your own business."

Despite their differences, Lorant says, many in the media and business share characteristics such as "...a propensity for arrogance, a reluctance to admit shortcomings and a tendency to take themselves too seriously."[41]

Business coverage nationwide is expanding rapidly, and reporters are asking what Lorant calls "unwelcomed questions," penetrating the business world as never before, pursuing executives unaccustomed to being pursued, and turning the spotlight on areas never previously opened to the public. And some of the writing is tough. Here, for example, is how the *New York Times* discussed a well-known hotel owner in a major profile on the front page of its business news section:

> But [the hotel owner] has another, more private face and it is a far darker one. Those who have been in management positions at his hotels say he is a quarrelsome, overbearing employer—and many of them have quit after brief stays. And although [he] insists his properties are flourishing, key associates say they are losing money steadily.... What's more, for years [he] has paid platoons of lawyers to defend a welter of lawsuits by those who claim he owes them money...$30 million of loans ...reportedly are overdue...today, he often postpones paying even the most paltry bills and is said to be in the throes of a deepening cash squeeze....[42]

Civil servants, politicians, and baseball managers may have grown accustomed, albeit reluctantly, to being treated that way in print. But for many business executives, having their "private face" exposed is a new experience, and they don't like it.

Business journalists tackle stories that create great unease in financial circles. In 1985, for example, the media covered savings-and-loans crises in two states—and were criticized both times for starting withdrawal runs on S&L institutions. In Ohio, the *Cincinnati Post* and *Enquirer* both reported on their front pages that the collapse of a securities firm in Florida left in jeopardy a Cincinnati S&L which had loaned it money; a local television station reported a "run" on the institution—and, sure enough, there was a run. Eventually, $154 million was withdrawn by panicky customers. That, in turn, undermined the state's deposit guarantee fund and threatened other Ohio S&Ls.[43] For editors, the question was how to discharge the media's first responsibility, to inform readers and viewers, yet not cause panic. One TV reporter said, "The facts created the panic, not us." S&L officials claimed *any* reporting of the story would create panic. In Maryland, the *Baltimore Sun* reported an S&L changed management because its "rapid growth had created serious difficulties." The next morning, customers lined up outside the S&L, waiting to withdraw funds. Again, S&L and state banking officials blamed the media for causing panic. But not Maryland Attorney General Stephen Sachs. He said that to suggest the media caused the S&L's difficulty by covering the story was "like blaming Pearl Harbor on The Associated Press," which also covered "bad news" that fateful Dec. 7, 1941.[44]

VIEWPOINT 10-8

CRISIS COVERAGE AT THE S&L

"There is no question that press coverage exacerbated the crisis. Without the kind of intense coverage they gave it, there wouldn't have been a crisis."

   Kenneth Elshoff, president, Ohio Savings and Loan League, following that state's 1985 S&L financial crisis

"Certainly by informing the public that banks were facing difficulties we might have influenced some people to pull their money out. But with our responsibilities to our readers we couldn't have done it any other way."

   Editor George Blake, *Cincinnati Enquirer*

"We were in a hot box. How do you cover runs on a bank without creating more runs on a bank?...We thought hard about how to play it. Do we lead with the runs? Do we put them further down in the story? We opted not to lead with them....My major concern was that I didn't want to create any more panic."

   Editor Paul Knue, *Cincinnati Post,* Source: *Washington Journalism Review*

It is reporting "bad news" that most upsets the business community. One study of network business coverage showed 60 percent devoted to "strikes, environmental threats, health hazards, product recalls, industrial accidents and illegal financial dealings."[45] But is that due to media bias or, rather, a definition of news as being the unusual, the aberrant, the deviation from the normal? In other words, is it news that S&Ls *don't* have financial difficulties, hotel owners *don't* have mounting debts, or that some do? This, of course, is an ethical question at the heart of all news coverage, not just business news coverage. It enters the media versus business equation at this time because newspapers and television are coming up to speed with discerning, hard-hitting coverage of business as they did long ago in covering politics, sports, government—and any number of other large, important American institutions.

   In great measure, the relatively recent turn by the media toward business coverage is a response to advertiser demands for more affluent readers and viewers, those interested in stock market reports and business news, and in the corporate *and* private lives of business leaders. So, in many parts of the country (not just business centers such as New York City, Chicago, or Boston) rapid—and costly—expansion of business news staffs is under way. This in itself could eliminate some business world complaints about media coverage as business reporters become more sophisticated and better trained. Coverage could be improved if more newspaper and television editors recruited reporters specially trained in the basics of economics, finance, and general business. It is not true that any sound general assignment reporter, even one untrained in business, can move into a complex business story and, under deadline pressure, sort out a savings-and-loan crisis in Ohio, or a hotel chain's financial difficulties in New York. The news instincts, willingness to work hard, and attention to detail displayed by a good general assignment reporter *are* essentials in business news, as in any news sector. But a reporter who opens an interview by asking a banker what the prime rate is or the chairman of an industrial firm what "earnings" means will not do much to reduce the feeling in the business world that when it comes to business news, the media simply don't know what they are doing.

Business sometimes creates problems for itself: people and companies with things to sell subject the media to multimillion dollar public relations barrages that never quit. From earliest cub reporter days, journalists grow up expecting business to push for free space and favorable mention, and to shade or distort the truth. (An American Management Association survey found 47 percent of public relations representatives admitted deliberately withholding information from the media. Predictably, the survey found one-third of responding journalists believed business people often lie to reporters; they unanimously accused top managers of withholding information).[46] The media often are vulnerable to such pressure. In a report on corporate PR practices in its region, the *San Francisco Chronicle* described how a manufacturer produced a sophisticated sound and light show to announce a new camera. The company "even created a Polynesian village, where the mostly male contingent of 160 reporters and ninety [financial] analysts used the [camera] to snap pictures of bikini-clad models." Rubbing salt in its own wound, the *Chronicle* reported, "The techniques work more often than many journalists like to think." The story said Apple Computer, "the most PR-savvy company" in nearby Silicon Valley, was mentioned in the *Chronicle* 359 times between January 1985 and April 1986.[47] (The important role of public relations practitioners in media operations is discussed more deeply in Chapter 11.)

NEWSPAPERS VERSUS TELEVISION

In his farewell speech as outgoing ASNE president, Creed Black posed a paradox:

"On one hand," he told society members convening in Washington, "most thoughtful students of the American press agree that our newspapers are doing a better job today than ever before in this nation's history. On the other, we are buffeted almost daily with new pronouncements of a crisis of public confidence....

"How do we explain this?" asked Black, a long-time editor and chairman of Knight-Ridder's *Lexington* (Ky.) *Herald-Leader*.

The answer Black delivered to his own question caused a furor in the media that hasn't ended yet. Black acknowledged that many American institutions suffer public distrust, that newspapers sometimes are made scapegoats for carrying bad news, that their watchdog role offends some people, and that newspapers are fallible and do make errors. But, then:

"Finally, I come to what I have become increasingly convinced is one of the major reasons our public standing seems to have declined while our performance as an institution has improved.

"It is that the public lumps the printed press and television together in something called 'the media' and make little distinction between the two. The result is that we are blamed for the sins and shortcomings of what television—which remains basically an entertainment medium—calls news."

Television executives were furious. A low-grade intramural quarrel had simmered for decades between print and broadcast journalists over whether TV truly presented news or "show biz," and, of course, there had been spirited competition for reader/viewer time and advertising dollars. But Black very publicly rubbed television's nose in it, using his position as president of the prestigious editors' society to do so. He took public a divisive quarrel that shows newspapers and television are far from united in how they relate to other institutions in our society.

Black told his colleagues he received many criticisms of newspapers, adding:

"A striking thing about all this is that when these critics get down to specifics, more often than not they unleash a litany of complaints about television ...if all those folks out there who are unhappy with 'the media' sometimes fail to make distinctions between our newspapers and television, that doesn't mean there aren't any. There are distinctions—and they are profound."

First, Black said, "television is no small part show biz."

Second, what is "breathlessly introduced on TV...often is not news at all— or at least not significant news presented in enough depth to give it meaning."

Third, Black continued, "television provides little opportunity for dissent or criticism by its viewers or the subjects of its coverage. The networks have no such mechanism at all. Some local television stations do permit limited viewer reaction, but the time they give to it doesn't begin to compare with the space devoted by any newspaper to letters to the editor."

Fourth, television has developed no standard mechanism for correcting its errors.

Black urged newspapers to "curb the use of that troublesome word 'media' ...make sure our readers understand the distinction between newspapers and TV. There's no reason we have to suffer in silence under the heavy load of television's baggage."

A final barb: "And we can always hope that television news will improve as it grows up."[48]

The theme was picked up by other newspaper executives. Richard J. V. Johnson, president of the *Houston Chronicle* and then chairman of the American Newspaper Publishers Association, complained that "arrogant TV reporters" helped create public feeling that all journalists are arrogant.[49] *Editor & Publisher,* a newspaper trade journal, said in an editorial "television's credibility problem is worse than newspapers'" and called on print and broadcast executives to work together to improve public perceptions.[50]

Some television executives also complained. Ralph Renick, for more than thirty years news director of WTVJ-TV, Miami, and a nationally recognized television journalist, said many ills in television news trace to poor management: "[T]o many in newsroom management, news is Entertainment Tonight: 'A little song, a little dance, a little seltzer down the pants.' We have filler stories designed to make you feel good all over. I'm not talking about features that have a legitimate place, but filler segments more suited for cooking shows or do-it-yourself hobby programs."[51]

CBS correspondent Charles Kuralt said one problem was television station managers who "don't know anything about news and don't care...." News consultants, Kuralt said, show stations how to improve ratings for news by using an anchorperson who often is "an attractive young person who would not know a news story if it jumped up and mussed his coiffure."[52] The dean of all newscasters, CBS's Walter Cronkite, also voiced reservations:

"What I'm afraid of, with polls showing most of the people getting most of their news from television, is that they're really not getting enough information. And yet at the same time, I see on the news an attempt to make the news more popular.

"There's no sense in doing a program nobody watches. But I'm afraid that there's an increasing amount of trivialization creeping into the news. More feature stories and less real digging for the stories that make a difference in people's lives."[53]

Some broadcasters launched a bitter counterattack. Don Hewitt, executive producer of CBS's *60 Minutes,* charged newspapers with "video envy," responding to Creed Black: "You may get your jollies by saying that television is no small part show biz. But it's your *Lexington* [Ky.] *Herald-Leader,* not CBS, that runs Sidney Omarr's Horoscope, Omar Sharif's Bridge Game, Garfield the Cat, Blondie, Beetle Bailey, Mary Worth, Ann Landers *and* Dear Abby, 39 column inches called 'Miss Manners' that last week told me when it's proper and when it's not proper for someone to bathe naked in my hot tub."

Hewitt continued: "How did we get on your enemies list? I think it's because you think we want to crash your club. Newspaper people have long be-

---

VIEWPOINT 10-9

IMAGE AND THE SONY SHEPHERDS

"In this country, we have armed with microphones a lot of fetuses in Gucci loafers. They are Sony shepherds, and they go around sticking mikes up people's nostrils, and that doesn't do much for our image."

Sander Vanocur, veteran NBC and ABC correspondent

lieved that getting a job at a newspaper was akin to joining the priesthood, that journalists, not our kind but your kind, are not hired but ordained. And that we who broadcast the news instead of printing it are somehow not worthy...one of the things I do take seriously is this constant sniping at us by publishers who should know better. The fallout is beginning to poison all of us, high-priced anchor and ink-stained wretch alike...."[54]

Van Gordon Sauter, then executive vice president of CBS's broadcasting group and a veteran television newsman, joined Hewitt in the counterattack: "I suspect those who work in television are increasingly uninterested in the anti-TV bias of many newspaper people. We have read more than our share of newspaper criticism of television news. With notable exceptions, it is done by insipid, ill-informed people who reflect the disdain or fear their editors feel toward the medium. Most of the material is petty gossip or snide derogatory articles, sourced by anonymous insiders. The major issues are rarely ever touched, apparently left for the adults to discuss at their journalistic seminars."[55]

So, from all directions, there is venom aplenty. That aside, what fundamentals fuel the newspaper versus television quarrel?

- In only three decades, television grew from birth as a commercial medium to newspapers' major competitor. Tempers flared as television went for newspapers' lifeblood—reader time and advertiser dollar. To some extent, television created new advertising support of its own. But every viewing minute given television, every dollar spent for commercials, is a dollar or minute newspapers don't get. In 1985, television's ad revenue hit $20.6 billion or 21.7 percent of the total, compared with $25.4 billion and 26.8 percent for newspapers. And, newspaper executives who long had assumed newspapers were perceived as journalistically superior got a shock: A survey by their own ASNE showed about half of the respondents would turn to television if they "had to choose one source for local news"; one-third chose newspapers. Asked which news media they would trust to help them understand national news, 57 percent chose TV, 29 percent newspapers. Clearly, there is an underlying economic conflict behind the "show biz" controversy, although both sides tend to cloak it in loftier terms, preferring instead to argue about journalistic ethics, quality, and so forth.
- There *is* a ratings-driven "show biz" aura around television news. Is any *journalist* worth the $2.5 million annually CBS paid (1986) Dan Rather? Or, the $1.8 million NBC paid Tom Brokaw, even the $900,000 Peter Jennings was paid by ABC?[56] Experienced reporters at even premier papers such as the *New York Times* are in only the $60,000 range; *Newsday,* a paper of world-class journalistic quality, made news in newspaper circles in 1986, by putting a $52,000 floor under annual salaries for reporters with five years experience. Obviously, in television's scheme of things, on-camera personalities are worth huge salaries if they pull high ratings which, of course, translate into millions of dollars in advertising revenue. In 1986, each network evening news show generated $150 million to $175 million in annual revenue. What television does to protect such enormous revenue can add to the "show biz" aura. In 1983, it was charged in

federal court in Kansas City that KMBC-TV had demoted a female anchor, Christine Craft, because she was "too old, unattractive and not deferential enough to men," and thus was costing the station viewers. After two trials, a jury awarded her $325,000 (the verdict later was overturned).[57] Commenting on TV's need for ratings, Gene F. Jankowski, president, CBS/Broadcast Group, once put it this way: "We are among the very few American industries that depend not on the customer's pocketbook but solely on the customer's interest and approval. That interest and approval must be won, over and over again, amid an ever-widening field of choice, for us to survive."

• There is "show biz" taint when networks buy news events. It wasn't journalism but something else when ABC paid $10 million for exclusive TV rights to much of "Liberty Weekend," the 1986 Independence Day unveiling of the renovated Statue of Liberty. (Ed Turner, senior vice president of Cable News Network, commented, "You don't license the Statue of Liberty to anybody. They practically want to put the ABC logo on the Statue of Liberty, for God's sake." For ABC, dividends were handsome: its ratings were double the combined CBS and NBC audiences July 3 to 4.)[58] Networks say they protect the sanctity of news by producing such extravaganzas in their entertainment divisions, but that is a nuance missed by the public who, as Creed Black said, tend to lump it all in with the "media." "Checkbook journalism" creates ethical problems when practiced in news departments. CBS News paid $500,000 for conversations between former President Nixon and a onetime aide, Frank Gannon. Of thirty-eight hours of conversations, the Nixon/Gannon team selected two-and-a-half hours from which CBS used ninety minutes. CBS surrendered its editorial responsibilities and prerogatives.[59] ABC News paid $25,000 for eighteen minutes of videotape of Soviet dissident Andrei Sakharov, and acknowledged the footage probably was produced by the Soviet internal security police, the KGB, to show Sakharov as being well treated.[60]

• Television's aggressive, intrusive nature—the camera focused tightly on grieving face, correspondents shouting questions at no less than the President of the United States and leader of the free world—*does* create public perception of arrogant invasion of both privacy and decency; a picture of irreverent, uncaring, unmannerly news hounds. Also, television's technical limitations at times create shallow, snap-crackle-pop journalism that seems unfair and unbalanced. And, print journalists feel they are tarred with the same brush when public opinion reacts negatively.

The resultant tension became obvious during this exchange between print and television journalists at a seminar sponsored by the Poynter Institute for Media Studies in St. Petersburg, Florida:

Tony Schwartz, media critic and editor: "There's nothing the matter with Sam Donaldson's yelling at the President, but then why do you show it? Why don't you just report what the President said? Why do you show yourselves looking like jerks?"

John Chancellor, NBC commentator: "That's a good question, a perfectly valid question. But, as I said, we are saps. I don't think we should be doing it and, in that sense, I agree with you. But it is impossible to take the Donaldson voice out of it if you're going to see the reality of the exchange.''

Schwartz: ''Well, why do you show it? Why can't you have Dan Rather say it?''

Don Hewitt, executive producer, 60 Minutes: ''No. We're in the reality business. If somewhere in all that yelling and screaming, the President says something newsworthy, and you can't extract it from all the shouting, you go ahead and figure it's your responsibility to put on what he said; and we're going to look bad because a couple of guys are screaming around him.''

Jack Nelson, Los Angeles Times *Washington bureau chief:* ''You put it on the air because you think the public does like to see Sam Donaldson holler over and the President holler back, because you think it's good television. I don't understand why all three networks put it on the air.... What purpose does it serve?''

However, there are other views of all this.

• Good journalism versus poor is the issue, not newspapers versus television. There *is* good journalism on TV; some poor. Some newspapers are great, some lousy. Some newspaper reporters are arrogant, some aren't.

VIEWPOINT 10-10

POINT AND COUNTERPOINT

''Does no one in charge of television care enough about either news or fiction to halt this corruption?''

New York Times editorial on *The Atlanta Child Murders,* a CBS ''docudrama'' combining fact and fiction

''How can you be so Goody-Two shoes Sunday morning [in the editorial] about a broadcast you don't think is fit to be shown and then go out Sunday night and show it on your three New York Times stations?

''The answer newspapers usually give is: We don't have anything to do with the television stations. That doesn't wash. If a publisher wants to allow his newspaper to beat up on television, he owes it his readers to let them know that as a station owner he, too, is part of the crowd his newspaper is beating up on.''

Don Hewitt, CBS executive producer, letter to *Times* noting the ''docudrama'' was shown on New York Times Co., stations

---

• Television is limited sometimes by its technology, but that very technology makes it a far superior medium for some types of coverage. The picture story, spectacle, or human drama—all come across better in living color than on newsprint. Television, however, is not at its best with in-depth, interpretive coverage. Do critics expect too much when they look to TV for excellence in this type of coverage? Don't television and print complement each other, and shouldn't each be accepted for what it is?

• *Both* newspapers and television are profit-oriented. One pushes for ratings, the other for circulation; one sells commercials, another advertising columns. Newspaper critics of television's profit orientation unfairly attack TV on that score, particularly since most newspaper-based companies own television stations (of the fifteen largest media companies in America, ten own both newspapers and broadcast stations).[61]

Why is warfare among journalists important? Because it emphasizes differences separating the media when they should be pulling together toward a common goal: vastly improved public support for *all* the media, which alone can buttress the First Amendment against a wide array of forces that would like to see it eroded. William Paley, CBS's founder, saw this need years ago. He told the newspaper-controlled Associated Press:

"It is imperative, in my view, that print and broadcasting people understand they have a common cause, and that cause is the removal of government intrusion in the editorial process. We must make our case not only to the courts and to the legislators, but most important, to the public itself."[62]

The American Newspaper Publishers Association, representing companies that own broadcast as well as newspaper properties, now states officially it believes "the concepts of press freedom should apply to electronic speech," and that it "opposes government influences on electronic information content." ANPA, like its broadcast brethren, opposes any government interference in advertising content. Many of television's critics, including Creed Black, say the First Amendment should cover broadcast as well as print.[63]

But, newspapers and television present a divided front as they head for the 1990s, a decade that could be dangerous for the free flow of information in this country.

CHAPTER SUMMARY

Serious problems disrupt institutional relationships between the huge and powerful media and other important groups in our society. Some create roadblocks between media and public understanding of each other.

In covering hijackings, the media—particularly television—have shown themselves vulnerable to manipulation by terrorists. Television's extraordinary technology, its ability to reach living rooms all over the world with live coverage of terrorism, at times outruns its masters' ability to use it ethically and responsibly. Television must cover such events and resist government attempts to control the news, but it also must practice self-restraint so it doesn't inspire more terrorism aimed at grabbing worldwide public attention.

Covering national security stories, such as espionage and the CIA, creates special problems in this era of big-power confrontation and intercontinental ballistic missiles. Should editors decide on their own which stories will jeopardize national security and which won't? Editors must retain final decision on what to print, but prior consultation with government seems indicated on particularly sensitive national security information.

New communications technology permits live broadcasts from battlefields. Hundreds of reporters inexperienced in military affairs now demand to follow U.S. troops into battle. The media should insist on covering U.S. military involvement abroad, but may have to reach an accommodation with the military on how many reporters can go at any one time and whether live broadcasting might jeopardize the mission and soldiers' lives.

Covering the presidency, Washington's single most important power center, poses special problems for the media. White House news can be manipulated with carefully staged "media events" and "photo opportunities." All presidents manipulate the news; those with strong public popularity are more successful.

The media are accused of antibusiness bias, but the problems really might be inadequately trained reporters who produce superficial, inaccurate coverage, and business executives who fail to understand the news selection process and who regard any coverage of bad news as proof of bias. For the media, improved training of business reporters is a must.

Newspapers and television don't present a united front in such matters. They spend much time quarreling with each other. Some newspaper executives accuse TV news of being "show biz." The intramural quarrel could weaken the media's defense against threats to the free flow of information.

CHAPTER 10

Notes

1 Coverage of this incident was widespread. The author found helpful: John Corry, "Must TV Be at the Mercy of Terrorists?" *New York Times,* July 21, 1985, p. H1; Margaret Genovese, "Terrorism," *presstime,* August 1986, p. 26; John Corry, "Critic's Notebook," *New York Times,* July 22, 1985, p. C14; "Taking the Cameras Hostage," a *Wall Street Journal* editorial, July 22, 1985, p. 42; Morton Dean, "TV's Duty to Cover Terror," *New York Times,* July 12, 1985, p. A27; Hodding Carter, "More Is Better But..." *Washington Journalism Review,* September 1985, p. 56; Fred W. Friendly, speech to Association for Education in Journalism and Mass Communications, reproduced in *AEJMC News,* October 1985, p. 3.

2 John Corry, "Must TV Be at the Mercy of Terrorists?" op. cit.

3 "Caught by the Camera," *Time,* May 19, 1986, p. 90; also, "State Department Rips NBC for Using Interview," an Associated Press dispatch for afternoon papers of Wednesday, May 7, 1986, published by *Athens* (Ga.) *Banner-Herald,* p. 25.

4 Michael J. Davies, speech to Associated Press Managing Editors Association, San Francisco, Oct. 28, 1985.

5 ABC News Policy Book, ABC News, 7 West 66th St., New York, N.Y., 10023; Larry Grossman, NBC News, 30 Rockefeller Plaza, New York, N.Y., 10112, memo to NBC News staff, July 24, 1985, p. 1.

6 Joseph Albright, "Survivors Recall Terror, Desperation of Hijack," *Atlanta Constitution,* Nov. 27, 1985, p. 1.

7 Katharine Graham, Churchill Lecture, English-Speaking Union of the Commonwealth, London, Dec. 6, 1985.

8 Ralph Izard, "Citizenship: Independence Vital—But Some Cooperation Needed," 1984–85 Ethics Report, Society of Professional Journalists, Sigma Delta Chi, 840 N. Lake Shore Drive, Suite 801, Chicago, Ill., 60611.

9 In this case, the author drew heavily on a variety of sources. More detail is available in a detailed report by executive editor Ben Bradlee in *Washington Post*'s "Out-

look'' section, May 26, 1986; ''Questions of National Security,'' *Time,* June 2, 1986, p. 67; ''Inside the Post's Pelton Story,'' *Editor & Publisher,* June 14, 1986, p. 11; ''Paper's Role in Pelton Case Is Defended,'' a UPI dispatch, *Atlanta Journal,* June 9, 1986, p. 2A; ''The Casey Offensive,'' *Columbia Journalism Review,* July/August 1986, p. 18.

10 ''CIA Chief Wants NBC Prosecuted Over News Report,'' a *New York Times* dispatch published in *Atlanta Constitution,* May 20, 1986, p. 6A.

11 Bradlee's May 26, 1986, ''Outlook'' explanation, op. cit.

12 ''Questions of National Security,'' *Time,* op. cit.

13 Bradlee's May 26, 1986, ''Outlook'' explanation, op. cit.

14 ''Magazine Suspends Column Naming Secret CIA Agent,'' *New York Times,* March 13, 1982, p. 19; Jay Peterzell, ''Can You Name that Agent?'' *Columbia Journalism Review* November/December 1984, p. 46; ''Press Groups Mount Opposition to Agent-Identity Legislation,'' *presstime* August 1981, p. 10.

15 Alex S. Jones, ''Press Warily Welcomes CIA Offer to Cooperate,'' *New York Times,* June 1, 1986, p. 18.

16 William Safire, ''Spilling the NID,'' *New York Times,* May 12, 1986, p. 17.

17 Daniel Schorr, ''Why Did CIA's Casey Want To Squelch Old-News Story,'' *Atlanta Journal and Constitution,* May 24, 1986, p. 17A.

18 Background on Grenada is available from ''ANPA, Other Press Groups Decline To Serve on Sidle Committee,'' *presstime,* February 1984, p. 34; Jonathan Friendly, ''U.S. Press Curbs in Grenada May Affect International Debate,'' *New York Times,* Nov. 8, 1983, p. 6; Jonathan Friendly, ''Naval Aide Says Old Rules for War Reporting Don't Apply,'' *New York Times,* Feb. 8, 1985, p. 9.

19 Caspar Weinberger, speech to International Association of Business Communicators, San Francisco, July 18, 1985.

20 Jerry W. Friedheim, speech to International Federation of Newspaper Publishers, Lisbon, Portugal, May 27, 1986.

21 Jonathan Friendly, ''Naval Aide Says Old Rules for War Reporting Don't Apply,'' op. cit.

22 Commodore Jack A. Garrow, U.S. Navy chief of information, letter to *Editor & Publisher,* July 14, 1984, p. 7.

23 Ibid.

24 Jonathan Friendly, ''Naval Aide Says Old Rules for War Reporting Don't Apply,'' op. cit.

25 Helen Thomas, UPI White House Correspondent, ''Presidents and the Press,'' *Editor & Publisher,* April 19, 1986, p. 160.

26 ''ANPA, Other Press Groups Decline To Serve on Sidle Committee,'' op. cit.

27 Laurie McGinley, ''Satellites May Give Journalists Powerful Tool, Lead to Showdown on National Security Issue,'' *Wall Street Journal,* July 2, 1986, p. 58; also see William J. Broad, ''Activity Reported at Soviet Test Site,'' *New York Times,* Aug. 4, 1986, p. A13; and David Hill, ''Ku-band Gridlock,'' *Washington Journalism Review,* August 1986, p. 8. Wider view of information technology and its impact on ethics in the nuclear age is available in Hans Jonas, *The Imperative of Responsibility: In Search of an Ethics for the Technological Age,* University of Chicago Press, 1984.

28 Gerald M. Boyd, ''Speakes and the Press: There They Go Again,'' *New York Times,* Aug. 8, 1985, p. A20.

29 James Reston, "Presidents, Doctors, Reporters," *New York Times,* July 21, 1985, p. E21.

30 White House figures, Aug. 15, 1986.

31 Helen Thomas, "Presidents and the Press," op. cit.

32 Peter W. Kaplan, "Networks Alter Policy on Off-record Remarks," *New York Times,* Aug. 15, 1984, p. C22; "'Lousy Bums' Remark Raises Washington Stir," *New York Times,* Oct. 11, 1982, p. 1.

33 Francis X. Clines, "President Assails Coverage of News on Latin Policies," *New York Times,* Aug. 16, 1983, p. 1.

34 George E. Reedy, "There They Go Again," *Columbia Journalism Review,* May/June 1983, p. 35.

35 Robert Timberg, "Benefitting from the Black-Out," *Washington Journalism Review,* January 1986, p. 14.

36 S. Prakash Sethi identified these attitudes in "The Schism Between Business and American News Media," *Journalism Quarterly,* Summer 1977, p. 240.

37 Robert Peterson, George Kometsky, Isabella C.M. Cunningham, "Perceptions of Media Bias Toward Business," *Journalism Quarterly,* Autumn 1982, p. 461.

38 Dorothy Lorant, "Can We Talk?" *Washington Journalism Review,* July/August 1984, p. 45.

39 Herbert Schmertz, "Turned Off," *Washington Journalism Review,* July/August 1984, p. 45.

40 Ibid.

41 Dorothy Lorant, "Can We Talk?" op. cit.

42 N. R. Kleinfield, "The Curious Case of John R. Coleman," *New York Times,* Aug. 10, 1986, p. 1F.

43 Of many stories on this incident, the author found particularly helpful Mike Kelly's "Runs For The Money," *Washington Journalism Review,* October 1985, p. 12.

44 Eleanor Randolph wraps up this incident nicely in her, "Media and the S&L Crisis," *Washington Post,* May 19, 1985, p. 2C.

45 Joseph R. Dominick, "Business Coverage in Network Newscasts," *Journalism Quarterly,* Summer 1981, p. 180.

46 Andrew Radolf, "Study Finds CEOs View Press Coverage Favorably," *Editor & Publisher,* July 18, 1981, p. 12.

47 Mark Lacter, "Manipulating the Media," *San Francisco Chronicle,* April 21, 1986, p. 23.

48 Creed Black, speech to American Society of Newspaper Editors, Washington, May 9, 1984.

49 Richard J. V. Johnson, interview, *USA Today* "Inquiry," May 7, 1985, p. 9A.

50 "Everyone Flunked," *Editor & Publisher,* editorial, April 20, 1985, p. 4.

51 Ralph Renick, "A Little Song, A Little Dance, Film at 11," *Quill,* April 1985, p. 12.

52 Charles Kuralt, Scripps Lecture in Journalism, University of Nevada-Reno, March 19, 1984.

53 Ben Brown, "Busy: That's the Way It Is for Walter," *USA Today,* Jan. 14, 1984, p. 1.

54 This exchange is from a seminar on news credibility conducted Jan. 24–25, 1985, by the Poynter Institute for Media Studies, and reproduced in "Believing the News," edited by Don Fry, available at the Institute, 801 Third St. South, St. Petersburg, Fla., 33701.

55 Ibid.

56 For anchor series see Alex S. Jones, "The Anchors," *New York Times Magazine,* July 27, 1986, p. 11.

57 This case and its wider implications are rounded up nicely by Sally Bedell Smith in "TV Newswoman's Suit Stirs Debate on Values in Hiring," *New York Times,* Aug. 6, 1983, p. 1; also see Smith's "News vs. Entertainment," *New York Times,* Aug. 11, 1983, C. 20; and two *Times* editorials, "Succumbing to Stereotypes," Aug. 17, 1983, and "Is She a Mutt," Aug. 11, 1983.

58 Peter J. Boyer, "ABC's Rivals Challenge 'Liberty' Exclusivity," *New York Times,* June 4, 1986, p. 1, and Boyer, "ABC's Liberty Weekend Coverage a Ratings Hit," *New York Times,* July 8, 1986, p. C18.

59 John Corry, "Questions of Journalism in Nixon Talks on CBS," *New York Times,* March 14, 1984, p.14.

60 Peter J. Boyer, "ABC News Pays $25,000 for Sakharov Videotape," March 25, 1986, p. 21.

61 *Advertising Age,* June 30, 1986, p. S-10.

62 William S. Paley, speech to Associated Press annual meeting, New York City, April 16, 1980.

63 "An Overview of Current Issues," American Newspaper Publishers Association, Box 17407 Dulles Airport, Washington, D.C., 20041.

PUBLIC RELATIONS, THE MEDIA, AND SOCIETY

By some estimates, 40 percent or so of the daily news diet the American media serve their readers or viewers is first created and shaped, packaged, or handled, by public relations practitioners.[1] Well over 100,000 persons nationwide are engaged in the process, which in its totality is a multibillion dollar industry.[2] With varying degrees of honesty and integrity, they attempt to influence media and public views of governments and individuals, companies and products, ideas and causes. Practitioners also research media and public attitudes toward the governments, organizations, and individuals they serve, and thus are instrumental in formulation of policies and strategies guiding some of this nation's most important institutions.

All to say our study of media ethics cannot ignore the huge public relations industry. Within the context of our study, essential issues are 1) the sense of ethics and personal conscience associated with conduct of *individual* public relations practitioners, 2) *institutional or corporate* attitudes toward socially responsible and ethical conduct in the marketplace, which must correspond closely to public interest, and 3) public relations *industry* standards of integrity and social responsibility for the public relations effort as a whole in its relationship with the media and the publics they serve.

Scott M. Cutlip, an early and noted researcher in the field, describes public relations as an "organized calling...a management function that identifies, establishes and maintains mutually beneficial relationships between an organization and the various publics on whom its success or failure depends."[3]

Ethical questions arise in each major public relations function practitioners perform as in-house employees, as members of outside PR agencies, or in management: *publicity,* releasing to the news media information about a corporation or product, for example; *advertising,* an allied function that involves paying the media to reach an audience and enhance reputation; *public affairs,* attempting to influence or lobby the political process on behalf of, say, a corporation, the government, or the military; *press-agentry,* helping publicize individuals, such as movie stars, or entertainment companies; *investor and financial community relations,* such as representing a company in its dealings with shareholders, banks, or brokerage houses; and *internal relations,* such as recruiting or operating information systems for employees.

Practitioners face many ethical stresses in the employ of corporations, governments, educational systems, labor unions, trade associations, religious groups—every type organization with a product or cause to push, a reputation to promote and enhance. Practitioners serve in management or as high-level public relations advisers to their clients or companies, a function that should carry a high degree of integrity, and on a lower level perform technical functions—writing and editing, contacting media, arranging special events such as press conferences or trade shows, producing annual reports or information booklets, conducting research, managing public relations efforts.

For individual practitioners, Cutlip acknowledges, a fundamental ethical problem is "how to maintain credibility...how to represent the client, yet stay separate and independent to tell the truth."[4]

For society, an ethical question, obviously, is how much of what pours out of a mammoth, often slick public relations effort is truthful, legitimate pleading on behalf of a client or employer, an idea or cause, and how much is designed—without truth, without principle—to cajole, wheedle, or sell something in disguise.

For newspaper or broadcast journalists honest enough to acknowledge it, getting the paper out on time or the newscast on the air would be supremely difficult without assists from public relations practitioners (one analysis indicated 45 percent of 188 news items in a single edition of the *Wall Street Journal* came from public relations sources).[5]

These and other issues will be examined in the chapter ahead. Let's start with a case study examining one practitioner's crisis of conscience in government public relations that illustrates some ethical questions individual practitioners confront.

THE PRACTITIONER AND PERSONAL ETHICS

Unusual quiet descended over the U.S. State Department auditorium as Bernard Kalb briefed assembled reporters. He had appeared before them many times, but this was Oct. 8, 1986, and high drama with international implications was at play. Kalb was publicly quitting as the nation's principal foreign policy spokesman in protest over a Reagan administration program which he otherwise would be obliged to explain and defend before the media and American public.

It was obvious to every reporter in that room that Bernie Kalb sincerely desired to serve his country as a member of the administration. He had put aside a career of substantial renown as a journalist (the *New York Times,* CBS, and NBC) to do so. But he made clear that to continue in the state department would force him to lie, and that he would not do.

It is an extraordinary example of a fundamental dilemma that can arise for public relations practitioners when their sense of personal integrity makes it impossible to believe in and thus wholeheartedly represent their client organization, idea, or cause. Not only that, the Kalb affair illustrates vividly how wrong a government effort can go when based on shaky ethical principles and without expert advice on possible public relations fallout. To explain:

On April 14, 1986, U.S. warplanes bombed Libya in retaliation for what Washington said was sponsorship of international terrorism by the regime of Col. Muammar el-Qaddafi. The United States tried to stoke worldwide condemnation of Qaddafi, and in early August, three months prior to the Kalb drama, U.S. diplomats began a secret campaign of deception—a "disinformation program"—against Libya. It was a campaign designed to confuse world public opinion and mislead the media. Word was put out that Qaddafi still was supporting terrorism and that the United States was about to move once more against him militarily. On August 25, the *Wall Street Journal,* quoting intelligence officials, reported "The U.S. and Libya are on a collision course again." Then, ABC, NBC, CBS, the *Washington Post,* and others picked up those reports and, as the disinformation experts had hoped, aired and published stories that helped focus worldwide pressure on Libya.

As the story gained momentum, more than a dozen officials in Washington were quoted separately as saying—anonymously—that Qaddafi again was supporting terrorists. White House spokesman Larry Speakes, artfully choosing his words, said the *Journal* story was "authoritative but not authorized." When pressed, Speakes said—in a statement attributed to "a senior White House official"—that there was "hard evidence" against Qaddafi.

That all this flowed into the media—and thus into living rooms across America—from a secret, tightly coordinated effort wasn't known publicly until October 2. On that day, the *Washington Post* published excerpts from what it said was a White House memorandum written by Vice Adm. John M. Poindexter, President Reagan's national security adviser. The memo counseled a strategy that "combines real and illusionary events—through a disinformation program—with the basic goal of making Qaddafi think that there is a high degree of internal opposition to him within Libya, that his key trusted aides are disloyal, that the U.S. is about to move against him militarily."

VIEWPOINT 11-1

SUNRISE AND THE ROOSTER

"It's like trying to sneak sunrise past a rooster."

John Trattner, State Department official, on trying to sell the press a story it doesn't want to buy

---

In sum, the outcome was a public relations disaster: to protect his own integrity, the U.S. State Department's principal spokesman publicly—and, for the Reagan administration, embarrassingly—quit; the U.S. government and its wider information programs stood revealed to the American public and the world as untrustworthy; and the media were furious at having been suckered by a secret disinformation program orchestrated internationally.[6]

Lessons are several:

Lesson No. 1: Aside from being revealed as unethical and unprincipled, a government (or corporation, group, or cause) that engages in a Big Lie will—almost inevitably in our open society—end up with egg on its face. There are too many willing leakers inside any institution, and too many probing reporters outside, for such things as worldwide disinformation programs to stay secret for long. Participating in fabrication quite simply is bad policy for any institution.

Lesson No. 2: For the individual public relations practitioner, credibility is a most precious asset. Protecting personal credibility is not only a principled and ethical thing to do, but it is absolutely essential to continued professional effectiveness. Kalb said, "I have been agonizing about this thing [the disinformation program]. I knew nothing about it. I was concerned with the impact of any such program on the credibility of the United States and the word of America and what the word of America means. And I was concerned about my own integrity....I didn't want my own integrity to get scooped up in this controversy." On the other hand, spokesman Larry Speakes apparently saw no conflict of conscience in his role in the affair. He continued at the White House before stepping down Jan. 30, 1987, to join a Wall Street brokerage firm.

Lesson No. 3: Misleading or lying to the media and thus embarrassing them with their reading/viewing publics will draw furious media attack. The Qaddafi affair drew media criticism from across the land against the Reagan administration: "Despicable..." Roone Arledge, president of ABC News; "Deplorable..." Eugene Roberts, executive editor, *Philadelphia Inquirer;* and "Pretty disgusting..." William Thomas, editor of the *Los Angeles Times.* The *New York Times,* in an editorial, "Lies Wound America, Not Libya," hit hard: "However desirable it may be to get rid of this unstable, dangerous dictator [Qaddafi], the chosen technique was worthy of the K.G.B. [Soviet secret police]. To the Reagan administration's shame, the 'disinformation' worked all too well, but only here in the land of the free."[7] ASNE telegraphed Reagan its "outrage and alarm" over "this calculated technique of falsehood...."[8]

Lesson No. 4: When the game is up, if deception is revealed, come clean. The only ethical—and effective—public relations response is to tell what happened and *why*. Early on, the Reagan administration actually had much public support for its anti-Qaddafi tactics. The April 14 bombing raid drew praise. But administration spokespersons failed to capitalize on that foundation of public support by forthrightly revealing details of what it regarded as justifiable U.S. aims. Wider damage resulted when officials fudged their explanations of the disinformation program. Secretary of State George Shultz didn't endear himself to the media by saying:

> If I were a private citizen...and I read that my government was trying to confuse somebody who was conducting terrorist acts and murdering Americans, I'd say, "Gee, I hope it's true." I know of no decision to go out and tell lies to the media. I think, however, that if there are ways in which we can make Qaddafi nervous, why shouldn't we? That is not deceiving you [reporters], but just using your predictable tendencies to report things that we try to keep secret, so we'll label it a big secret and you'll report it. We know that. The higher the classification, the quicker you'll report it. So you're predictable in that sense.

Well, then, for the public relations practitioner—and the media and public—are the ethical conflicts in handling such a case as the Qaddafi affair neatly divided between "right" and "wrong" and "good" and "bad"? Are "bad guys" those who deceive, and "good guys" those who uncover and publish? Hardly. Many questions remain that are answerable only in each situation by each individual practitioner. For example, is misleading or lying *ever* justifiable? Should a practitioner ever deceive or lie on behalf of what he or she regards as a greater good? How about in time of war, when a nation's fate can hang in the balance? (In his statement, Shultz said the United States was "pretty darn close" to a state of war with Libya).[9] The question is an old one. It surfaced with international impact when Arthur Sylvester, Pentagon spokesman under the Kennedy and Johnson administrations, defended official management of news during a period of enormous tension that developed in 1962 between the United States and Soviet Union because Moscow had placed missiles in Cuba capable of hitting American targets. Said Sylvester: "In the kind of world we live in, the generation of news by actions taken by the government becomes one weapon in a strained situation. The results justify the methods we used..." And then: "I think the inherent right of the government to lie—is basic, basic." Being involved in such news management—lying—creates huge ethical problems for many practitioners.

However, the reality is that few press secretaries on the Washington level either faced such matters of conscience—or felt compelled to resign over them. Only three resigned on principle in the thirteen years preceding the Qaddafi affair—Les Janka, deputy White House press secretary for foreign affairs, quit Oct. 28, 1983, to protest Reagan administration restrictions on the media during the Grenada invasion; Jerald F. terHorst resigned Sept. 8, 1974, as President Ford's press secretary on grounds he was misled by White House officials over the

---

VIEWPOINT 11-2

THE WIDER DAMAGE

"In considering 'disinformation' as a means to undermine the Libyan leader, the Reagan administration has not only risked damage to its credibility but also cast doubt over its overall news policy."

Bernard Weinraub, news analysis, *New York Times,* Oct. 3, 1986, p. 1

President's pardon of former President Nixon; Charles W. Bray 3d, deputy assistant secretary for state department press relations, quit Aug. 24, 1973, over appointment of Henry Kissinger as secretary of state (because, Bray said, Kissinger had ordered wiretapping of aides).[10]

In such situations, do practitioners have a responsibility to the institution they represent to resign? Jerald terHorst says yes: "Whenever a spokesman reaches a conclusion that he is in a position in which he must defend or endorse or carry on policies or actions with which he personally disagrees or believes not to be truthful, *he owes it to his government to step down* [author's emphasis]." But, must a practitioner *always* resign when his or her conscience is in conflict with the message or aim of the employer? Or, can a practitioner ethically continue to serve as, say, spokesperson and take no moral responsibility for the message? (Courts have held the messenger has *legal* responsibility for the message if, for example, it commits a libel.) Lawyers serve even patently guilty clients, and physicians treat condemned murderers. Should public relations practitioners be similarly nonjudgmental in representing employers or clients who dispense disinformation or who pollute the environment or who sell products, such as tobacco, that are harmful? Should practitioners be nonjudgmental toward representing in this country foreign governments hostile to U.S. interests? What ethical questions arise if a practitioner represents, say, Iran, whose government has declared the United States an enemy, the "Great Satan"? As we shall see in Chapter 12, American practitioners earn millions annually representing foreign regimes.

Another question: How far should practitioners go in insisting public relations or ethical factors be pivotal in their employers' decision-making process? For example, should corporate practitioners attempt to veto a proposed course of action by their company on grounds it will be perceived negatively by the public? Some, Cutlip among them, argue the most a practitioner can expect of an employer is that public relations factors be considered before a major de-

---

VIEWPOINT 11-3

DISINFORMATION: THREE VIEWS

"[I] would dodge, not lie, in the national interest.... There are 10,000 ways to say 'no comment' and I have used 9,999...."

Larry Speakes in interviews with The Associated Press and *New York Times* before his resignation in 1987 as President Reagan's press spokesman

"The whole question comes down to: 'Is deception going to be a tool that the government can use in combating a very significant national security problem,' and I think the answer...has to be yes."

John M. Poindexter, White House author of memo outlining disinformation program against Libya

"We suggest that the other news media grow up and get back to the business they're in and stop using their news columns to try to run the government. Disinformation is a fact of life."

Advertising Age, editorial following the Qaddafi affair, Oct. 20, 1986, p. 17

cision is taken or policy formulated—but not that public relations considerations must be controlling factors. Cutlip argues there are times, in its own best interests, when an institution should ignore public opinion, and the practitioner's job then becomes one of explaining and justifying to gain public acceptance of the unpopular decision or action.

TerHorst says practitioners must step aside when in conflict with the client or mission. If so, can they *step aside quietly and let a lie continue?* Or, are they morally bound to "blow the whistle," as Bernie Kalb did? These, too, are questions answerable only by individual practitioners who must construct their own personal codes of ethics. We later will discuss industry efforts to lay down at least broad guidelines for practitioners trying to sort out all this. For now, suffice it to say they must decide for themselves what is right or wrong in the practice of public relations, what they personally will do—and won't do—for the government, corporation, product, or cause they represent.

Now, let's turn from the *individual* practitioner's ethics to a case study of *institutional* attitudes toward ethical behavior in public relations.

INSTITUTIONAL PUBLIC RELATIONS ETHICS

For Johnson & Johnson, worldwide distributor of pharmaceuticals and other products, Sept. 30, 1982, was the precise date it was challenged to turn a public relations disaster into a business success story—and do it with a high degree of institutional ethics and social responsibility.

Larry Foster, vice president-public relations, got first word. He was in his New Brunswick, New Jersey, office that day when a reporter telephoned from Chicago: Cyanide had been found in a bottle of Extra-Strength Tylenol, marketed by McNeil Consumer Products, a Johnson & Johnson subsidiary. People had died after taking the pain reliever.[11]

For Johnson & Johnson, the stakes were enormous. An estimated 100 million Americans used Tylenol; the product captured 37 percent of the market with $400 million annual sales and was highly profitable. Foster had to move quickly.

At such a moment in any public relations crisis, a corporation's options include evading the press, meeting reporters but stonewalling and saying nothing substantive, issuing vague "we-are-looking-into-it" statements—many are the devices to protect corporate image or product reputation, and ignore any larger social responsibility the corporation might have.

Foster recalls Johnson & Johnson decided automatically how to proceed even without a meeting of executives: "Since the extent of the contamination was not immediately known, there was grave concern for the safety of the estimated 100 million Americans who were using Tylenol. The first critical public relations decision, taken immediately and with total support from company management, was to cooperate fully with the news media. *The press was key to warning the public of the danger* [author's emphasis]."

Ethical guidance came from Johnson & Johnson's corporate credo (much as communications companies discussed in Chapter 5 operate in accordance with broad corporate codes of ethics). The Johnson & Johnson credo called for complete openness with media and public.

The company halted production of the product, recalled 22 million bottles from retailers nationwide, warned through the media against taking the capsules—and saw Tylenol begin a slide from its 37 percent market share to 6 percent, which resulted in an after-tax loss of $50 million. Foster pulled scores of public relations executives into headquarters from throughout the Johnson & Johnson system, installed extra telephone lines, and began taking what turned out to be thousands of calls from reporters seeking information.

"During the crisis phase of the Tylenol tragedy," Foster says, "virtually every public relations decision was based on sound, socially responsible business principles, which is when public relations is most effective."

Within a week, answering the corporate imperative to get business back on track, Johnson & Johnson began a public relations effort to restore Tylenol's market position. The company's chief executive officer, James Burke, made himself available to reporters. A press conference was held in thirty cities linked by satellite. Foster says surveys show that within one week, 90 percent of the public knew of the Tylenol crisis; after the second week, 90 percent knew Johnson & Johnson was not to blame, and that the cyanide that eventually killed seven persons had been inserted in capsules on the shelves of retail stores. Tylenol quickly regained more than 30 percent of the total market—and CEO Burke publicly thanked the media for fair, responsible coverage.

Says Foster: "The Tylenol tragedy proved once again...that the best public relations decisions are closely linked to sound business practices and a responsible corporate philosophy."[12]

Compare Johnson & Johnson's handling of its crisis with the Reagan administration's handling of the Libyan disinformation affair:

Lesson No. 1: Johnson & Johnson had an established corporate credo which, although it obviously could not anticipate an event such as the Tylenol crisis, did require frank, open—truthful—revelation of details to customers, media, and the wider public. Media faith in Johnson & Johnson's handling grew, and the public sensed the company was as much a victim as those who died. And Foster, by being so forthcoming, in effect controlled how the media developed the news story.

Lesson No. 2: Johnson & Johnson and Foster not only protected their corporate and personal credibility with media and public, they came away from the near-disaster with *enhanced* reputations and image. For Foster, the Tylenol affair was opportunity to serve as public relations adviser in a principled manner that not only protected his own personal sense of ethics and responsibility but also buttressed the business fortunes of his company.

Lesson No. 3: Johnson & Johnson avoided adversarial relationships with reporters and, indeed, employed open, principled tactics that in effect permitted it to use the media to warn Tylenol users and even use newspapers and television to rebuild public confidence in the company and product. Contrast that with the Reagan administration's decision to launch a secret disinformation program that could only result in misleading the media, embarrassing them with their reading/viewing publics, and creating a sense of betrayal that brought down on administration heads a storm of newspaper and television criticism. When his crisis passed, Johnson & Johnson's CEO Burke thanked the media for fair and accurate handling; when the disinformation crisis broke, Secretary of State Shultz virtually taunted reporters by suggesting they easily could be set up to report any story as long as it carried a security classification. Which approach was ethical, responsible—and, in a public relations sense, effective?

VIEWPOINT 11-4

KEY TO SUCCESS?

"Successful publicity, over the long pull, must be grounded in works that the public defines as good, motives that the public accepts as honest, and presentation that the public recognizes as credible."

  Cutlip, Center, and Broom, *Effective Public Relations,* Prentice-Hall, 1985

Now, it would be comforting to suggest corporate public relations is dominated by the ethics and social responsibility displayed by Johnson & Johnson. But, of course, it isn't. The Tylenol affair, in fact, must be put forward to illustrate what corporate public relations *should* be, not what it universally *is*.

Many public relations practitioners are strongly career-oriented, in hot pursuit of higher salaries and greater corporate prestige, and thus open to compromise over ethics and principle. In their authoritative *Public Relations Practices,* Allen Center and Frank Walsh, both experienced practitioners as well as researchers and writers, comment bluntly:

"Ethical standards have tended to be reflections of the employers and clients served. Putting it another way, the public relations voice has generally emerged publicly more as the echo of an employer's standards and interests than of a professional discipline applied to the employer's problems. The practitioner comes on as narrowly organizational rather than broadly professional."[13]

And, of course, employer "standards and interests" by definition are directed at influencing public opinion to more favorably regard a company, product, idea, individual, or cause. Certainly, in the corporate world, where management's first obligation is to enhance shareholder return on investment—to increase profits—the basic mission of public relations is to help improve business fortunes. Ethical or moral considerations often enter the equation only secondarily or as important to, frankly, higher profits. Scott Cutlip notes that in his forty years of research into the public relations function he finds top management too often "instinctively inclined to keep decisions secret, to work out of public view, to make only favorable news known."[14] And, too often, the public relations function stands indicted—"with some validity"—for cynically "loading our channels of communication with noise and clogging them with the clutter of manufactured stories."[15]

The very term "public relations" carries with some a heavy connotation of practices sometimes unprincipled and unethical, rather than constructive contributions to free flow of information with a legitimate role in the nation's decision-making process. Public perceptions of public relations often are negative, and media attitudes sometimes poisonous.

Journalists often view public relations as a massively financed, slick effort to manipulate the news—in fact, create it—to penetrate news columns or air-time, and thus obtain free advertising and the patina of respectability, the legitimacy of appearing in a newspaper's news pages, or on a broadcast news program. Journalists sometimes feel chagrin and anger at being reliant on practitioners for so much information and repeatedly susceptible to their manipulation. For example, Washington correspondents are furious—but helpless—when herded away from the President by White House news managers who then stage "photo opportunities" and otherwise ensure a story of their choosing receives widespread coverage and that the President is linked only to favorable news. (It is not happenstance that bad news is released in other departments of government, whereas good news comes from the White House or the President himself.)

Many are the devices unethical practitioners use to suppress news or give it a spin favorable to a client. For example, in corporate public relations, practitioners sometimes simply sit on bad news, release only part of it—or time its release for a day and hour when it likely will get little notice. Bad news released at 10 P.M. on Saturday is too late for many Sunday newspapers (which have earlier deadlines), and there won't be another newspaper on the streets before Monday morning. NBC, CBS, and ABC will only lightly touch the news on their Monday morning entertainment shows, and won't get down to serious news coverage until Monday night—and by that time the world likely will have gone on to other things. Sometimes, bad news is held until front pages and broadcasts are dominated by a major news story, then quietly released in hopes it will be overlooked. Conversely, "good news" timed for Sunday release is perfect for Monday morning newspapers, *always* short of hard news because relatively little news breaks on Sunday and, anyway, most reporters have the day off.

Many practitioners consider it standard—and not particularly unethical—procedure to use such devices and manipulate the media through intimate understanding of their mechanical limitations, or to bar reporters from direct access to news or newsmakers. But, of course, practitioners often have legitimate complaints about the media—that public relations brings into view valid news which reporters unfairly refuse to recognize as legitimate, or that it in fact assists the media in doing their own job. And, practitioners complain, too many journalists fail to realize times have changed—that not all practitioners are disreputable flacks, that not all information channeled through the public relations function is disguised propaganda. Nevertheless, many reporters see themselves as targets of unprincipled, unethical attempts to manipulate the news.

Obviously, the public relations function *can* serve with social utility. If conducted with motives openly revealed, it can assist public debate by legitimately, ethically pleading a point of view in the marketplace of ideas; properly and ethically employed, it can inject clarifying fact and reliable information into a media and public dialogue burdened by misinformation and lack of true communication; and, importantly, a socially responsible public relations effort can influence conduct of the individual, company, or group it serves by representing in executive policymaking circles the external public's attitudes and demands. Optimum business conditions often exist when corporate policy and public attitudes are consonant.

But, can these seemingly disparate goals—serving, say, corporate interest yet remaining true to a personal sense of ethics—be reached simultaneously? Let's look, in the final section of this chapter, at how the public relations industry has tried to lay down guidelines for individual practitioners desiring to achieve both.

THE INDUSTRY AND ETHICAL STANDARDS

The individual practitioner who seeks guidance in matters of ethics from current practices in the public relations industry may be disappointed. The industry was late in coalescing as a recognized discipline with any coherent approach to questions of conscience, and even today demonstrates uncertainty over how to treat such issues. The individual practitioner still is left with responsibility for developing and following his or her own personal code.

Public relations generally became identified as an "organized calling" only in the 1920s, after other business disciplines such as sales and advertising were solidly entrenched in American corporate design and public awareness.[16] Only in the mid-1930s did practitioners form major industry groups; not until 1948 did two of the largest, in New York City and San Francisco, form today's leading industry organization, the Public Relations Society of America (PRSA).

After PRSA was formed, ethics and matters of conscience were opened more widely for discussion throughout the industry. PRSA adopted a code of standards in 1954, and subsequently revised it four times (the current version is an addendum to this book); another industry group, International Association of Business Communicators (IABC), adopted in 1976 a code of standards; industry conferences featured seminars on public relations ethics; and universities taught the subject. Yet, practitioners today are divided on even whether there should be codes, let alone what should be in them or how—indeed, if—they should be enforced.

Some say codes not only provide behavorial standards for individual practitioners in matters of ethics and principle, but also create for employers and the general public an image of principled behavior distinct from the disreputable "flackery" of old. For others, ethics is a subject far too personal, depending altogether too much on each situation, for comprehensive or meaningful treatment in any code. For some, even voluntary codes are objectionable because there is danger of adherence to them one day becoming a *condition* of practice, which could lead to government control and licensing (which the society describes as offending the American tradition of free speech).

A code of ethics and social responsibility, subscribed to by practitioners, is among criteria necessary before public relations can achieve "professionalism" in the generally accepted sense of the word. That would include a requirement that practitioners adhere to industry standards—*not* to employer standards if they contradict the code—in questions of ethics and conscience, as well as operational technique. Clearly, neither public relations practitioners nor employers are ready for that. For many individual practitioners who are employees or for outside public relations firms which are retained by an employer, the secret to career success is adapting to, not bucking against, the employer's business thrust and ethical stance. For many individual practitioners, particularly those with home mortgages and children in expensive colleges, the penalty for nonconformance—being fired—is too stiff. But even large, prosperous public relations firms, presumably somewhat insulated against financial punishment by a single client, rarely "resign the account" over ethical disputes.

Other characteristics generally regarded as essential to achieving professionalism are:

Subordination of private profit and interest to achieving social good and serving the public interest—or, at least, being strongly motivated in that direction *and* being recognized for it by the general public. Actually, few of the recognized true professions can claim for all their members such selflessness. And, it would be a concept slow to take root in the public relations industry or public mind.

A sense of independence and personal accountability by members. As discussed, individual practitioners often tend to reflect employer attitudes and ethics, and there is no widespread notion, particularly among employers, that this should change.

Special education and training or apprenticeship, followed by accreditation or licensing by an appropriate industry or government authority. Universities do offer public relations education, special training is available—but neither is

---

VIEWPOINT 11-5

ETHICAL CODES: ANOTHER VIEW

"Not needed: A namby-pamby code of ethics that will be given only lip service. People engaged in public relations need hard-headed morality that will make top management feel they are as devoted to the company's interests as any lawyer. At the same time, however, this morality must cause those engaged in public relations to be proud of what they do."

Alec Benn, "The 23 Most Common Mistakes in Public Relations," American Management Association, New York, 1982

required for entry into the field. And, although both PRSA and IABC offer accreditation to members, few seek it. Of PRSA's approximately 12,000 members (1986), about 26 percent are accredited members with the designation ''APR''— Accredited Public Relations. To receive that, a member must have five years experience in practice or teaching public relations, must pass written and oral examinations, and have two sponsors who testify to the applicant's integrity. Fewer than 5 percent of IABC's 11,500 members have gone through that group's accreditation procedure to win the designation of ''Accredited Business Communicator.''

So, public relations as practiced is far from professionalism in the classic sense. Yet, there is considerable desire within the industry to reach that goal. It is reflected notably in PRSA's efforts to maintain a code of ethics and behavorial standards that, in theory at least, takes precedence over standards established by an employer and that is enforced by colleagues within the industry.

The PRSA code, for example, requires (Article One) members to ''deal fairly with clients or employers, past and present, with fellow practitioners and the general public,'' and (Article Two) to ''conduct his or her professional life in accord with the public interest.'' Members pledge ''truth, accuracy, fairness and responsibility to the public.''

However, some code language is wide open to liberal interpretation. For example, Article Three states, ''A member shall adhere to truth and accuracy and to *generally accepted standards* of good taste [author's emphasis].'' That permits virtually any conduct if enough practitioners engage in it to make it ''generally accepted.''

And, PRSA enforces its code very unevenly. Complaints about practitioner behavior go before six-member panels in each of nine PRSA regions, then to the board of directors serving as a national grievance board. The proceedings are confidential. The penalties are censure, suspension, or expulsion from PRSA. Complaints are few and deal mostly not with matters affecting the public, but, rather, quarrels between members. In the entire decade of the 1970s, only forty-six complaints were filed with the grievance board. Four were tried (a fifth became inoperative when the member resigned from the society). Of the four complaints tried, one was withdrawn during the proceedings by the complainant, two were thrown out for incomplete evidence, and one resulted in a PRSA member being suspended—for pirating another member's account.[17]

Because PRSA procedures directly affect only members, most practitioners in the industry are untouched by either the code or its enforcement. And, even members can avoid action by resigning from the society. In 1986, that course was followed by none other than the society's own president, Anthony Franco. He resigned as the board of directors was meeting to consider whether he had violated the code. (Franco shortly before had signed a consent decree with the Securities and Exchange Commission in a case involving allegations of insider trading based on information gained from a client.[18])

There have been, then, steps backward as well as forward for practitioners striving for ethical, principled professionalism in public relations. However, if we synthesize specific ethical principles raised in the PRSA and, to a lesser degree, IABC codes, as well as in current writing by leading practitioners and scholars, we note considerable progress toward at least defining exactly what is ethical, principled behavior in the practice of public relations.

The codes and leading textbooks counsel principled behavior toward three major constituencies—clients, the media/public, and other practitioners.[19]

With clients, the effort is to establish a professional relationship similar to that between physicians and patients, or lawyers and their clients. The PRSA code requires members to "safeguard the confidences of present and former clients." (Societal acceptance of that principle has not yet reached the point where practitioners can refuse in court to divulge client confidences, as can physicians, lawyers, and, sometimes, journalists.) Practitioners are counseled to avoid conflict of interest with duty to clients, and generally disclose fully any circumstances that might disadvantage the clients. It's considered unethical to promise clients specific results from a public relations campaign—guaranteeing, for example, a news release will appear in a certain number of newspapers.

Much attention is paid ethical relationships between practitioners and the media/public. Consistent themes in codes and writings on the subject include: don't conceal the client's identity, purpose, or motive; openly identify your role as a public relations practitioner; be truthful, accurate, and fair in what you say, write, or do on behalf of the client; conduct your professional life, as the PRSA code puts it, "in accord with the public interest"; don't corrupt the integrity of communication (with, for example, false or misleading news releases); and don't corrupt the processes of government (by, for example, unethically lobbying or bribing officials). Despite their dependence on each other—practitioners need the media to reach the public, the media need information from practitioners—the relationship between the two disciplines is, as noted, sharply adversarial. Ethical codes and scholarly writings counsel practitioners to exercise principled professionalism in relations with the media by ensuring reporters never are lied to and news releases never falsified. (In addition to such *ethical* considerations, practitioners operate under *legal* constraints in dealing with both the media and public. The Securities and Exchange Commission, for example, requires publicly owned companies to fully and promptly disclose information—good or bad—on such things as earnings, dividends, mergers, new products, or, that is, anything that might affect the company's stock price. The Fair Trade Commission patrols against deceptive promotion and advertising, fraudulent testimonials, and unsubstantiated claims. The Food and Drug Administration regulates promotion of food and drugs.)

In defining ethical relations between practitioners, codes and writings generally make two broad points: First, do nothing to injure the business of another practitioner; don't pirate accounts, for example, or libel another's reputation. Second, do all you can to enforce adherence by others to ethical standards. The latter point is difficult to make stick. PRSA requires members (Article Ten) to report to the society any "unethical, illegal or unfair practices'' by other members and (Article Eleven) appear if summoned as a witness in society investigations of unethical conduct. Yet, PRSA is demonstrably uneasy about enforcing its own code, as we have seen, and many practitioners question the need or feasibility of codes.

Perhaps the public relations industry's fundamental ethical challenge can be stated this way: Practitioners insert themselves into the information flow in America as champions of institutions, causes, and ideas with a right to be heard. They demand access to the marketplace of ideas, and claim a legitimacy equal to that of, say, print or broadcast media in influencing public attitudes. And, it must be said, many particularly adroit practitioners carve out influential—not to say operative—roles in how the nation makes its political, economic, social, and cultural decisions. Enormous responsibilities attend such claims for legitimacy and adoption of such influential roles—and surely those responsibilities include helping guarantee the integrity of the information system and its ethical, principled operation. Should not those who live by influencing the nation's decision-making process undertake to conduct themselves in accord with the highest of principles?

So, in sum, ethics in public relations is a very personal thing each practitioner must work out for himself or herself. But because of their strong influence on the free flow of information in America, how those practitioners work it out is of crucial interest to society at large. We'll look, in Chapter 12, at this wider picture of information flow in America.

CHAPTER SUMMARY

No study of media ethics is complete without considering the multibillion dollar public relations industry and its enormous impact on news and information reaching the American reading/viewing publics. An estimated 40 percent of news is created, shaped, packaged, or handled by public relations practitioners.

For individual practitioners, ethical conflict can arise in trying to vigorously represent a client, yet remain independent in matters of conscience and principle.

For media and society, an ethical question is how much of the public relations output is truthful, legitimate pleading in the marketplace of ideas on behalf of a client, employer, idea, or cause, and how much is untruthful and unprincipled.

Bernard Kalb revealed a classic case of ethical conflict when he publicly resigned as U.S. State Department spokesman, rather than front for a Reagan administration secret disinformation campaign which enticed newspaper and broadcast journalists to write untrue stories about U.S.-Libya relations. A public relations disaster flowed from the Libyan affair, underscoring the fundamental weakness of any public relations effort structured on untruths.

By contrast, Johnson & Johnson, a worldwide distributor of pharmaceuticals, achieved a stunning public relations success by fully and openly explaining to the media and public exactly what happened when some of its Extra-

Strength Tylenol capsules were poisoned in Chicago-area retail stores, resulting in seven deaths.

The public relations industry has made considerable progress in defining ethical standards for practitioners, notably through efforts of the Public Relations Society of America and International Association of Business Communicators. These groups and writers in public relations counsel standards for three main constituencies: *Clients* (practitioners should create a professional relationship similar to that between physicians and patients, safeguard client confidences, and disclose to a client any possible conflict of interest); *media/public* (don't conceal the client's identity or motive; identify yourself as a practitioner; be truthful, accurate, and fair; and conduct your professional life in accord with public interest); and *other practitioners* (do nothing to injure another's business or reputation; and do all you can to enforce adherence by others to ethical standards).

However, the public relations industry is far from achieving widespread adherence to such principles or true professionalism.

CHAPTER 11

Notes

1 Scott M. Cutlip, Allen H. Center, Glen M. Broom, *Effective Public Relations,* sixth ed., Prentice-Hall, Englewood Cliffs, N. J., 1985, p. 429. For those interested in an authoritative overview of the public relations industry, this text is excellent.
2 Allen H. Center and Frank H. Walsh, *Public Relations Practices,* Prentice-Hall, Englewood Cliffs, N. J., 1985, p. 7.
3 Cutlip, Center, Broom, *Effective Public Relations,* op. cit.
4 Scott M. Cutlip, interview with author, Athens, Ga., Dec. 7, 1986. For discussion of ethical issues also see two books by Michael Schudson: *Discovering the News,* Basic Books, New York, 1978 (particularly pages 134–144), and *Advertising, The Uneasy Persuasion,* Basic Books, New York, 1984 (p. 99–128).
5 A *Columbia Journalism Review* study published in March 1981 and quoted by Dennis L. Wilcox, Phillip H. Ault, and Warren K. Agee in *Public Relations Strategies and Tactics,* Harper & Row, New York, 1986, p. 238. This text offers an excellent overview of the public relations industry.
6 For more details on the Kalb affair see David K. Shipler, "Spokesman Quits State Dept. Post on Deception Issue," *New York Times,* Oct. 9, 1986, p. 1; "Defining Disinformation Dispensers," an editorial, *Advertising Age,* Oct. 20, 1986, p. 17; "Editors Protest to White House," an AP dispatch for morning papers, published in *New York Times,* Oct. 13, 1986, p. 4; John Walcott, "U.S. Credibility on Libya Is Damaged by White House Campaign of Deception," *Wall Street Journal,* Oct. 6, 1986, p. 7.
7 "Lies Wound America, Not Libya," *New York Times,* Oct. 3, 1986, p. 22.
8 Associated Press dispatch for morning papers of Oct. 13, 1986, published that day in *New York Times,* p. 4.
9 Bernard Gwertzman, "Shultz Justifies Scaring Qaddafi by Use of Press," *New York Times,* Oct. 3, 1986, p. 1.
10 "A Most Exclusive Club: Others Who Quit," *New York Times,* Oct. 9, 1986, p. 8.

11 Foster describes the Tylenol affair in the March 1984 issue of *Public Relations Journal,* and it is expertly discussed in both Cutlip, Center, and Broom, *Effective Public Relations,* op. cit., and Wilcox, Ault, and Agee, *Public Relations,* op. cit.

12 Foster's quotations are from his description in *Public Relations Journal,* op. cit.

13 Center and Walsh, *Public Relations Practices,* op. cit., p. 345.

14 Scott Cutlip, interview with author, op. cit.

15 Cutlip, Center, and Broom, *Effective Public Relations,* op. cit., p. 452.

16 For early chronology see Ivan Hill, *The Ethical Basis of Economic Freedom,* American Viewpoint, Chapel Hill, N. C., 1976. Broader background is in David F. Linowes, *The Corporate Conscience,* Hawthorne Books, New York, 1974, and Thomas Donaldson, *Corporation and Morality,* Prentice-Hall, Englewood Cliffs, N. J., 1982.

17 Thorough research into code complaints in the 1960s and 1970s is in Cutlip, Center, and Broom, *Effective Public Relations,* op. cit.

18 The Franco resignation is discussed in a letter dated Oct. 5, 1986, from PRSA's new president, John W. Felton, to society members and in a news release from PRSA of the same date. Further details are in Jack Bernstein, "The Franco Fiasco—The Wages of Sin," *Advertising Age,* Oct. 27, 1986, p. 28, and the weekly newsletter *pr reporter,* Sept. 1, 1986, p. 1.

19 Superb scholarly discussions are in Cutlip, Center, and Broom, *Effective Public Relations,* op. cit.; Center and Walsh, *Public Relations Practices,* op. cit.; writing of a more topical nature often appears in *pr reporter,* a weekly newsletter, PR Publishing Company, Inc., Dudley House, P.O. Box 600, Exeter, N. H., 03833-0600, and *PRSA News,* Public Relations Society of America, 845 Third Avenue, New York, N. Y., 10022.

THE MEDIA, FREEDOM OF INFORMATION, AND THE LAW

Soon after Johann Gutenberg popularized movable type in his print shop in Germany in the mid-1440s, established authority in the Western world recognized unrestricted printing as a threat to its power. Printing permitted relatively rapid and easy exchange of information; information equalled power. Better to put the technique under wraps, keep it tightly controlled, and limit it to approved work. Ever since, Gutenberg's successors have fought to win and protect the right to print without licensing, censorship, or prior restraint by anyone—governments or special issue pressure groups —and to engage in the free exchange of information.

The early battles over the free flow of information in the English-speaking world were fought in the United Kingdom. Generations of printers and writers struggled against restrictions laid down soon after William Caxton developed that country's first printing operation in the 1470s. In 1534, Henry VIII proclaimed that royal permission was required for all print shops. It was a restrictive licensing act Parliament finally allowed to die in 1694. Thus was established a concept central to the First Amendment to the U.S. Constitution, which reads, "Congress shall make no law respecting an establishment of religion, or prohibiting the free exercise thereof; or abridging the freedom of speech, or of the press; or the right of people peaceably to assemble, and to petition the government for a redress of grievances."

The First Amendment was passed by Congress on Sept. 25, 1789, and ratified by three-fourths of the states on Dec. 15, 1791, to become the foundation beneath the freest, most vigorous journalism in the world. But, it is not in itself a *guarantee* of a free press, or of a free exchange of information, and never has been. No constitutional language, however venerated, could guarantee any principle so hard won as this one was and which today remains so radical, so subversive, in so many left-wing and ultraconservative minds throughout the world.

Rather, the First Amendment is an expression of hope, of determination. For the media, it is a rallying point around which they and those who believe in the free exchange of information must gather the societal support and nurturing that alone can translate that hope, that determination, into the reality of a truly free press.

Society at times wavers in its support of these principles, occasionally standing by passively as relatively small but powerful disciplined forces move to restrict the media. Although the media claim right of access to official information as surrogates of the people, there are many in government and out who believe journalists have no constitutional right of access and, indeed, no legal basis for the assumed role of surrogates. Official attempts to restrict information are increasing and, clearly, a battle is shaping up for which the media will need full public understanding and support.

In our final chapter we will look first at the broad question of access to information, then touch on areas of the law where important skirmishes are being fought.

Rising tensions between the media and other institutions in our society point to a fundamental—and worsening—confrontation over the free flow of information in the United States.

Consider, for example, increasing federal restrictions on how journalists cover stories involving national security, military affairs, and the presidency. Are these restrictions just more of the ups and downs that have marked relations between officialdom and the media since days of the Founding Fathers? Are we to believe the new restrictions discussed in Chapter 10 are designed to be only temporary, and that if international tensions ease a bit the military/intelligence community will liberalize its relations with the media? More likely, the Pentagon and other agencies intend to hold permanently the ground gained, and will continue the effort to cast a cloak of "national security" over their operations.

Will future presidents tear down barriers the Reagan administration erected between reporters and the "Great Communicator"? More likely, such highly successful news management techniques as the "shout line" restricting movement of reporters will continue as standard operating procedures at the White House.

VIEWPOINT 12-1

WHOSE GOVERNMENT IS IT, ANYWAY?

"It's incongruous in a democracy for the government to know more about its people than the people know about their government. Yet this pattern has been established. I fear that news from the White House will continue to be manipulated and distorted as in a Hollywood script."

  Thomas Winship, then editor of the *Boston Globe*

What will be the future relationship between the media and the individual thrust into the news? All signs point toward officials and private citizens alike using libel law or its threat not only to protect reputation, but also to "chill" the media in hopes of restraining coverage prior to publication, and to punish them afterward. Many First Amendment skirmishes will be waged in the courts in decades ahead.

Isn't it curious: The media today enjoy unprecedented economic support in the marketplace. Advertising revenue for newspapers and television alone is well over $46 billion annually; nearly 63 million supportive votes are cast each day by those who buy daily newspapers, and millions more tune in television's newscasts. And, many qualified observers feel news coverage never was better, nor the media never more responsible. Yet, the U.S. government with near impunity can bar reporters from covering military activities and even an invasion of Grenada; it can wield the "top secret" stamp, and manage, withhold, and manipulate much news of what it is doing.

There obviously are battles to be fought in that complex, if loosely defined, area of law and administrative procedures governing the flow of official information in America.

THE FREEDOM OF INFORMATION BATTLE

In 1967, a law was passed giving U.S. citizens for the first time the right to see, within limits, what is in the files of eight federal agencies. President Lyndon B. Johnson, never one to lay all his administration's cards on the table for anyone, reluctantly signed the Freedom of Information Act (FOIA) under congressional pressure and added substantial *right of access* to the rights of free speech and press established back in 1791. In was an historic development, for there always had been—and still is—argument over whether the First Amendment implies guarantee of the right to gather news as well as print it. Some legal scholars say no, that the Constitution means only what it says—and it doesn't say anything about the right of access to news; others say the Constitution means what the U.S. Supreme Court says it means, and that the law which has developed since the First Amendment was written clearly *implies* the right of access. Otherwise, they ask, how could we have a truly free press? What the Constitution's drafters intended never will be known. They drafted the Constitution in secrecy, and the deliberations over actual wording are unrecorded.

VIEWPOINT 12-2

IT IS THE PEOPLE'S AMENDMENT

"All the talk about the First Amendment rights of the press is not about special privileges for newspaper reporters and publishers, but about rights of the public—the right to be kept informed, the right of the governed to have a surrogate watching the governors. The First Amendment wasn't drafted for the publishers' benefit but for the public's."

Warren Phillips, chairman, Dow Jones & Co., publisher, *Wall Street Journal*

In any event, FOIA, stiffened by amendments in 1974 and 1986, orders open all but highly sensitive records in eight agencies.

Two decades after FOIA became law, the eight combined receive *250,000 to 300,000 requests annually* for documents. In 1984, for example, with some requests withdrawn and others eliminated for procedural reasons, such as non-payment of fees, the agencies had 226,193 requests to handle; 207,978 requests were fulfilled—a huge flow into the public domain of information previously withheld.[1]

However, the federal government continues stamping secrecy classifications on millions of documents. No one possibly can know for sure, but by some estimates 20 million or so are classified. As many as 350,000 carry "top secret" classification to indicate government feeling that disclosure would cause "exceptionally grave damage" to national security.[2] And, throughout the federal bureaucracy, there is definite tightening of the information flow—talk of lie detector tests for government employees and lifetime censorship agreements for 100,000 of them; restrictions on the media by the Justice, Defense, and State departments; and CIA threats of legal action against the media.[3]

Significant erosion of FOIA and the spirit of free flow of information is constantly threatened in the federal government. One problem is the discretion FOIA gives the agencies it covers—the departments of State, Justice, Defense, Commerce, Treasury, Education, Energy, and Health and Human Services. When information is requested, an agency decides whether it falls within nine categories of documents which legally can be withheld. Broadly, they are documents classified to protect national security, records on personnel matters, business or trade secrets obtained from a business firm or person, law enforcement investigations, records kept in regulation of financial institutions, and geologic and other data on oil and gas wells. In 1984, 17,007 requests were denied on grounds they fell within one of those categories. Additionally, 21,775 requests were rejected for procedural reasons, including inability to find the requested documents. So, even though the eight agencies fulfilled an impressive 91.9 percent of all requests that year, considerable discretion was permitted them.[4] If challenged over a rejection, an agency has the legal burden of justifying its action—but that requires an expensive lawsuit to bring about.

An agency unwilling to deliver information can explain documents aren't available or that it cannot perform quickly due to the huge administrative workload FOIA creates. (Health and Human Services alone received 103,110 requests in 1984, the Defense Department, 81,179.) Also, until it was prohibited by 1986 amendments, agencies could charge substantial fees for document search, and costs sometimes were high for private individuals or small news organizations.

Despite problems, however, FOIA brings to light much government information that otherwise never would be published or broadcast. In 1986 alone, three newspapers won Pulitzer prizes with information unlocked through FOIA. The *San Jose* (Calif.) *Mercury News* obtained bank documents that led its reporters to the transfer of wealth out of the Philippines by former President Ferdinand Marcos; The *Pittsburgh Press* learned of deficiencies in the Health Care Financing Administration for a series on organ transplants; and the *Dallas Morning News* used government documents for a prize-winning series on racial discrimination in public housing. Edward Cony, associate editor of the *Wall Street Journal*, said, "There's absolutely no doubt that a great deal of information has become available to the press and to other citizens that otherwise would have been kept from the American public."[5]

However, the media, often on deadline and unable to wait for time-consuming file searches, actually are relatively minor users of FOIA. One estimate is that fewer than 5 percent of requests are from the media.[6] Some in the federal government would like to restrict FOIA on grounds many requests for information come not from the media or general public, but from business firms—foreign as well as American—seeking proprietary information from competitors, and from foreign governments, including the Soviet Union, which find it an inexpensive form of espionage. Iran's Ayatollah Khomeini once employed an American law firm to ask the CIA through FOIA for all its information on the ousted Shah of Iran. The Secret Service reports a decline in the number of informants who fear their identities can become known to criminal elements through FOIA. The cost of meeting FOIA requests is of concern, too. Some estimate it at $60 million or more annually. (A sample letter for requesting information under FOIA is an addendum to this book.)

Successive administrations tried to weaken FOIA since President Johnson—his hand forced by a 307-0 roll-call vote in the House and a voice vote in the Senate—signed it into law. President Gerald Ford in 1974 vetoed amendments that ended some outright abuses of FOIA by federal agencies; Congress overrode his veto. The Reagan administration attempted to broaden provisions for exempting material and to increase agency discretion in rejecting requests. Congressman Glenn English of Oklahoma, chairman of the House Government-Operations Subcommittee on Government Information, Justice, and Agriculture said, "While much information is disclosed under the FOIA, sometimes the disclosures only come after long and tortured administrative consideration. For a reporter with a deadline, information delayed is information denied."[7] Carl Stern of NBC News, a frequent user of FOIA, says government employees violate the act's spirit by improperly using the nine exemptions or inventing a tenth: "I don't want to give it to you so I won't give it to you." Steve Weinberg, executive editor of *Investigative Reporters & Editors,* with headquarters at the University of Missouri School of Journalism, and an expert in FOIA matters, says bureaucrats under the Reagan administration had little fear of punishment and were free to make "excessive absurd deletions" from requested material."[8]

The spirit of FOIA at times chokes in a wider atmosphere of secrecy in Washington. Howard Simons, curator of the Nieman Foundation and former managing editor of the *Washington Post,* says the first thing a Washington journalist learns is that "it is impossible, not just improbable, but impossible to do your daily job without bumping into a secret...it is a constant wonder how any of the four million Americans who have access to classified information can remember what is secret and what is not secret...in short, if you are to know anything about government, you have to know secrets—there are so many of them."[9]

Obviously, the battle for the free flow of information extends far beyond the Freedom of Information Act and the eight federal agencies it covers.

The Battle for Information Widens

Many are the devices those who hold information about the people's government can employ to keep it from the people. Some are illustrated in a "report card" issued in 1985 by the Society of Professional Journalists, Sigma Delta Chi, on the Reagan administration's relations with news media.[10] After analyzing administration devices to control information in twelve broad areas, the society issued ten "F" grades for failing, and two "P" grades for passing (see Table 12-1).

Also in 1985, the Reporters Committee on Freedom of the Press, based in Washington, charged the Reagan administration had taken fifty-one "executive actions" in its first five years to restrict the flow of information, and said they were the most significant restrictions since World War II censorship. Among them were efforts to deny reporters news sources within the administration and permit infiltration of the media (along with political and academic groups), with the attorney general's approval, if national security is involved. The pattern thus revealed shows clearly the ability of any politically strong president to move against the free flow of information without ever directly and openly challenging the Constitution or Freedom of Information Act. Jack Landau, executive director of the reporters committee said, "More threats are coming. Public apathy is being read by the Administration and other conservative press critics as approval for new government censorship policies."[11]

VIEWPOINT 12-3

SECRETS WALK OUT THE FRONT DOOR

"[T]he very best secrets never appear in American publications. Rather, they walk out the front door when humans—several in the employ of the Defense Department and the Central Intelligence Agency—steal them and give them to an enemy, usually for money or ideological reasons.

"This is what happened during World War II when Russian espionage agents penetrated the Manhattan atomic bomb project. This is what seems to happen with increasing frequency these days as the FBI announces arrest after arrest of persons selling or attempting to sell the nation's most sensitive secrets.

"To the best of my knowledge, no American newspaper editor or newspaper reporter ever has been prosecuted for espionage."

Howard Simons, Nieman Foundation curator and former managing editor, the *Washington Post*

Congress supported FOIA initially after one of its own, Rep. John E. Moss (D-Calif.), had difficulty getting information from the Justice Department and Civil Service Commission for use while he served on the Post Office and Civil

Service Committee. In sum, President Dwight D. Eisenhower's Republican administration was holding back information from Democrats. Moss, who became known as the "father" of FOIA, designed the act to unlock for Congress information being restricted by agencies under executive control. At other times, with its own interests not so directly involved, Congress helped slow the information flow. In the early 1980s, for example, Congress in three separate

TABLE 12-1
JOURNALISTS FLUNK REAGAN

The Society of Professional Journalists, Sigma Delta Chi, gave President Reagan failing grades in 1985 for his administration's limits on the free flow of information. The "report card":

F—The administration pushed through Congress a bill providing criminal penalties for anyone who discloses names of present or former CIA operatives "regardless of the sources of that information or its value to the public."

F—Breaking longstanding tradition, the administration barred civilian reporters and photographers from the Grenada invasion.

F—"Guidelines" were issued through the Justice Department to encourage all federal agencies to be more restrictive in their release of information under FOIA, and to deny fee waivers to journalists and others.

F—The administration called FOIA "a highly overrated instrument," and "began a drive for amendments that would broaden the opportunities for federal agencies to withhold information, increase the expense of making FOIA requests and increase the time for agencies to respond."

F—Reagan signed an executive order making it easier for federal agencies to classify information, and thus withhold it from the public, and much harder to get information declassified.

F—The President issued a directive, "later partly withdrawn under congressional pressure," requiring all federal employees with access to sensitive government information "to sign away their First Amendment rights for life and agree to obtain prior government approval for any books, articles or speeches they might write."

F—The administration won congressional passage of a bill largely exempting CIA operational files from disclosure under FOIA.

F—The Justice Department "sought to restrict the flow of ideas across U.S. borders by labeling as propaganda three Canadian films dealing with nuclear war and acid rain, and by denying unconditional visas to a number of writers and political figures with anti-administration views."

F—Reagan "continued his slow pace of holding news conferences" and "White House staffers restricted access to the President on the campaign trail."

F—Under guise of national security, the administration adopted policies to stem politically embarrassing leaks and use lie detector tests to trace sources of leaks.

In just two categories did the Reagan administration win "P" for passing from the society:

P—The state department resisted UNESCO efforts to establish international regulation of journalists.

P—Chairman Mark Fowler of the Federal Communications Commission campaigned for repeal of regulations impinging upon First Amendment rights of broadcast journalists.

moves helped tighten the secrecy lid: it gave the CIA broader discretion on information it will release, and permitted the Defense Department and Department of Energy wider latitude in withholding certain *un*classified information about military, space, and nuclear activities. Supporters of the measures argue the information must be prevented from reaching the Soviet Union or terrorists. Threats posed by both are used frequently to justify tighter information policies. FOIA supporters argue unclassified information should be available for publication or broadcast, and that information crucial to national security can be classified under appropriate regulations.[12]

When Glitter Creates Coverups

At times, the media are dazzled by government public relations glitter that creates an information coverup as effective as any "top secret" stamp. So it was with the U.S. space program prior to Jan. 28, 1986, when space shuttle *Challenger* rose in the sky over Cape Canaveral and exploded. The accident killed not only the seven astronauts aboard, but also an aura of technical invincibility the National Aeronautics and Space Administration had created around itself, and which the media generally failed to penetrate.

For years, NASA scored one astonishing technical triumph after another. Astronauts cavorted on the moon, walked in space. The spectacle, the enormity of it all, was overwhelming. National pride soared. Few reporters had engineering or scientific background to cover the space story in knowledgeable, discerning depth, and it was easiest to do the "human interest" story—where the astronauts went to high school, or what they ate for breakfast. NASA public relations officials dutifully supplied all the details for each handsome man and woman who cracked the frontiers of space and became a national hero. Some technical journals and a few newspapers assigned truly qualified reporters to NASA, but many newspaper and television reporters, some with years of covering NASA, never heard of an "O-ring" until investigations after the accident revealed one failed, causing the explosion.

Ironically, however, media coverage in its superficiality helped create public pressure later blamed for pushing NASA into a *Challenger* launch despite safety concerns. The aura of invincibility the media helped shape became in the end a performance standard some in NASA felt compelled to meet. In a postmortem, *Columbia Journalism Review* found a record of media "carping" against NASA for delays in getting Challenger airborne. The evening before *Challenger* finally got off the ground, Dan Rather opened his CBS newscast by saying, "Yet another costly, red-faces-all-around space shuttle launch delay. This time a bad bolt on a hatch and a bad-weather bolt from the blue are being blamed." ABC reported, "Once again a flawless lift-off proved to be too much of a challenge for the *Challenger*." The *New York Times* referred to NASA's "comedy of errors." Richard Smith, Kennedy Space Center director, said such coverage created 98 percent of the pressure to launch. Looking back, associate editor David Ignatius of the *Washington Post* said the media should have been questioning whether *Challenger* should be launched, rather than criticizing NASA for delays.[13]

Some reporters were quick to accept blame. Robert Drogin of the *Los Angeles Times:* "We are the people who did not tell you everything you wanted to know about the shuttle program....We are the folks who pushed and believed NASA's mythology and hype." Bruce Hall of CBS News: "We had become lackadaisical. We were being spoon-fed by a very good NASA public affairs office. And when we did turn up something, editors and show producers had no interest...it appeared the only one who was losing interest quicker than the media was the public."[14]

The *Challenger* incident is recounted here to illustrate that merely demanding the "free flow of information" does not discharge the media's responsibility for covering—discerningly and in depth—the federal government in all its complexities for readers and viewers. The media must ensure they obtain the *correct* information—O-ring details, not just breakfast menus—and, importantly, that they are equipped to analyze and report it properly once it is in hand. That requires not only truly qualified reporters, but also understanding at highest corporate levels in both newspapers and television that money and time are needed to do the job properly. And, it means covering some stories on a methodical, regular basis even if public interest wanes and even if the stories don't always hit the front pages or boost ratings (just one network, CNN, was covering *Challenger* live when it blew up).

Another lesson from the *Challenger* incident is that federal information officers sometimes learn little from their own public relations disasters, and the media must keep pressing for news the public is entitled to have. Although *Challenger* blew up in view of thousands and instantly became a news story of great international concern, NASA's immediate reaction was a secrecy lid. It locked up almost all information about *Challenger* and instructed employees not to talk to reporters, even off the record. Asked for a transcript of final cockpit conversations between *Challenger* astronauts during this very abnormal mission, NASA spokesperson Barbara Schwartz said news organizations should file a request under the Freedom of Information Act: "We don't normally release intercom voice tapes from missions."[15]

SPECIAL ISSUE PRESSURE GROUPS

The media in America today are caught in the middle of arguments for or against the women's movement, school prayer, racial equality, homosexuality, abortion, pornography, capital punishment, arms control, military aid to Latin America—and dozens more emotional issues. Nothing new in that. As a hodgepodge of nationalities, religious beliefs, and customs, America always has felt the tug and pull of opposing ideas, and first newspapers, then television as well, have been tugged and pulled in the process.

Now, however, some special issue pressure groups, particularly conservative religious and political elements, strike directly at media ownership and financial stability in intimidation campaigns to influence the flow of news and shape what is reported about them. Their techniques include exerting marketplace pressure by organizing reader or viewer boycotts to frighten off advertisers, and even attempting actual takeover of a company which, if only a bluff that fails, can destabilize its management. Consider CBS:

Throughout the mid-1980s, a competitively difficult time, CBS's management was trying to run the network on a day-by-day basis and improve its long-range prospects while simultaneously fighting off repeated takeover attempts on one hand and, on the other, responding to conservative charges that it is staffed by unpatriotic reporters and anchors bent on giving the news a liberal twist. At the 1986 CBS annual meeting, leaders of three special issue pressure groups dominated floor questions: Accuracy in Media charged that CBS "goes out of its way to undermine confidence in the United States," and attacked anchor Dan Rather; Fairness in Media, part of a conservative bloc supporting Sen. Jesse Helms (D-N.C.), rose to make sure CBS was aware of the threat from the Soviet Union and leftist insurgencies; and Rev. Jesse Jackson criticized lack of blacks in both management and anchor ranks at the network and local CBS stations. Recounting the crescendo of special interest arguments, one reporter noted, "A soft-spoken gentleman shocked everyone by actually asking a question about company business."[16]

It is ability to mobilize considerable public support and hit the media where it hurts—in their business affairs—that marks today's special issue pressure groups. Helms, for example, seized attention by announcing in 1985 he was leading an effort to buy CBS so that conservatives could end what he called the network's "liberal bias" and "become Dan Rather's boss." The move aroused enormous concern among investors on Wall Street, and Gene Jankowski, CBS/Broadcast Group president, said it seriously distracted him and others responsible for improving the network's programming and faltering news ratings.[17] There were other efforts to take over CBS, one by Atlanta entrepreneur Ted Turner, who spoke of a combination of business and ideological motives. (Turner was quoted once as saying "the greatest enemies America has

---

VIEWPOINT 12-4

CRITICS ATTEMPT TO INTIMIDATE

"Often when I meet with critics of the news, I find that many of them mistake any coverage of an event or person as being supportive of that event or person. These critics would prefer we ignore the events they do not approve of—even when reporting on them is vital to keeping a free society informed.... In convention years, when we cover the Republicans, the Democrats complain. When we cover the Democrats, the Republicans complain. We expect this. After all, complaining about the coverage you get—or about the coverage your opponents get—is part of the political game. But frankly, it is often an attempt to manipulate the press. And sometimes it is an attempt to intimidate."

  Thomas Wyman, then (1986) chairman and chief executive officer, CBS Inc.

ever had, posing a greater threat to our way of life than Nazi Germany or Tojo's Japan, are the three television networks."[18])

Helms and Turner failed to gain control of the company, but in the process both helped destabilize it so badly that CBS never will be the same again. To fight the takeover CBS management enacted a series of defensive maneuvers, including purchase of the company's own stock on the open market, that cost nearly $1 billion. That enormous cost, in turn, forced an expense reduction program which, among other things, led to a hefty 8.7 percent staff reduction—the elimination of more than 700 jobs, well over 100 in the news division alone.[19] Before the dust settled, Loew's Corp., bought 24.9 percent of CBS's common stock, becoming the largest shareholder, and Loew's chairman, Laurence Tisch, in 1986 became CBS's president and chief executive officer. Those were tangible effects of destabilization. Were there others, more intangible? Do conservative attacks "chill" the CBS newsroom? Do reporters, even subconsciously, more cautiously rethink the stories they will cover, and how they will cover them? Does knowing his every word, every gesture, is being monitored by conservative groups change the way Dan Rather views the news?

Special issue pressure groups intervened decisively in how two major newspapers, the *Washington Post* and *Dallas Times Herald,* do things. When the *Post* launched a revitalized Sunday magazine in 1986, blacks dumped thousands of copies at the newspaper's front door, complaining it stereotyped blacks as criminals and showed no blacks in advertising. Executive editor Ben Bradlee apologized for the offense "that first issue plainly—if inadvertently—gave to certain segments of our audience." At the *Times Herald,* about 350 members of Dallas's black community protested remarks about blacks in a column, "Joe Bob Briggs Goes to the Drive-in." After tense negotiations the paper cancelled the column, added a minority person to its editorial board, hired a minority associate editor with senior policy responsibilities, and agreed ten of the next twenty editorial department employees hired would be minorities. In addition, the Los Angeles Times Syndicate, owned by the *Times Herald*'s then parent, Times Mirror Co., agreed to cancel the column, which was distributed to fifty-seven newspapers. The protesters' leverage, of course, was a threatened boycott by readers and advertisers.[20] ("Joe Bob Briggs" eventually was picked up by another syndicate.)

Strong pressure is exerted on the networks by conservative religious groups. For example, Rev. Donald Wildmon, a United Methodist minister in Tupelo, Miss., and director of the National Federation for Decency, claimed the backing of more than 600 religious leaders in eighty-four denominations when he charged the networks with "anti-Christian bias," and accused them of featuring immoral sex, gratuitous violence, and profanity. He threatened to boycott products of "offending sponsors" who supported programming that he said rarely portrays modern Christians positively.[21] It is impossible to measure the dollar effect of such efforts on network revenue, or its subconscious impact on advertisers and network personnel. But the impact surely is considerable in any industry so responsive to public mood as television.

Conservative groups frequently seek ammunition in studies of journalists by three social scientists, Stanley Rothman, S. Robert Lichter, and Linda Lichter.[22] In 1980, the researchers interviewed and tested a sample of 240 journalists and news executives at ABC, CBS, NBC, the Public Broadcasting Service, *Time, Newsweek, U.S. News and World Report,* the *New York Times,* the *Washington Post,* and the *Wall Street Journal.* The researchers reported many journalists term themselves liberal and vote Democratic in presidential elections. Conservatives seized the findings as evidence journalists are, among other things, hostile to business, supportive of homosexuality and adultery, and that many (56 percent of the sample) feel the United States exploits the Third World and generally are left-wing in their attitudes. The studies were used in attacks on the media by, among other groups, the National Conservative Foundation, which launched a $1-million campaign to alert the public to "media bias," and the American Legal Foundation, which works through the courts and Federal Communications Commission against what it calls the media's "liberal outlook." George Keyworth, President Reagan's science adviser, charged national journalists come mainly from a far-left fringe element which "is intent on trying to tear down America."

The studies and conclusions reached from them, however, were strongly criticized. For example, Herbert J. Gans, Columbia University professor of sociology and senior fellow at the Gannett Center for Media Studies, said media critics "hide a political argument behind a seemingly objective study, highlighting the data which support that argument."[23] Albert Hunt, *Wall Street Journal* Washington bureau chief, wrote that careful analysis of journalists reporting on the national level would show some bad journalism is practiced at times and that the media "sometimes lack discipline and are swept away by the passions of the moment," but that journalists as a group are not ideologically biased or unpatriotic.[24] Nevertheless, the Rothman/Lichter studies are firmly embedded in conservative thinking, and likely will influence future attacks on the media by special issue pressure groups.

Many journalists are concerned the uniquely conservative drive behind some recent attacks on the media will gain support on the U.S. Supreme Court, where so many battles still are to be fought over First Amendment issues. President Nixon placed conservatives on that highest bench. And a 1986 report on freedom of information by The Associated Press Managing Editors Association comments that President Reagan's appointments of William H. Rehnquist as chief justice and Antonin Scalia as associate justice "raised questions of what will happen to

---

VIEWPOINT 12-5

ATTACKS FROM RIGHT AND LEFT

"The New Right and the New Left, the pro-nukes and the anti-nukes, the National Conservative Political Action committee and the National Abortion Rights Action League have found a common enemy. It is us—the press."

Fred Barnes, national political correspondent, *Baltimore Sun,* writing in *Washington Journalism Review*

media cases that may reach the Supreme Court in years ahead.'' Both are regarded as holding conservative views of the media. (Ohio State University researcher Guido Stempel III in 1986 said Rehnquist voted against the press 77 percent of the time in First Amendment cases.) However, it is impossible to say whether conservative pressure groups will be able to escalate their currently well-financed campaigns in the court of public opinion to the highest court in the land. Supreme Court justices have a history of finding their own way once appointed to the bench, and there is question a truly conservative bloc in First Amendment thinking is developing on the court.

FOREIGN REGIMES PURSUE U.S. MEDIA

Because they want to influence public opinion and official policy in a nation so pivotal in world affairs, foreign governments intervene in the flow of information in America. The media are special targets. Embassies and public relations experts retained by them spend millions of dollars annually in the United States in vigorous attempts to influence how foreign news is covered. Abroad, a much more sinister campaign to control the flow of information is under way, engineered primarily by the Soviet Union and eastern bloc countries. Their aim is a "new order" of world communications that would subject all correspondents, Americans included, to licensing and other restrictions best suited for captive journalists of totalitarian countries.

In dealing with American journalists in this country, some foreign governments are openly aggressive. Israel, for example, publicly charged NBC misrepresented its motives and tactics in the 1982 war in Lebanon, even producing an hour-long film purporting to show the network did not report the truth. Israel also publicly rated leading newspapers on their coverage. (It said the *Washington Post* was most "negative" toward Israel during the war, and the *Atlanta Constitution* most "positive.") Among other countries trying to influence American media, South Africa, Saudi Arabia, Canada, and Taiwan are counted among the big spenders. American University researchers found, for example, Saudi Arabia paid $400,000 one year to a public relations firm spreading its story in Washington, and $300,000 to a lawyer with media contacts in the capital. Canada launched a $650,000 campaign against U.S. trade restrictions. Taiwan, struggling to maintain its identity alongside the People's Republic of China, offered junkets to as many as 600 journalists from around the world—and even held reunions of junketeers.[25] Such efforts often are cumbersome and unsophisticated.

The effort for a "new order" of world communications is more sophisticated, more difficult for American reporters to deflect, and, certainly, requires more patience. It has been under way for years.[26]

Pressure arises primarily from two sources:

First, there is ideological distrust in the Soviet bloc of any free flow of information anywhere in the world. In any communist country, the media are propaganda arms of the state, and trying to harness world media to international communist policy is consistent with the role given Soviet newspapers and television at home.

Second, however, there is strong feeling in some Third World countries that the international flow of information has a Western slant. Four large news agencies dominate the international flow: all are Western—The Associated Press, a New York City-based cooperative of American newspapers and broadcast stations; United Press International which, although principally owned by a Mexican, is in news orientation an American agency; Reuters, London-based and owned primarily by investors in Britain, the United States, Australia, and New Zealand; Agence France Press, with headquarters in Paris. Television news operations with most international impact are American and British. Now, each of these news organizations employs many foreign nationals. They operate "world service" divisions which cover Third World news for Third World countries. But, unquestionably, the agencies cover the world primarily for their financially important newspaper and television constituencies in the West. Foreign correspondents for AP and UPI spend most of their time serving the news interests of editors in the United States. This creates Third World feeling that news of and for their regions is not covered fully or, even worse, is covered primarily through Western eyes.

Third World nations have made numerous efforts to launch international news collection and distribution systems by expanding their own national agencies. But costs are enormous, Western agencies are competitively dominant—and bickering between Third World countries often prevents cooperation in news exchange. Consequently, even large nations with active domestic media of their own—India, and many countries in Asia, Africa, and Latin America—must depend for international news coverage primarily on agencies that in news orientation are American, British, and French. The considerable frustration arising from all that creates receptive conditions for the "new order" campaign.

One major Soviet effort, along with East Germany and like-thinking Third World governments, was to construct the "new order" through UNESCO—the United Nations Educational, Scientific, and Cultural Organization. The Soviets mixed with their positions on human rights, arms control, and other issues a proposal for an "International Commission for the Protection of Journalists." The Soviets proposed international "rules of ethics" in journalism and said journalists, for their own protection, should carry internationally recognized identity cards. The goal, of course, was a communist-dominated licensing procedure under which only friendly journalists would be permitted to report the news. Western journalists were quick to object. Dana Bullen, executive director, World Press Freedom Committee, said, "In more than 200 such cases, I so far have failed to find a single instance in which an additional identification card would have saved a journalist's life or otherwise kept him or her from harm....Police, paramilitary groups, terrorists and others know exactly who they are killing, wounding, jailing and expelling."

Angered by the Soviet move and other operational and financial problems, the United States and Britain withdrew from UNESCO. They charged, among other things, it had become a forum for Soviet and radical Third World attacks on the free flow of information. The Soviet campaign did not die there, however. A group called the "International Organization of Journalists" surfaced in Prague, Czechoslovakia, with proposals in 1985 that it supply journalists with identity cards.[27] In 1986, the sixty-nine-nation United Nations Committee on Information, chaired by an East German, adopted a resolution for "a new, more just and more effective world information and communication order intended to strengthen peace and international understanding and based on the free circulation and wider and better balanced dissemination of information." The resolution, inevitably, proposed international rules of ethics for journalists. Not one Western country voted for the resolution.[28]

The Soviets shrewdly propose licensing journalists under the guise of "protecting" them. There is international concern over the reality that being a journalist is an increasingly dangerous business. The American Newspaper Publishers Association says that in 1984 alone, 23 journalists were killed worldwide, 81 wounded, 205 jailed or detained, and 50 expelled or denied the right to report. Red Cross figures show about 300 journalists killed in the period from 1950 to 1985.[29] (In 1986, the Soviet Union added a statistic by imprisoning for two weeks and detaining for two more Nicholas Daniloff, Moscow correspondent of *U.S. News & World Report* who was seized by secret police on espionage charges after a Russian acquaintance gave him an envelope said to contain two "top secret" maps. U.S. officials said Daniloff's detention was a "set-up," the Soviet response to the arrest a few weeks earlier of a Russian physicist in New York City on espionage charges.)

Despite many such pressures, American journalists generally are far more worried that what is happening these days in U.S. courtrooms will have greater impact on the free flow of information than clumsy Soviet intrigue abroad or efforts by Washington bureaucrats to hide government documents.

THE MEDIA AND THE LAW

Much of the tension surrounding the media stems from two First Amendment considerations: attempts to outright censor or restrain the media prior to publication, which is specifically prohibited by the First Amendment, and increasing use of libel law to indirectly achieve the same result and "chill" reportorial vigor by threatening to punish the media with heavy financial penalties.

First, although the Constitution explicitly forbids prepublication licensing or censorship, there have been numerous attempts to accomplish just that, particularly by the government in national security cases. In one of many battles over the issue, the U.S. Supreme Court strongly affirmed the freedom to publish without prior restraint in a 1931 landmark case, *Near versus Minnesota*. That ruling extended First Amendment press guarantees to the state level. However, in 1971, the principle was seriously weakened in the Pentagon papers case.

The Nixon administration won in a lower court a temporary order restraining the *New York Times* from further publication of a series it had started on a confidential government study of the Vietnam war. Upon appeal, the Supreme Court stunned the media by continuing the temporary order; *Times* lawyers sidestepped a direct confrontation on what many experts felt was the court's serious dilution of the First Amendment. The lawyers argued instead the government could not prove publication would harm national security, and the *Times* was permitted to proceed with the series. The court stated, "Any system of prior restraint of expression comes to this court bearing a heavy presumption against its constitutional validity." But the ruling, nevertheless, widely was interpreted as meaning the government might be able to argue successfully for prior restraint in some future case. In 1979, the Justice Department, citing secrecy provisions of the Atomic Energy Act, obtained a preliminary injunction to prevent the *Progressive,* a small Madison, Wisconsin, magazine, from publishing an article on how to make a hydrogen bomb. The issue never got higher than a U.S. District Court because the government withdrew its suit when it was learned information in the article was publicly available in libraries and elsewhere. The basic issue of prior restraint was not resolved, therefore, and the battle over such censorship clearly is not finished.

Second, although the Constitution establishes the right to speak and write as we please without prior restraint, it of course left everyone who does so subject to punishment after the fact for what they say or write. For that purpose, society devised libel laws covering those who harm the reputation of an individual or corporation by publishing or broadcasting a falsehood. Society also has laws to punish those who offend it in other ways, by publishing obscenity, for example, or seditious material. Libel law is of particular concern to us here because Americans are using it with unprecedented vigor, sometimes frivolously, sometimes harshly and openly threatening—and often with the intent of "chilling" coverage. Consider:

• In an era of multimillion dollar libel suits and soaring legal costs, Frank Sinatra's attorneys ask Universal Press Syndicate for the names of newspapers that published its "Doonesbury" comic strip satirizing him. They just asked, mind you—but get the point? Quickly, verbal battle is joined, and a First Amendment issue arises with free speech implications for anyone who prints or broadcasts opinion. Before the matter fades from public view, cartoonist Garry Trudeau's defenders go vigorously on record that he is entitled to his opinion, as is any political commentator; Sinatra's attorneys say just as vigorously Sinatra's rights were violated—and editors all over the country start looking at comic strips just a little more carefully. (Universal, which refuses to divulge names, says thirty newspapers did not print all or part of the Sinatra series; two papers cancelled the popular strip altogether.)[30]

• An indian tribe sues Gannett's *Santa Fe* (N.M.) *New Mexican* for $3.6 million because it published two photos of a private tribal dance. To settle, the *New Mexican* makes two apologies, and, when both are rejected as inadequate, makes a third—and promises $20,000 for a tribal college scholarship fund, internships for tribal students, free advertising for some tribal enterprises, and assigns a reporter to cover indian affairs.[31]

• A Chinese restaurant owner in New York City sues a reviewer who wrote, among other things, his sweet and sour pork "contained more dough than meat" and his fried rice was "soaking" in oil. A jury awards the restaurant $20,000 damages; only on appeal is the verdict overturned on the grounds that "the natural function of the review is to convey the critic's opinion of the restaurant reviewed."[32]

• Use of libel law is escalated as Gen. William C. Westmoreland sues CBS for $120 *million* on the grounds that a documentary defamed him by accusing his command in Vietnam of engaging in a "conspiracy" to understate enemy capabilities in reports to Washington. Westmoreland and supporters spend about $3.25 million pursuing the case; CBS, $5 million. Then, both sides settle with a joint statement that CBS respects Westmoreland's "long and faithful service to his country" and the general notes CBS's "distinguished journalistic tradition."[33]

• Gen. Ariel Sharon, former defense minister of Israel, comes into U.S. courts to sue *Time* magazine for $50 million on the grounds that a story about fighting in Lebanon contained a paragraph that defamed him by falsely accusing him of encouraging a massacre by Phalangists. After a legal battle that lasts months and costs more than $3 million, a jury says the article indeed did contain a false and defamatory paragraph and *Time* was "negligently and carelessly" wrong in its reporting. But, it says *Time* didn't libel Sharon because it didn't publish the information with "serious doubts as to its truth." Both *Time* and Sharon claim victory.[34]

What's happening here? It is this:

As illustrated by these cases, many Americans regard the media as negligent and insensitive, cold and distant, and offering no self-correcting mechanism under which an offended individual can seek redress. The word "arrogant" keeps popping up. Those who feel harmed often say they don't have access to the media for their side of the story. The public has no legal "right of access" to newspapers; the U.S. Supreme Court overturned in *Miami Herald Co. versus Pat L. Tornillo* a Florida law that required it. And, what do newspapers offer those who feel harmed by coverage? A letter to the editor, perhaps, or if pressed, a correction buried on an inside page. The networks and most television stations only rarely offer even those limited remedies.

For many persons seeking to be heard, then, the courtroom is their only forum, the law their only weapon for restoring reputation and punishing the media they feel harmed them.

For the media, the result is an unprecedentedly litigious atmosphere in which enormous legal costs and potentially crippling damage awards are real and present dangers in everyday journalism.

For society, as well as the media, a major question is how expensive litigation—or merely its threat—is "chilling" news coverage and slowing the free flow of information.

Does Law of Defamation "Chill"?

This is the law: Defamation is communication that subjects a person to contempt, ridicule, or hatred; it is falsehood printed ("libel") or spoken ("slander") which harms the reputation of an individual or corporation, which lowers persons in the esteem of their fellows, which causes them to be shunned, or which injures them in business or their calling.

These are conflicting and broadly representative views of the law and its impact on the media and the free flow of information:

Floyd Abrams, constitutional law specialist who represents print and broadcast clients:

> [N]o country in the world has offered more legal protection for those wishing to speak out frankly and fearlessly. Yet today, American libel law manages to achieve the worst of two worlds: It does little to protect reputation. It does much to deter speech ...neither side wins much from the way libel law works today. The law effectively chills both the press and private citizens who wish to speak out on public issues. It does this by imperiling those who cannot afford to risk the possibility of huge court judgments or the certainty of ever-increasing defense fees. From the point of view of most plaintiffs, the law provides a bit of psychic gratification in being in court at all, but little more.[35]

James E. Beasley, Philadelphia lawyer noted for successfully representing the plaintiffs in product liability, medical malpractice, and defamation cases:

> News is for sale. It's a product. Nobody lets General Motors put a defective product on the street. Why should a newspaper be allowed to put out a defective product with impunity?...If they [the media] are truthful, they have an absolute defense. But if they want to sell newspapers based on falsity, then somebody should have a right to say, "You're not going to make a profit at my expense."...The only way you can make people do right is to hit them in the pocketbook...[newspapers complaining about "chilling"] make it appear they are poor little lambs being taken to slaughter. What they are saying is, "We don't want to have the same cost of doing business as others."[36]

The cost of defending against libel charges—and the chance, even if remote, of losing—is slowing a great deal of vigorous reporting. Many small newspapers and television stations openly acknowledge reluctance to engage in aggressive reporting that might draw legal problems. Richard Schmidt, general counsel for ASNE, says he sometimes discusses legal ramifications of stories with editors who then say, "Oh hell, let's drop the thing; it's not worth it to me. I can't afford the risk." Even editors known for hard-hitting investigative techniques show concern. Gene Roberts, executive editor of the *Philadelphia Inquirer,* whose staff has produced numerous Pulitzer prize-winning stories, notes eight libel suits were filed against his newspaper in one forty-six-day period in 1985. A "First Amendment crisis" has developed, Roberts says, adding, "We as a society, have now delivered into the hands of government officials the nation over—indeed, the world over—a simple but effective weapon against freedom of expression. It is the capability of using protracted litigation to harass, intimidate and punish the press and private citizen alike for views and reports that officials do not like. The weapon has been there for some years now. The trend toward using it has been growing steadily. The Sharon and Westmoreland cases simply spotlighted the trend."[37]

James Batten, president of Knight-Ridder, Inc., sees possibly fundamental change arising from the legal battles: "I believe we are seeing the emergence of libel suits as a weapon which public officials, senators, generals, judges and county commissioners are seizing upon to recast their relationship with the press, radio and television. And they are finding, in many cases, enthusiastic allies in those ordinary citizens who serve on American juries and are eager, it seems, to cut us down to size. In the process, fundamental First Amendment values may also get cut down."[38]

Representatives of conservative groups monitoring the media say complaints about legal costs chilling the media are a smokescreen; most citizens, they say, are less able to afford litigation than newspapers or television networks. Anyway, they say, there is nothing wrong with a little chilling. Reed Irvine, chairman of Accuracy in Media: "What is wrong with chilling any propensity of journalists to defame with reckless disregard of the truth? Isn't that supposed to be what professional journalists are taught to avoid doing? Isn't that what editors are supposed to do? If journalists fail to observe the ethical codes of their profession, and if editors fail to do their job, why shouldn't there be a penalty for malpractice in a possible libel judgment?"[39]

Some experienced journalists have different views:

Lester Bernstein, former editor of *Newsweek* commenting on the CBS/Westmoreland trial:

> Would CBS News or its counterparts in big-league journalism shrink from exercising their freedom to uncover malfeasance in high places or to undertake any story that serves the ultimate end of a free press—namely to give people the information they need to govern themselves? Don't you believe it. Having worked in that league most of my life, I find it inconceivable that any verdict under existing libel law could turn off the innate professional zeal or the competitive imperative that drive the news

---

VIEWPOINT 12-6

THREAT OF ECONOMIC SELF-CENSORSHIP

"Public officials and politicians across the land seem to have found new reasons for trying to threaten, aggravate, or even close a newspaper if they can win a big libel case. Economic self-censorship is a serious threat to freedom of expression."

Stephen A. Cousley, editor and publisher, whose *Alton* (Ill.) *Telegraph* sought protection in bankruptcy while settling for $1.4 million a record $9.2 million libel judgment against it

A REPORTER WHO QUIT

"I finally had to make a choice: I decided to abandon my obligation to the First Amendment and run my newspapers as businesses. I'm completely out of the investigative reporting business. It's worked. I haven't been sued since."

Irving Lieberman, weekly publisher in suburban Philadelphia sued for libel eleven times in seven years

media irresistibly into their role as watchdogs. What would indeed be chilled, and one hopes is already being chilled, is the feverish pursuit of sensation without taking pains to be scrupulously fair and accurate. A story can be unfair without being libelous, but it is very hard to commit libel if you try to be fair...as the framers of the First Amendment saw it, the highest goal of a free press is to keep government honest. What will keep the press honest? The best answer is the law of libel....[40]

Commenting on the Sharon case, Richard Clurman, former chief of correspondents for *Time* and *Life*, notes *Time* declared itself the winner even though found "negligently and carelessly" wrong in its reporting. Says Clurman:

> In journalism, there is only one sin worse than being found wrong: an unwillingness to admit it....We do not need to revise our laws or tamper with First Amendment principles. But the press must change many of its ways. For example, if the media make a serious factual charge against a public figure, they had better be able to offer proof that it is true. If they cannot—as *Time* could not—whether they believe it or not, they should retract the charge. And then if a Sharon—or other officials—still choose to sue, let them face the weight of the press's vital constitutional protection.[41]

Sharon insists it was a retraction, not financial reward, he sought from *Time:* "[T]here would have been no lawsuit had *Time* magazine published a retraction and apologized for its blood libel—this vicious, absolutely untrue charge that I instigated the massacres in Sabra and Shatila [Lebanon]. That *Time* refused to retract and still refuses in the face of overwhelming evidence that the charge was utterly false and unsubstantiated only proves that its arrogance is unremitting...."[42]

Westmoreland says he had no place but the courtroom to go: "[T]his country and its citizens, public and private alike, need some nongovernmental, nonjudicial forum where complaints against the media can be heard, judged and redressed...sometimes an overzealous reporter or producer gets carried away with what he or she perceives or believes to be the facts and comes up with what one would consider irresponsible reporting. When this occurs, where can the victim go for redress? Given the power of the media, which tend to act as their own judge and jury insofar as their own acts are concerned, there is only the court of law." Westmoreland says he found the courtroom unsuitable for his defense of his role in Vietnam history and, he imagines, it was unsuitable for CBS, too. He argues for a forum similar to the now-defunct National News Council.[43]

Many libel cases are instituted by people who, like Sharon and Westmoreland, feel harmed not financially but *emotionally*. A study by the University of Iowa Libel Research Project finds plaintiffs sue not for financial reward, but "to restore their reputations or punish the media."

Many Americans are sympathetic to them and prove it as jurors in libel cases. The Libel Defense Resource Center in New York City says media defendants lost 83 percent of jury trials in the period 1979 to 1983. The percentage dropped somewhat in later years (to 64 percent between 1984 and 1985), but the message from jurors clearly is that plaintiffs against the media can get a sympathetic hearing in courtrooms, if not in newsrooms. By contrast, the center says, defendants in medical malpractice cases lose 33 percent of the time,

---

VIEWPOINT 12-7

PRESSURE GROUPS PLAY HARDBALL

"Hard-ball intervention—whether by expensive libel suits or threatening stock takeovers—is, I believe, likely to affect reporting, likely to affect coverage of the news. Editors are bound to ask themselves, 'Is it worth it to print that extra fact and open us up to a libel suit, which can be costly and time-consuming?' The end result is that the paper discloses less. And the pressures are not one-time things: special interests hammer and hammer and papers tend to become less daring, more intimidated."

Sam Zagoria, *Washington Post* ombudsman

"Care and caution are giving way to timidity in newsrooms across the land."

Osborne Elliott, former editor of *Newsweek* and dean of Columbia University Graduate School of Journalism

"It scared the hell out of the publisher and editor. That definitely trickled down to us—to the point of near hysteria."

David Crowder, *El Paso* (Tex.) *Times* reporter after $3.5 million libel judgment (later reduced to $600,000) against newspaper

---

and defendants in product liability cases, 38 percent. Jury awards in libel cases *averaged* $2,043,702 in 1980 to 1984, compared with $785,651 in product liability cases and $665,764 in medical malpractice cases. (A federal jury in Las Vegas on December 18, 1986, skewed the picture even more: It awarded entertainer Wayne Newton $19.2 million in damages on grounds he had been defamed in NBC News broadcasts on organized crime. Of the total, $5 million was in punitive damages—the jury's way of punishing NBC beyond $14.2 million in damages for what it said was Newton's suffering and loss of reputation and income.)

Disparity between libel judgments on the one hand and liability cases and malpractice on the other is a clear signal of *juror sentiment* toward the media; the *law* is something else—70 percent or so of jury verdicts against the media are overturned by appeals courts. Damages are trimmed by four-fifths or more even when jury verdicts are allowed to stand. The largest award affirmed by an appeals court is $400,000. (Some media defendants settled out of court for more than that, however. The 38,000-circulation *Alton*

(Ill.) *Telegraph* settled with a local businessman for $1.4 million when a jury awarded him $9.2 million damages for a memo two reporters wrote to government officials but never published.)

Libel law offers many defenses for those who publish. For example, in reporting on public officials and public figures, particularly those who thrust themselves into public debate or who obtain general fame or notoriety, the media are not liable for damaging falsehoods unless they act with "actual malice." That means publishing with knowledge the story was false or publishing in "reckless disregard for whether it was true or false." The media have privilege in reporting from official court or government proceedings, and official sources such as police authorities. Truth is a defense, and opinion may be published freely. The Supreme Court affirmed these defenses many times. In 1964, in *New York Times versus Sullivan,* the Court held public officials must prove actual malice to recover damages for a defamatory falsehood in coverage of their official conduct; in 1986, the Court strengthened that by ruling in *Philadelphia Newspapers, Inc., versus Hepps* that those suing news organizations must prove damaging statements are false, at least "on matters of public concern." That reversed a Pennsylvania statute that required journalists to prove contested statements were true. Also that year, the Court ruled in *Anderson versus Liberty Lobby* that libel suits by public officials and figures in federal courts must be dismissed before trial unless evidence suggests they can prove libel with "convincing clarity."

Although libel law thus is weighted heavily in favor of the media, there are suggestions courtrooms be made even more unattractive for plaintiffs. Attorney Abrams, for example, notes the "sole purpose of libel law is restoration of unjustly lost reputation." He suggests damages for libelous error be limited if it is corrected promptly; punitive damages be abolished and limits established on damages for injury; anyone who brings or defends a suit without sufficient basis and loses should pay the winner's legal fees; libel law should be interpreted to permit the "harshest commentary of the performance of those in power"; public officials or figures should be able to sue for a declaratory judgment that what had been printed or said was false but not to seek monetary damages.

However, there is sentiment that the solution to the libel onslaught must be found outside the law, through substantive changes in the way newspaper and television journalists do things. There is feeling too many journalists for too long have been simply shouting "First Amendment" and proceeding to publish and broadcast without sufficient care for the fairness and sensitivity that opinion polls—and libel verdicts—indicate the public demands. As Richard Clurman noted in the Sharon case, the media must offer proof with charge, and willingly retract the charge if proven wrong. Reporting that is *legally permissible* may not be *socially acceptable* if deemed by the public to be unfair, insensitive or, simply put, just plain lousy journalism.

The fight for the free flow of information extends into other areas of reporting crucial to newspaper and television journalists. Let's look at the most important.

Free Press/Fair Trial

Because the media claim the right not only to publish and broadcast, but also to gain access to news, conflict with other rights and institutions is inevitable. Nowhere is that more apparent than where the First Amendment meets Sixth Amendment guarantees to criminal defendants that they will receive speedy and public trial by an impartial jury or the Fourteenth Amendment guarantee of due process under the law for every citizen.

The most common conflict is whether news coverage prejudices juries and makes fair trial impossible. Judges sometimes close courtrooms or issue "gag orders" prohibiting reporting of certain details of a criminal proceeding. Most such restraints are struck down by the U.S. Supreme Court, and the First Amendment generally is given preferred status. *Richmond Newspapers versus Commonwealth of Virginia* was a landmark case in which the Court ruled, in 1980, that the public has the right to attend criminal *trials*. But it left *pre*trial hearings subject to closing. This is a serious problem for the media in this era of plea-bargaining because pretrial hearings often are the only forum for criminal proceedings. ASNE acknowledges "there may be occasions when what is published will be false or misleading or perhaps even prejudicial." It adds, "The publication of erroneous material is liable to punishment, and remedies exist to mitigate the damage that may result. But rumor and gossip, and the ignorance and prejudice they promote, are not subject to any control, nor are they liable to punishment." ASNE argues judges can permit coverage *and* prevent potential prejudice by isolating jurors, giving them explicit instructions or, even, moving the trial to another venue. As for pretrial hearings, ASNE says closing them makes "a mockery of the public's First Amendment right to attend criminal trials."[44]

Others, including the American Bar Association, argue every effort must be made to ensure trials are held in courtrooms, not in newspapers or on television. The ABA warns member attorneys not to make statements to the media if they "reasonably should know that it will have a substantial likelihood of materially prejudicing the proceeding." That warning, embodied in the ABA's "Model Rules of Professional Conduct," has been adopted in several states where voluntary guidelines have been written by judges, attorneys, and journalists.

VIEWPOINT 12-8

A TRIAL, NOT A CIRCUS

"It is the integrity of our judicial process that is fundamentally at stake. This trial will not become a circus show played out on the steps of this courthouse."

U.S. District Court Judge David Kenyon, Jr., barring attorneys from talking to reporters covering Los Angeles trial in 1985 of three persons charged with spying for the Soviet Union

---

Guidelines, even if "voluntary," are highly controversial among journalists. Some fear they eventually could be judicially imposed and become mandatory. The U.S. Supreme Court long held such guidelines could not become mandatory. Then, in 1981, the Washington State Supreme Court ruled in *Federated Publications Inc. versus Swedberg* that reporters could be required to agree to "voluntary" guidelines drawn up by journalists and the state bar association as a condition for gaining access to pretrial hearings. The U.S. Supreme Court declined to hear Federated's appeal, so that question is left open.

The free press/fair trial issue became heated in 1966 when the U.S. Supreme Court overturned the murder conviction of an Ohio physician, Dr. Sam Sheppard, on the grounds that pretrial publicity compromised his Sixth Amendment rights. Many similarly sensational trials since then have kept the issue alive, but judges generally take steps to protect rights of both the media and defendants without closing their courtrooms. In 1985, for example, a judge in Providence, Rhode Island, ordered jurors sequestered to prevent them from reading or seeing media coverage of the retrial of Claus von Bulow, charged (and later acquitted) with killing his wife.

Television coverage itself became news with charges of John Z. DeLorean's drug-trafficking. CBS in 1983 broadcast—before the trial—FBI tapes showing the auto-maker being arrested, and the trial judge in Los Angeles said the network interfered with the judicial process. He postponed the trial, saying the broadcast could have "devastating effect." CBS countered that "Not only was the story newsworthy, the underlying facts had already been extensively reported by the press." In the same case, an ABC staff member called the homes of six jurors to try to arrange their appearance on the network after the verdict (which was that DeLorean was innocent). Amid charges of jury-tampering, ABC warned its staff against repeating the incident.

Television's Special Problem

Cameras are banned in federal courts, but television coverage in state courts has been a live issue since 1963. That year, one Wilbert Rideau was filmed admitting to a sheriff in Louisiana that he robbed a bank and was a kidnapper and killer. The twenty-minute film was shown by a local television station once each day for three consecutive days. The U.S. Supreme Court, in *Rideau versus Louisiana,* overturned Rideau's subsequent conviction: "For anyone who has ever watched television the conclusion cannot be avoided that this spectacle, to the tens of thousands of people who saw and heard it, in a very real sense was Rideau's trial—at which he pleaded guilty to murder. Any subsequent court proceedings in a community so pervasively exposed to such a spectacle could be but a hollow formality."

The Court thus drew attention to the impact of such "sight and sound" coverage by television—although two dissenting justices said the Court should not have inferred Rideau's trial was meaningless unless adverse publicity was shown to have "fatally infected the trial."

In *Rideau versus Louisiana,* the Court held Rideau had been denied due process, guaranteed by the Fourteenth Amendment. ("No state shall make or enforce any law which shall abridge the privileges or immunities of citizens of the United States; nor shall any State deprive any person of life, liberty, or property, without due process of law; nor deny to any person within its jurisdiction the equal protection of the laws.") The Court affirmed that position in *Estes versus Texas* in 1985, overturning a conviction in a trial that had been filmed and televised. In Estes, however, the Court went even further, stating that proving jurors actually had been prejudiced by TV coverage was not a prerequisite for overturning the conviction.

Some states experiment with television coverage of trials, and out of one in Florida came a 1981 case, *Chandler versus Florida,* in which Supreme Court

Chief Justice Warren Burger said the court in *Estes* had not placed "an absolute ban on *state* experimentation with evolving technology...." He stated, "An absolute constitutional ban on broadcast coverage of trials cannot be justified simply because there is a danger that, in some cases, prejudicial broadcast accounts of pretrial and trial events may impair the ability of jurors to decide the issue of guilt or innocence uninfluenced by extraneous matter. The risk of juror prejudice does not justify an absolute ban on news coverage of trials by the printed media; so also the risk of such prejudice does not warrant an absolute constitutional ban on all broadcast coverage." However, this issue also is open, for other justices indicated in their opinions they feel the court in *Estes* indeed had banned television coverage of trials, and, Burger himself, speaking outside his court, said in 1984 that television in the courtroom was the "most destructive thing in the world.... There will be no cameras in the Supreme Court of the United States while I sit there.... Show business and judicial business just won't mix."[45]

Even with Burger now retired, how—or whether—television fits into courtrooms is far from settled.

Sources, Notes, and Confidentiality

Watergate and countless other important stories would not have unfolded quite the same way if the media had been forced to publicly identify every source. For that reason, there has developed in American journalism a tradition of granting anonymity to some sources and protecting their identity.

In 1972, when it rejected separate appeals from two newspaper reporters and one television journalist, the U.S. Supreme Court held that journalists, like other citizens, must respond to grand jury subpoenas and provide information in criminal cases. That is, the First Amendment grants journalists no special immunity when what they know is needed in criminal proceedings. Dissenting, Justice William O. Douglas wrote what many journalists know to be fact: If a reporter is forced to testify, "his sources will dry up and the attempted exposure, the effort to enlighten the public, will be ended. If what the court sanctions today becomes settled law, then the reporter's main function in American society will be to pass on to the public the press releases which the various departments of government issue."

The cost of protecting sources can be high. Richard Hargreaves, then of the *St. Louis Globe-Democrat,* was jailed for three days in 1984 because he refused to identify sources for an editorial he wrote four years earlier for the *Bellview* (Ill.) *News-Democrat.* In the 1970s, Myron Farber of the *New York Times* spent forty days in a New Jersey jail for refusing to turn over documents in a murder case, and William Farr of the *Los Angeles Herald-Examiner* spent forty-six days in a Los Angeles jail.

Some states have "shield" laws that legislatures enacted in an effort to protect journalists from being forced to divulge sources or turn over confidential notes or documents. They are far from panoramic in their coverage, however.

New Jersey had such a law when Farber went to jail. Many journalists are reluctant to lobby for shield laws for fear they would weaken what many regard as absolute guarantee of a free press in the First Amendment.

Officials sometimes subpoena television videotape during investigations, hoping it will help identify criminals or solve crimes. Networks generally resist, fearing that would endanger reporters and photographers who subsequently would be considered tools of the police. Yet, the question: Does a network—or any journalist—have the responsibility of assisting officials if that will help solve a crime? After days of debating that question, all four networks turned over tape to federal officials in 1985 investigating the hijacking to Beirut of TWA Flight 847. Says Lyle Denniston who covers the Supreme Court for the *Baltimore Sun:* "Editorial independence was challenged by the government and editorial independence suffered …the news organizations surrendered.…" Denniston and many other journalists felt the networks should have resisted the subpoenas to maintain their distance from officialdom in such matters.[46]

Because their notes also can be subpoenaed in libel cases, many reporters now discard them after a story is written.

One of the most disturbing assaults on journalists' right to protect confidential material came in 1971 when police raided the student-run *Stanford Daily* at Stanford University, looking for photographs they could use in identifying protesters who had staged a sit-in on campus. In 1978, in *Zurcher versus Stanford Daily,* the U.S. Supreme Court ruled the First Amendment gave the press no special protection from such raids. As a consequence, President Jimmy Carter in 1980 signed legislation banning police raids on newsrooms. The law requires officials—local, state, or federal—to request permission to enter newsrooms or to use subpoenas, which require advance notice and permit court appearance to fight the order, and not search warrants, which can be used without notice.

It is on many fronts, then, that the battle for the free flow of information is fought. And, unfortunately, it is a battle in which victory never is won conclusively.

VIEWPOINT 12-9

FREE BECAUSE IT MUST BE

"The American press is extraordinarily free and vigorous, as it should be. It should be, not because it is free of inaccuracy, oversimplification and bias, but because the alternative to that freedom is worse than those failings."

  Judge Robert Bork, U.S. Court of Appeals for District of Columbia

---

CHAPTER SUMMARY

Despite unprecedentedly strong support in the marketplace from advertisers, readers, and viewers, the media constantly must struggle for access to official information without which there can be no truly free press. The Freedom of Information Act opens to public view hundreds of thousands of documents from eight federal agencies. But the federal government continues stamping secrecy classifications on millions of documents, and throughout the federal government there are efforts to restrict the flow of information.

Special interest pressure groups attempt not only to influence coverage of controversial news stories, but also strike directly at the ownership and financial stability of the media. Conservative groups did this with CBS, starting a sequence of events that fundamentally changed the network. Foreign governments pursue U.S. media because they influence public opinion and official policy in a nation pivotal in world affairs. The Soviet Union and some Third World countries are attempting to institute a "new order" of world communications that, among other things, would require licensing of all journalists.

Much legal tension surrounding the media stems from official attempts to restrain them prior to publication or broadcast, which is prohibited by the First Amendment, and use of libel law by private citizens and officials alike to indirectly achieve the same result by "chilling" reportorial vigor under threat of expensive lawsuits. Many Americans who feel harmed by the media regard the courtroom as their only forum for telling their side of the story.

A concern for society is how much news coverage is being restricted voluntarily by journalists who fear lawsuits. Particularly in smaller newspapers and television stations, newsrooms are getting very cautious.

Other restrictions on the free flow of information arise from conflict between the First Amendment and the Sixth Amendment's guarantee of a fair trial and the Fourteenth's assurance that each citizen must receive due process under the law. There is a "chilling" effect in the U.S. Supreme Court's stance that journalists, like any other citizens, must respond to grand jury subpoenas and provide information in criminal cases. Many journalists feel that could cause their confidential sources to "dry up," and more than one has gone to jail to protect a source's identity.

CHAPTER 12

Notes

1 House Subcommittee on Government Information, quoted by David Burnham, "Assessing the Freedom of Information Act," *New York Times,* Aug. 29, 1985, p. B10.
2 Howard Simmons, curator, Nieman Foundation, speech to ASNE, Washington, D.C., April 16, 1986.
3 Fine summaries of Freedom of Information Act and related developments are by Margaret Genovese, "Reagan Administration Information Policies," *presstime,* April 1985, p. 14; Genovese, "FOIA," *presstime,* July 1986, p. 22; Steve Weinberg, "Hits and Misses, FOIA at 20," *Washington Journalism Review,* September 1986, p. 38; Weinberg, "Trashing the FOIA," *Columbia Journalism Review,* January/February 1985, p. 21.
4 David Burnham, "Assessing the Freedom of Information Act," op. cit.
5 Margaret Genovese, "FOIA," op. cit.
6 Richard Huff, codirector of the Justice Department's Office of Information and Privacy, quoted by Genovese, "FOIA," op. cit.

7 Steve Weinberg, "Trashing the FOIA," op. cit.

8 Steve Weinberg, "Trashing the FOIA," op. cit.

9 Howard Simmons, speech to ASNE, op. cit.

10 The "report card," is reproduced in the society's "Freedom of Information '84–'85," p. 7.

11 "Reporters Committee Raps Reagan Administration," *Editor & Publisher*, April 6, 1985, p. 12.

12 Helpful background is in "Comment," *Columbia Journalism Review*, November/December 1983, p. 31; Stuart Taylor, Jr., "Administration Seeks a Stronger Lock on 'Classified' Files," *New York Times*, March 24, 1985, p. E5; Margaret Genovese, "FOIA," op. cit.

13 William Boot, "NASA and the Spellbound Press," *Columbia Journalism Review*, July/August 1986, p. 23.

14 Comments were made during a panel discussion at the annual convention of Investigative Reporters and Editors, Portland, Ore., June 17, 1986.

15 John Noble Wilford, "Shuttle's Tapes Show Crew Had No Hint of Fate," *New York Times*, July 18, 1986, p. 1. For a superb and more detailed view of NASA's information policies, see Alex S. Jones, "The Shuttle Inquiry: NASA and News Coverage," *New York Times*, Feb. 9, 1986, p. 20.

16 Michael Massing, "The Annual CBS Free-For-All," *Columbia Journalism Review*, July/August 1986, p. 45; also see Charles Babington, "Helms & Co.: Plotting to Unseat Dan Rather," *Columbia Journalism Review* July/August 1985, p. 47; John Corry, "Is TV Unpatriotic or Simply Unmindful?" *New York Times*, May 12, 1985, p. 1, section 2.

17 Peter Boyer, "Loew's Increases Its Stake in CBS," *New York Times*, Aug. 12, 1986, p. C18.

18 John Corry, "Is TV Unpatriotic or Simply Unmindful?" op. cit.

19 Timothy Layer, "CBS Is Offering Early Retirement to 2,000 Workers," *Wall Street Journal*, Sept. 4, 1985, p. 11; also, Peter Kaplan, "CBS News Facing Internal Turmoil," *New York Times*, Oct. 23, 1985, p. 44.

20 "Confrontation with Local Blacks Leads to Cancellation of Column," Southern Newspaper Publishers Association Bulletin, May 8, 1985, p. 5.

21 Maurine Christopher, "Wildmon Airing Network Gripes," *Advertising Age*, June 17, 1985, p. 83.

22 S. Robert Lichter and Stanley Robinson, "Media and Business Elites," *Public Opinion*, October/November 1981, p. 42; Linda Lichter, S. Robert Lichter, Stanley Rothman, "The Once and Future Journalists," *Washington Journalism Review*, December 1982, p. 26.

23 Herbert J. Gans, "Are U.S. Journalists Dangerously Liberal?" *Columbia Journalism Review*, November/December 1985, p. 29.

24 Albert R. Hunt, "Media Bias Is in Eye of the Beholder," *Wall Street Journal*, July 23, 1985, p. 32.

25 James Buie, Maura Casey, Gregory Enns, Vandana Mathur, and Mark Williams did this study under the guidance of Prof. Richard T. Stout, and published their findings in, "Foreign Governments Are Playing Our Press," *Washington Journalism Review*, October 1983, p. 21. For details of Israel's charges against NBC, see Edward Walsh, "NBC's Mideast Conflict," *Washington Journalism Review*, October 1983, p. 22.

26 "Free-Press Groups Denounce 'Rules of Ethics' for Journalists," *presstime*, March 1981, p. 25; "Britain Pulls Out of UNESCO, Following U.S. Lead of a Year Ago,"

an Associated Press dispatch for afternoon papers of Dec. 6, 1985, published in that day's *Atlanta Constitution.*

27 "Battle Reporters: Red Cross to Act," *New York Times,* April 25, 1985, p. 5.

28 Dana Bullen, executive director, World Press Freedom Committee, "Press Debate May Start Anew at UN," *presstime,* June 1986, p. 54.

29 "Battle Reporters: Red Cross to Act," *New York Times,* op. cit.; also see, Edward Cony, "Government-Issued IDs Won't Save Journalists' Lives," *Wall Street Journal,* July 25, 1985, p. 20.

30 The Sinatra incident, which quickly faded from public view, is summarized in *SNPA Bulletin,* July 3, 1985, p. 4.

31 This incident involved indians of the Santo Domingo Pueblo and extended over many months. Final settlement is recounted in *"New Mexican* Reaches Settlement with Indians," *Editor & Publisher,* Feb. 16, 1985, p. 23.

32 See Arnold H. Lubasch, "Court Rejects Libel Award Over Critical Food Review," *New York Times,* March 31, 1985, p. 21; also, "Away with the Libel Hash," an editorial in *New York Times,* April 3, 1985, p. 24.

33 Coverage was voluminous; in publications of record generally available, note summaries: M. A. Farber, "A Joint Statement Ends Libel Action by Westmoreland," and Peter Kaplan, "'Best I Could Get,' General Asserts," *New York Times,* Feb. 19, 1985, p. 1; Karen Rothmayer, "Westmoreland v. CBS," *Columbia Journalism Review,* May/June 1985, p. 25; *USA Today* devoted its Feb. 21, 1985, editorial page to five differing views of the Westmoreland trial.

34 Note Stuart Elliott, *"Time* Fights 'Malice in Blunderland' Image," *Advertising Age,* Feb. 4, 1985, p. 4; Arnold Lubasch, *"Time* Cleared of Libeling Sharon But Jurors Criticize Its Reporting," *New York Times,* Jan. 25, 1985, p. 1; David Margolick, "Sharon Case and the Law," *New York Times,* Jan. 25, 1985, p. 13.

35 For Abrams' views in detail, see his article, "Why We Should Change the Libel Law," *New York Times Magazine,* Sept. 29, 1985, p. 34.

36 Andrew Radolf, "Represener of 'Defamed People,'" *Editor & Publisher,* April 6, 1985, p. 10.

37 Gene Roberts, speech to William Allen White Foundation, reprinted in, "Shop Talk at Thirty," *Editor & Publisher,* March 9, 1985, p. 52.

38 Sam Zagoria, *Washington Post* ombudsman, in speech to New Jersey Press Association, reprinted in "Shop Talk at Thirty," *Editor & Publisher,* April 13, 1985, p. 48.

39 Reed Irvine, letter to editor, *New York Times,* Dec. 30, 1984, p. 12E.

40 Lester Bernstein, "'Chilling Effect' or Fresh Air?" *New York Times,* Dec. 23, 1984, p. E13.

41 Richard M. Clurman, "Fallout from the Sharon Trial," *New York Times,* Jan. 30, 1985, p. 23.

42 Ariel Sharon, "'Sharon, Get Lost,' They Say. I Won't," *New York Times,* Dec. 16, 1984, p. E21.

43 William C. Westmoreland, "A Court's No Forum," *New York Times,* Feb. 24, 1985, p. E19.

44 ASNE and the American Newspaper Publishers Association in 1982 issued jointly a superb summary of this issue—"Free Press & Fair Trial," available at the Newspaper Center, Box 17407, Dulles Airport, Washington, D.C., 20041.

45 Associated Press dispatch for morning papers, Nov. 13, 1984, reprinted in *Atlanta Constitution* on that date, p. 3A.

46 Lyle Denniston, "War of Independence," *Washington Journalism Review,* October 1985, p. 17.

AMERICAN SOCIETY OF NEWSPAPER EDITORS STATEMENT OF PRINCIPLES

PREAMBLE

The First Amendment, protecting freedom of expression from abridgment by any law, guarantees to the people through their press a constitutional right, and thereby places on newspaper people a particular responsibility.

Thus journalism demands of its practitioners not only industry and knowledge but also the pursuit of a standard of integrity proportionate to the journalist's singular obligation.

To this end the American Society of Newspaper Editors sets forth this Statement of Principles as a standard encouraging the highest ethical and professional performance.

ARTICLE I: RESPONSIBILITY

The primary purpose of gathering and distributing news and opinion is to serve the general welfare by informing the people and enabling them to make judgments on the issues of the time. Newspapermen and women who abuse the power of their professional role for selfish motives or unworthy purposes are faithless to that public trust.

The American press was made free not just to inform or just to serve as a forum for debate but also to bring an independent scrutiny to bear on the forces of power in the society, including the conduct of official power at all levels of government.

ARTICLE II: FREEDOM OF THE PRESS

Freedom of the press belongs to the people. It must be defended against encroachment or assault from any quarter, public or private.

Journalists must be constantly alert to see that the public's business is conducted in public. They must be vigilant against all who would exploit the press for selfish purposes.

ARTICLE III: INDEPENDENCE

Journalists must avoid impropriety and the appearance of impropriety as well as any conflict of interest or the appearance of conflict. They should neither accept anything nor pursue any activity that might compromise or seem to compromise their integrity.

ARTICLE IV: TRUTH AND ACCURACY

Good faith with the reader is the foundation of good journalism. Every effort must be made to assure that the news content is accurate, free from bias and in context, and that all sides are presented fairly. Editorials, analytical articles and commentary should be held to the same standards of accuracy with respect to facts as news reports.

Significant errors of fact, as well as errors of omission, should be corrected promptly and prominently.

ARTICLE V: IMPARTIALITY

To be impartial does not require the press to be unquestioning or to refrain from editorial expression. Sound practice, however, demands a clear distinction for the reader between news reports and opinion. Articles that contain opinion or personal interpretation should be clearly identified.

ARTICLE VI: FAIR PLAY

Journalists should respect the rights of people involved in the news, observe the common standards of decency and stand accountable to the public for the fairness and accuracy of their news reports.

Persons publicly accused should be given the earliest opportunity to respond.

Pledges of confidentiality to news sources must be honored at all costs, and therefore should not be given lightly. Unless there is clear and pressing need to maintain confidences, sources of information should be identified.

These principles are intended to preserve, protect and strengthen the bond of trust and respect between American journalists and the American people, a bond that is essential to sustain the grant of freedom entrusted to both by the nation's founders.

This Statement of Principles was adopted by the ASNE Board of Directors on Oct. 23, 1975; it supplants the 1922 "Cannons of Journalism."

APPENDIX **TWO**

SOCIETY OF PROFESSIONAL JOURNALISTS, SIGMA DELTA CHI, CODE OF ETHICS

The Society of Professional Journalists, Sigma Delta Chi, believes the duty of journalists is to serve the truth.

We believe the agencies of mass communication are carriers of public discussion and information, acting on their Constitutional mandate and freedom to learn and report the facts.

We believe in public enlightenment as the forerunner of justice, and in our Constitutional role to seek the truth as part of the public's right to know the truth.

We believe those responsibilities carry obligations that require journalists to perform with intelligence, objectivity, accuracy and fairness.

To these ends, we declare acceptance of the standards of practice here set forth:

RESPONSIBILITY

The public's right to know of events of public importance and interest is the overriding mission of the mass media. The purpose of distributing news and enlightened opinion is to serve the general welfare. Journalists who use their professional status as representatives of the public for selfish or other unworthy motives violate a high trust.

FREEDOM OF THE PRESS

Freedom of the press is to be guarded as an inalienable right of people in a free society. It carries with it the freedom and the responsibility to discuss, question and challenge actions and utterances of our government and of our public and private institutions. Journalists uphold the right to speak unpopular opinions and the privilege to agree with the majority.

ETHICS

Journalists must be free of obligation to any interest other than the public's right to know the truth.

1 Gifts, favors, free travel, special treatment or privileges can compromise the integrity of journalists and their employers. Nothing of value should be accepted.

2 Secondary employment, political involvement, holding public office and service in community organizations should be avoided if it compromises the integrity of journalists and their employers. Journalists and their employers should conduct their personal lives in a manner which protects them from conflict of interest, real or apparent. Their responsibilities to the public are paramount. That is the nature of their profession.

3 So-called news communications from private sources should not be published or broadcast without substantiation of their claims to news value.

4 Journalists will seek news that serves public interest, despite the obstacles. They will make constant efforts to assure that the public's business is conducted in public and that public records are open to public inspection.

5 Journalists acknowledge the newsman's ethic of protecting confidential sources of information.

ACCURACY AND OBJECTIVITY

Good faith with the public is the foundation of all worthy journalism.

1 Truth is our ultimate goal.

2 Objectivity in reporting the news is another goal, which serves as the mark of an experienced professional. It is a standard of performance toward which we strive. We honor those who achieve it.

3 There is no excuse for inaccuracies or lack of thoroughness.

4 Newspaper headlines should be fully warranted by the contents of the articles they accompany. Photographs and telecasts should give an accurate picture of an event and not highlight a minor incident out of context.

5 Sound practice makes clear distinction between news reports and expressions of opinion. News reports should be free of opinion or bias and represent all sides of an issue.

6 Partisanship in editorial comment which knowingly departs from the truth violates the spirit of American journalism.

7 Journalists recognize their responsibility for offering informed analysis, comment and editorial opinion on public events and issues. They accept the obligation to present such material by individuals whose competence, experience and judgment qualify them for it.

8 Special articles or presentations devoted to advocacy or the writer's own conclusions and interpretations should be labeled as such.

FAIR PLAY

Journalists at all times will show respect for the dignity, privacy, rights and well-being of people encountered in the course of gathering and presenting the news.

1 The news media should not communicate unofficial charges affecting reputation or moral character without giving the accused a chance to reply.

2 The news media must guard against invading a person's right to privacy.

3 The media should not pander to morbid curiosity about details of vice and crime.

4 It is the duty of news media to make prompt and complete correction of their errors.

5 Journalists should be accountable to the public for their reports and the public should be encouraged to voice its grievances against the media. Open dialogue with our readers, viewers or listeners should be fostered.

PLEDGE

Journalists should actively censure and try to prevent violations of these standards, and they should encourage their observance by all newspeople. Adherence to this code of ethics is intended to preserve the bond of mutual trust and respect between American journalists and the American people.

Adopted 1926, Revised 1973

THREE

RADIO/TELEVISION NEWS DIRECTORS ASSOCIATION CODE OF BROADCAST NEWS ETHICS

The members of the Radio/Television News Directors Association agree that their prime responsibility as journalists—and that of the broadcasting industry as the collective sponsor of news broadcasting—is to provide to the public they serve a news service as accurate, full and prompt as human integrity and devotion can devise. To that end, they declare their acceptance of the standards of practice here set forth, and their solemn intent to honor them to the limits of their ability.

ARTICLE ONE

The primary purpose of broadcast journalists—to inform the public of events of importance and appropriate interest in a manner that is accurate and comprehensive—shall override all other purposes.

ARTICLE TWO

Broadcast news presentations shall be designed not only to offer timely and accurate information, but also to present it in the light of relevant circumstances that give it meaning and perspective.

This standard means that news reports, when clarity demands it, will be laid against pertinent factual background; that factors such as race, creed, nationality or prior status will be reported only when they are relevant; that comment or subjective content will be properly identified; and that errors in fact will be promptly acknowledged and corrected.

ARTICLE THREE

Broadcast journalists shall seek to select material for newscast solely on their evaluation of its merits as news.

This standard means that news will be selected on the criteria of significance, community and regional relevance, appropriate human interest, service to defined audiences. It excludes sensationalism or misleading emphasis in any form; subservience to external or "interested" efforts to influence news selection and presentation, whether from within the broadcasting industry or from without. It requires that such terms as "bulletin" and "flash" be used only when the character of the news justifies them; that bombastic or misleading descriptions of newsroom facilities and personnel be rejected, along with undue use of sound and visual effects; and that promotional or publicity material be sharply scrutinized before use and identified by source or otherwise when broadcast.

ARTICLE FOUR

Broadcast journalists shall at all times display humane respect for the dignity, privacy and the well-being of persons with whom the news deals.

ARTICLE FIVE

Broadcast journalists shall govern their personal lives and such nonprofessional associations as may impinge on their professional activities in a manner that will protect them from conflict of interest, real or apparent.

ARTICLE SIX

Broadcast journalists shall seek actively to present all news the knowledge of which will serve the public interest, no matter what selfish, uninformed or corrupt efforts attempt to color it, withhold it or prevent its presentation. They shall make constant effort to open doors closed to the reporting of public proceedings with tools appropriate to broadcasting (including cameras and recorders), consistent with the public interest. They acknowledge the journalist's ethic of protection of confidential information and sources, and urge unswerving observation of it except in instances in which it would clearly and unmistakably defy the public interest.

ARTICLE SEVEN

Broadcast journalists recognize the responsibility borne by broadcasting for informed analysis, comment and editorial opinion on public events and issues. They accept the obligation of broadcasters, for the presentation of such matters by individuals whose competence, experience and judgment qualify them for it.

ARTICLE EIGHT

In court, broadcast journalists shall conduct themselves with dignity, whether the court is in or out of session. They shall keep broadcast equipment as unobtrusive and silent as possible. Where court facilities are inadequate, pool broadcasts should be arranged.

ARTICLE NINE

In reporting matters that are or may be litigated, the journalist shall avoid practices which would tend to interfere with the right of an individual to a fair trial.

ARTICLE TEN

Broadcast journalists shall not misrepresent the source of any broadcast news material.

ARTICLE ELEVEN

Broadcast journalists shall actively censure and seek to prevent violations of these standards, and shall actively encourage their observance by all journalists, whether of the Radio/Television News Directors Association or not.

FOUR

ASSOCIATED PRESS MANAGING EDITORS CODE OF ETHICS

This code is a model against which newspaper men and women can measure their performance. It is meant to apply to news and editorial staff members, and others who are involved in, or who influence news coverage and editorial policy. It has been formulated in the belief that newspapers and the people who produce them should adhere to the highest standards of ethical and professional conduct.

RESPONSIBILITY

A good newspaper is fair, accurate, honest, responsible, independent and decent. Truth is its guiding principle.

It avoids practices that would conflict with the ability to report and present news in a fair and unbiased manner.

The newspaper should serve as a constructive critic of all segments of society. Editorially, it should advocate needed reform or innovations in the public interest. It should vigorously expose wrongdoing or misuse of power, public or private.

News sources should be disclosed unless there is clear reason not to do so. When it is necessary to protect the confidentiality of a source, the reason should be explained.

The newspaper should background, with the facts, public statements that it knows to be inaccurate or misleading. It should uphold the right of free speech and freedom of the press and should respect the individual's right to privacy.

The public's right to know about matters of importance is paramount, and the newspaper should fight vigorously for public access to news of government through open meetings and open records.

ACCURACY

The newspaper should guard against inaccuracies, carelessness, bias or distortion through either emphasis or omission.

It should admit all substantive errors and correct them promptly and prominently.

INTEGRITY

The newspaper should strive for impartial treatment of issues and dispassionate handling of controversial subjects. It should provide a forum for the exchange of comment and criticism, especially when such comment is opposed to its editorial positions. Editorials and other expressions of opinion by reporters and editors should be clearly labeled.

The newspaper should report the news without regard for its own interests. It should not give favored news treatment to advertisers or special interest groups. It should report matters regarding itself or its personnel with the same vigor and candor as it would other institutions or individuals.

Concern for community, business or personal interests should not cause a newspaper to distort or misrepresent the facts.

CONFLICTS OF INTEREST

The newspaper and its staff should be free of obligations to news sources and special interests. Even the appearance of obligation or conflict of interest should be avoided.

Newspapers should accept nothing of value from news sources or others outside the profession. Gifts and free or reduced-rate travel, entertainment, products and lodging should not be accepted. Expenses in connection with news reporting should be paid by the newspaper. Special favors and special treatment for members of the press should be avoided.

Involvement in such things as politics, community affairs, demonstrations and social causes that could cause a conflict of interest, or the appearance of such conflict, should be avoided.

Outside employment by news sources is an obvious conflict of interest, and employment by potential news sources also should be avoided.

Financial investments by staff members or other outside business interests that could conflict with the newspaper's ability to report the news or that would create the impression of such conflict should be avoided.

Stories should not be written or edited primarily for the purpose of winning awards and prizes. Blatantly commercial journalism contests, or others that reflect unfavorably on the newspaper or the profession, should be avoided.

No code of ethics can prejudge every situation. Common sense and good judgment are required in applying ethical principles to newspaper realities. Individual newspapers are encouraged to augment these guidelines with locally produced codes that apply more specifically to their own situations.

(Adopted 1975)

DOW JONES & COMPANY CONFLICTS OF INTEREST POLICY

Growth of business and financial reporting by newspapers and television forces editors to consider more carefully ethical implications in handling that type news and, particularly, possible conflicts of interest. Dow Jones & Company, Inc., publisher of the *Wall Street Journal* and other newspapers, has a detailed policy each employee must adhere to as a condition of employment. Pertinent excerpts:

CONFLICTS OF INTEREST POLICY

This policy statement is designed to provide all employees with guidelines which will enable them to avoid conflicts of interest that might be construed to be detrimental to the best interests of Dow Jones. It is important for all employees to keep in mind the tremendous embarrassment and damage to the Company's reputation and that of fellow employees that could come about through a lapse in judgment by one person, or someone closely associated with that person, no matter how well-intended that person may be. Because we think it is so essential that every employee be above suspicion, we consider any slip in judgment in the areas covered in this policy statement to be serious enough to warrant dismissal.

CONFIDENTIAL INFORMATION

1 Employees should not use, directly or indirectly, for their own or any other person's financial gain, any information about Dow Jones which the employee obtained in connection with Dow Jones employment. Further, employees should not disclose to anyone confidential information obtained in connection with Dow Jones employment until such information has been made available to the public...

SECURITY TRANSACTIONS

6 Dow Jones has always had a strict policy on security transactions by employees who have access to inside information regarding unpublished stories or advertising schedules. It also has had a strict related policy on the conduct of news and advertising staff members dealing with corporations we cover or whose advertising we carry. Each employee is expected to bend over backwards to avoid any action, no matter how well-intentioned, that could provide grounds for suspicion:

a that an employee, his family or others close to the employee made financial gains by acting on the basis of inside information gained through a position on our staff, before it was available to the general public. Such information includes hold-for-release material, our plans for running stories, items that may affect price movements, or projected advertising campaigns;

b that the writing of a news story or item or scheduling of advertising was influenced by a desire to affect the stock's prices;

c that an employee is financially committed in the market so deeply or in such other way as to create a temptation to biased writing or scheduling of advertising;

d that an employee is beholden to brokers or any other group we cover or advertisers. Such indebtedness could arise through acceptance of favors, gifts or payments for performing writing assignments or other services for them;

e that an employee is beholden for any tips, allocations or underwritten new issues or in any other way to anyone in the financial community.

We do not want to penalize our staff members by suggesting that they not buy stocks or make other investments. We do, however, want employees to avoid speculation or the appearance of speculation. Members of the Management Committee, national department heads, and members of the news and advertising departments must not engage in short-term trading; they must hold securities a minimum of six (6) months, unless they get prior approval from the Vice President/Legal or his designee to meet some special need. They must not buy or sell basically speculative instruments such as futures or options. No employee of the Company should engage in short selling of securities.

We reiterate that it is not enough to be incorruptible and act with honest motives. It is equally important to use good judgment and conduct one's outside activities so that no one—management, our editors, an SEC investigator, or a political critic of the Company—has any grounds for even raising the suspicion that an employee misused a position with the Company.

With these general propositions in mind, here are some further specific guidelines:

i First and foremost, all material gleaned by you in the course of your work for Dow Jones is deemed to be strictly the Company's property. This includes not only the fruits of your own and your colleague's work, but also information on plans for running items and articles on particular companies and industries and advertising schedules in future issues. Such material must never be disclosed to anyone outside the Company, including friends and relatives. Viewing information as the Company's property should avoid a great many of the obvious pitfalls.

ii No employee regularly assigned to a specific industry should invest, nor should his family, in any company engaged in whole or significant part in that industry.

iii No employee with knowledge of a forthcoming article, item or advertisement concerning a company or industry should, prior to the publication of such article, item or advertisement, invest or in any way encourage or assist any other person in selling a security in that company prior to publication without the approval of the appropriate Management Committee member.

iv Further, any employee having prior knowledge of a forthcoming article, item or advertisement, should delay buying or selling the securities of the company involved, as should his family, until the general public has an opportunity to read and digest the information contained in any Dow Jones publication or news service. Employees should wait two full trading days after an article or advertisement first appears in a Dow Jones publication or news service.

v If an employee thinks there is a possibility he or a family member may have inadvertently violated any of the above guidelines, or if an employee should buy a security prior to publication, and then acquire knowledge of a proposed article, item or advertisement, the employee should notify his or her department head as soon as practical. In the case of a purchase, the employee or family member should hold the security for six months.

SERVING ON THE BOARD OF DIRECTORS OF OTHER COMPANIES

7 Dow Jones' employees are prohibited except with written approval of the chief executive officer from serving as directors or officers of any other company devoted to profit-making. This prohibition, of course, does not apply to employees appointed to serve as directors or officers of companies in which Dow Jones has a significant equity interest. If an employee is involved in a family-owned profit-making business, clearance should be obtained from the appropriate member of the Management Committee...

...Should any question ever arise in your mind as to the propriety of your activity, you are urged to consult in confidence with your national department head or any Dow Jones officer.

We would like to emphasize that we have complete confidence in all our employees. It is essential, however, that all of us maintain the highest standards of ethics in the conduct of Dow Jones' business in actuality and also in appearances by acting within the framework of these guidelines. Please retain this policy statement in your files.

Your cooperation is greatly appreciated.

Warren E. Phillips
Chairman
Dow Jones & Company, Inc.

THE ADVERTISING CODE
OF AMERICAN BUSINESS

1 *Truth*. Advertising shall tell the truth, and reveal significant facts, the concealment of which would mislead the public.

2 *Responsibility*. Advertising agencies and advertisers shall be willing to provide substantiation of claims made.

3 *Taste and Decency*. Advertising shall be free of statements, illustrations or implications which are offensive to good taste or public decency.

4 *Disparagement*. Advertising shall offer merchandise or service on its merits and refrain from attacking competitors unfairly or disparaging their products, services or methods of doing business.

5 *Bait Advertising*. Advertising shall offer only merchandise or services which are readily available for purchase at the advertised price.

6 *Guarantees and Warranties*. Advertising of guarantees and warranties shall be explicit. Advertising of any guarantee or warranty shall clearly and conspicuously disclose its nature and extent, the manner in which the guarantor or warrantor will perform and the identity of the guarantor or warrantor.

7 *Price Claims*. Advertising shall avoid price or savings claims which are false or misleading, or which do not offer provable bargains or savings.

8 *Unprovable Claims*. Advertising shall avoid the use of exaggerated or unprovable claims.

9 *Testimonials*. Advertising containing testimonials shall be limited to those of competent witnesses who are reflecting a real and honest choice.

This code was developed by the American Advertising Federation and Association of Better Business Bureaus International. It has been endorsed by International Newspaper Advertising and Marketing Executives, Association of Newspaper Classified Advertising Managers, National Newspaper Association, Magazine Publishers Association, American Association of Advertising Agencies, National Association of Broadcasters and many other trade groups.

SEVEN

PUBLIC RELATIONS SOCIETY OF AMERICA CODE OF PROFESSIONAL STANDARDS FOR THE PRACTICE OF PUBLIC RELATIONS

Members of the Public Relations Society of America base their professional principles on the fundamental value and dignity of the individual, holding that the free exercise of human rights, especially freedom of speech, freedom of assembly and freedom of the press, is essential to the practice of public relations.

In serving the interests of clients and employers, we dedicate ourselves to the goals of better communication, understanding and cooperation among the diverse individuals, groups and institutions of society, and of equal opportunity of employment in the public relations profession.

We pledge:

To conduct ourselves professionally, with truth, accuracy, fairness and responsibility to the public;

To improve our individual competence and advance the knowledge and proficiency of the profession through continuing research and education;

And to adhere to the articles of the Code of Professional Standards for the Practice of Public Relations as adopted by the governing Assembly of the Society.

ARTICLES OF THE CODE

These articles have been adopted by the Public Relations Society of America to promote and maintain high standards of public service and ethical conduct among its members.

1 A member shall deal fairly with clients or employers, past and present, or potential, with fellow practitioners and the general public.

2 A member shall conduct his or her professional life in accord with the public interest.

3 A member shall adhere to truth and accuracy and to generally accepted standards of good taste.

4 A member shall not represent conflicting or competing interests without the express consent of those involved, given after a full disclosure of the facts; nor place himself or herself in a position where the member's interest is or may be in conflict with a duty to a client, or others, without a full disclosure of such interests to all involved.

5 A member shall safeguard the confidences of present and former clients, as well as those of persons or entities who have disclosed confidences to a member in the context of communications relating to an anticipated professional relationship with such member, and shall not accept retainers or employment that may involve disclosing using or offering to use such confidences to the disadvantage or prejudice of such present, former or potential clients or employers.

6 A member shall not engage in any practice which tends to corrupt the integrity of channels of communication or the processes of government.

7 A member shall not intentionally communicate false or misleading information and is obliged to use care to avoid communication of false or misleading information.

8 A member shall be prepared to identify publicly the name of the client or employer on whose behalf any public communication is made.

9 A member shall not make use of any individual or organization purporting to serve or represent an announced cause, or purporting to be independent or unbiased, but actually serving an undisclosed special or private interest of a member, client, or employer.

10 A member shall not intentionally injure the professional reputation or practice of another practitioner. However, if a member has evidence that another member has been guilty of unethical, illegal or unfair practices, including those in violation of this Code, the member shall present the information promptly to the proper authorities of the Society for action in accordance with the procedure set forth in Article XIII of the By-laws.

11 A member called as a witness in a proceeding for the enforcement of this Code shall be bound to appear, unless excused for sufficient reason by the Judicial Panel.

12 A member, in performing services for a client or employer, shall not accept fees, commissions or any other valuable consideration from anyone other than the client or employer in connection with those services without the express consent of the client or employer, given after a full disclosure of the facts.

13 A member shall not guarantee the achievement of specified results beyond the member's direct control.

14 A member shall, as soon as possible, sever relations with any organization or individual if such relationship requires conduct contrary to the articles of this Code.

(Adopted 1954; Revised 1959, 1963, 1977, 1983)

FREEDOM OF INFORMATION SERVICE CENTER SAMPLE LETTER

The following sample letter is recommended by the Freedom of Information Service Center, Washington, D.C., for requesting documents under the Freedom of Information Act.

Business telephone number
Return address
Date

Name of Public Body
Address

To the FOI Officer:

This request is made under the federal Freedom of Information Act, 5 U.S.C. 552.

Please send me copies of (*Here, clearly describe what you want. Include identifying material, such as names, places, and the period of time about which you are inquiring. If you wish, attach news clips, reports, and other documents describing the subject of your research.*)

As you know, the FOI Act provides that if portions of a document are exempt from release, the remainder must be segregated and disclosed. Therefore, I will expect you to send me all nonexempt portions of the records which I have requested, and ask that you justify any deletions by reference to specific exemptions of the FOI Act. I reserve the right to appeal your decision to withhold any materials.

I promise to pay reasonable search and duplication fees in connection with this request. However, if you estimate that the total fees will exceed $_____ , please notify me so that I may authorize expenditure of a greater amount.

(*Optional*) I am prepared to pay reasonable search and duplication fees in connection with this request. However, the FOI Act provides for waiver or reduction of fees if disclosure could be considered as "primarily benefiting the general public." I am a journalist (*researcher or scholar*) employed by (*name of news organization, book publishers, etc.*), and intend to use the information I am requesting as the basis for a planned article (*broadcast or book*). (*Add arguments here in support of fee waiver.*) Therefore, I ask that you waive all search and application fees. If you deny this request, however, and the fees will exceed $_____ , please notify me of the charges before you fill my request so that I may decide whether to pay the fees or appeal your denial of my request for a waiver.

As I am making this request in the capacity of a journalist (*author or scholar*) and this information is of timely value, I will appreciate your communicating with me by telephone, rather than by mail, if you have any questions regarding this request. Thank you for your assistance, and I will look forward to receiving your reply within ten business days, as required by law.

Very truly yours,

(Signature)